THE
DRAMATIC WORKS OF
THOMAS DEKKER

THE
DRAMATIC WORKS OF
THOMAS DEKKER

EDITED BY
FREDSON BOWERS
Professor of English Literature
University of Virginia

VOLUME IV

CAMBRIDGE
AT THE UNIVERSITY PRESS
1961

PUBLISHED BY
THE SYNDICS OF THE CAMBRIDGE UNIVERSITY PRESS

Bentley House, 200 Euston Road, London, N.W. 1
American Branch: 32 East 57th Street, New York 22, N.Y.
West African Office: P.O. Box 33, Ibadan, Nigeria

Printed in Great Britain at the University Press, Cambridge
(Brooke Crutchley, University Printer)

CONTENTS

FOREWORD

WITH this fourth volume the textual editor's assignment is completed. Herein are presented two Lord Mayor's Entertainments and one play, *The Sun's Darling*, that have always been a part of the Dekker canon. In addition I have selected three plays from the list that at one time or another has been attributed to him. *Lust's Dominion*, *The Noble Spanish Soldier*, and *The Welsh Embassador* are in my opinion certainly Dekker's, either in whole or in part, and should be printed in any complete edition.

Two plays that on stylistic grounds have some claim to serious consideration have been omitted. I can speak only impressionistically, but I believe that there is fairly good evidence for seeing Dekker's hand in some scenes of *Blurt Master Constable* and perhaps less good but still sufficient evidence in some scenes of *The Family of Love*. However, two main reasons dictated the omission of these texts. First, of the three attributed plays in this volume, one was entered in the Stationers' Register as Dekker's, one was assigned to him in an early play list that may have transcribed the lost first leaf of the preserved manuscript of the play, and the third may reasonably be equated with a play for which Dekker was in part paid. Thus in each case there is some evidence other than from parallel passages, stylistic analysis, and impressions of personality to warrant inclusion.

Nothing of the sort has been found for the two excluded plays, and what studies of them that have been published have not, I think, demonstrated Dekker's authorship by evidence so persuasive in method or detail as to require a textual editor to add them on his own authority to the generally established Dekker canon.

Second, whether or not Dekker collaborated in *Blurt* and *The Family of Love*, it is most improbable (again I write impressionistically) that he was the major contributor. Instead, these two plays seem to belong most appropriately in the Middleton canon where, without useless duplication from me, they can appear in the edition proposed for that dramatist.

FOREWORD

At the end of this volume a number of notes and corrections to the earlier plays will be found. Of greatest interest, the preservation in the Bute Collection, now a part of the National Library of Scotland, of the only perfect copy of *The Converted Courtesan* has enabled me to reproduce the previously missing title-page and to give the details of still another copy, especially the revisions from the final two leaves that had been wanting. Some errors in transcription in various plays that have been called to my attention are recorded, but I have not re-collated the texts in search of further sins except for the collation of the Bute *Converted Courtesan*. Dr Johan Gerritsen kindly informs me that the Royal Library, The Hague, has a copy of *If This Be Not a Good Play* that corresponds to the Dyce copy in its mixture of corrected and uncorrected formes. Some readings in the earlier volumes are looked at again in the light of second thoughts and the suggestions of critics. I especially wish to acknowledge the valuable queries offered by Messrs J. C. Maxwell and J. George in this connexion.

The illustrations in this, as in earlier volumes, are reduced from the size of the originals.

F. B.

THE
Sun's-Darling:
A Moral Masque.

As it hath been often presented at *Whitehall*, by
their Majesties Servants; and after at the Cock-pit
in *Drury Lane*, with great Applause.

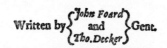

Written by ⎰*John Foard*⎱ Gent.
⎱ and ⎰
⎱*Tho. Decker*⎰

LONDON,
Printed by *J. Bell*, for *Andrew Penneycnicke,*
Anno Dom. 1656.

I

TEXTUAL INTRODUCTION

THE SUN'S DARLING (Greg, *Bibliography*, no. 767) appeared in 1656 printed by J. Bell for the actor Andrew Pennycuicke, who together with another actor, Theophilus Bird, signed the dedicatory address. Certain details of the printing and publishing history of this quarto are obscure. In most copies the dedication is to Thomas Wriothesley, earl of Southampton. However, three press-variant headings to the same text are preserved, each in a unique example. In a Bodleian copy the heading reads: 'To the Right Honorable | *Robert Peirpont* Earle of *Kingston* upon | *Hull*, Viscount *Newark*, and Lord *Peirpont*, | of Holmes *Peirpont*, and Marquesse | of *Dorchester*.' In the Ashley copy in the British Museum: 'To the Right Honorable | ALGERNOWNE PERCY, *Earl of Northum-*|*berland*, Lord *Piercy*, *Lucy*, *Poynings*, *Fitz-*|*Paine*, *and Bryan*, Knight *of the most* | *Noble Order of the Garter*.' A Dyce copy in the Victoria and Albert Museum has the heading: 'To the Right Honorable | My very good Lady, the Lady *Newton*, | Wife to the worshipfull Sir *Henry Newton*, Knight.' This version necessitated the alteration of the text to the following readings: 1 MADAM! | 3 *your Ladyship* | 9 *Madam* | 12 (*Madam*,) | 17 MADAM | 22 Ladyships | 23 Servant |. However, in line 21 *my Lord* was inadvertently retained, though heavily deleted by hand in the Dyce copy. Andrew Pennycuicke signed this dedication alone.

Greg suggests that these variants to the standard Southampton dedication may have been printed as presentation copies. Certainly the survival of only a single example of each is an indication that they were not printed for public sale in any large number, if for public sale at all. The incomplete changes made in the text of the dedication to Lady Newton demonstrate that the sheet in this copy was run off after the other copies containing the standard form of the text, and hence presumably as the last sheet(s) printed.[1] If this is so, it still need not be a necessary inference that the other recorded variant headings were machined in order just before this Lady

---

[1] Since alterations take place in sigs. A2 and A2ᵛ, both inner and outer formes, such sheets would need to have been segregated for special perfecting.

Newton state and after the major run of the Southampton form had been completed. What seems to be an authentic press-variant occurs on sig. A2^v, the only known uncorrected state (*Forloru* for *Forlorn*) being found in the Ashley copy where it backs the inner forme that on sig. A2 recto contained the variant heading to Northumberland. If we could count on sheets being perfected in the same order that they were printed, the combination would indicate that the Northumberland dedication was printed off at the start of the run and before any of the other dedications.[1] This is not necessarily an unusual procedure, for the number of special headings may not have been firmly settled before printing started: and indeed we have no evidence whether the Dorchester heading followed on the Northumberland or immediately preceded the Lady Newton, although the odds may perhaps favour the latter.

Fortunately, an editor can take a somewhat academic interest in the purely technical and very likely insoluble problem of the precise order and chronology of the variant headings, for no textual question is involved. However, an editorial problem does exist for the text of the dedication itself. A unique copy is preserved in the Pierpont Morgan Library with the text of the Southampton dedication in a completely variant typesetting that exhibits different compositorial characteristics from the common form. Influenced perhaps by the odd fact that the heading is in the same setting in each and that only the text on sigs. A2 and A2^v (less the ornamental

---

[1] Unfortunately there is plenty of evidence that the whole heap of sheets was not invariably perfected as a unit in the exact order of printing. The case is complicated by the difficulty that ordinarily the direction of change in a single variant of this nature cannot be demonstrated: an original error may have been corrected in press but on the other hand an ink-ball might have pulled the type and it been put back in the turned position. In this example, however, one may infer that the variant is a true press-alteration. Since *Forlorn* is correct in the forme backing the dedication to Lady Newton, and since this sheet must have been perfected in its normal order, we can be sure that *Forlorn* was the reading in the last sheet(s) to be machined. This presupposes that *Forloru* was the earlier and presumably the original reading. The only alternative is to speculate that *Forlorn* was original, that the type was jerked out and replaced incorrectly so that the form *Forloru* resulted, and that the error was discovered and corrected before the Lady Newton state was printed. Although this hypothesis would put all the variant headings together, it has an undesirable complexity, especially since it fails to explain (assuming seriatim perfecting in order of printing) why what would be the immediately adjacent Dorchester dedication does not contain the misprint.

initial) is reset, the remainder of the preliminaries being printed from standing type without any variation, Greg suggested that the anomaly could represent a trial setting. If this is so, its text would be the one composed directly from manuscript and would, therefore, be chosen by an editor as of greater authority, at least for the forms of its accidentals.

So long as there was any doubt whether copies of *The Sun's Darling* had press-variant and not cancellans title-pages when the setting is the same except for the altered date 1657 for 1656 (see below), Greg's suggestion was equally uncertain. That is, if these titles had been press-variant, the Pierpont Morgan example, which has the 1656 date, would necessarily represent a trial sheet since it could not have been last through the press. But since one can now confirm that the title-leaves of these few copies with the altered date but the same title-page setting are indeed cancels, Greg's explanation is not mandatory and another possibility may be considered.[1]

The evidence is so very slight that there can be no real certainty in the matter, but I take it that the balance tips slightly towards the priority of the common setting of the text, and hence I have chosen to reproduce this form in the present edition.

Not much can be made, perhaps, of the want of analogies for trial settings in early printing, especially for such commercial work as a cheap play quarto. One could argue, I suppose, that the entrepreneurs doubtless anticipated being well paid for their multiple dedication and may have required proofs to insure that they had an attractive typographical layout for the pleasure of their patrons. Yet such a plea may import modern sensibilities into the matter; and, in fact, the Pierpont Morgan typesetting in the fount of the play text, although it is perhaps not so well calculated as the standard form with its larger types, is by no means so unattractive as to be in any way unusual.

The chief difficulty is that if we are to take it that this copy holds a

[1] In assigning these copies as a true variant issue, with a cancel title-leaf, Greg was forced to rely on his own observation of the British Museum copy and reports of the Huntington and Yale copies. Re-examination of these two, for which I am indebted respectively to Professor Sears Jayne and Miss Marjorie Wynne, establishes that their title-leaves are truly disjunct. The case is completely settled by the report of Miss Marion Linton that the National Library of Scotland copy is also disjunct.

trial sheet, we must also accept two other propositions: (*a*) the sheet in the Morgan copy is very probably a proof that was not discarded but was economically bound up;[1] and (*b*) the sheet in the Ashley copy with the misprint backing the Northumberland dedication was printed at the end and not at the beginning of the run.[2] Secondly, Dr Hinman's identification[3] of the two compositors who set the text of the play, starting with sig. B 1, shows that compositor *A* set 25 pages, including the last three, and compositor *B* set 18. He very properly remarks that since *B* can be identified as the compositor of the standard form of the preliminaries (including the verses as well as the dedication), the *B* setting of the preliminaries would bring his share in the book to exactly 25 pages too.

The compositor of the Pierpont Morgan dedication is quite certainly not *B*. One cannot definitely establish that he is *A*, because of the small amount of text, or whether he was another compositor in the shop with somewhat similar characteristics; but the evidence is not inconsistent with *A* and it is probable that he was the workman. No one can prove that *B* did not temporarily drop out after sig. F 4^v, leaving *A* to set the three pages of half-sheet G and the two pages of dedication on A 2–2^v of the preliminaries. But the division of labour in the play text certainly represents continuous typesetting,

---

[1] That is, since the two pages of the dedication are in the inner and the outer formes respectively, a trial would be proofed for both formes but would not be printed and perfected as part of the regular routine until the proof was passed by the authors of the dedication. The only alternative would be to conjecture that printing did indeed start with the Morgan setting and that some sheets of one forme were run off before the press was stopped to reset the dedication. Then in order to save paper (the most costly item in printing), the sheets in the first setting were segregated and were perfected by the forme containing the other page of the smaller type. Such perfecting could have been managed either at the regular time (followed by the substitution of the larger type) or while the resetting was in progress. This hypothesis requires one or other of the two actors to have arrived at the printing house within minutes of the start of printing the initial forme of the preliminary sheet. To conjecture such convenient visitations was more popular in the past than is presently the custom.

[2] That is, one would be hard put to explain a trial setting of the Southampton form followed by a decision to reset with a variant heading for Northumberland and then the main printing with a return to the original setting of the heading to Southampton, all this accomplished without signs of change between the Pierpont Morgan heading and the regular form. Nevertheless, the weight of evidence favours the Northumberland form as the first through the press for the inner forme.

[3] C. J. K. Hinman, 'Principles Governing the Use of Variant Spellings as Evidence of Alternate Setting by Two Compositors', *The Library*, 4th ser., XXI (1940), 78–94.

and the quickest way of getting the quarto off the press would have been to equalize the shares and to put *B* to work simultaneously setting the preliminaries while *A* was engaged with the last of the text in half-sheet G. If *A* thereupon undertook the routine duties that would otherwise have engaged *B* after he had set sig. F4^v, the preliminaries might well have been finished by the time he had completed his own and *B*'s routine.

This appeal to normality can only suggest a probable procedure, of course, and it must be viewed in connexion with other evidence. For instance, the setting of the standard form of the dedication by *B*, who then continued with the Tatham verses on sig. A3 in the very same fount, is a natural sequence. The typography thus suggests that the form of the preliminary sheet set exclusively by *B* is more 'normal' than the form in which (if we may trust the evidence of the spelling *Masque*) *B* set the title on sig. A1, *A* set the dedication on sigs. A2–2^v in an anomalous type, and *B* finished the sheet by setting sigs. A3–4^v. Any attempt to rationalize this division and its typographical units and to make it as efficient a procedure as concluding the book by simultaneous composition in different founts would seem to end in difficulty.

If the Morgan setting of the dedication is not the original, however, we must identify what it may be, instead. Here common experience suggests that this typesetting could have been made to repair a faulty estimate and to bring an underprinting of sheet *A* with the original, or standard, typesetting up to the correct number of copies. If this were true, we should need to suppose that distribution had started before the error was discovered, but that not much time had elapsed between the end of printing and the resetting that was designed to make up the full edition-sheet.[1]

[1] There is no particular difficulty in this supposition. If the type used in the dedication had been required for some other book, it would have been distributed at the earliest opportunity and the type-cases would not have been available for a resetting. But if the rest of the type in the preliminaries had not been required immediately, it might have awaited distribution at better convenience. Of course, we cannot tell (especially since the multiple variant headings do not appear to have been printed one after another) whether Pennycuicke and Bird had not proposed to underprint sheet *A* slightly, and to have the type held standing for a time while they investigated the possibility of securing more money by further specially printed dedications. If so, the dedication type could still have been distributed if it had been required for another

Possible evidence from their texts bearing on the order of the two dedications is so slight and subject to mere opinion that it is substantially worthless as compared to the accumulation of bibliographical argument.[1] However, since the editorial choice of the standard dedication remains in the area of probability and not of demonstration, a full collation has been provided so that the exact details of both forms of the dedication can be reconstructed.

Dr Hinman's study of the two compositors was based on their differences in spelling habits in dealing with (1) twenty words that vary between *i* (medially) or *ie* (finally) and *y*, such as *air-ayre*, *diet-dyet*, *eie-eye*, *follie-folly*, *glorie-glory*; (2) four words that vary between *-ear* and *-eer*, such as *dear-deer*; (3) three words varying between *-k* or *-ck* and *-que*, such as *mask-masque* and *musick-musique*; (4) thirteen more or less unrelated words, such as *altar-alter*, *cristal-*

---

operation in Bell's shop but the remainder left undisturbed. Such a speculation, indeed, would remove the most awkward feature of the underprinting hypothesis: the almost immediate discovery if a short run had been made by accident. Usually a short run of a sheet is not discovered until the latter stages of binding, or at least of the collation of the sheets before binding. Yet it must be emphasized that we know nothing of the actual length of time the type for the preliminaries was held standing, and we do not know how long a time elapsed between the machining of sheet A and the printing from standing type but with altered date of the first cancel title-leaf. Thus elaborate theories to account for the partial distribution of sheet A are not required, since normal distribution may have been started for all we know. Distribution of title-pages and of the special types in preliminaries was not necessarily a matter of hours. For example, from the use in the cancel title-page of Shakespeare's *Troilus and Cressida* Q1 of the typesetting of the original title-page, printed perhaps a fortnight earlier, we can tell that non-text types might be kept standing for a considerable interval.

[1] On the one hand it might be guessed (although we do not know enough about compositor *B* in Bell's shop even to speculate) that faced with concord in noun and verb in the Morgan *present*, line 3, he would be unlikely to set *presents*. But this is mere fantasy, for we cannot estimate the effect on a compositor of the singular *Wrapping their Dead*, even if we could generalize that ordinarily, in a resetting, a text is likely to be sophisticated by enforcing concord instead of the reverse. On the other hand, if the Morgan text were the resetting, we might have difficulty in explaining the quite anomalous commas that were introduced after *under* (l. 14) and *Demetrius* (l. 16) if the text had been the standard setting (as we have supposed), and perhaps the introduction of a colon for a full stop after *Eternity* in l. 5. Such eccentric punctuation is not a habit of compositor *A* in the body of the quarto, and, offhand, would be more readily explained as caused by a compositor struggling with manuscript copy than reading a clear and sensibly punctuated print. Nevertheless, all such suppositions are fundamentally undemonstrable and cannot be taken seriously as arguments in favour of one or other order.

8

christal, guid-guide. To these he added pieces of evidence from stage-directions and speech-prefixes to construct a case that would appear to be an excellent one. The division is in such units as led Dr Hinman to conjecture that setting was continuous in order to speed the work, and the second compositor would take over while his fellow was distributing, imposing, rinsing the formes, and performing other necessary duties. Only two skeleton-formes were used per sheet, and it is likely that the quarto was printed on one press.

We may take it from the evidence that compositor *A* set sigs. B1–2ᵛ (I.i.1–113 [...now and then his |]), C1–3 (II.i.39 [| *Spr. Thou*...]–II.i.211), D1ᵛ–3 (*c.* line 18) (III.i.28–III.iii.1), D4ᵛ–E3 (III.iv.46–IV.i.136), F1ᵛ–3 (IV.i.274–V.i.120), and G1 (line 8)–G2 (V.i.234–342). In turn, compositor *B* set sigs. B3–4ᵛ (I.i.113 [| working-day...]–II.i.39 [...falls from me. |]), C3ᵛ–D1 (II.i.212–III.i.27), D3 (*c.* line 19)–D4 (III.iii.2–III.iv.45), E3ᵛ–F1 (IV.i.137–273), and F3ᵛ–4ᵛ (V.i.121–233 S.D.).

The rest of the publishing history is soon told. Four copies are known in which the title-page is from the same setting of type as the original, and the only difference is that the date 1656 has been changed to 1657. These title-leaves are cancels, not press-variants. It seems clear that printing must have concluded towards the end of 1656; and that too late to change the date in press, but early enough to anticipate distribution of the title setting, the proprietors decided that a small number of copies should be prepared looking forward to 1657 sale. That the four known examples all contain the standard setting of the Southampton dedication has nothing to do with the question of the order of the dedication typesettings, for the last sheets off the press would not necessarily be selected for cancellation.[1]

That sale was slower than anticipated is very likely indicated by a third issue, in which a number of copies have a cancel title-page with the date 1657, but in a different typesetting that omits the reference to performances at Whitehall. This is presumably a later printing.

---

[1] All that can be said is that if the Morgan state of the dedication is the second type-setting, the fact that its title-page is dated 1656 indicates that the extra copies of preliminary sheet A must have been printed earlier than the machining of the cancel title-leaf from the original title setting but with altered date.

9

In his consideration of this play in *The Jacobean and Caroline Stage*, III, 459–461, G. E. Bentley surveys the different theories that have been advanced about the authorship and date, and comes to the conclusion that 'there is no considerable evidence' for the hypothesis that *The Sun's Darling* is a revision by Ford of an early masque by Dekker: real internal evidence for an early date does not exist, and the connexion of the work with the lost *Phaethon* that Dekker wrote in 1598 for Henslowe is most speculative.

The earliest reference that we have is the Herbert licence of 3 March 1623/4, 'For the Cockpit Company; *The Sun's Darling*; in the nature of a masque by Deker and Forde' (Adams, *Herbert*, p. 27). Bentley also reports the reference on 10 August 1639: '"The Sunnes Darling" is one of a list of forty-five plays which William Beeston said belonged to the repertory of the King and Queen's Young Company at the Phoenix, and which the Lord Chamberlain accordingly forbade any other London company to act.' Finally, the song in II.i.48 is found in a variant form in Lyly's *Alexander and Campaspe*, V.i, but its first appearance there was in the 1632 edition, and Bentley concludes, 'Whatever the origin of the songs in Blount's 1632 edition of Lyly's plays, it does not seem probable that the cuckoo song was copied from Lyly's play into Dekker and Ford'.

Bentley rightly finds the masque 'as a whole...an odd piece for a London theatre'. However, it is questionable whether, as he asserts, scenery would be required, or whether there is 'quite a bit' of spectacle ordinarily associated with court masques. Perhaps, as he seems to feel, the masque was originally written in 1623/4 for normal production as a play at the Cockpit, and the new staging effects, as well as the passage about the Scottish troubles (see below), were added in 1638/9 for court performance and then 'the whole new production was transferred as something of a feat to the Phoenix'. He concludes, 'Such a sequence of events would fit the new passage, the curiously elaborate staging, and the title-page statement, but one would expect an event of this nature to have attracted some contemporary comment'.

That revisions in an earlier form of the play have been made in 1638 or early in 1639 is very clear. In some considerable part the fifth act, and the last few lines of the fourth which introduce it, refer unmistakably to preparations for the Bishops' Wars. Since Charles's entry into Scotland is anticipated, the date of writing is very likely between 28 November 1638 when the Duke of Hamilton dissolved the Scottish assembly and 30 March 1639 when Charles arrived in York on his way to Scotland. That the date was perhaps in late 1638 may be indicated by Folly's remark to Time in I.i.137, 'Farewell 1538, I might have said five thousand, but the others long enough a Concience to be honest Condition'd'. I take this to be a sarcastic reference to Time as a century old (although Folly might have said 5000 years, the approximate time of the creation of the world). Of course, Folly may be using the legal year rather than the calendar dating; but it is tempting to associate a revision with performance at court during the Christmas festivities of 1638 and early 1639 before Charles had left London.

Still, the question of the form of the original play remains. It is obvious that the manuscript given to the printer in 1656 was a prompt-book, or a copy made from the prompt-book. Thus the directions for music and the preparations for the maskers must certainly represent what was acted at Whitehall in 1638/9. Yet despite Beeston's list, there is no actual evidence that the play was ever acted at the Phoenix after its production at court. It may have been, but we really do not know whether it was. The quarto text, then, in all probability represents the actual prompt-book used at court in 1638/9, unmodified by any possible subsequent public performance.[1]

Whether the Sun's address to the audience in I.i.199–212 was part of the original production or was added in 1638/9 is not to be determined, perhaps. Yet if these lines could be firmly associated with a 1623/4 production at Whitehall, we should be able to do a little more than guess about the relation of a hypothetical court performance in 1623/4 to public performances at the Cockpit.[2]

Since we can only speculate, my own guesses may be briefly

---

[1] It is true that the masque would need no modification from its 1638 Whitehall version for public performance. But the present fifth act, which must replace an earlier text, would have been timely for only a short period.

[2] The language of this passage is that suitable for the court, but once having been written it would have been appropriate enough for delivery in a public theatre.

offered. I have difficulty in following Bentley's objections to a court performance in 1623/4 preceding public representation. It is true that this would be a reversal of the usual procedure, in which plays from the public stage were selected for production at court. But *The Sun's Darling* is no ordinary public play. Moreover, if the title-page of the 1656 edition refers to the 1638/9 Whitehall production, it is odd that the play's connexion with the Phoenix is omitted in favour of the quite obsolete Cockpit. I take it as at least possible that this title was made up from the facts of the 1623/4 performances. If a court performance, revised for a timely political event, could precede (hypothetical) public performances in 1638/9, the same progression could hold in 1623/4, given something of the same circumstances.

Here we return to the question that *The Sun's Darling* is no ordinary play, certainly not one that would have been written for the public theatre directly. One of the oddities about the plot is the invention of Raybright to perform the duties that would ordinarily be assigned to the Sun, the travel through the four seasons. The 1638/9 revision in associating Raybright with Charles I promoted the Sun to divinity, perhaps with some strain. Usually the Sun would be the king, and Raybright, as his son, would be the prince. It is tempting to speculate that *The Sun's Darling* was written for performance at Whitehall in 1623 sometime after Prince Charles's return from Spain on 5 October, that it was intended basically as a compliment to James I and his son Prince Charles, and that it was subsequently produced at the Cockpit, probably in March 1624, as indicated by Sir Henry Herbert's Office Book. If this is so, it is natural to assume that the 1638/9 revisions are largely if not exclusively confined to a rewriting of the fifth act and that the bulk of the play as it was printed in 1656 (perhaps even including the end of Act I) represents the text as originally written by Dekker and Ford in 1623. Whether Ford or someone else made the 1638/9 revision of the fifth act has not been determined.

The Sun's Darling has been edited in modernized form by Henry Weber, *Dramatic Works of John Ford* (1811), vol. II; William Gifford, *Dramatic Works of John Ford* (1827), vol. II; Hartley Coleridge, *Dramatic Works of Massinger and Ford* (new ed., 1848);

and *Works of John Ford*, ed. Gifford, with additions to the text and
to the notes by Alexander Dyce (1869), vol. III.

The following sixteen copies have been collated in the prepara-
tion of the present text: British Museum, copy 1 (Ashley 620)
Northumberland dedication, copy 2 (644.b.41), copy 3 (1478.d.29),
copy 4 (644.b.42), copy 5 (C.12.g.3[8]); Bodleian Library, copy 1
(Mal. 238[8]), copy 2 (Mal. 172[1]) Kingston dedication, copy 3
(Linc A.6.11), copy 4 (Mal. B.165[6]); Dyce (Victoria and Albert
Museum) Lady Newton dedication; Eton College; Library of
Congress (Longe), wants A2.3; Harvard University, copy 1
(*14424.41.3), copy 2 (*14424.41.4); Princeton University, Pierpont
Morgan Library (variant setting of Southampton dedication).

Only a single press-variant was observed, that on sig. A2^v, except
for the variant headings to the dedication on sig. A2. There is some
difficulty in establishing the exact nature of a variant on sig. F4
(V.i.186) between the error *inhabitant* and the correct *inhabitants*;
but on the whole the difference is more probably due to worked-up
type that has not inked than to press-correction.

To the Right Honorable
THOMAS WRIATHESLEY
Earle of *Southampton,* Lord
WRIATHSLEY, of *Tichfield, &c.*

MY LORD!

Herodotus *Reports that the Ægyptians by Wrapping their Dead in Glasse, presents them lively to all Posterity; But your Lordship will do more, by the Vivifying beames of your Acceptation, Revive the parents of this Orphan Poem, and make them live to Eternity. While the Stage florisht, the* POEM *liv'd by the breath of Generall Applauses, and the Virtuall Fervor of the Court; But since hath languisht for want of heate, and now neere shrunk up with Cold, creepes (with a shivering feare) to Extend it selfe at the Flames of your Benignity. My Lord, though it seems Rough and Forlorn, It is the issue of Worthy parents,* 10 *and we doubt not, but you will find it accomplisht with their Vertue. Be pleased then (my Lord) to give it entertainement, the more Destitute and needy it is, the Greater Reward may be Challenged by your Charity; and so being shelter'd under your Wings, and Comforted by the Sunshine of your Favoure, it will become Proofe against the Injustice of Time, and like one of* Demetrius *statues appeare fresher and fresher to all Ages. My Lord, were we not Confident of the Excellence of the Peece, we should not dare to Assume an impudence to preferr it to a Person of your* HONOR, *and* KNOWN JUDGMENT; *whose* HEARTS *are ready* SACRIFICES, *to your* NAME *and* HONOR, 20 *Being my Lord,*

> Your Lordships most humble, and most
> Obligedly, Submissive Servants,
>
> *Theophilus Bird.*
> *Andrew Penneycuicke.*

Upon the SUN'S DARLING.

Is he then found? *Phœbus* make holliday;
Tye up thy Steeds; And let the *Cyclops* Play;
Mulceber leave thy Anvile, and be trim;
Combe thy black Muzle, be no longer Grim;
Mercury be quick, with mirth furnish the heavens,
Jove, this day let all run at six and seavens;
And *Ganimede* be nimble, to the Brim
Fill Boules of *Nectar*, that the Gods may swim,
To solemnize their healths that did discover
The oscure being of the *Suns* fon'd lover.   10
That from the Example of their liberall mirth
We may enjoy like freedome upon Earth.

John Tatham.

*10 oscure] *stet* Q   12 upon] on Q

READER.

It is not here intended to present thee with the perfect Analogy betwixt the World and man, which was made for Man; Nor their Co-existence, the World determining with Man: this I presume hath bin by others Treated on, But drawing the Curtain of this Morall, you shall finde him in his progression as followeth.

The first Season.

Presents him in the Twy-light of his age
Not Pot-gun-proofe, and, yet hee'l have his page:
This smale Knight-Errant will encounter things
Above his pearch, and like the partridge Springs.   10

The second Season.

Folly, his Squire, the Lady *Humor* brings,
Who in his eare farr sweeter Novells sings.
He follows them; forsakes the Aprill Queene,
And now the Noone-tide of his age is seene.

The third Season.

As soone as *Nerv'd* with strength, he becoms *Weake*,
Folly and *Humor*, doth his reason breake;
Hurries him from his Noone-tide to his even;
From *Summer* to his *Autumne* he is driven.   20

The fourth Season.

And now the *Winter*, or his nonage takes him;
The sad remembrance of his errours wakes him;
Folly and *Humour*, Faine hee'd cast away,
But they will never leave him, till hee's *Clay*.
Thus Man as Clay *Descends*, *Ascends* in spirit;
Dust, goes to dust, The soule unto It's Merit.

THE NAMES OF THE PERSONS.

Phœbus the Sun,
Raybright the suns Darling.
Lady Spring.
Youth,
Delight,
Health.
[*Lady Humor.*]
Summer.
Plenty.
Pomona.
Cupid.
Fortune.
Autumne.
Bacchanalian.
Bounty.

Winter.
Conceit.
Detraction.
Time.
Priest of the Sun.
Folly.

A Souldier.
A Spanyard.
An Italian Dancer.
A French Taylor.
A Forrester.
Æolus.
Maskers.
3 Clowns.

THE
Sun's-Darling.

ACT. I. [SCENE i]

AN ALTAR

Enter the Priest *of the* Sun.

Raybright *discovered sleeping.*

Priest. Let your tunes, you sweet-voic'd sphears,
        overtake him:
  Charm his fancies, ope his ears,
        now awake him. Begin.

SONG.

Fancies are but streams
  of vain pleasure:
They who by their dreams
  true joies measure;
Feasting, starve; laughing, weep;
  playing, smart. Whilst in sleep   10
fools with shadows smiling,
  wake and finde
  hopes like winde,
Idle hopes beguiling.
Thoughts flie away, Time hath past 'em;
Wake now, awake, see and taste 'em.

Raybright. That I might ever slumber, and enjoy
Contents as happie as the soul's best wishes

---

1 sphears] Weber; spears Q   *4 Begin.] Weber; begin. Q
12 *wake*] Q cw is *makes*   12 *and*] Weber; *and and* Q

Can fancie or imagine, 'tis a crueltie
Beyond example, to usurp the peace   20
I sate inthron'd in. Who was't pluck'd mee from it?
Priest.   Young man look hither.
Raybright.   Good; I envie not
The pomp of your high office; all preferment
Of earthly glories are to me diseases,
Infecting those sound parts which should preserve
The flattering retribution to my thankfulness;
The times are better to mee, there's no taste
Left on the pallate of my discontent
To catch at emptie hopes, whose onely blessedness
Depends on beeing miserable.
Priest.   *Raybright*!   30
Thou drawst thy great descent from my grand patron
The *Sun*; whose priest I am.
Raybright.   For small advantage;
Hee who is high-born never mounts yon battlement
Of sparkling stars, unless hee bee in spirit
As humble as the childe of one that sweats
To eat the dear-earn'd bread of honest thrift.
Priest.   Hast thou not flow'd in honors?
Raybright.   Honors, I'de not bee baited with my fears
Of loosing em, to bee their monstrous creature
An age together, 'tis beside as comfortable   40
To die upon the embrodrie of the grass,
Unminded, as to set a world at gaze,
Whilst from a pinacle I tumble down
And break my neck, to bee talk'd of, and wonder'd at.
Priest.   You have worn rich habits.
Raybright.   Fine Ass-trappings.
A Pedler's heir turn'd gallant, follows fashion,
Can by a cross-legg'd Tailor bee transform'd
Into a Jack a napes of passing bravery:
'Tis a stout hapiness to wear good clothes,
Yet live and die a fool — mew.

34 hee] Weber; I Q   45 *Raybright.*] Weber; *om.* Q

Priest.   You have had choice
Of beauties to enrich your marriage-bed.
Raybright.   Monkyes and Parakeetoes are as prettie
To play withall, tho not indeed so gentle.
Honestie's indeed a fine jewel, but the *Indies*
Where it grows is hard to bee discovered, troath sir
I care for no long travels with lost labor.
Priest.   Pleasures of every sence have been your servants,
When as y'ave commanded them.
Raybright.   To threaten ruine,
Corrupt the puritie of knowledg, wrest
Desires of better life, to those of this,   60
This scurvie one, this life scarce worth the keeping.
Priest. 'Tis melancholy, and too fond indulgence
To your own dull'd affections, sway your judgment:
You could not else bee thus lost, or suspect
The care your ancestor the *Sun* takes of yee.
Raybright.   The care, the scorn hee throws on mee.
Priest.   Fie, fie;
Have you been sent out into strange lands,
Seen Courts of forreign Kings, by them been grac'd,
To bring home such neglect?
Raybright.   I have reason for't.
Priest.   Pray shew it.
Raybright.   Since my coming home I have found   70
More sweets in one unprofitable dream,
Then in my lives whole pilgrimage.
Priest.   Your fantasie
Misleads your judgment vainly, sir in brief
I am to tell you, how I have receiv'd
From your Progenitor, my Lord, the *Sun*,
A token, that he visibly will descend
From the celestial orbe to gratifie
All your wilde longings.
Raybright.   Very likely, when pray:
The world the whiles shall be beholding to him

60 this,] Weber; these_∧ Q   *67 strange] *stet* Q

For a long night, new married men will curse,   80
Tho their brides tickle for't, oh! candle and lanthorn
Will grow to an excessive rate i'th Citie.
Priest.   These are but flashes of a brain disordered.
Contein your flout of spleen in seemly bounds,
Your eies shall bee your witness.
Raybright.   Hee may come.

Enter Time *with a whip, whipping* Follie *before him.*

Time.   Hence, hence, thou shame of nature, mankindes foil:
Time whipps thee from the world, kicks thee, and scorns thee.
Folly. Whip me from the world, why whip? am I a dog, a cur,
a mungrel: baw waw. Do thy worst, I defie thee.

Sings.   *I will rore and squander,*   90
                    Cozen, and bee drunk too;
                    I will maintein my Pander,
                    Keep my Hors, and Punck too;
                         brawl and scuffle,
                         shift and shuffle,
                    Swagger in my Potmeals:
                         Dammes rank with,
                         do mad pranck with
                    Roaring boies and oatmeals.

                    Pox a time, I care not,   100
                         being past 'tis nothing:
                    I'le be free and spare not.
                         Sorrows are lives loathing:
                              melancholy
                              is but folly,
                    Mirth and youth are plotters.
                         Time go hang thee,
                         I will bang thee,
                    Though I die in totters.

---

*84 flout] float Q   97 *Dammes*] *i.e.* damn-me's
*109 *totters*] Weber; *cotters* Q

And what think you of this, you old doting moth-eaten bearded 110
rascal; as I am *Follie* by the mothers side, and a true-bred Gentleman,
I will sing thee to death, if thou vex mee: Cannot a man of fashion,
for his pleasure, put on now and then his working-day robes of
humility, but he must presently be subiect to a Beadles rod of
Correction; goe mend thy selfe Caniball, 'tis not without need,
I am sure the Times were never more beggerly and proud, waiting-
women flant it in Cast-suits, and their Ladies fall for em; knaves
over-brave wise men, while wise men stand with cap and knee to
fooles: Pitifull *Time*! pitifull *Time*!

Time.   Out foul, prodigious, and abortive birth;   120
Behold the sand glasse of thy dayes is broke.

Folly.   Bring me another, I'le shatter that too.

Time.   No; th'ast mispent thy hours, lavish'd fool-like
The circuit of thy life, in ceaselesse riots;
It is not therefore fit that thou shouldst live
In such a Court as the *Sunnes* Majesty
Vouchsafes to illuminate with his bright beames.

Folly.   In any Court, father bald-pate, where my granam the *Moon*
shews her hornes, except the Consistory Court, and there she
need not appeare; Cuckolds carry such sharp Stelettoes in their 130
fore-heads. I'le live here and laugh at the bravery of ignorance,
mauger thy scurvie and abhominable beard.

Time.   Priest of the *Sunne* 'tis neere about the minute,
Thy Patron will descend, scourge hence this trifle;
Time is ne're lost, till in the common Schools
Of impudence, *Time* meets with wilfull fooles.   *Exit.*

Folly.   Farewell 1538, I might have said five thousand, but the
others long enough a Concience to be honest Condition'd, pox
on him; it's a notable railing whipper, of a plain Time whipper.

Priest.   You heard the charge he left.   140

Folly.   I, I, a may give a charge, a has been a petty Court-holder
ever since he was a minute old, he tooke you for a fore-man of
a Jurie.

Raybright.   Pray sir, what are you?

123 lavish'd fool-like] Gifford; lavish fool, like Q
136 *Time*] time Q

23

Folly.   Noe matter what, what are you?

Raybright.   Not as you are, I thank my better fates,
I am grand child to the *Sun.*

Folly.   And I am Cosen german, some two or three hundred
removes off, to the *Moon,* and my name is *Folly.*

Raybright.   *Folly,* sir, of what quality?   150

Folly.   Quality; any quality in fashion: Drinkeing, Whoring,
Singing, Dancing, Dicing, Swearing, Roring, Foisting, Lying,
Cogging, Canting, *et cetera,* will you have any more?

Raybright.   You have a merry heart, if you can guid it.

Folly.   Yes faith; so, so, I laugh not at those whome I feare, I fear
not those whom I love, and I love not any whom I laugh not at,
pretty strange humor, is't not?

Raybright.   To any one that knowes you not, it is.

Priest.   You must avoid.   *Enter Recorders.*

Folly.   Away away, I have no such meaning indeed-la.   160

Priest.   Hark the faire hour is com, draw to the Alter,   [*Music.*]
And with amazement, reverence, and comfort
Behold the broad ey'd lamp of heaven descending, —
Stand —

                                                    The Sunne *above.*

Folly.   Oh brave!

Priest.   Stand.

SONG.

Glorious and bright, loe here we bend
Before thy throne, trembling, attend
Thy sacred pleasures, be pleased then
To shower thy comforts downe, that men   170
May freely taste in lifes extreams
The influence of thy powerfull beams.

Raybright.   Let not my fate too swiftly runne,
Till thou acknowledge me thy sonne.
Oh theres no joy even from the wombe,
Of frailty: till we be called home.

172 beams] Gifford; *dreams* Q   174 sonne] Weber; sunne Q

Folly.　Now am I an arrant rascall, and cannot speak one word for
　my selfe, if I were hang'd.
Sun.　Raybright.
Priest.　　　　　It calles yee, answer.
Raybright.　　　　　　　　Lord and Father.
Sun.　We know thy cares, appear to give release,　　　　　180
　Boldly make thy demands, for we wil please
　To grant what ere thou suest for.
Raybright.　　　　　　　　Fair beam'd sir;
　I dare not greedily prefer
　Eternitie of earths delights,
　Before that dutie which invites
　My filial pietie; in this
　Your love shall perfect my hearts bliss,
　If I, but for one onely year,
　Enjoy the several pleasures here,
　Which every season in his kinde,　　　　　190
　Can bless a mortal with.
Sun.　　　　　　　I finde
　Thy reason breeds thy appetite, and grant it,
　Thou master'st thy desire, and shalt not want it;
　To the spring garden let him bee convey'd,
　And entertain'd there by that lovely maid:
　All the varieties the *Spring* can shew,
　Be subject to his will.
Priest.　　　　　Lights Lord, wee go.
Folly.　And I will follow, that am not in love with such fopperies.
　　　　　　　　　　　　　Exeunt. [*Manet* Sun.]
Sun.　We must descend, and leav a while our sphere
　To greet the world — ha, there does now appear　　　　　200
　A circle in this round, of beams that shine,
　As if their friendly lights would darken mine:
　No, let em shine out still, for these are they,
　By whose sweet favors, when our warmths decay,
　Even in the storms of winter, daily nourish

　　　　182 suest] Gifford; saist Q　　190 Which] Weber; With Q
　　　　193 shalt] Weber; shall Q　　198 S.D. *Exeunt.*] Gifford; *Exit.* Q

Our active motions, which in Summer flourish
By their fair quickning dews of noble loves:
Oh may you all like stars, whilst swift time moves,
Stand fixt in firmaments of blest content:
Mean while the recreations wee present,   210
Shall strive to please; I have the foremost tract;
Each season else begins and ends an Act.

Exit.

ACTUS SECUNDUS. [SCENE i]

Enter Spring, Raybright, Youth, Health *and* Delight.

Spring.　Welcom! the mother of the year, the *Spring*,
　That mother on whose back age ne're can sit,
　For age still waits upon her; that *Spring* the Nurse,
　Whose milk the *Summer* sucks, and is made wanton;
　Physitian to the sick, strength to the sound;
　By whom all things above, and under-ground
　Are quickned with new heat, fresh blood, brave vigor;
　That *Spring* on thy fair cheeks, in kisses laies
　Ten thousand welcoms, free as are those raies
　From which thy name thou borrowest: glorious name!   10
　Raybright, as bright in person as in fame.
Raybright.　Your eies amaz'd mee first, but now mine ears
　Feel your tongues charms, in you move all the sphears.
　Oh Ladie! would the *Sun*, which gave mee life,
　Had never sent me to you.
Spring.　　　　　　　　　Why! all my veins
　Shrink up, as if cold Winter were com back,
　And with his frozen beard have numm'd my lips
　To hear that sigh fly from you.
Raybright.　　　　　　　　　Round about mee
　A firmament of such full blessings shine,

209 content] Weber; contents Q　　　210 the] Weber; *om.* Q
1 Welcom!...Spring,] Weber (substantially); ~ ‸ ... ~ ; Q
6 under-ground] Weber; under-round Q

I in your sphear seem a star more divine　　　　　　　20
　Than in my Fathers Chariot; should I ride
　One year about the world in all his pride.
Spring.　Oh that sweet breath revives mee! if thou never
　Part'st hence (as part thou shalt not) bee happie ever.
Raybright　I know I shall.
Spring.　　　　　　　　Thou (to buy whose state,
　Kings would lay down their crowns) fresh *Youth* wait,
　I charge thee, on my darling.
Youth.　　　　　　　　Madam I shall,
　And on his smooth cheek such sweet roses set,
　You still shall sit to gather them, and when
　Their colours fade, as brave shall spring agen.　　　　30
Spring.　Thou (without whom they that have hills of gold
　Are slaves and wretches) *Health* that canst nor be sold
　Nor bought, I charge thee make his heart a tower
　Guarded, for there lies the *Springs* paramour.
Health.　One of my hands is writing still in heaven,
　(For that's *Healths* librarie) t'other on the earth
　Is Physicks treasurer, and what wealth those lay
　Up for my queen, all shall his will obay.
Raybright.　Mortalitie sure falls from me.
Spring.　　　　　　　　　　Thou! to whose tunes
　The five nice Sences dance; thou that dost spin　　　40
　Those golden threds all women love to winde,
　And but for whom, man would cut off mankinde;
　Delight not base, but noble, touch thy Lire,
　And fill my Court with brightest Delphick fire.
Delight.　Hover, you wing'd Musicians, in the air;
　Clouds leav your dancing, no windes stir but fair.
Health.　Leav blustring *March.* ———

SONG.

What bird so sings, yet so does wail,
'Tis Philomel the Nightingale;

29 them] Weber; then Q　　　　　　　*30 as] *om.* Q

Jugg, Jugg, Jugg, Terue she cries, 50
And hating earth, to heaven she flies — Cuckow.
Ha, ha, hark, hark, the Cuckows sing
Cuckow, to welcom in the Spring.
Brave prick-song; who is't now we hear!
'Tis the Larks silver leer a leer:
Chirup, the Sparrow flies away;
For hee fell too't ere break of day.
Ha, ha, hark, hark, the Cuckcows sing
Cuckow, to welcom in the Spring.

Spring. How does my sun-born sweet-heart like his queen; 60
Her court, her train.
Raybright.   Wondrous, such ne're were seen.
Health. Fresher and fresher pastimes, one delight
Is a disease to th' wanton appetite.
Delight. Musick take Ecchoes voice, and dance quick rounds
To thine own times in repercussive sounds.   *Exit.*

Eccho of Cornets.

Spring. Enough! I will not weary thee, pleasures change:
Thou, as the Sun in a free zodiack range. —

Enter Delight.

Delight. A company of rural fellows, fac'd
Like lovers of your Laws, beg to bee grac'd
Before your Highness, to present their sport.   70
Spring. What is't?
Delight.   A Morris.
Spring.   Give them our Court:
Stay, these dull birds may make thee stop thine ear,
Take thou my lightning, none but Laurel here
Shall scape thy blasting; whom thou wilt confound
Smite; let those stand, who in thy choice sit crown'd.
Raybright. Let these then, I may surfet else on sweets.
Sound sleeps do not still lie in Princes sheets.

59 *in*] Weber; *in in* Q

28

Spring.   Becken the Rurals in, the Country-gray
  Seldom ploughs treason, shouldst thou be stoln away
  By great ones, that's my fear.
Raybright.   Fear it not Lady;   80
  Should all the worlds black sorceries bee laid
  To blow mee hence, I move not.
Spring.   I am made   *Morris.*
  In that word the earths Emperesse. —
                              Are not
  These sports too rustick?
Raybright.   No; pretty and pleasing.
Spring.   My youngest girle, the violet-breathing *May*,
  Being told by *Flora* that my love dwelt here,
  Is com to do you service, will you please
  To honor her arrival?
Raybright.   I shall attend.
Spring.   On then, and bid my rosie-finger'd *May*
  Robs hills and dales, with sweets to strow his way.   90
                  Exeunt [Spring, Health, Delight, *and*] *Morris.*
Raybright.   An Empress, saist thou, faln in love with me?
Folly.   Shee's a great woman, and all great women wish to be
  Empresses; her name, the Ladie *Humor.*
Raybright.   Strange name, I never saw her, know her not:
  What kinde of creature is shee?
Folly.   Creature! of a skin soft as Pomatum, sleek as Jellie, white
  as blanch'd Almonds; no Mercers wife ever handled yard with
  a prettier hand; breath sweet as a Monkies; lips of cherries, teeth
  of pearle, eies of diamond, foot and leg as ——
Raybright.   And what's thy name?   100
Folly.   'Tis but a folly to tell it, my name is *Folly.*
Raybright.   *Humor* and *Folly*; to my listning ear
  The Ladies praises often have been sung,
  Thy trumpet sounding forth her graceful beauties,
  Kindles high flames within me to behold her.

90 S.D. *Exeunt....*] Gifford; Q reads at the right of lines 89–90: *Morris* | *Exit.*
94 know] Weber; knew Q   98 hand;] Gifford; *om.* Q
103 The] Gifford; Thy Q   104 Thy] Gifford; The Q

Folly.   Shee's as hot as you for your heart.

Raybright.   This Ladie, call'd the *Spring*, is an odd trifle.

Folly.   A green sickness thing. I came by the way of a hobby-horse
letter of Attorney, sent by my Ladie as a spie to you: *Spring* a hot
Ladie, a few fields and gardens lass, can you feed upon sallets and
tanzies, eat like an Asse upon grasse? every day at my Ladies,
coms to you now a Goose, now a Woodcock, nothing but fowl;
fowl pies, platters all cover'd with fowl, and is not fowl very
good fare?

Raybright.   Yea marry is't sir, the fowl being kept clean.
My admiration wastes it self in longings
To see this rare piece, I'le see her; what are Kings,
Were not their Pleasures varied; shall not mine then?
Should day last ever, 'twould bee loath'd as night.
Change is the sawce that sharpens appetite;   120
The way, I'le to her.

Folly.   The way is windie and narrow; for look you, I do but winde
this Cornet, and if another answer it, she coms.

Raybright.   Be quick then.   *Cornets.*

Enter Humor, *a Souldier, a Spaniard, an Italian Dancer,*
a French Tailor.

Humor.   Is this that flower the *Spring* so dotes upon?

Folly.   This is that hony-suckle, she sticks in her ruffe.

Humor.   A bedfellow for a Fairie.

Raybright.   Admir'd perfection!
You set my praises to so high a tune,
My merits cannot reach em.

Humor.   My heart-strings shall then;
As mine eie gives that sentence on thy person,   130
And never was mine eie a corrupt Judg,
That Judg to save thee would condemn a world,
And lose mankinde to gain thee; 'tis not the *Spring*,
With all her gawdy arbors, nor perfumes
Sent up in flattering incense to the Sun,

*111 grasse?] ∼ ∧ Q
113 with fowl] Weber; with foul Q

For shooting glances at her, and for sending
Whole quires of singers to her every morn,
With all her amorous fires, can heat thy blood
As I can with one kisse.
Raybright.   The rose-lipp'd dawning
Is not so melting, so delicious.   140
Turn mee into a bird that I may sit
Still singing in such boughs.
Folly.   What bird, a Ring-tayl?
Humor.   Thou shalt be turn'd to nothing but to mine,
My Mine of pleasures which no hand shall rifle
But this, which in warm Nectar bathes thy palm:
Invent som other tyres; musick; stay; none.
Folly.   Hoy-day.
Humor.   New gowns, fresh fashions, I am not brave enough
To make thee wonder at me.
Raybright.   Not the Moon   150
Riding at midnight in her cristal Chariot,
With all her Courtiers in their robes of stars
Is half so glorious.
Humor.   This feather was a bird of Paradice,
Shall it bee yours?
Raybright.   No Kingdom buies it from mee.
Folly.   Being in fools paradice he must not lose his bawble.
Raybright.   I am wrapt.
Folly.   In your mothers smock.
Raybright.   I am wrapt above mans being, in being spher'd
In such a globe of rarities, but say Ladie   160
What these are that attend you.
Humor.   All my attendants
Shall be to thee sworn servants.
Folly.   *Follie* is sworn to him already, never to leav him.
Raybright.   Hee?
Folly.   A French Gentleman that trayls a Spanish pike. A Tailor.

---

136 glances] Weber; gleames Q
*143 *Folly.* What bird, a Ring-tayl?] *Fol.* What bird? | *Sol.* A Ring-tayl. Q
146 thy] the Q

31

Tailor. Wee Mounsieur, hey nimbla upon de crosse caper, me
takea de measure of de body from de top a de noddle to de heel
and great toe, oh stish be fine: dis coller is cut out in anger scurvie,
oh dis breeshes pincha de bum, me put one French yard into de
toder hose.   170

Folly. No French yards, they want an English yard at least.

Raybright. Shall I bee brave then?

Humor.   Golden as the sun.

Raybright. What's hee that looks so smickly?

Folly. A Flounder in a frying-pan, still skipping, one that loves
mutton so well, he alwaies carries capers about him; his brains lie
in his legs, and his legs serve him to no other use then to do tricks,
as if he had bought em of a Jugler, hee's an Italian dancer, his
name ——

Dancer. *Signior Lavolta* (Messer mio) me tesha all de bella
Corantoes, galliardaes, pianettaes, capeorettaes, amorettaes dolche 180
dolche to declamante de bona robaes de Tuscana.

Raybright. I ne're shall be so nimble.

Folly. Yes, if you powr quick-silver into your shin-bones, as he
does.

Raybright. This now?

Folly. A most sweet Spaniard.

Spaniard. A Confecianador, which in your tongue is, a Comfit-
maker, of *Toledo*, I can teach sugar to slip down your throat
a million of waies.

Folly. And the throat has but one in all, oh *Toledo*!   190

Spaniard. In Conservs, candies, marmalades, sinkadoes, panadoes,
marablane, Bergamotu, aranxues muria, lymons, berengenas of
Toledo, oriones, potatoes of *Malaga*, and ten millions more.

Folly. Now 'tis ten millions, a Spaniard can multiply.

Spaniard. I am your servidor.

Raybright. My pallate pleas'd to, what's this last?

Soldier. I am a Gun that can rore, two stelettoes in one sheath,

168 be] Gifford; de Q   169 breeshes] beeshes Q
171 an English yard] Gifford; a yard Q
180 pianettaes] Gifford; piamettaes Q   181 de bona] do bona Q
191 panadoes] ponadoes Q   193 potatoes] Dyce; potataes Q

I can fight and bounce too, my Ladie by mee, presents this sword
and belt to you.

Raybright.   Incomparable Mistresse.

Humor.   Put them on.   200

Soldier.   I'le drill you how to giue the lie, and stab in the punto;
if you dare not fight, then how to vamp a rotten quarrel without
ado.

Raybright.   How: dare not fight! there's in me the *Suns* fire.

Humor.   No more of this, dances! awake the musick.

Folly.   Oyes! Musick!

Raybright.   No more of this, this sword arms me for battel.

Humor.   Com then, let thou and I rise up in arms,
The field embraces, kisses our alarms.

Folly.   A dancer and a Tailor, yet stand still: strike up.   *Dance.* 210

Enter Spring, Health, Youth, Delight.

Spring.   Oh! thou inticing strumpet, how durst thou
Throw thy voluptuous spells about a Temple
That's consecrate to me.

Humor.   Poor *Spring*, goodie herb-wife;
How dar'st thou cast a glance on this rich jewel
I ha bought for mine own wearing.

Spring.   Bought! art thou sold then?

Raybright.   Yes, with her gifts, she buyes me with her graces.

Health.   Graces! A Witch.

Spring.   What can she give thee.

Raybright.   All things.

Spring.   Which I for one bubble cannot add a sea too?

Folly.   And shew him a hobbie-horse in my likeness.   220

Spring.   My *Raybright*, hear me; I regard not these.

Raybright.   What dowrie can you bring me?

Spring.   Dowrie! ha!
Is't com to this? am I held poor and base?
A girdle make, whose buckles stretch'd toth' length
Shall reach from th'artick to th'antartick pole:
What ground soever thou canst with that inclose

205 dances!] Weber; ~ ∧ Q   206 *Folly.*] *om.* Q

I'le give thee freely, not a Lark that calls
The morning up, shall build on any turf
But shee shall be thy tenant, call thee Lord,
And for her rent pay thee in change of songs.   230
Raybright.   I must turn bird-catcher.
Folly.   Do you think to have him for a song?
Humor.   Live with mee still, and all the measures
Plaid to by the spheres, I'le teach thee;
Let's but thus dallie, all the pleasures
The Moon beholds, her man shall reach thee.
Raybright.   Divinest!
Folly.   Here's a Lady.
Spring.   Is't come to who gives most?
The self same Bay tree into which was turnd   240
Peneian Daphne, I have still kept green;
That tree shall now be thine: about it sit,
All the old poets with fresh Lawrel Crownd,
Singing in verse the praise of chastity;
Hither when thou shalt come, they all shall rise,
Sweet Cantoes of thy love, and mine to sing:
And invoke none but thee as *Delian King*.
Raybright.   Live by singing ballets?
Folly.   Oh! base, turn poet, I would not be one my self.
Humor.   Dwell in mine armes, aloft wee'l hover,   250
And see fields of armies fighting:
Oh! part not from mee, I will discover
There, all but books of fancies writing.
Delight.   Not far off stands the *Hipocrenian* well,
Whither i'le leade thee, and but drinking there,
To welcome thee, nine Muses shall appear:
And with full bowles of knowledge thee inspire.
Raybright.   Hang knowledge, drowne your muses.
Folly.   I, I, or they'l drown themselves in Sack and Claret.
Humor.   Do not regard their toyes,   260
Be but my darling, age to free thee
From her curse, shall fall a dying;

258 muses] Gifford; muse Q

34

Call me thy Empresse; *Time* to see thee
Shall forget his art of flying.
Raybright.　Oh! my all excellence.
Spring.　Speake thou for me; I am fainting.
Health.　Leave her, take this and travel through the world;
　I'le bring thee in to all the Courts of Kings,
　Where thou shalt stay, and learn their languages:
　Kisse Ladies, revell out the nights in dancing,　　　　　　270
　The day in manly pastimes; snatch from *Time*
　His glasse, and let the golden sands run forth
　As thou shalt jogg them, riot it, go brave;
　Spend halfe a world, my Queen shall beare thee out:
　Yet all this while, tho thou climb hills of yeares,
　Shall not one wrinckle sit upon thy brow,
　Nor any sicknesse shake thee; *Youth* and *Health*,
　As slaves, shall lackie by thy Chariot wheeles;
　And who, for two such jewelles, would not sell
　The *East*, and *West Indies*; both are thine, so that ——　280
Raybright.　What?
Folly.　All lies! gallap o're the world, and not grow old, nor be
sick; a lie; one gallant went but into *France* last day, and was never
his own man since, another stept but into the low Countries, and
was drunk dead under the table, another did but peep into *England*,
and it cost him more in good morrows blowne up to him under
his window, by Drums and Trumpets, then his whole voiage,
besides he run mad upon't.
Humor.　Here's my last farewel; ride along with me,
　I'le raise by art, out of base earth, a pallace;　　　　　　290
　Whither thy selfe, waving a Christal stream,
　Shall call together the most glorious spirits
　Of all the Kings that have been in the world;
　And they shall come onely to feast with thee.
Raybright.　Rare!
Humor.　At one end of this pallace shalbe heard

　263 thy] Gifford; their Q　　　267 travel through] Gifford; travel, tell Q
　271 day in manly] Weber; day, manly Q
*291 waving a Christal stream] *stet* Q

That Musique which gives motion to the Heaven;
And in the midle *Orpheus* shall sit and weep,
For sorrow that his Lute had not the charmes
To bring his faire *Euredice* from hell;   300
Then at an other end ——
Raybright.   I'le hear no more;
This ends your strife, you onely I adore.
Spring. Oh! I am sick at heart; unthankfull man
'Tis thou hast wounded mee, farewel.   *She is led in.*
Raybright.   Farewell!
Folly. *Health*, recover her; sirrah *Youth*, look to her.
Health. That bird that in her nest sleeps out the spring
 May fly in Summer, but with sickly wing.   *Exit.*
Raybright. I owe thee for this pill, Doctor.
Humor. The *Spring* will Dye sure.
Raybright.   Let her!
Humor.   If she does,
 Folly here is a kind of a foolish poet,   310
 And he shall write her Epitaph.
Raybright.   Against the morning
 See it then writ, and I'le reward thee for it.
Folly. It shall not need.
Raybright. 'Tis like it shall not need, this is your *Folly*.
Humor. He shall be ever yours.
Folly. I hope ever to be mine own folly,
 Hee's one of our fellows.
Humor. In triumph now I lead thee; no, be thou *Cesar*,
 And lead me.
Raybright. Neither; wee'l ride with equall state
 Both in one Chariot, since we have equall fate.   320
Humor. Each do his office to this man your Lord;
 For tho *Delight*, and *Youth*, and *Health* should leave him,
 This Ivory gated pallace shall receive him.
             Exeunt.

   323 S.D. *Exeunt.*] Weber; *Exit.* Q

ACTUS TERTIUS. [SCENE i.]

Enter Raybright *Melancholy.*

Raybright.   Oh my deer love the *Spring*, I am cheated of thee;
Thou hadst a body the four elements
Dwelt never in a fairer; a minde princely:
Thy language like thy fingers, Musical.
How coole wert thou in anger, in thy dyet
How temperate, and yet sumptuous; thou wouldst not waste
The waight of a sad violet in excesse;
Yet still thy board had dishes numberlesse.
Dumbe beasts even lov'd thee; once a young Lark
Sate on thy hand, and gazing on thine eyes   10
Mounted and sung, thinking them moving skies. ——

Enter Follie.

Folly.   I ha don my Lord: my Muse has pump'd hard for an
Epitaph upon the late departed *Spring*, and here her lines spring up.
Raybright.   Read.
Folly.   Read; so I will, pleas you to reach mee your high ears.

> *Here lie's the blith* Spring,
> *Who first taught birds to sing;*
> *Yet in April herself fell a crying:*
> *Then May growing hot*
> *A sweating sickness shee got,*   20
> *And the first of June lay a dying.*
> *Yet no month can say*
> *But her merry daughter May*
> *Stuck her Coffin with flowers great plenty.*
> *The Cuckow sung in verse*
> *An Epitaph o're her herse,*
> *But assure you the lines were not dainty.*

Raybright.   No more are thine, thou Ideot; hast thou none
To poison with thy nastie jiggs but mine,

My matchless frame of nature, Creations wonder,   30
Out of my sight.
Folly.   I am not in't, if I were, you'd see but scurvily; you finde
fault as Patrons do with books, to give nothing.
Raybright.   Yes ball'd one, beastly base one, blockish, away;
Vex me not fool, turn out a doores your rorer,
French Tailor, and that Spanish ginger-bread,
And your Italian skipper; then sir, your self.
Folly.   My self! Carbonado me, bastinado me, strapado me, hang
me, I'le not stir; poor *Follie*, honest *Follie*, jocundary *Follie* forsake
your Lordship; no true Gentleman hates me, and how many 40
women are given daily to me (if I would take em) some not far
off know; Tailor gon, Spanish figg gon, all gon but I ——

Enter Humor.

Humor.   My waiters coited off by you, you flea them;
Whence com these thunder-bolts, what furies haunt you?
Raybright.   You.
Folly.   Shee!
Raybright.   Yes, and thou.
Folly.   Baw waw.
Raybright.   I shall grow old, diseas'd, and melancholy;
For you have robb'd me both of *Youth* and *Health*,   50
And that *Delight* my *Spring* bestow'd upon me:
But for you two, I should be wondrous good;
By you I have been cozen'd, baffled, and torn
From the embracements of the noblest creature.
Humor.   Your *Spring*.
Raybright.   Yes she, even she, onely the *Spring*:
One morning spent with her, was worth ten nights
With ten of the prime beauties in the world:
She was unhappie never, but in two sons,
March a rude roring fool—
Folly.   And *April* a whining puppie.   60
Humour.   But *May* was a fine piece.
Raybright.   Mirror of faces.

34 ball'd] *i.e.* bald

38

Folly.   Indeed *May* was a sweet creature, and yet a great raiser
of May-poles.

Humor.   When will you sing my praises thus?

Raybright.   Thy praises, that art a common creature.

Humor.   Common!

Raybright.   Yes, common:
I cannot passe through any Princes Court,
Through any Countrie, Camp, Town, Citie, Village,
But up your name is cried, nay curs'd; a vengeance
On this your debauch'd Humor.   70

Folly.   A Vintner spoke those very words last night, to a company
of roring boies, that would not pay their reckoning.

Raybright.   How many bastards hast thou?

Humor.   None.

Raybright.   'Tis a lie, bee judg'd by this your squire else.

Folly.   Squire! worshipful Master *Follie.*

Raybright.   The Courtier has his Humor, has he not *Follie?*

Folly.   Yes marry has he, follie; the Courtier's humor is to bee
brave, and not pay for't; to bee proud, and no man cares for't.

Raybright.   Brave Ladies have their humors.   80

Folly.   Who has to do with that, but brave Lords.

Raybright.   Your Citizens have brave humors.

Folly.   Oh! but their wives have tickling humors.

Humor.   Yet don?

Folly.   Humor Madam, if all are your bastards that are given to
humor, you have a companie of as arrant rascals to your children,
as ever went toth' gallows; a Collier being drunk, jossell'd a
Knight into the kennel, and cry'd 'twas his humor; the Knight
broke his coxcomb, and that was his humor.

Raybright.   And yet you are not common.

Humor.   No matter what I am: 90
Rail, curse, be frantick, get you to the tomb
Of your rare Mistresse; dig up your dead *Spring*
And lie with her, kisse her; me, have you lost.

Folly.   And I scorn to be found.

Raybright.   Stay: must I lose all comfort, dearest stay;

75 judg'd] Gifford; judg Q   86 humor, you] humor you, you Q

There's such a deal of magick in those eies,
I'me charm'd to kisse these onely.
Folly.   Are you so? kisse on, I'le be kiss'd som where I warrant.
Raybright.   I will not leav my *Follie* for a world.
Follie.   Nor I you for ten.   100
Raybright.   Nor thee my love, for worlds pil'd upon worlds.
Humor.   If ever for the *Spring* you do but sigh,
I take my bells.
Folly.   And I my hobby-horse, — Will you be merry than, and
jawfand.
Raybright.   As merry as the Cuckows of the spring.
Folly.   Again.
Raybright.   How Ladie, lies the way?
Humor.   I'le be your convoy,
And bring you to the Court of the *Suns* queen,
(*Summer* a glorious and majestic creature)   110
Her face out-shining the poor *Springs*, as far
As a sun-beam doe's a lamp, the moon a star.
Raybright.   Such are the spheres I'de move in, attend us *Follie.*

                                                    Exeunt.

[ACT III. Scene ii]

Enter Raybright *and* Humor.

Raybright.   I muse, my nimble *Follie* staies so long.
Humor.   Hee's quick enough of foot, and counts (I swear)
That minute cast away, not spent on you.
Raybright.   His companie is musick, next to yours;
Both of you are a Consort; and I, your tunes
Lull me asleep, and when I most am sad,
My sorrows vanish from me in soft dreams:
But how far must we travel, is it our motion
Puts us in this heat; or is the air
In love with us, it clings with such embraces,   10
It keeps us in this warmth.

*105 jawfand] *stet* Q

40

Humor.　　　　　　　　This shews, her Court
　Is not far off, you covet so to see:
　Her subjects seldom kindle needlesse fires,
　The *Sun* lends them his flames.
Raybright.　　　　　　　Has she rare buildings?
Humor.　Magnificent and curious; every noon
　The horses of the day bait there; whilst he
　(Who in a golden Chariot makes them gallop
　　In twelve hours o're the world) alights a while,
　To give a love-kisse to the *Summer*-queen.
Raybright.　And shall we have fine sights there?
Humor.　　　　　　　　　Oh!
Raybright.　　　　　　　　　And hear 20
　More ravishing musick?
Humor.　　　　　All the quiristers
　That learn't to sing i'th Temple of the *Spring*;
　But there attain such cunning, that when the windes
　Rore and are mad, and clouds in antick gambols
　Dance o're our head, their voices have such charms,
　They'l all stand still to listen. ——
Raybright.　　　　　　　Excellent.

Enter Follie.

Folly.　I sweat like a pamper'd jade of *Asia,* and drop like a
　Cob-nut out of *Africa.*

Enter a Forrester

Forrester.　Back: whither go you?
Folly.　Oyes! this way.　　　　　　　　　30
Forrester.　None must passe:
　Here's kept no open Court; our Queen this day
　Rides forth a hunting, and the air being hot,
　She will not have rude throngs to stifle her —
　Back.

　　　　　　　　　　　　　　　　Exeunt.

*23 there] Q her　　　　30 *Folly.*] Weber; *om.* Q

41

[ACT III. Scene iii]

Enter Summer *and* Delight.

Summer.   And did break her heart then.

Delight.   Yes with disdain.

Summer.   The heart of my deer mother nurse the *Spring*,
    I'le breake his heart for't: had she not a face,
    Too tempting for a *Jove*?

Delight.   The graces sate,
    On her faire eye-lids ever, but his youth
    Lusting for change, so doted on a Lady,
    Phantastick, and yet fair; a peece of wonder:
    They call her *Humor*, and her parasite *Folly*;
    He cast the sweet *Spring* off, and turn'd us from him;
    Yet his celestial kinsman, for young *Raybright*   10
    Is the *Suns* darling: knowing his jorneying hither
    To see thy glorious Court, sends mee before
    To attend upon you, and spend all my hours
    In care for him.   *Recorders.*

Enter Sun.

Summer.   Obay your charge — oh thou builder,
    Of me thy hand maid! Landlord of my life,
    Life of my love, throne where my glories sit;
    I ride in tryumph on a silver clowd;
    Now I but see thee.

Sun.   Rise; is *Raybright* come yet?

Delight.   Not yet.

Sun.   Be you indulgent over him,   20
    And lavish thou thy treasure. —

Enter Plenty

Plenty.   Our princely Cosen *Raybright*,
    Your darling, and the worlds delight, is come.

Sun.   Who with him?

13 upon] on Q   24 him?] Weber; them. Q

42

Plenty.   A goddesse in a woman, attended
  By a prating sawcie fellow, called *Follie.*
Sun.   They'l confound him, but he shall run,
  Go and receive him.   [*Exit* Plenty.]
Summer.   Your sparkling eyes, and his arivall, drawes
  Heapes of admirers; earth it self will sweat
  To bear our weights; vouchsafe, bright power, to borrow   30
  Winds not too rough from *Æolus*, to fan
  Our glowing faces.
Sun.   I will: ho *Æolus*;
  Unlock thy jayle, and lend a winde or two,
  To fan my girle the *Summer.*
Æolus.   I will.
Sun.   No rorers.
Æolus.   No.
Sun.   Quickly.
Æolus.   Fly you slaves, *Summer* sweats; cool her.

  Hoboyes, [*exeunt omnes.*] *The* Sun *takes his seat above.*

                [ACT III. Scene iv]

  Enter Summer, Raybright, Humor, Plenty, [Delight,]
      Folly, *Country-fellows and Wenches.*

                    SONG.

  Hay-makers, Rakers, Reapers and Mowers,
      Waite on your Summer-Queen,
  Dresse up with Musk-rose her Eglentine bowers,
      Daffadills strew the greene,
        Sing, dance and play,
        'Tis Holy day.
          The Sun does bravely shine
          on our ears of corn.

        *26 run] *stet* Q   33 thy] the Q

                    43

Rich as a pearle
coms every girle,
   this is mine, this is mine, this is mine;
Let us die, ere away they be born.

Bow to the Sun, to our Queen, and that fair one
  com to behold our sports,
Each bonny lasse here is counted a rare one,
  as those in Princes Courts.
   These and wee
   with Countrie glee
    will teach the woods to resound,
    and the hills with eccho's hollow:
   skipping lambs
   their bleating dams
    'mongst kids shall trip it round,
    for joy thus our wenches we follow.

Winde, jollie Hunts-men, your neat Bugles shrilly,
  Hounds make a lustie crie:
Spring up, you Faulconers, the Partridges freely,
  then let your brave Hawks flie.
   Horses amain
   over ridg, over plain,
    the Dogs have the Stag in chace;
    'tis a sport to content a King.
   So ho ho, through the skies
   how the proud bird flies,
    and sowcing kills with a grace,
    Now the Deer falls, hark how they ring. —

   The Sun *by degrees is clowded* [*and Exit*].

Summer.   Leav off, the *Sun* is angry, and has drawn
 A clowd before his face.
Delight.   He is vex'd to see
That proud star shine near you, at whose rising

     38 *Delight.*] Gifford; *Hu.* Q

44

The *Spring* fell sick and dy'd; think what I told you,   40
His coynes will kill you else.
Summer.   It cannot — fair Prince!
Though your illustrious name has touch'd mine ear:
Till now I never saw you, nor never saw
A man whom I more love, more hate.
Raybright.   Hate Ladie!
Summer. For him I love you, from whose glittering raies
You boast your great name, for that name I hate you,
Because you kill'd my mother, and my nurse.
Plenty. Kill'd he my grandmother, *Plenty* will never
Hold you byth' hand again.
Summer.   You have free leave
To thrust your arm into our treasurie   50
As deep as I my self: *Plenty* shall wait
Still at your elbow, all my sports are yours,
Attendants yours, my state and glorie's yours;
But these shall be as sun-beams from a glasse
Reflected on you, not to give you heat;
To dote on a smooth face, my spirit's too great. *Exit* [*attended*].
                                                   Florish.

Raybright. Divinest!
Humor. Let her go.
Folly. And I'le go after, for I must and will have a fling at one
of her plum-trees.   60
Raybright. I ne're was scorn'd till now.
Humor.   This is that *Alteza*,
That Rhodian wonder, gaz'd at by the *Sun*:
I fear'd thine eies should have beheld a face,
The *Moon* has not a clearer: this! a dowdie.
Folly. An Ouzle; this a queen-apple, or a crab she gave you?
Humor. She bid's you share her treasure, but who keeps it?
Folly. She point's to trees great with childe with fruit, but when
delivered? grapes hang in ropes, but no drawing, not a drop of
wine: whole ears of corn lay their ears together for bread, but the
divel a bit I can touch.   70

44 Hate] Ha Q   65 Ouzle; . . .-apple, . . .you?] Weber; ∼ , . . . ∼ ; . . . ∼ . Q

Humor.   Be rul'd by me once more, leave her.

Raybright.   In scorn, as she doe's me.

Folly.   Scorn! If I be not deceived, I ha seen *Summer* go up and
   down with hot Codlings; and that little baggage, her daughter
   Plenty, crying six bunches of Raddish for a peny.

Humor.   Thou shalt have nobler welcoms, for I'le bring thee
   To a brave and bounteous house-keeper, free *Autumne*.

Folly.   Oh! there's a lad — let's go then.

[*Enter* Summer *and* Plenty.]

Plenty.   Where's this Prince; my mother, for the *Indies*
   Must not have you part —

Raybright.   Must not?

Summer.   No; must not.   80
   I did but chide thee like a whistling winde
   Playing with leavie dancers: when I told thee
   I hated thee, I lied; I doat upon thee.
   Unlock my garden of th'Hesperides,
   By draggons kept (the Apples beeing pure gold)
   Take all that fruit, 'tis thine.

Plenty.   Love but my mother,
   I'le give thee corn enough to feed the world.

Raybright.   I need not golden apples, nor your corn;
   What land soe're, the worlds surveyor, the *Sun*
   Can measure in a day, I dare call mine: 90
   All kingdoms I have right to, I am free
   Of every Countrie; in the four elements
   I have as deep a share as an Emperor;
   All beasts whom the earth bears are to serv me,
   All birds to sing to me, and can you catch me
   With a tempting golden Apple?

Plenty.   Shee's too good for thee;
   When she was born, the *Sun* for joy did rise
   Before his time, onely to kisse those eies,
   Which having touch'd, he stole from them such store
   Of light, he shone more bright then e're before: 100

72 she] Weber; he Q   100 he] Weber; she Q

46

At which he vow'd, when ever shee did die,
Hee'd snatch them up, and in his sisters sphere
Place them, since she had no two stars so clear.
Raybright.   Let him now snatch them up; away.
Humor.   Away, and leav this Gipsie.
Summer.   Oh! I am lost.
Raybright.   Love scorn'd, of no triumph more then love can boast.

             Exeunt.

Plenty.   This strumpet will confound him.   *Recorders.*

      Enter Sun.

Summer.   Shee has me deluded.
Sun.   Is *Raybright* gon?
Summer.   Yes, and his spightfull eies
Have shot darts through me.
Sun.   I, thy wounds will cure,
And lengthen out thy daies; his followers gon?   110
Cupid and *Fortune* take you charge of him.
Here thou, my brightest Queen, must end thy reign,
Som nine months hence I'le shine on thee again.

             Exeunt.

ACTUS QUARTUS. [SCENE i]

  Enter Pomona, Raybright, Cupid *and* Fortune.

Raybright.   Your entertainment, *Autumns* bounteous queen,
Have feasted me with rarities as delicate,
As the full growth of an abundant year
Can ripen to my palate.
Pomona.   They are but courtings
Of gratitude to our dread Lord the *Sun*,
From whom thou draw'st thy name; the feast of fruits
Our gardens yield, are much too course for thee;
Could we contract the choice of natures plenty

  105 *Summer*] Weber; *Sun.* Q   *106 Love scorn'd,] *stet* Q
  106 S.D. *Exeunt.*] *Exit.* Q   107 strumpet] Weber; strump Q

        47

Into one form, and that form to contein
All delicacies, which the wanton sence   10
Would relish: or desire to invent to please it:
The present were unworthie far to purchase
A sacred league of friendship.
Raybright.   I have rioted
In surfets of the ear, with various musick
Of warbling birds; I have smelt perfumes of roses,
And every flower with which the fresh-trim'd earth
Is mantled in: the *Spring* could mock my sences
With these fine barren lullabies, the *Summer*
Invited my then ranging eies to look on
Large fields of ripen'd corn, presenting trifles   20
Of waterish pettie dainties, but my taste
Is onely here pleas'd, t'other objects claim
The style of formal, these are real bounties.
Pomona.   We can transcend thy wishes: whom the creatures
Of every age and qualitie posts, madding
From land to land, and sea to sea to meet,
Shall wait upon thy nod, *Fortune* and *Cupid.*
Love yield thy quiver, and thine arrows up
To this great Prince of Time, before him *Fortune,*
Powr out thy mint of treasures, crown him sovereign   30
Of what his thoughts can glorie to command:
He shall give paiment of a roial prize;
To *Fortune,* Judgment, and to *Cupid* eies.
Fortune.   Be a Merchant, I will fraight thee
With all store that time is bought for.
Cupid.   Bee a lover, I will wait thee
With successe in life most sought for.
Fortune.   Be enamored on bright honor,
And thy greatnesse shall shine glorious.
Cupid.   Chastitie, if thou smile on her,   40
Shall grow servile, thou victorious.
Fortune.   Be a warrior, conquest ever
Shall triumphantly renown thee.

10 delicacies] Gifford; delicates Q   33 *Cupid*] Gifford; Cupids Q

Cupid.   Be a Courtier, beauty never
 Shall but with her duty crown thee.
Fortune.   *Fortunes* wheel is thine, depose me,
 I'me thy slave, thy power hath bound me.
Cupid.   *Cupids* shafts are thine, dispose me,
 Love loves love, thy graces wound me.
Fortune and Cupid.   Live, reign, pitie is fames jewel;   50
 We obay, oh! be not cruel.
Raybright.   You ravish me with infinites, and lay
 A bountie of more sovereigntie and amazement,
 Then the Atlas of mortalitie can support. —

                        Enter Humor *and* Follie.

Humor.   Whats here.
Folly.   Nay pray observe.
Raybright.   Be my hearts Empresse, build your kingdom there.
Humor.   With what an earnestnesse he complies.
Folly.   Upon my life he means to turn *Costermonger*, and is pro-
 jecting how to forestall the market; I shall crie Pippins rarely.   60
Raybright.   Till now, my longings were ne're satisfied,
 And the desires of my sensuall appetite
 Were onely fed with barren expectations,
 To what I now am fill'd with.
Folly.   Yes we are fill'd and must be emptied, these wind fruits
 have distended my guts into a Lenten pudding, theres no fat in
 them, my belly swells, but my sides fall away, a month of such
 diet would make me a living Anatomie.
Pomona.   These are too little, more are due to him,
 That is the patterne of his fathers glorie;   70
 Dwell but amongst us, industrie shall strive,
 To make another artificiall nature;
 And change all other seasons into ours.
Humor.   Shall my heart breake, I can containe no longer.
Raybright.   How fares my lov'd *Humor*?
Humor.   A little stirr'd, no matter, i'le be merry:
 Call for some Musick, do not; i'le be melancholly.

                    62 of] Weber; *om.* Q

Folly. A sullen humor, and common, in a dicer that has lost all his money.

Pomona. Lady! I hope 'tis no neglect of Courtesie 80
In us, that so disturbs you, if it rise
From any discontent, reveal the cause,
It shall be soone removed.

Humor. Oh! my heart, helpe to unlace my gowne.

Folly. And unlace your peticoate.

Humor. Sawcie, how now! 'tis well you have some sweet heart,
Some new fresh sweet heart; i'me a goodly foole
To be thus plaid on, stall'd, and foyl'd.

Pomona. Why Madam?
We can be courteous without staine of honor;
'Tis not the raging of a lustfull blood 90
That we desire to tame with satisfaction:
Nor hath his masculine graces in our brest
Kindled a wanton fire, our bounty gives him
A welcome free, but chaste and honorable.

Humor. Nay 'tis all one, I have a tender heart,
Come, come, let's drink.

Folly. A humor in fashion with gallants, and brought out of the
low Countries.

Humor. Fie! there's no musick in thee, let us sing.

Folly. Here's humor in the right trim, a few more such toies 100
would make the little world of man runne mad, as the *Puritan* that
sold his conscience for a May pole. *Florish: showte.*

Raybright. The meaning of this mirth?

Pomona. My Lord is coming.

Raybright. Let us attend, to humble our best thanks,
For these high favours. —

Enter Autumne *and* Bacchanalian.

Pomona. My dearest Lord, according to th'injunction
Of your command, I have with all observance,
Given entertainement to this noble stranger.

105 S.D. Bacchanalian.] Q *adds:* Humor *and* Follie.

Autumn.   The Sun-born *Raybright*, minion of my love,
Let us be twins in heart, thy grandsires beames   110
Shine graciously upon our fruits, and vines:
I am his vassail-servant, tributarie:
And for his sake, the kingdomes I possesse,
I will devide with thee; thou shalt command
The *Lidian Tmolus*, and *Campanian* mounts,
To nodd their grape-crownd heads into thy bowles,
Expressing their rich juice: a hundred graines
Both from the *Beltick* and *Sicilian fields*,
Shall be Congested for thy sacrifice
In *Ceres* fane. *Tiber* shall pay thee Apples,   120
And *Sicyon* Olives, all the Choicest fruits,
Thy Fathers heat doth ripen.
Raybright.   Make me but treasurer
Of your respected favours, and that honor
Shall equall my ambition.
Autumn.   My *Pomona*,
Speed to prepare a banquet of novelties;
This is a day of rest, and we the whiles,
Will sport before our friends, and shorten time
With length of wonted revels.
Pomona.   I obay:
Will't please you Madam, a retirement
From these extreames in men, more tollerable,   130
Will better fit our modesties.
Humor.   I'le drink,
And be a *Bacchanalian*; no, I will not;
Enter, i'le follow; stay, i'le go before.
Pomona.   Ee'ne what humor pleaseth.   *Exeunt. Florishes.*
Autumn.   *Raybright*, a health to *Phœbus*.   *Drinks.*
These are the Peans which we sing to him,
And yet we wear no baies, our cups are onely
Crowned with *Lyeus* blood, to him a health.   *Drinks.*
Raybright.   I must pledge that too.

134 *Exeunt.*] *Exit.* Q   137 yet we] Weber; ye Q

Autumn.   Now one other health,   140
To our grand *Patron*, called, good fellowship;
Whose livery, all our people hereabout
Are clad in.   *Drinks.*
Raybright.   I am for that too.
Autumn.   'Tis well,
Let it go round, and as our custome is
Of recreations of this nature, joyne,
Your voices, as you drink, in lively notes;
Sing *Ios* unto *Baccus.*
Folly.   Hey hoes, a god of windes, there's at least four and twenty
of them imprisoned in my belly; if I sigh not forth some of them,
the rest will break out at the back door; and how sweet the Musick
of their roring will be, let an Irishman judge.   150
Raybright.   He is a songster too.
Folly.   A very foolish one; my Musiques naturall, and came by
inheritance; my father was a French Nightingall, and my mother
an English wagtaile; I was born a Cuckow in the Spring, and lost
my voice in Summer, with laying my egges in a sparrowes nest;
but I'le venture for one, fill my dish; every one take his own, and
when I hold up my finger, off with it.
Autumn.   Begin.

Folly.   *Cast away care, hee that Loves sorrow,*
Lengthens not a day, nor can buy to morrow: 160
Money is trash, and he that will spend it,
let him drink merrily, Fortune will send it.
Merrily, Merrily, Merrily, Oh ho.
Play it off stiffly, we may not part so:
Merrily &c.

Wine is a Charme, it heates the blood too,
Cowards it will arm, if the wine be good too;
quickens the wit, and makes the back able;
scornes to submit to the watch or Cunstable.
Merrily, &c.   170

142 clad] Weber; call'd Q

52

> *Pots fly about, give us more Liquor;*
> *Brothers of a rowt, our braines will flow quicker;*
> *emptie the Cask, score up, wee care not,*
> *fill all the Pots again, drink on, and spare not.*
> *Merrily, &c.*

Now have I more air then ten Musicians, besides there is a whirl-
winde in my brains, I could both caper and turn round.

Autumn.   Oh! a Dance by all meanes,
Now cease your healths, and in an active motion
Bestir yee nimbly, to beguile the hours.   180

Folly.   I am for you in that too, 'twill jogge down the lees of these
rowses into a freer passage; but take heed of sure footing, 'tis
a slippery season: many men fall by rising, and many women are
raised by falling.   *Dance.*

Autumn.   How likes our friend this pastime?

Raybright.   Above utterance,
Oh! how have I in ignorance and dullnesse,
Run through the progresse of so many minutes;
Accusing him, who was my lifes first author,
Of slacknesse and neglect, whilst I have dream't
The *folly* of my daies in vaine expence,   190
Of uselesse taste and pleasure; pray my Lord
Let one health passe about, whilst I bethink me
What course I am to take, for being denison
In your unlimited courtesies.

Autumn.   Devise a round,
You have your liberty.

Raybright.   A health to *Autumns* selfe.
And here let *Time* hold still his restlesse glasse,
That not another golden sand may fall
To measure how it passeth.   [*Drinks.*]

Autumn.   Continue here with me, and by thy presence
Create me favorite to thy faire progenitor;   200
And be mine heire.

Raybright.   I want words to expresse
My thankfullnesse.

Autumn.   What ere the wanton *Spring*,
When she doth diaper the ground with beauties,
Toils for, comes home to *Autumne*, *Summer* sweats
Either in pasturing her furlongs, reaping
The cropp of bread, ripening the fruits for food.
Autumnes garners house them, *Autumnes* jollities
Feeds on them; I alone in every land
Traffique my usefull merchandize; gold and jewells,
Lordly possessions, are for my commodities   210
Morgag'd and lost; I sit Cheefe moderator
Between the cheek-parch'd *Summer*, and th'extreames
Of *Winters* tedious frost; nay, in my selfe
I do containe another teaming *Spring*:
Surety of health, prosperity of life
Belongs to *Autumne*, if thou then canst hope
T'inherit immortality in frailty,
Live here till time be spent, yet be not old.
Raybright.   Under the *Sun*, you are the yeers great emperor.
Autumn.   On now, to new veriety of feasts;   220
Princely contents are fit for princely guests.   *Exit.*
                                                              Florish.

Raybright.   My Lord I'le follow; sure I am not well.
Folly.   Surely I am halfe drunk, or monstrously mistaken, you
mean to stay here belike.
Raybright.   Whither should I go else?
Folly.   Nay, if you will kill your selfe in your own defence, I'le
not be of your Jurie. —

Enter Humor.

Humor.   You have had precious pleasures, choice of drunkennesse;
Will you be gon?
Raybright.   I feele a warr within me,
And every doubt that resolution kills   230
Springs up a greater; in the years revolution
There cannot be a season more delicious,

204 *Summer*] Gifford; *Summers* Q

54

When *Plenty* (*Summers* daughter) empties daily
Her *cornucopia*, fill'd with choisest viands.

Folly.   *Plenties* horne is alwaies full in the City.

Raybright.   When temperate heat offends not with extremes;
When day and night have their distinguishment
With a more equall measure.

Humor.   Ha! in contemplation.

Folly.   Troubling himself with this windy-gutts; this belly-aking 240
Autumne; this Apple *John Kent*, and warden of Fruiterers hall.

Raybright.   When the bright *Sun*, with kindly distant beames
Guilds ripen'd fruit.

Humor.   And what fine meditation
Transports you thus, you study some *Encomium*
Upon the beauty of the gardens Queene,
You'd make the palenesse to supply the vacancie
Of *Cinthia's* dark defect.

Folly.   Madam! let but a green sicknesse chamber-maid be
throughly steel'd, if she get not a better color in one month, I'le
bee forfeited to *Autumne* for ever, and fruite-eat my flesh into 250
a consumption.

Humor.   Come *Raybright*, whatsoer'e suggestions
Have won on thy apt weakenesse, leave these empty
And hollow sounding pleasures, that include
Onely a windy substance of delight,
Which every motion alters into ayre:
I'le stay no longer here.

Raybright.   I must.

Humor.   You shall not,
These are adulterate mixtures of vain follies;
I'le bring thee
Into the Court of *Winter*, there thy food   260
Shall not be sicklie fruits, but healthfull broathes,
Strong meat and dainty.

Folly.   Porke, Beefe, Mutton, (very sweet Mutton), veale, Venson,
Capon, fine fat Capon, partridge, Snite, plover, larkes, Teale,
admirable Teale, my Lord.

Humor.   Mistery there, like to another nature,

Confects the substance of the choisest fruits,
In a rich candy, with such imitation
Of forme and colour, 'twill deceive the eye:
Untill the taste be ravished.   270

Folly. Comfits and Carawaies, Marchpaines and Marmalades,
Suger-plums and Pippin-pies, ginger bread and Walnuts.

Humor. Nor is his bounty limited, hee'le not spare
T'exhaust the treasure of a thousand *Indies.*

Folly. Two hundred pound suppers, and neither fidlers nor
broken glasses reckoned, besides, a hundred pound a throw, ten
times together, if you can hold out so long.

Raybright. You tell mee wonders!
Be my conductresse, I'le flie this place in secret;
Three quarters of my time is almost spent,   280
The last remains to crown my full content.
Now if I fail, let man's experience read me;
'Twas *Humor,* join'd with *Follie,* did mislead me.

Humor. Leav this naked season,
Wherein the very trees shake off their locks,
It is so poor and barren.

Folly. And when the hair fall's off, I have heard a Poet say, 'tis
no good sign of a sound bodie.

Raybright. Com let's go taste old *Winter's* fresh delights,
And swell with pleasures our big appetites.   290
The *Summer, Autumne, Winter* and the *Spring,*
As 'twere conjoin'd in one conjugal ring;
An embleme of four Provinces we sway,
Shall all attend our pastimes night and day,
Shall both be subject to our glorious state,
While wee enjoy the blessings of our fate:
And since wee've notice that som barbarous spirits
Mean to oppose our entrance, if by words
They'l not desist, wee'l force our way with swords.

                                                      Exeunt.

291 *Winter*] Weber; *om.* Q

56

ACTUS QUINTUS. [SCENE i]

Enter three Clowns.

1. Clown. Hear you the news neighbor?

2. Clown. Yes, to my grief neighbor; they say our Prince *Raybright* is coming hither, with whole troops and trains of Courtiers; wee'r like to have a fine time on't neighbors.

3. Clown. Our Wives and Daughters are, for they are sure to get by the bargain; tho our barn be emptied, they will be sure to bee with barn for't: Oh! these Courtiers, neighbors, are pestilent knaves; but ere I'le suffer it, I'le pluck a Crow with som of em.

1. Clown. Faith neighbor, let's lay our heads together, and resolve to die like men, rather then live like beasts.   10

2. Clown. I, like horn-beasts, neighbor; they may talk and call us Rebells, but a figg for that, 'tis not a fart matter; let's be true amongst our selvs, and with our swords in hand resist his entrance.

Enter Winter.

Winter. What, such murmurings does your gall bring forth,
Will you prov't true, no good coms from the North;
Bold sawcie mortals, dare you then aspire
With snow and ice to quench the sphere of fire:
Are your hearts frozen like your clime, from thence
All temperate heat's fled of obedience: 20
How durst you else with force think to withstand
Your Princes entrie into this his land;
A Prince who is so excellently good,
His virtue is his honor, more then blood;
In whose clear nature, as two Suns, do rise
The attributes of Merciful, and Wise:
Whose laws are so impartial, they must
Be counted heavenly, cause th'are truly just:

---

1 *1. Clown.*] *this and similar speech-prefixes in* Q *in this scene distinguish the speakers only as:* 1., 2., *and* 3.

*15 What, such murmurings] *stet* Q

Who does with princely moderation give
His subjects an example how to live;   30
Teaching their erring natures to direct
Their wills, to what it ought most to affect:
That as the *Sun* does unto all dispence
Heat, light, nay life from his full influence,
Yet you wilde fools, possess with gyant rage,
Dare, in your lawlesse furie, think to wage
War against heaven, and from his shining throne
Pull *Jove* himself, for you to tread upon;
Were your heads circled with his own green Oak,
Yet are they subject to his thunder-stroak;   40
And he can sink such wretches as rebell,
From heaven's sublime height, into the depth of hell.

1. Clown.   The divel a can as soon, we fear no colors, let him do
his worst; there's many a tall fellow besides us, will die rather
then see his living taken from them, nay even eat up; all things
are grown so dear, there's no enduring more mouths then our own,
neighbor.

2. Clown.   Thou'rt a wise fellow, neighbor, prate is but prate;
they say this Prince too would bring new laws upon us, new rights
into the Temples of our gods, and that's abominable, wee'l all   50
bee hang'd first. —

Winter.   A most fair pretence,
To found rebellion upon conscience;
Dull stubborn fools, whose perverse judgments still
Are govern'd by the malice of your will,
Not by indifferent reason, which to you
Coms, as in droughts the elemental dew
Does on the parch'd earth, 'twets, but does not give
Moisture enough to make the plants to live:
Things void of soul, can you conceive that he,   60
Whose every thought's an act of pietie,
Who's all religious, furnish'd with all good
That ever was compris'd in flesh and blood,
Cannot direct you in the fittest way
To serv those powers, to which himself does pay

True zealous worship, nay 's so near ally'd
To them, himself must needs be deified.

Enter Follie.

Folly.   Save you Gentlemen! 'tis very cold, you live in frost,
y'ave Winter still about you.

2. Clown.   What are you sir?   70

Folly.   A Courtier sir: but you may guesse, a very foolish one, to
leav the bright beams of my Lord, the Prince, to travel hither;
I have an Ague on me, do you not see me shake: Well, if our
Courtiers, when they com hither, have not warm young wenches,
good wines, and fires to heat their bloods, 'twill freez into an
Apoplexie; farewell frost, I'le go seek a fire to thaw me, I'me all
ice I fear already.   *Exit.*

1. Clown.   Farewel and be hang'd, ere such as these shall eat what
we have sweat for, wee'l spend our bloods; com neighbors, let's
go call our company together, and go meet this Prince he talks 80
so of.

3. Clown.   Som shall have but a sowr welcom of it, if my Crab-tree
cudgel hold here.

Winter.   'Tis, I see,
Not in my power to alter destinie:
You'r mad in your rebellious mindes, but hear
What I presage, with understanding clear,
As your black thoughts are mistie: take from me
This as a true and certain augurie.
This Prince shall com, and by his glorious side   90
Lawrel-crown'd conquest shall in triumph ride,
Arm'd with the justice that attend's his cause,
You shall with penitence embrace his laws:
Hee to the frozen northern clime shall bring
A warmth so temperate, as shall force the *Spring*
Usurp my privilege, and by his Ray
Night shall bee chang'd into perpetual day.
Plentie and happinesse shall still increase,
As does his light; and Turtle-footed Peace
Dance like a Fairie through his realms, while all   100

That envie him, shall like swift Comets fall,
By their own fire consum'd, and glorious he
Ruling, as 'twere, the force of destinie,
Shall have a long and prosperous reign on earth,
Then flie to heaven, and give a new star birth.   *Florish.*

            Enter Raybright, Humor, Bountie, *and* Delight.

But see, our star appear's, and from his eie
Flie thousand beams of sparkling majestie.
Bright son of *Phebus*! welcom, I begin
To feel the ice fal from my crisled skin;
For at your beams the Waggoner might thow   110
His Chariot, axell'd with *Riphean* snow;
Nay, the slow moving North-star having felt
Your temperate heat, his isicles would melt.
Raybright. What bold rebellious Catives dare disturb
The happie progresse of our glorious peace.
Contemne the Justice of our equall lawes,
Prophane those sacred rights, which stil must bee
Attendant on monarchall dignitie.
I came to frolick with you, and to chear
Your drouping soules by vigor of my beams;   120
And have I this strange welcom! reverend *Winter*!
I'me come to be your guest; your bounteous free
Condition does assure me, I shall have
A welcom entertainment.
Winter. Illustrious sir! I am not ignorant
How much expression my true zeale will want
To entertain you fitlie, yet my love,
And hartie dutie, shall be farr above
My outward welcome; to that glorious light
Of heaven, the *Sunne* which chaces hence the night,   130
I am so much a vassaile, that I'le strive,
By honoring you, to keep my faith alive
To him, brave Prince, thro you, who do inherit

105 S.D. Bountie,] Weber; Bountie, Winter Q   123 me] Weber; *om.* Q
125 not] Gifford; *om.* Q   133 thro] Gifford; tho Q

Your fathers cheerefull heat, and quickning spirit;
Therefore as I am *Winter*, worne and spent
So farre with age, I am *Tymes* monument,
Antiquities example; in my zeale,
I, from my youth, a span of Tyme will steale
To open the free treasures of my Court,
And swell your soul with my delights and sport.   140
Raybright.   Never till now
Did admiration beget in me truly
The rare match'd twins at once, pittie and pleasure;
So royall, so aboundant in earth's blessings,
Should not partake the comfort of those beames,
With which the *Sun* beyond extent doth cheere
The other seasons, yet my pleasures with you,
From their false charmes, doth get the start as farr
As heaven's great lamp from every minor starr.
Bounty.   Sir! you can speak wel: if your tongue deliver   150
The message of your heart, without some cuning
Of restraint, we may hope to enjoy
The lasting riches of your presence hence,
Without distrust or change.
Raybright.   *Winters* sweet bride,
All Conquering *Bounty*, queen of harts, life's glory,
Natures perfection; whom all love, all serve;
To whom *Fortune*, even in extreame's a slave,
When I fall from my dutie to thy goodness,
Then let me be ranck'd as nothing.
Bounty.   Come, you flatter mee.   160
Raybright.   I flatter you! Why Madam? you are *Bounty*;
Sole daughter to the royall throne of peace.
Humor.   He minds not mee now.
Raybright.   Bounties self!
For you he is no souldier dares not fight,
No Scholar he, that dares not plead your merites,
Or study your best Sweetness, should the *Sun*,
Eclips'd for many yeares, forbeare to shine

> 144 So royall] *i.e.* that one so royal

Upon the bosome of our naked pastures,
Yet where you are, the glories of your smiles   170
Would warm the barren grounds, arm hartless misery,
And cherish desolation. Deed I honor you,
And as all others ought to do, I serve you.
Humor.   Are these the rare sights, these the promis'd Complements.
Winter.   Attendance on our revells, let delight
  Conjoyn the day with sable-footed night;
  Both shall forsake their orbes, and in one sphere
  Meet in soft mirth, and harmlesse pleasures here;
  While plump *Lyeus* shall, with garland crown'd
  Of triumph-Ivie, in full cups abound   180
  Of Cretan wine, and shall dame *Ceres* call
  To waite on you, at *Winters* festivall:
  While gawdy *Summer*, *Autumne*, and the *Springe*,
  Shall to my Lord their Choycest viands bring.
  Wee'l robb the sea, and from the subtill ayre,
  Fetch her inhabitants, to supply our fare.
  That were *Apicious* here, he in one night
  Should sate with dainties his strong appetite.
  Begin our revells then, and let all pleasure
  Flow like the Ocean, in a boundlesse measure.   *Florish.* 190

                Enter Conceit *and* Detraction.

Conceit.   Wit and pleasure, soft attention,
  Grace the sports of our invention.
Detract.   *Conceit* peace, for *Detraction*
  Hath already drawn a faction,
  Shall deride thee.
Conceit.   Antick leave me;
  For in laboring to bereave me
  Of a scholars praise, thy dotage
  Shall be hist at.
Detract.   Here's a hot age;
  When such pettie penmen covet
  Fame by folly, on, I'le prove it   200

                *176 sable-footed] *stet* Q

                        62

Scurvie by thy part, and trie thee
By thine owne wit.
Conceit.   I defie thee,
Here are nobler Judges, wit
Cannot suffer where they sit.
Detract. Pri'thee foolish *Conceit*, leave off thy set-speeches, and
come to the conceit it selfe in plain language; what goodly thing
is't, in the name of laughter?
Conceit. *Detraction* doe thy worst, *Conceit* appears,
In honour of the *Sunne*, their fellow-friend,
Before thy censure; know then that the spheres,   210
Have for a while resigned their orbes, and lend
Their seats to the Four Elements, who joyn'd
With the Four known Complexions, have atton'd
A noble league, and severally put on
Materiall bodies; here amongest em none
Observes a difference; Earth and Ayre alike
Are sprightly active; Fire and Water seek
No glory of preheminence; Phlegm and Blood,
Choler and Melancholy, who have stood
In contrarieties, now meet for pleasure,   220
To entertain Time in a courtly measure.
Detract. Impossible and improper; first to personate insensible
Creatures, and next to compound quite opposite humors; fie, fie,
fie, it's abominable.
Conceit. Fond ignorance! how darest thou vainly scan
Impossibility; what reignes in man
Without disorder; wisely mixt by nature,
To fashion and preserve so high a creature.
Detract. Sweete sir! when shall our mortall eyes behold this new
peece of wonder;   230
We must gaze on the starres for it doubtlesse.
Conceit. See, thus the clouds flie off, and run in chase,
When the *Sun's* bountie lends peculiar grace.

206 language] Weber; languages Q
227 Q *prints in right margin the S.D.:* Maskers.

The Maskers discover'd.

Detract. Fine ifaith; pretty, and in good earnest; but sirrah scholar; will they come down too?

Conceit. Behold em well, the foremost represents
Ayr, the most sportive of the Elements.

Detract. A nimble rascall, I warrant him some Aldermans son; wonderous giddy and light-headed; one that blew his patrimony away in feather and Tobacco. 240

Conceit. The next near him is Fire.

Detract. A cholerick gentleman, I should know him, a younger brother and a great spender, but seldom or never carries any money about him; he was begot when the sign was in *Taurus*, for a rores like a Bull, But is indeed a Bell-weather.

Conceit. The third in rank is Water.

Detract. A phlegmatick cold piece of stuff, his father me thinks should be one of the Dunce-table, and one that never drunk strong beer in's life but at festival times, and then he caught the heart-burning a whole vacation and half a Term after. 250

Conceit. The fourth is Earth.

Detract. A shrewd plodding-pated fellow, and a great lover of news; I guesse at the rest, Blood is placed near Air, Choler near Fire, Phlegme and Water are sworn brothers, and so are Earth and Melancholie.

Conceit. Fair nymph of Harmonie, be it thy task
To sing them down, and rank them in a mask. —

SONG.

See the Elements conspire,
Nimble Air doe's court the Earth,
Water doe's commix with Fire, 260
To give our Princes pleasure birth;
Each delight, each joy, each sweet,
In one composition meet.
All the seasons of the year,
Winter *doe's invoke the* Spring,
Summer *doe's in pride appear,*

Autumn *forth its fruits doth bring,*
And with emulation pay
Their tribute to this Holy-day;
In which the Darling *of the* Sun *is com,*   270
To make this place a new Elisium.
                                    Dance [*and exeunt*].

Winter.   How do these pleasures please?
Humor.   Pleasures!
Bounty.   Live here,
And be my Lord's friend, and thy sports shall vary
A thousand waies, invention shall beget
Conceits as curious as the thoughts of change
Can aim at.
Humor.   Trifles: progresse o're the year
Again my *Raybright,* therein like the *Sun,*
As he in heaven runs his circular course,
So thou on earth run thine, for to be fed
With stale delights, breeds dulnesse and contempt;   280
Think on the *Spring.*
Raybright.   She was a lovely Virgin.
Winter.   My roial Lord!
Without offence, be pleas'd but to afford
Me give you my true figure, do not scorn
My age, nor think, cause I appear forlorn,
I serve for no use, 'tis my sharper breath
Doe's purge grosse exhalations from the earth;
My frosts and snows do purifie the air
From choking foggs, makes the skie clear and fair:
And though by nature cold and chill I be,   290
Yet I am warm in bounteous charitie;
And can, my Lord, by grave and sage advice,
Bring you toth' happie shades of Paradice.
Raybright.   That wonder; Oh! can you bring me thither?
Winter.   I can direct and point you out a path.
Humor.   But where's the guide?
Quicken thy spirits, *Raybright,* I'le not leav thee,
Wee'l run the self same race again; that happinesse,

These lazie, sleeping, tedious winters nights
Becom not noble action.
Raybright.   To the *Spring*   *Recorders.* 300
I am resolv'd —— Oh! what strange light appears;
The *Sun* is up sure.

                    The Sun *above.*

Sun.   Wanton Darling look,
And worship with amazement.
Raybright.   Yes! gracious Lord.
Sun.   Thy sands are numbred, and thy glasse of frailtie
Here runs out to the last: here in this mirror
Let man behold the circuit of his fortunes;
The season of the *Spring* dawns like the Morning,
Bedewing *Childhood* with unrelish'd beauties
Of gawdie sights; the *Summer,* as the Noon,
Shines in delight of *Youth,* and ripens strength   310
To *Autumns Manhood,* here the Evening grows,
And knits up all felicitie in follie;
Winter at last draws on the Night of Age;
Yet still a humor of som novel fancie
Untasted, or untry'd, puts off the minute
Of resolution, which should bid farewel
To a vain world of wearinesse and sorrows.
The powers from whom man do's derive his pedigree
Of his creation, with a roial bountie
Give him health, youth, delight for free attendants   320
To rectifie his carriage: to be thankful
Again to them, Man should casheer his riots,
His bosom whorish sweet-heart, idle *Humor;*
His Reasons dangerous seducer, *Follie;*
Then shall
Like four streight pillars, the four Elements
Support the goodly structure of mortalitie;
Then shall the four Complexions, like four heads
Of a clear river, streaming in his bodie,

303 *Raybright.*] Weber; *om.* Q   *303 Yes] Oes Q

66

Nourish and comfort every vein and sinew.   330
No sicknesse of contagion, no grim death
Or deprivation of healths real blessings
Shall then affright the creature built by heaven,
Reserv'd to immortalitie; henceforth
In peace go to our Altars, and no more
Question the power of supernal greatnesse,
But give us leav to govern as wee please
Nature, and her dominion, who from us,
And from our gracious influence, hath both being
And preservation; no replies but reverence.   340
Man hath a double guard, if time can win him;
Heavens power above him, his own peace within him.

332 Or] Weber; Of Q

FINIS.

TEXTUAL NOTES

Tatham. 10 oscure] Although the form *oscure* is not listed by the *O.E.D.*, it is possible that Tatham is using the Italian spelling, partly to flourish his learning but partly to call special attention to the patriotic allegory linking Charles I to the titular character.

I.i

4 Begin.] Weber, followed by all editors, takes Q 'begin' to be a stage-direction. Despite some white space between the end of the verse and this word, the compositor manifestly did not intend 'begin' to be a direction since he set it in roman. But fortunately we do not need to conjecture, for at IV.i.158 the use of the same word to order a song shows that 'begin' here is part of the text. Moreover, it is not a word used in prompt-markings for music.

67 strange] The line is metrically defective unless *Have* is given stress as the first foot. Weber suggested that the line would be metrical if *Fie, fie* were moved down from line 66. The other editors follow Gifford in emending *strange* to *stranger*. Neither expedient seems satisfactory: the metrics are not sound, as Weber believed; nor is *stranger lands* idiomatic or characteristic. Perhaps some word has been inadvertently omitted.

84 flout] Weber emended Q *float* to *flood*; but Gifford and other editors follow Q. *Float* is just barely possible in the sense of a wave, sea, or watercourse, but the expression would be highly strained and I have no confidence in it.

109 totters] Q *cotters* strains the sense, even in the *O.E.D.* meaning, from a much later time, of 'entanglement'. Weber's emendation seems to be a natural one.

II.i

30 as] Weber mended the metre by altering Q *brave* to *braver*; Gifford and the rest preferred to insert *like*.

111 grasse? every day at my Ladies] Q has no punctuation after *grasse* or *day*. Weber placed a query after *Lady's*, but Gifford and the rest inserted it after *day*. However, the question does not seem to be whether Raybright can eat grass every day, but whether he wants to eat such stuff at all. The profusion at the Lady Humor's house is indicated by the variety of fowl that is served *every day*. Moreover, the parallelism is confirmed by the present pointing: 'can you feed upon sallets and tanzies' followed by '[can you] eat like an Asse upon grasse'. The speech rhythm is also suggestive.

143 a Ring-tayle.] Although Q assigns this to 'Sol.', the speech-prefix is suspect since the Soldier is not formally noticed until line 196 and the attendants stay well in the background and are mute until the Tailor begins to speak at line 166. Gifford and the rest give *What bird?* to Humor and *A Ring-tayl* to Folly. But a serious query is pointless without the quip, and it seems more likely that Folly asks the question only in order that he may provide the answer.

291 waving a Christal stream] Weber emends *stream* to *wand*, whereas Gifford, followed by the rest, supposes a complicated eyeskip and a lost line or so in two different parts. The text seems to be hopelessly corrupt, although 'weaving a christal dream' is possible.

III.i

105 jawfand] This unknown word would seem to cry out for emendation, but the cure is not necessarily better than the disease. Weber tried *jawsand*, deriving it from French *joyeusement* or *jouissant*. The *O.E.D.* gives various examples of the sixteenth- and seventeenth-century uses of *jouisance*, and so it may be that *jouisant* or *jouisand* is intended by Folly's word. Gifford suggested *joysome*, although he and the rest print *jocund*. The *O.E.D.* lists only one early use of *joysome*. Obviously the compositor was struggling with some unfamiliar word: if emendation is to be made, either *jouisant* (or *jouisand*) or *joysome* is palaeographically possible. However, it may be significant that in *The Welsh Ambassador* IV.ii.52–55 Voltimar remarks that he will 'steale out of the kinges glasse one quarter of an hower to bee Iouiall'; and Eldred, in his Welsh dialect, responds, 'But where is wine and good seere to be Iawfall and pipes and fiddles to shake our heele at.' Even though *Iawfall* (or *Iawfull*) is a dialect pronunciation of *Iouiall* (a favourite Dekker word) it shows that in a certain pronunciation *jawf* can stand for *jov*. This is enough to give an editor pause in emending *jawfand*. It is true that Folly does not elsewhere speak in dialect. It is true that no known word readily suggests itself. Under the circumstances when no patently clear emendation is available to offer real satisfaction, it may be wiser to let Folly have his say. (*Jocund*, the natural word, is seemingly discouraged by palaeographical probability and by the *Ambassador* association of *jawf* with *jov*.)

III.ii

23 But there] Weber and the rest emend Q *But her* to *But here*, except for Dyce, who follows Gifford's query and prefers *By her*. No one reading is wholly satisfactory. *But here* gives contorted syntax and ellipsis. As for Dyce's emendation, there is no indication that the singers have been trained by Summer. If we accept *But hers* we may take it, with some strain, that Raybright is to hear all the Spring's singers who by transference to Summer's

region have attained further skill. The alternative is to read *But there* on the analogy of *there* in lines 16 and 20, a choice that offers the most natural language.

III.iii

26 run] Gifford, following Weber's query, adds *his course*, a reading accepted by other editors. Doubtless something like that is missing, as indicated by the short line.

III.iv

106 Love scorn'd,] Since this is the concluding line of a couplet, one may expect some strain in the expression. Gifford and the rest unnecessarily emended: '*Ray*. Lost? | *Sum*. Scorn'd! — | *Ray*. Of no triumph more then love can boast?' Weber paraphrased the line: 'If love be scorn'd, love can then no more boast of any triumphs.' This may be the sense, but it does not perfectly fit the context since Summer's capitulation has in fact provided an example of Love's triumphs. Very likely what we have is Raybright's justification of his rejection of Summer: 'When love is scorned, it can boast of no greater triumph than the offer of love which it can then reject.'

V.i

15 What, such murmurings] The quarto's *What such murmurings* was thought by Weber not to be 'consistent with metre and reason', and in altering *such* to *sullen* he was followed by all editors. Q can be defended if *What* is taken to be an ejaculation, and we paraphrase: 'What! does your gall bring forth such murmurings? Will you prove it true that no good comes from the North?' In this reading the stress on *What* straightens out what would otherwise be a metrical difficulty. Just possibly we may think of the syntax as: 'What! does your gall bring forth such murmurings *that* you will prove it true. . . .'

176 sable-footed] Dyce queries *sable-suited*, a more conventional figure than the odd one found in the text.

303 *Raybright*. Yes!] Q omits a speech-prefix and starts a new line with 'Oes'. Tempting as it may be to imagine that Folly interjects an *Oyes* here, the speculation must be resisted on the grounds of decorum. Humor and Folly are properly mute in this last scene after the appearance of the Sun. Weber added the speech-prefix for Raybright and altered *Oes* to *Oh!* Gifford and the rest print '*Omnes*. Gracious lord!'. It may be thought that *Oh* is weak, and that *Omnes* disregards the exclamation mark in Q after *Oes*. The emendation *Yes* is not wholly satisfactory but seems to suit the conditions most closely.

PRESS-VARIANTS IN Q

[Copies collated: BM¹ (British Museum Ashley 620), BM² (644.b.41), BM³ (1478.d.29), BM⁴ (644.b.42), BM⁵ (C.12.g.3[8]); Bodl¹ (Bodleian Library Mal. 238[8]), Bodl² (Mal. 172[1]), Bodl³ (Linc A.6.11), Bodl⁴ (Mal. B.165[6]); Dyce (Victoria and Albert Museum), Eton College, DLC (Library of Congress, wants A2.3); MH¹ (Harvard University 14424.41.3), MH² (14424.41.4) NjP (Princeton University), NNP (Pierpont Morgan Library).]

SHEET A (outer forme)

> Corrected: BM²⁻⁵, Bodl¹⁻⁴, Dyce, Eton, MH¹⁻², NjP.
> Uncorrected: BM¹.

Sig. A2ᵛ.
Dedication
10 *Forlorn*] Forloru

VARIANTS IN THE DEDICATION

[The Pierpont Morgan Library copy presents the dedication to Southampton in a completely different typesetting, recto and verso. In this collation of the two texts, the first reading is that of the present edition, and the second the reading of the unique Pierpont Morgan typesetting.]

2 *Ægyptians*] *Ægiptians*
3 *presents*] *present*
4 *the-parents*] *the parents*
5 *Eternity.*] *Eternity:*
6 *Generall*] *General*
7 *languisht*] *languisht*
8 *neere*] *near*
8 *creepes*] *creeps*
11 *and*] *&*
11 *find*] *finde*
12 *Destitute*] *Destitute,*
13 *is,*] *is*
14 *under*] *under,*
16 Demetrius] Demetrius,
16 *appeare*] *appear*
18 *we*] *wee*
18 *dare*] *dare,*
20 HONOR,] HONOR (*point doubtful*)

71

EMENDATIONS OF ACCIDENTALS

Dedication

4 the parents] the-|parents
10 issue] jssue

14 Sun-|shine] Sun-shine
19 and KNOWN] andKNOWN

Reader

3 their Co-] theirCo-
4 Curtain] Gurtain

20 Summer] Snmmer
22 him;] the semi-colon clear in Dyce

I.i

10 playing, smart. Whilst] playing⌄ smart, whilst
15 'em;] ~ ⌄
16 and] aud
21 in. Who] in, who
21 it?] ~ .
31–32 Thou...am.] prose in Q
33 battlement] battlemen
42 Unminded] Unwinded [turnedm]
46 fashion,] comma inks in MH and few others
57 your] yonr
63 affections, ...judgment:] ~ : ...~ ,
69 neglect?] ~ .
78 All] all
103 Sorrows] sorrows
112 thou] thon
116–117 waiting-|women] waiting-women
120 abortive] a bortive

124 riots;] ~ ⌄
130 carry] Carry
131 fore-heads.] ~ ,
134 Thy] thy
148 I] J
150 sir,] ~ ⌄
153 more?] ~ .
154 You] you
155 Yes] Ycs
159 avoid] a void
162 amazement] a mazement
164 Stand —] Q runs-on with line above
172 powerfull] powerfnll
173 Raybright.] Roy.
179 Raybright] Ray-bright
186 pietie;] ~ ,
187 bliss,] ~ ;
192 it,] ~ ⌄
203 No,] ~ ⌄

II.i

2 sit,] ~ .
3 her; ...Nurse,] ~ ⌄ ...~ ;
4 wanton;] ~ .
7 vigor;] ~ ,
9 thousand] thonsand
13 tongues] tougues

25 (to buy⌄ ...state,] ⌄ ~ ~ , ...~ ?
26 crowns)] ~ ,
28 smooth] smeoth
42 mankinde;] ~ .
51 heaven] heauen

56 *Chirup,*] ~ ∧
66 change:] *the point may be a full stop*
66 Enough!] ~ ?
83–84 Are...rustick?] *one line in* Q
83 Emperess.] Empress∧
88 arrival?] ~ .
91 me?] ~ .
108 thing.] ~ ,
108 hobby-horse] hobby-|horse
113 very] yery
117–119 To see...night.] Q *lines:* To see...not their | Pleasures... day | Last...night.
124 S.D. *Dancer*] Dance
129 then;] ~ ,
130 person,] ~ ;
139 As] as
155 yours?] ~ .
162 thee] the
164 Hee?] ~ .
167 takea] take a
187–188 Comfit-|maker] Comfit-|maker
201 punto;] ~ ,

206 Oyes] O yes
210 S.D. *Delight*] Delighe
219 too?] ~ .
222–223 Dowrie...base?] *one line in* Q
240 turnd∧] ~ :
242 thine: ...sit,] ~ , ...~ :
253 fancies] fances
259 themselves] themseves
263 *Time*] time
264 forget] for get
267 world;] ~ ∧
268 Kings,] ~ ;
269 languages:] ~ ;
270 dancing,] ~ ;
271 *Time*] time
282 lies!] ~ ∧
287 Drums] Drnms
289 farewel;...me,] ~ , ...~ ;
289 along] a long
304 Farewell!] ~ ?
309–310 If she...poet,] *one line in* Q
309 her!] ~ ?

III.i

8 Yet] yet
11 skies.] ~ ∧
17 *taught*] tanght
29 jiggs] iggs
34 blockish,] ~ ∧
51 *Delight*] delight

59 fool —] ~ .
66–67 Yes...Court,] *one line in* Q
84 don?] ~ .
87 drunk,] ~ ∧
102–103 If...bells.] *one line in* Q

III.ii

2 counts (] ~ ,
14 buildings?] ~ .
20–21 And...musick?] *one line in* Q

20 *Raybright.*] Roy.
26 listen.] ~ ∧
34–35 *one line in* Q

III.iii

4 *Jove?*] ~ .
8 *Humor, ...Folly;*] ~ ; ...~ ,
11 *Suns*] Snns
18 tryumph] trynmph

19 yet?] ~ .
21 treasure.] ~ ∧
24 Who] who

73

III.iv

5 *Sing, ...play*,] ~ ∧ ... ~ ∧
7 *The*] the
14 *behold*] bebold
17 *These*] these
20 *hollow*] hollaw
55 heat;] ~ ∧
64 clearer:] ~ ,
66 it?] ~ .

68 delivered?] ~ ∧
79 Prince; ... mother,] ~ , ... ~ ;
86–87 Love...world.] *one line in* Q
96 Apple?] ~ ,
104 up;] ~ ∧
108 gon?] ~ .
110 daies; ...gon?] ~ , ... ~ .

IV.i

11 it:] ~ ,
24 wishes:] ~ ,
27 *Cupid.*] ~ ,
32 prize;] ~ ∧
54 support.] ~ ∧
80 Courtesie] Conrtesie
87–88 Some...foyl'd.] *prose in* Q
103 mirth?] ~ .
105 favours.] ~ ∧
105 S.D. Bacchanalian] Baccanalion
113 kingdomes] knigdo mes
114 thee;] ~ ,
120 fane.] ~ ,
121 Olives] *Olives*
131–132 I'le...not;] *one line in* Q
132 *Bacchanalian*] *Bacehanalion*
142–143 'Tis...is] *one line in* Q
150 Irishman] *Irishman*
153 French] *French*
154 Spring] *Spring*
155 Summer] *Summer*
165 Q *runs on with line above*
174 *not.*] ~ ,

176 whirl-|winde] whirl-|winde
192 bethink] be think
196 *Time*] time
202 My] my
209 merchandize;] ~ ,
211 lost;] ~ ,
218 Live] live
221 guests. *Exit.*] guests, *Exit* —
227 Jurie.] ~ ∧
229 Will] will
231 greater; ...revolution∧] ~ ∧
             ... ~ ;
240 belly-aking] belly-|aking
243 Guilds] guilds
243–244 And...*Encomium*] Q *lines:*
             And...thus,|You...*Encomium*
258–260 These...food] Q *lines:*
             These...thee | Into...of |
             Winter...food
260 food∧] ~ :
263 Mutton), veale,] ~ ∧ , ~ ∧
264 Teale,] ~ ∧
271 Marmalades] ~ ∧

V.i

6 bargain;] ~ ,
51 first.] ~ ∧
57 droughts] droughs
87 clear,] ~ :
88 mistie:] ~ ,
89 augurie.] ~ ,

99 light;] ~ ,
101 him,] ~ .
129 welcome;] ~ ,
130 night,] ~ ;
136 monument,] ~ ;
137 example;] ~ ,

150 wel:] ~ ,
160 Come, you~] ~ ~ ~ ,
171 Would] would
188 dainties] danties
191 pleasure,] ~ ~
197–198 Of...at.] *one line in* Q, *with*
     a long dash after dotage
206 it] if
224 it's] i'ts

250 heart-burning] heart-|burning
298 again;   ...happinesse,]   ~ ,
     ... ~ ~
302–303 Wanton...amazement] *one*
     line in Q
316 resolution] resolutiou
324–325 His...shall] *one line in* Q
334 immortalitie;] ~ ,

75

Brittannia's Honor:

Brightly Shining in ſeuerall Magnificent
Shewes or Pageants, to Celebrate the Solemnity of
the Right Honorable R I C H A R D D E A N E,
At his Inauguration into the Majoralty of the Ho-
nourable Citty of *London*, on Wedneſday,
Oꝏber the 29ᵗʰ. 1628.

At the particular Coſt, and Charges of the Right VVorſhip-
full, Worthy and Ancient Society of *Skinners*.

Mart. lib. 7. Ep. 5. *Rurſus 18, Magnos clamat noua-Troia Triumphos.*

Inuented by T H O. D E K K E R.

TO GOD ONLY BE ALL GLORY

A NOTE ON THE TEXT

Britannia's Honour (Greg, *Bibliography*, no. 419) would have been printed shortly before 29 October 1628, the day of the Lord Mayor's inauguration. Although the imprint is cropped in the only preserved copy, the names of Nicholas Okes and John Norton can be read. G. E. Bentley (*Jacobean and Caroline Stage*, III, 248) has a note on the little that is known of this pageant.

The piece has not been previously edited except for the reprint in the Pearson *Dekker*. The present text has been prepared from the only known copy, that in the British Museum (C.33.e.7[10]).

To the Right Honorable, *Richard Deane* Lord
Maior of the most Renowned Citty of *London*:
And to the two worthy Sheriffes, Mʳ. *Rowland
Backhouse*, and Mʳ. *William Acton*.

Honorable Prætor:

Noble Consuls.

You *are* (this Yeare) *the* Subiect *of my Verse*,
In You *lye hid the* Fires *which heate my Braines*,
To You, my Songs Triumphant I rehearse:

From You, *a* thankes *brings in a golden Gaines*,
Since You *are then the* Glory *of my Muse*,   5
But You, *whom can shee for her* Patrons *chuse?*

Whilst I rest,
Deuoted
To your Lordship,
And Worships
In all seruice,

Tho. Dekker.

Brittania's Honor:

Brightly shining in seuerall Magnificent Shewes or Pageants, to Celebrate
the Solemnity of the Right Honorable Rɪ-
CHARD DEANE, at his Inauguration
into the Majoralty of the Honorable
City of *London*, on Wensday
the 29. of *October*. 1628.

What *Honor* can bee greater to a *Kingdome*, than to haue a *Citty*
for *beauty*, able to match with the *Fairest* in the World? A *Citty*,
renowned Abroad, *admired* at Home. *London*, and her Royall

Daughter (*Westminster*) are the *Representatiue* body of the *general State*; for, here our *Kings* and *Queenes* keepe their Courts; heere are our *Princes*, the *Peeres*, *Nobility*, *Gentry*, Lords *Spirituall* and *Temporall*, with the Numerous *Communalty*.

London in Forraine Countries is called the *Queene* of Cities, and the *Queene-mother* ouer her owne. She is her Kings *Chamber-royall*, his *Golden-Key*: His *Store-house*: The *Magazine* of *Merchandize*; the *Mistris* of *Sciences*; a *Nurse* to all the *Shieres* in *England*. 10

So famous shee is for her *Buildings*, that *Troy* has leap'd out of her own Cinders, to build Her Wals. So *remarkable* for *Priority* and *Power*, that *hers* is the Master-wheele of the whole Kingdome: As *that* moues, so the *maine* Engine works.

London is *Admirall* ouer the *Nauy royall* of Cities: And as she sayles, the whole *Fleete* of them keepe their course.

Fully to write downe all the *Titles*, *Stiles*, and *Honors* of this our *Metrapolis*, would weary a thousand pennes: *Apollo* shall haue a *New* Garland of *Bayes*, to vndertake it. 20

As thus in State, shee her selfe is *Glorious*; so haue all our Kings held it fit to make her chiefe *Ruler* eminent, and answerable to her *greatnesse*. The *Prætorian* Dignity is therefore come from the ancient *Romans*, to inuest with Robes of Honor, our *Lord Maior* of *London*: Their *Consuls* are our *Sheriefes*: their *Senators* our *Aldermen*.

The extention of a Lord Maiors power, is euery yeare to bee seene both by Land and Water: Downe as low as *Lee* in *Essex*: Vp, as high as *Stanes* in *Middlesex*: In both which places, he keepes personall Courts. His House is a *Chancery*: He the *Chancellor* to mittigate the fury of Law: Hee the *Moderator* betweene the griping *Rich* and the wrangling *Poore*. 30

All the *City-Orphans* call him *Father*: All the Widdowes call him their *Champion*. His *Table* lyes spread to *Courtiers*, and *Free* to all Gentlemen of fashion.

More to Proclaime his Greatnesse, what *Vice-roy* is install'd with louder popular acclamations? What *Deputie* to his Soueraigne goes along with such *Triumphes*? To behold them, *Kings*, *Queenes*, *Princes*, and *Embassadors* (from all parts of the World) haue with Admiration, reioyced.

These *Triumphall passages* are full of *Magnificence* for State, 40

Munificence for Cost, and *Beneficence* for doing good. For, besides all the twelue *Companies*, (euery one of which is a gayner by this imployment:) it would puzzle a good memory to reckon vp all those *Trades-men* (with other extraordinary Professions which liue not in the City) who get money by this Action.

Then by this meanes, are euery Yeare added to those that were before, three Faire, Spacious, and Pallacious Houses, Beautified, Painted, and Adorned.

The Lord Maior of *London* (like a Prince) hath likewise his Variety of Noble Recreations: As Hunting, Shooting, Wrastling, 50 before him, and such like.

Thus hauing (as it were in Lantschip) a farre off shewne you the Toppes onely of our *City-Buildings*; and in a little Picture drawne the Face of her *Authority*, giuing but a glimpse of her *Prætor* as hee passes by; let mee now open a Booke to you, of all those Ceremonies, which this great *Festiuall* day hath prouided to Attend vppon him, and doe him Honor.

The first Shew, is called a Sea-Consort.

The first Salutation being on the Water, is furnished with Persons and Properties fitting the quality of that Element. An Artificiall 60 *Rocke* therefore is queintly contriued: On whose highest Ascent sits *Amphitrite* Queene of the Seas, habited to her State; a Mantle frindg'd with siluer crossing her Body: Her hayre long, and disheuelled; on her head, a phantasticke dressing made out of a Fishes writhen shell, interwouen with Pearle, the shell is siluer, on the top of it stands an Artificiall moouing Tortoyse: On each side of her, swimme two *Mermaides*. These two intic'd by the variety of seuerall instruments (ecchoing to one another) haue followed the Sea-Soueraigne, and waite vppon her, as Maides of Honor.

Round about the Rocke are Sea-Nimphes, and in places con- 70 uenient for them are bestowed our three famous Riuers, *Humber*, *Trent*, and *Seuerne*, aptly attired according to the quality of such Marine Persons, who play vpon Cornets.

Amphitryte is the Speaker. From whom are *deliuered these lines.*

Haile *worthy* Prætor, *(Haile Graue* Senators*)*
The Queene *of* Waues *(leauing Gray* Neptunes *Bowres)*
Waites here (Faire Lord) *to serue you.* Fames *Report,*
(So farre as old Oceanus *Christall Court)*
What Tryumphes Ceremony *forth would Call*   80
To Swell *the Ioyes of This* Grand Festiuall,
Intic'de me with my Mermaydes *and a* Traine
Of Sea-Nymphes *hither. Here (this day) shall Reigne*
Pleasures in State Maiesticke: *And to lend*
A brighter Splendor to them, do Attend
Three of my Noblest Children, Humber, Trent,
And Seuerne *(Glorious made by Punishment.)*
The Siluer-footed Thames *(my eldest sonne)*
To grace your Tryumphes *by your* Barge *shall runne.*
Your Fortunes *(led by a white-handed* Fate   90
Vp to this High Fame) I Congratulate:
Glad am I to behold you Thus Set Round
With Glories, Thus with Acclamations Crownd,
So Circled, and Hembd in, on Euery side
With Ecchoing Musicke, Fishes euen take pride
To Swimme along, and listen. Goe, and Take
The Dignity *stayes for you, Whilst I make*
Smooth way Before you, on This Glassy Floore,
Vshering your glad Arriuall to the Shore.
To Honors Temple *now you haue not farre,*   100
Hye, and Come backe more Great *than yet you Are,*
On.

And so the Cornets playing one to Another, they goe forward.
If her *Maiestie* be pleased on the Water, or Land, to Honor These
Tryumphes with her Presence; This following Speech in *French* is
then deliuered to her, with a Booke of the Presentations, All the
Couer, being set thicke with *Flowre de Luces* in Gold.

MADAME,

Voicy, maintenant les Quatre Elements qui vos Attendent pour vous faire Honneur. L'eau est Couverte de Triomphes flottans, pour Dancer 110 *en L'Air: E' L'Air est Remply de Mille Echos, et Retentit de la doulce Musique, que leur voix resonne, pour Attirer vos oreilles fauorables à les Escouter. Puis vous aue₂ sur la Terre, dix mille Mains qui vous Applaudissent pour Ioy et Allegresse quelles ressentent de voir vostre Maieste dans la Ville. L'Element du Feu, Bruit et Tonne vostre Bien Venue. Vos Subjects accourent à grand Foulle, rauis de voir les Graces qui ont choisi leur Throsne sur vostre Front. Toutes les Delices d'Amour se Iouënt sur vos paupieres, La Rose d' Angleterre, et les Fleurs de lis de France S'entrebaisent sur le Vermeil de vos Iouës. Soye₂ Saine comme le printemps, Glorieuse comme l'Este, Autant* 120 *Fructeuse que la vigne. Que Seurte guarde, et Enuironne vostre Chariot de Iour: Et le Sommeil d'ore Dresse et orne vostre Chambre de Nuict. Viue₂ longuement: Viue₂ Heureu₂e: Viue₂ aimee, et Cherie. Bonte vous guarde; Vertu vous Couronne; Et les Anges vous guident.*

Thus Englished.

ROYALL LADY,

Behold, the foure *Elements* waite vpon you to do you Honor: *Water* hath prouided Floating Tryumphes to Dance in the *Aire*: In the *Aire* are a Thousand Ecchoes with Musick in their Mouthes, to Intice you to heare them: On the Shore shall ten thousand paire 130 of hands giue you Plaudits in the *Citty*: The Element of *Fire*, Thunders aloud your welcomes. Thronges of Subjects here, are glad to see the *Graces* Inthroand on your *Forehead*: All the *Delicacies* of *Loue*, playing on your *Eye-lids*, The *Roses* of *England*, and the *Lillies* of *France*, Kissing one Another on your *Cheekes*. Be you healthfull as the *Spring*; Glorious as *Summer*: Fruitfull as the *Vine*: Safety runne along your *Chariot* by Day; *Golden Slumbers* dresse vp your *Chamber* at Night.

Liue long,	Goodnesse Guard you,
Liue happy,	*Vertues* Crowne you,
Liue beloude;	*Angels* Guide you.

140

122 *de Iour*] *le Iour* Q

85

The second Presentation, *New Troyes Tree of Honor*.

A *Person* in a rich *Romane* Antique Habit, with an ornament of Steeples, Towers, and Turrets on her head, Sits in a queint Arbor, Interwouen with seuerall Branches of Flowers.

In her *Left* hand, she holds a golden Truncheon (leaning on the ground) to shew that shees a *Leader* and *Conductresse* of a *Mighty People*: Her *Right Hand* (thrusting through the *Arbor*) takes hold of a Tree, out of which spread *Twelue Maine* and *Goodly Branches*.

This *Lady* (thus sitting) Represents *London*: The Tree (guarded, 150 and supported by her) The twelue *Superior Companies*.

Vpon euery particular *Branch*, is bestowed the *Armes* of some One of the *Twelue*, exprest in the True Cullors within a faire shield. The highest *Branch* of all (as ouer-topping the Rest at *This Time*) bearing the *Armes* of the *Skinners* in a more large and glorious *Escuchion*.

Among the *Leaues* in the *Top*, is a *Tablet*, in which is written, in letters of gold, *Viuite Concordes*, *Liue in Loue*: or *Agree in one*.

Ouer the Person, Representing *London*, is likewise Inscribed in golden Capitals, This,   160

> *Me cunctus Lauro perducit ad astra Triumphus.*
> Each Triumph Crown'd with Bayes,
> Mee to the Starres does raize.

In places conuenient, and in a Triangular forme, vnder the twelue branches of the Tree, are seated *Minerua*, (Inuentresse and Patronesse of Artes, Handy-crafts, and Trades) in Ornaments proper to her quality: And not farre from her, is *Bellona* goddesse of Warre, in a Martiall habit, on her head a Helme and Plume, in her hands a golden Speare and Shield, with *Medusaes* head. Heereby intimating, that both *Artes* and *Armes*, are (in a high degree and fulnesse of 170 honor,) nurc'd vp and maintain'd by and in the City: And, that either of them flourish brauely vnder the shaddow and protection of the *twelue Branches*, shooting forth from that, *New Troy's Tree of Honor*.

Vpon a border of Flowers, inclosing this Tree, are fitly bestowed

86

the *Armes* of as many of the inferior Companies in lesse Escucheons, as for the quantity of roome, can there be hansomely placed.

Within the same Border, (where lesse Trees also grow) are presented *Peace, Religion, Ciuill Gouerment, Iustice, Learning, Industry,* and close to *Industry, Honor.* For as all these are golden 180 Columnes, to beare vp the *Glories* of the City, so is the City an indulgent and carefull Mother, to bring vp them to their Glories. And as these twelue *Noble Branches* couer these Persons, (as it were with the wings of Angels,) so the Persons watch day and night to defend the twelue *Branches.*

These Persons are adorned fitting their state and condition, and hold such properties in their hands, as of right belong vnto them.

1. *Peace* hath a *Doue* on her fist, and a Palme-tree Branch in her hand.

2. *Religion* is in a white glittering roabe, with a Coronet of 190 Starres on her head, holding in one hand, a Booke open, in the other, a golden ladder, (embleme of prayer, by whose steppes wee climbe to Heauen.)

3. *Ciuill Gouernment* is in a roabe full of eyes, and a Dyall in her hand to expresse her Vigilance: For shee must watch euery houre, and keepe all eyes open, yet all little enough.

4. *Iustice* holds a Sword.

5. *Learning* a Booke, and a *Iacobs* Staffe.

6. *Industry,* a golden Hammer, and a Sea-mans Compasse, as taking paines to get wealth, both by Sea and Land. 200

7. *Honor* sits in Scarlet.

The Person, in whom is figured *London,* is the Speaker, *who thus salutes his Lordship.*

Ten thousand welcomes Greete you on the shore,
(My long expected Prætor,*) O before*
You looke on Others, fixe your eyes on Mee,
On Mee, your second Mother, (London.) Shee
Whom all Great Brittaines Citties, stile their Queene,
For still I am, and haue her Darling beene.

87

The Christian World, in Me, *reads* Times *best stories.* 210
And Reading, *fals blind at my da*z*ling Glories,*
But now the Snow *of age, couers my head:*
As therefore you, by Mee *haue vp bin bred,*
You (Sir) *must* Nurse *me* now: *With a quicke eye*
View then my Tree *of* Honor, *branching high*
For hundreds of past yeares, with twelue large Stems,
Twelue *Noble* Companies, *which like twelue Iems*
So shine, they adde new Sun-beames *to the Day:*
 Guard all these twelue main-Boughes; *but you must lay*
A soft hand, on the Topping-branch, *for there* 220
(Thriue the Roote well*) your Selfe grows al this yeare:*
The lesser *twigges which lowly runne along*
My tall Trees Border, *you must shield from wrong,*
There the poore Bee, *(the sweating* Trades-man*) flies*
From Flower *to* Flower, *and home with* Honey *hyes.*
 With me Minerua, *and* Bellona *come,*
For Artes *and* Armes, *must at your Board haue roome,*
Your Gates will spred, the Rich *to entertaine,*
But whilst the Mighty ones *within remaine,*
And feast: Remember *at the same* Gate *stands* 230
The Poore, *with crying Papers in their hands,*
To watch when Iustice *vp the Glasse shall turne.*
Let those sands runne, the Poore can neuer mourne.
 Place in your eyes two Beacons, to descry
Dangers farre off, which strike ere home they flie;
Kisse Peace; *let* Order *euer steere the Helme,*
Left-handed Rule, *a* State *does ouer-whelme.*
 You are your Soueraignes Gardner *for one yeare,*
The Plot *of* Ground, *y'are trusted with, lies here,*
(A Citty,*) and your* care *must all bee spent,* 240
To prune and dresse the Tree *of* Gouernment.
 Lop off Disorders, Factions, Mutiny,
And Murmurations *against those sit high,*
May your yeares last day, end *as this beginnes,*
Sphær'd in the loues of Noble Citizens.

Our third presentation is call'd,
The Glory of Furres.

This is a *Chariot Triumphant*, garnished with Trophies of Armors.
It is drawne by two *Luzernes*, The Supporters of the Skinners
Armes. On the two *Luzernes* ride two Antickes, who dance to a 250
Drum beating before them, there aptly placed. At the vpper end
of this Chariot, in the most eminent Seate, carrying the proportion
of a Throne, are aduanced a *Russian Prince* and *Princesse*; richly
habited in Furres, to the custome of the Country.

1. Vnder them, sits an old Lord, Furred vp to his chin in a short
cloake.
2. By him, a Lady with Martin skinnes about her necke, and her
hands in a Muffe.
3. Then, a *Iudge* in Robes Furred.
4. Then, an Vniuersity *Doctor*, in his Robes furred.   260
5. Then, a *Frow* in a short furred Cassocke, girt to her.
6. Then a *Skipper* in a furred Cap.

In all these Persons, is an implication of the necessary, ancient,
and general vse of *Furres*, from the highest to the lowest.

On the Top of this Throne, (at the foure corners) are erected the
Armes of the *Citty*, in foure Pendants: On the point of the fore-
front, a large square Banner plaies with the wind, which *Fame*
(who is in this Chariot,) holds in her hand, as she stands vpright,
Being the Speaker.

> Fame's *turne is now to Speake; for who but* Fame   270
> *Can with her thousand Tongues abroad Proclaime,*
> *Your this dayes Progresse (rising like the Sunne,)*
> *Which through the yearely* Zodiacke *on must runne.*
> Fame *hath brought hither from great* Mosco's *Court,*
> *(The seauen-mouth'd* Volga, *spreading the report,)*
> *Two* Russian *Princes, who to feast their eies,*
> *With the rich Wonders of these rarities,*
> *Ride in this glorious Chariot: How amazde*
> *They looke, to see streetes throng'd, and windowes glaz'd*

With beauties, from whose eyes such beames are sent, 280
Here moues a second starry Firmament.
   Much, on them, startling admiration winnes,
To see these Braue, Graue, Noble Citizens,
So stream'd in multitudes, *yet* flowing *in State,*
For all their Orders *are* Proportionate.
   Russia, *now enuies* London, *seeing (here) spent*
Her richest Furres, *in gracefull ornament,*
More Braue, and more Abounding, than her owne:
A golden Pen he earnes, that can make knowne
The vse of Furres, *so Great, so Generall,* 290
All men, may these, their Winter Armors call.
   Th'inuention of warme Furres *the* Sunne *did fret,*
For Russians *lap'd in these, slighted his heate,*
Which seene, his fiery Steedes he droue from thence,
And so the Muss *has dwelt in cold ere since.*
   What royalties, adde Furres *to Emperors, Kings,*
Princes, Dukes, Earles, in the distinguishings,
Of all their seuerall Robes? *The* Furres *worne here,*
Aboue th'old Romane State *make* Ours *appeare:*
The reuerend Iudge, *and all that climbe the trees* 300
Of sacred Artes, ascend to their Degrees,
And by the colours chang'd of Furres *are knowne:*
What Dignity, each Corporation,
Puts on by Furres, *witnesse these infinite eyes,*
Thanke then the bringers of these Rarities.
   *I wish (*Graue Prætor*) that as Hand in Hand,*
Plenty and Bounty bring you safe to Land,
So, Health may be chiefe Caruer at that Board,
To which you hasten. Bee as Good a Lord
I'th'eyes of Heauen, as this day you are Great 310
In Fames *applause: Hye to your Honor'd Seate.*

The fourth Presentation is Called Brittannia's Watch-Tower.

This is a Magnificent Structure, Aduancing it selfe from the Platforme, or Ground-worke vpward, with the Bewty of eight Antique Termes, By whose strength is supported a Foure square Building; The Toppe of which is a Watch-Tower, or Lanthorne, with eight Columnes of siluer: And, on the Highest poynt of this Watch-Tower, is Aduanced a Banner, bearing the Cullors of the Kingdome.   320

At foure Corners of the vpper Square, stand foure Pendants; In which are the Armes of the foure Companies of which his Lordship is Free.

At each end of this Platforme, stands a great *Corynthian Brazen Pillar*, on a *Pedestall* of *Marble*.

On the *Capitals* of those Pillars, stand two *Angels*, in Postures ready to flye: holding Garlands of Victory in one hand, stucke with White and Red Roses, and Branches of Palme in the other.

The Capitals and Bases of the Pillars are Gold, and are Emblemes of the two Houses of *Yorke* and *Lancaster*; once diuided, but now 330 Ioyned into One Glorious Building, to Support this Royal Kingdom, and Consequently This Citty.

At Night, in place of the *Angels*, are set two Great Lights: and so is the Watch-Tower at that Time, Filld with lighted Tapers.

Vpon the same Square, in foure seuerall Places, are Aduanced foure stately Pyramides, being Figures, of the foure Kingdomes Embellished with Escutcheons.

In the vpper seate of all (fashioned into a *Throne*) is placed *Britannia*, Maiestically attirde, fitting to her Greatnesse.

Beneath Her, and round about Her, are these Persons: *viz.* 340 *Magnanimity* with a drawne Sword.

A *Shipwright* with a Mallet, holding a Scutcheon, in which is drawne a Ship vnder sayle. Then,

A person representing *Victory*, with a Palme Tree.

Prouidence with a Trumpet, ready to Foresee Dangers, and awaken Men to meete them.

91

All These haue bene, and still are, Watch-Towers, and Lanthornes, in the Nights of Feare and Trouble, to Guard the Kingdome, and in the Kingdome, This Citty.

In other Eminent places are seated some of those Kinges of 350 *England* (in Robes Ermynd) whose loues and Royall fauors, in former times were Watch-Towers to Grace *London*, stucke full with Beames and Lights of Honors, Titles, Offices, Magistracies and Royalties, which they Bestowed vppon Her.

Edward Confessor, called *Londons* Chiefe Ruler, a Port-reue.

Richard I. appointed two Bayliffes ouer *London*.

King *Iohn* gaue the Citty a Lord Maior and two Sheriffes.

Henry 3. added Aldermen.

These were Tender ouer the Renowne of the Citty, and still heaped on her head, Royalties vpon Royalties.   360

And albeit most of our Kinges, haue in most of all of the twelue Companies, Entred their Names, as Free of the Societies, thereby to Royallize their Brotherhoods: And that many of our Kinges likewise, besides Princes and Great Personages, haue bin Free of *This Company*, whose Names I forbeare to set downe, because they haue in former yeeres beene fully exprest: yet no Company, did euer, or can hereafter, receiue such Graces from Kinges, as This *Antient*, and *Honord Corporation* of *Skinners*, hath had, and still haue, In regard that All our Kinges and Princes, sit in their high Courts of Parliament in Robes Ermynd, (being the richest Furre) 370 the workemanship of which goes through the *Skinners* fingers, wearing likewise vnder their Crownes, *Royall Caps* of Honor Ermynd.

Three of such Crownes, beeing the rich *Armes* of *This Company*, thereby expressing aswell their Honor, as Antiquity.

Britannia deliuers thus much.

Shall the Proud wife of Neptune, *or shrill* Fame,
Or Troynouant *her selfe, Ring out your Name:*
And I be Dumbe, or sparing, to Sound high,
The Glories of This Day? No, They shall Fly   380
Like Soaring Eagles, to That Curled Maine
Whose Head my Rocky Bridle, In does Reyne:

The Great Britannia, *Bred you in her Wombe,*
Heare then a Mothers *Counsell; You are Come*
Aboard a Goodly Ship, *where all your State,*
Fame, Honor *and* Renowne *(Imbarqu'd) must waite*
The voyage of twelue Moones. High Admirall
You are to All That Fleete, *which* Thus *you Call*
To sayle in This vast Ocean. Nor must you
Walke Heartlesse on the Hatches: Theres a New   390
State-Nauigation, to be studied Now,
With an High-rear'd, Vndanted, Fixed Brow.
    Be sure to haue Braue Ordnance, *and Chargd well;*
In this your Ship, Trust None, For Officers Sell
Their Captaines Trust; let None but your owne Eyes,
Rule Chart and Compasse, There your Safety lyes.
    Your Owne Hands steere the Helme, But strongly Steere,
And spite of stormes, be stoute when you stand There.
    Embleme of Mercy! Your Keene sword does sleepe,
But why a Sword, if not to Kill, and Keepe   400
Vices (like Slaues) in Awe? Fulnesse *of* Wine
Is a Fowle Dropsie, That and Lust Entwine:
Pride *a Swolne Timpany,* Sloth, *the Beggars Goute,*
(In Tradesmens Hands and Feete, It runnes about,)
No Cure for this! Oathes thicke as Small-shot flye
From Children, No Defence to Put this by!
    You May, you Must. I Counsell not, but Reade
A Lesson of my loue; By which Loue led
Ile on, and Bring you to your Honord Chaire,
Whilst Aues *(Round about you) Dance i'th' Aire.*   410

The last Presentation is called the Sun's Bower.

The vpper part of this, is adorned with seuerall Flowers, which
interwouen together, dresse vp a comely *Greene Arbor,* in which
the *Sunne* sits, with golden Beames about his Face; an Attire
glittering like gold; and a mantle bright as his garment, fringed with
gold, his haire curled and yellow. About him are plac'd *Spring,*

Summer, *Autumne*, and *Winter*, in proper Habiliments. Beneath these, is a Wildernesse, in which are many sorts of such *Beasts*, whose rich Skinnes serue for *Furres*: As the *Beare*, *Wolfe*, *Leopard*, *Luȝerne*, *Cat-A-Mountaine*, *Foxes*, *Sables*, *Connies*, *Ferrets*, *Squirrels*, 420 &c. Of these Beasts, some are climbing, some standing, some grin- ning, with liuely, naturall postures, In a Scrole, hanging on a Bough, This is written in Capitall letters.

> *Deus ecce Furentibus obstat.*
> See, for all some Beasts are fell,
> There's one, that can their curstnesse quell.

Sol *is the* Speaker.

Heauens bright Orientall Gates I op'd this Morne,
And Hither wheeld my Chariot *to adorne*
These splendors with my Beames: nere did the Sun   430
In his Cælestiall Circle faster runne
Than Now, to see these Sights: O how I ioy
To view a Kingdome, and a New-built Troy
So flourishing, so full, so faire, so deare
To th' Gods: they leaue Ioue's *Court to reuell here.*
    All o're the World, I trauell in one Day,
Yet oft am forc'd to leaue my beaten way,
Frighted with Vproares, Battailes, Massacres,
Famines, *and all that Hellish brood of Warres:*
    I meete no Peace *but here. O blessed* Land!   440
That seest fires kindling round, and yet canst stand
Vnburnt for all their flames; O Nation blest!
When all thy Neighbours shrike, none wound thy brest.
    To Crowne these ioyes, with me are come along,
The foure Lords of the yeare, who by a strong
Knit Charme, bring in this goodly Russian *priȝe,*
As earnest of a more rich Merchandiȝe:
Halfe of our Race, Time, and my Houres haue runne,
Nor shall they giue o're till the Goale be wonne.

94

The *Sunne* at Night being couered with a vaile of *Darknesse*: 450
The Person, representing *London*, thus takes leaue.

> *The Sunne is mantled in thicke Clouds of Blacke,*
> *And by his hidden Beames, threatens the wracke*
> *Of all these Glories: Euery pleasure dyes*
> *When Rauen-winged Night, from her Caue flyes;*
> *None but these Artificiall Starres keepe fire*
> *To Light you Home, these burne with a desire*
> *To lengthen your braue Triumphes; but their heate*
> *Must coole, and dye at length, tho ne're so Great.*
> *Peace therefore guide you on: Rest, charme your eyes,*   460
> *And Honors waite to cheere you when you Rise.*

Let it be no Ostentation in *Me* the Inuentor, to speak thus much
in praise of the workes, that for many yeares, none haue beene able
to Match them for curiosity: They are not Vast, but Neate, and
Comprehend as much Arte for Architecture, as can be bestowed
vpon such little Bodies. The commendations of which must liue
vppon Mr. *Gerard Chrismas* the Father, and Mr. *Iohn Chrismas*
the Sonne.

FINIS.

EMENDATIONS OF ACCIDENTALS

36 Soueraigne] So-|raigne
63–64 disheuelled;] ~ ,
66 Tortoyse] Torroyse
74 *Amphitryte*] *text; Amphitrite* cw
96 *listen.*] ~ ,
102 On.] ~ ,
113 *la*∧ *Terre,*] ~ , ~ ∧
118 *Delices*] *Deliees*
122 *d'ore*] *dore*
157 the *Top*] rhe *Top*
173 that,] ~ .
192 steppes] *text;* steps cw
219 *lay*∧] ~ :
227 *and*] *aud*
232 *turne.*] ~ ,
240 *and*] *and and*

250 *Luʒernes*] *Luʒerncs*
266–267 fore-|front] fore-front
269 Being the Speaker.] *Being the*
    Speaker.
306 *I wish*] Q *indents line* 305 *instead*
    of line 306
321 Pendants] *text;* -dents cw
324 each] rach
340 Persons] Petsons
348 Nights] Nighrs
350 Kinges] Kiuges
390 *Hatches:*] ~ ,
408 *led*] *lcd*
413 interwouen] inrerwouen
432 *Sights*] *Sight s*

Londons Tempe,

OR,

The Feild of Happines.

In which *Feild* are planted ſeuerall Trees of Magnifi-
cence, *State and Bewty*, to *Celebrate the Solemnity of the Right*
Honorable *Iames Campebell*, At his Inauguration into the Honorable
Office of Pretorſhip, or Maioralty of London, on Thurſday the 29 of October, 1629.

All the particular Inuentions, for the Pageants, Showes of Triumph, both by Water and land being here fully ſet downe, At the ſole Coſt,
and liberall Charges of the Right worſhipfull Society of *Ironmongers.*

Written by THOMAS DEKKER.

Quando magis Dignos licuit Spectare Triumphos?

A NOTE ON THE TEXT

London's Tempe (Greg, *Bibliography*, no. 421) would have been printed shortly before the Lord Mayor's inauguration on 29 October 1629. Bentley (*Jacobean and Caroline Stage*, III, 256) has a note on the little that is known of this pageant.

The cropped imprint in both preserved copies prevents us from knowing anything definite about the details of publication, but Greg identifies the ornamental initial on sig. A3 as belonging to Nicholas Okes.

The text has been edited previously by Frederick W. Fairholt in *Lord Mayor's Pageants* (Percy Society: Early English Poetry, Ballads, and Popular Literature of the Middle Ages, vol. x, 1843).

The present text has been prepared from a collation of the only two known copies: British Museum (C.34.g.11), which wants sigs. C1.2; and the copy in the Henry E. Huntington Library. As remarked, both have been cropped at the expense of the imprint.

To the Right honorable *Iames Campe-bell,* Lord
Maior of the most renouned Citty of
London.

Honorable Prætor:

The Triumphes which these few leaues of paper, present to your
vew, (Albeit their glories are but short-liued as glittering onely for
a day) Boldly shew their faces vnto the eye of the world, as Seruants
attending on your Lordship onely to doe you honor.

With much care, cost and curiosity are they brought forth; And,
with exceeding greatnes of Loue, *a free handed bounty of their* Purse,
a Noble and generous Alacrity of Spirit, *haue your worthy Fraternity,*
and much to be honored Brother-hood of Ironmongers, *bestowed them*
vpon you.   10

It much winnes vpon them, to haue such a Cheife; and you cannot
but be glad to haue such a Society: *By a free Election are you* Londons
Prætor; The Suffrages of Commoners *call you to your seate. A suc-*
cession to the place, Takes you by the hand, your Industry hath met with
Blessings, those blessings giuen you ability, and that ability makes you
fit for a Maiestrate.

Yet there is a musicke in your owne bosome, whose strings being
touchd yeilds as harmonius a sound to you, as All theis, And that is,
to see your selfe heire to that Patrician Dignity *with which your Father*
was Inuested. It was an honor to him to weare that Robe of Scarlet, 20
It is a double glory to you, in so short an age to haue his sword borne
before you.

You haue the voyce of Senators *breathing out your welcome,*
A confluence of Graue Citizens, *Adding state to your state, The*
acclamations of People, *vshering you along. Whilst I (the least part*
of this Triumphant day) spend such sand as I haue to helpe to fill vp
the houre glasse, my Seruice ronning.

Attending on your Lordship

Thomas Dekker.

Londons Tempe.

Were it possible for a Man, in the Compasse of a Day, to behold (as the Sunne does) All the Citties in the World, as if he went with Walking Beames about him; That Man should neuer see in any Part of the yeare, Any Citty, so Magnificently Adorned with All Sorts of Tryumphes, variety of Musicke, of Brauery, of Bewty, of Feastings, of Ciuill (yet Rich) Ceremonies, with gallant Lords and Ladies, and Thronges of People as *London* is inriched with, on the first Day, that Her Great Lord (or Lord Maior, for tis all one) Takes, That Office vpon him.

In former Ages, He was not Encompast with such Glories, 10 No such Firmaments of Starres were to be seene in *Cheape-side:* *Thames* dranke no such Costly Healthes to *London*, as hee does Now. But as *Troynouant* spred in Fame, so our *English* Kinges, shined vpon her with Fauours.

In Those Home-spun Times, They had no Collars of SS, no Mace, Sword, nor Cap of Maintenance, These came by Degrees, as *Additamenta Honoris*, additions or Ensignes of more Honour, Conferd by seuerall Princes on this Citty: For, in the time of *Edward Confessor*, the chiefe Ruler of the City was called *Reeue*, *Greeue*, or *Portreeue*: The next to him in authority, *Prouost*. 20

Then in the first of *Richard I.* two Bayliffes carried the sway: This continued till the ninth of King *Iohn*, who by Letters Patents gaue the Citizens power, yearely to choose themselues a Lord Maior, and two Sheriffes.

Then, King *Henry 3.* made the first *Aldermen* in *London* (yet the Name of *Ealdorman* was knowne in the *Saxons* time, for *Alwin* in the reigne of *Edgar*, was *Alderman of All England*, that is to say, *Chiefe Iustice*:) and those *Aldermen* of *London*, had Rule then (as Now) ouer the Wardes of the Citty, but were euerie yeare changed, as the Shreiffes are in these dayes. 30

Then *Edward I.* ordained that the Lord Maior, should in the Kings absence, sit in all Places within *London*, as Chiefe Iustice; And that euery *Alderman* that had bin Lord Mayor, should be a Iustice of Peace for *London* and *Middlesex* all his life after.

Then, in the reigne of *Henry 7. Sir Iohn Shaw* Goldsmith, being Lord Maior, caused the *Aldermen* to ride from the *Guild-hall* to the water side, when he went to take his Oath at *Westminster*, (where before they Rode by land thither,) and at his returne to ride againe to the *Guild-hall*, there to dine, all the Kitchens, and other Offices there, Being built by Him: since which time, 40 the Feast has there bin kept: for before, it was either at Grocers Hall, or the Merchantaylors.

Thus small Rootes grow in time to *Cædars*, shallow streames, to riuers, and a Hand of Gouerment to be the strongest Arme in a Kingdome. Thus you see *London* in her meane attyre, then in Robes Maiestical; and sitting in that Pompe, cast your Eye, vpon those alluring Obiects, which she her selfe Beholds with Admiration.

The first.

The first Scæne is a Water-worke, presented by *Oceanus*, King of the Sea (from whose Name the Vniuersall Maine Sea is called the 50 Ocean.) He, to celebrate the Ceremonies and Honors, due to this great Festiuall, and to shew the world his Marine Chariot, sits Triumphantly in the Vast (but Queint) shell of a siluer Scollup, Reyning in the heads of two wild Sea-horses, proportioned to the life, their maynes falling about their neckes, shining with curles of gold.

On his head, which (as his Beard) is knotted, long, carelesly spred, and white, is placd, a Diadem, whose Bottome, is a conceited Coronet of gold; The middle ouer that, is a Coronet of siluer Scollops, and on the top a faire spreading branch of Corrall, inter- 60 wouen thickly with Pearle. In his right hand, a golden Trident, or three forked Scepter.

His habit is *Antique*, the stuffe watchet, and siluer: a mantle crossing his body, with siluer waues, Bases, and Buskins cut likewise at the top into siluer scollups. And in this language he congratulates his Lordship.

Oceanus his Speech.

Thus Mounted, hither comes the King of waues,
Whose voyce Charmes roughest Billowes into slaues,
Whose Foote, treades downe their necks with as much Ease   70
As in my shelly Coach, I reyne vp These.
 Lowd Ecchoes cald me from my glittering Throne
To see the Noble Thamesis, — *A Sonne*
To this my Queene *and Me,* (Tethys) *whose Eare*
Ne're Ieweld vp such Musick as sounds Here.
For, our vnfaddomd World, Roares out with None
But Horrid Sea-fights, Nauies Ouerthrowne,
Ilands halfe-drownd in Bloud, Pyrates pell mell,
Turkes *slauish tugging Oares, The* Dunkerks *Hell,*
The Dutchmans *Thunder, And the* Spaniards *Lightning,*   80
To whom, the Sulphures Breath giues Heat and Heightning.
O! These are the Dire Tunes my Consort sings,
But here! old Thame *out shines the Beames of Kings.*
 This Citty Addes New Glories to Ioues *Court.*
And to All you, who to this Hall resort,
This Lactea via *(as a Path) is giuen,*
Being Pau'ed with Pearle, as that with Starres in heauen.
 I could (to swell my trayne) Becon the Rhine.
(But the wilde Boare has tusked vp his vine.)
I could Swift Volga Call, whose curld head lies   90
On seauen rich pillowes, (But, in merchandizes
The Russian, him imployes) — *I could to theis*
Call Ganges, Nilus, long haird Euphrates,
Tagus whose golden Hands claspe Lisbone walles,
Him could I call too, — *But what neede theis calles?*
Were they all here, they would weepe out there eyes,
Madde that new Troys *high towers on tiptoe rize*
To hit Heauens Roofe: Madde, to see Thames this day
(For all his age) in wanton windinges Play,
Before his new Graue Prætor, and before   100
Theis senators, — *Best fathers of the poore.*

That Grand Canale, where (stately) once a yeare
A Fleete of bridall Gondoletts appeare,
To marry with a golden Ring, (Thats Hurld,
Into the sea) That minion of the world
Venice to Neptune, — A poore Lantscip is,
To these full Braueries of Thamesis.
    Goe therefore vp to Cæasars Court, — And clayme
What honors there are left to Campe-bels *name*
As by disent, whilst we tow vp a tyde   110
Which shall ronne sweating vp by your barges side:
That done, Time *shall* Oceanus *Name Inroll,*
For guarding You to Londons *Capitoll.*

The second Presentation.

The Inuention is a Proud-swelling Sea, on whose Waues is
borne vp, a sea Lyon, as a proper and eminent Body, to Marshall
in the following Triumphes; In reguard it is one of the supporters
of the East Indian Company, of which his Lordship is free, and
a great aduenturer. And these Marine creatures, are the more fitly
imployed, In regard also, that his Lordship is Maior of the Staple, 120
Gouernour of the *French* Company, and free of the East-land
Company.

On this Lyon (which is cut out of wood to the life) rides *Tethys*,
wife to *Oceanus*, and Queene of the Sea; for why should the King
of waues be in such a glorious progresse without his Queene, or she
without him? They both therefore twin themselues together to
heighten these solemnities.

Her haire is long, and Disheuelled, on her head, an antique sea-
tyre, encompast with a Coronall of gold and pearle, her garments
rich, and proper to her quality, with a Taffaty mantle fringed with 130
siluer crossing her body. Her right hand, supporting a large
streamer, in which are the Lord Maiors armes.

On each side of this Lyon, attend a Mermaid, and Merman,
holding two Banners, with the Armes of the two New Shrieues,

seuerall fishes swimming as it were about the border. And these
two hauing dispatched on the water, hasten to aduance themselues
on Land.

The third.

The third show is an Estridge, cut out of timber to the life,
biting a horse-shoe. On this Bird rides an Indian boy, holding in 140
one hand a long *Tobacco pipe*, in the other a dart. His attire is
proper to the Country.

At the foure angles of the square where the Estridg stands, are
plac'd a *Turke*, and a *Persian*. A pikeman and a Musketeere.

The fourth.

The fourth presentation is called the *Lemnian Forge*. In it are
Vulcan, the *Smith* of *Lemnos*, with his seruants (the *Cyclopes*)
whose names are *Pyracmon*, *Brontes* and *Sceropes*, working at the
Anuile. Their habits are wast coates, and lether approns: their
haire blacke and shaggy, in knotted curles.   150

A fire is seene in the Forge, Bellowes blowing, some filing, some
at other workes; Thunder and Lightning on occasion. As the
Smiths are at worke, they sing in praise of Iron, the *Anuile* and
Hammer: by the concordant stroakes and soundes of which,
Tuballcayne became the first inuentor of Musicke.

The Song.

> *Braue Iron! Braue Hammer! from your sound,*
> *The Art of Musicke has her Ground,*
> *On the Anuile, Thou keep'st Time,*
> *Thy Knick-a-knock is a smithes Best Chyme,*   160
>   *Yet Thwick a-Thwack,*
>   *Thwick, Thwac a-Thwac-Thwac,*
>   *Make our Brawny sinewes Crack,*
>   *Then Pit a-pat-pat, pit a-pat-pat,*
>   *Till thickest barres be beaten flat.*

149 habits] habite Q

We shooe the Horses of the Sunne,
Harnesse the Dragons of the Moone,
Forge Cupids *Quiuer, Bow, and Arrowes,*
And our Dames Coach, thats drawne with Sparrowes.
    Till thwick-a-thwack, &c.   170

Ioues *Roaring Cannons, and his Rammers,*
We beate out with our Lemnian *Hammers,*
Mars *his Gauntlet, Helme and Speare,*
And Gorgon *Shield are all made here.*
    Till thwick-a-thwack, &c.

The Grate which (shut) the Day out-barres,
Those golden studdes which naile the starres,
The Globes-case, and the Axletree,
Who can Hammer these but Wee.
    Till thwick-a-thwack, &c.   180

A Warming-panne to heate Earth's bedde,
Lying i'th froʒen Zone halfe-dead,
Hob-nailes to serue the Man ith Moone,
And Sparrow-bils to cloute Pan's *shoone.*
    Whose worke but ours? Till thwic-a thwack, &c.

Venus *Kettles, Pots and Pannes,*
We make, or else she Brawles and Bannes,
Tonges, Shouels, Andirons haue their places,
Else shee scratches all our faces.
    Till thwick a-thwack, &c.   190

Cupid sits in one place of this Forge; on his head a curld yellow
haire, his eyes hid in Lawne, a Bow and Quiuer, his armour: Wings
at his backe; his body in light colours, a changeable silke mantle
crossing it: Golden and siluer arrowes, are euer and anon reached
vp to him, which hee shootes vpward into the aire, and is still supplied
with more from the Forge.

On the top sits *Ioue*, in a rich *Antique* habite, a long white
reuerend hayre on his head, a beard long and curld: A Mace of

186 *Pannes*] Fairholt; *Pennes* Q

Triple fire in his hand burning. Who calling to *Vulcan*, This language
passes betweene them.   200

Ioue.   *Ho* Vulcan.
Vulcan.   *Stop your Hammers: what ayles* Ioue?
  We are making arrowes for my slip-string sonne,
  Here, — reach him those two dozen; I must now
  A golden handle make for my wifes fann:
  Worke my fine Smugges.
Ioue.   *First heare; you shall not play,*
  The Fates would scold should you keepe Holiday.
Vulcan.   *What then?*
Ioue.   *Command thy Brawny-fisted slaues to sweate*
  At th' Anuile, and to dust their Hammers beate,
  To stuffe with Thunderbolts Ioues *Armoryes,*   210
  For Vices (mountain-like) in black heapes rize,
  My sinewes crack to fell them: — Ideot pride
  Stalkes vpon stilts, — Ambition, *by her side,*
  Climbing to catch Starres, breakes her necke it'h fall,
  The Gallant Roares, — Roarers drinke oathes and gall,
  The Beggar curses, — Auarice eates gold
  Yet ne're is fild, — Learning's a wrangling scold,
  Warre has a Fatall hand, — Peace, whorish Eyes,
  Shall not Ioue, *beate downe such Impieties?*
    Ist not high time, Ist not true Iustice then   220
  (Vulcan) *for thee, and thy tough Hammer-men*
  To beate thy Anuile, — and blow fires to flames
  To burne these Broodes, who kill euen with their Names?
Vulcan.   *Yes* Ioue, *tis more then Time.*
Ioue.   *And what helpes this, but Iron! O then, how high*
  Shall this Great Troy, *Text vp the Memory*
  Of you her Noble Prætor, and all Those
  (Your worthy Brotherhood) through whose Care goes
  That rare, rich prize of Iron, to the whole Land,
  Iron! farre more worth then Tagus *golden Sand.*   230
    Iron! best of Mettals! Pride of Minerals!

222 *beate*] Fairholt; *heate* Q

Hart of the Earth! Hand of the World, which fals
Heauy when it strikes home: — By Irons strong Charmes
Ryots lye bound: — Warre stops her rough Allarmes.
Iron; Earthquakes strikes in Foes: — Knits friends in loue,
Iron's that maine Hinge, on which the World doth moue:
No Kingdomes Globe can turne, Euen, Smooth and Round,
But that his Axletree in Iron is found:
For, Armies wanting Iron, are puffes of wind,
And, but for Iron, who thrones of peace would mind? 240
Were there no gold nor siluer in the land:
Yet Nauigation (which on Iron does stand)
Could fetch it in. — Gold's Darling to the Sunne,
But Iron, his hardy Boy, by whom is done
More than the Tother dare: The Merchants Gates
By Iron, barre out theeuish assassinates:
Iron is the Shop-keeper, both Locke and Kay,
What are your Courts of Guard, when Iron's away?
How would the Corne pricke vp her golden Eares:
But that Iron Plough shares, all the labour beares 250
In Earth's strange Midwiffry? Braue Iron! what praise
Deserues it? More tis beate, more it obayes;
The more it suffers: More it smoothes offence:
In Drudgery, it shines with Patience.
  This Fellowship, was then with Iudging Eyes
Vnited to the twelue great Companies:
It being farre more Worthy, than to Fill
A File inferiour; — Yon's the Sunne's guilt Hill:
Ontoot: Ioue *guardes you on:* Cyclopes, *a Ring*
Make with your Hammers, to whose Musicke Sing. 260

The Fift.

The fift Presentation is called *Londons Tempe*, or *The Field of Happinesse*; thereby reflecting vpon the name of *Campe-bell*, or *Le Beu Champe, A faire and glorious field.* It is an arbor, supported

248 *Courts*] Fairholt; *Cours* Q

by foure Great Termes: On the foure Angles, or corners ouer the Termes, are placed foure Pendants with armes in them.

It is round about furnished with trees and flowers: the vpper part with seuerall fruites: Intimating that as *London* is the best-stored Garden in the Kingdome for Plants, Herbes, Flowers, Rootes, and such like; So, on this day it is the most glorious Citty in the 270 Christian world.

And therefore *Tytan* (one of the names of the Sun) in all his splendor, with *Flora, Ceres, Pomona, Ver* and *Estas*, are seated in this *Tempe*; on the top of all stands a Lyons head, being the Lord Maiors Crest.

Tytan being the Speaker, does in this language court his Lordship to attention.

Tytan his Speech.

Welcome (great Prætor) Now heare Tytan *speake,*
Whose beames to Crowne this Day, through Clouds
            thus Breake.   280
My coach of beaten gold is set aside,
My Horses to Ambrosiall mangers tied,
Why is this done? why leaue I mine owne Sphære?
But here to circle You, for a whole Yeare:
Embrace then Tytans *Counsell: — Now so Guide*
The Chariot of your sway in a Iust Pace,
That All (to come hereafter) may with Pride,
Say, None like you did Noblier quit the Place:
Lower than Now you are in Fame, Neuer fall,
Note me (the Sunne) who in my Noone Careere,   290
Renders a shaddow, short or None at all,
And so, since Honors Zodiac is your sphære,
A shrub to you must be the tallest Pine,
On poore and rich you Equally must shine.
    This if you Doe, my Armes shall euer spread
About those Roomes you Feast in: — From her head
Flora, *her garlands plucke (beeing Queene of Flowers)*
To dresse your Parlors vp like summers Bowers:
Ceres, *lay golden sheaffes on your full boord,*

With fruit you from Pomona *shall be stoard,*   300
Whilst Ver *and* Estas (*Spring and Sommer*) *Driue*
From this your Tempe, *Winter, till he Diue*
I'th froẑen Zone, and Tytans *Radiant shield*
Guard Campe-bels *Beuchampe,* Londons *fairest field.*

The sixth and last Presentation.

This is called *Apollo's* pallace: because seuen persons representing the seuen liberall Sciences are richly Inthroned in this Citty. Those seuen are in loose roabes of seuerall cullors, with mantles according, and holding in their hands Escutcheons, with Emblemes in them proper to euery one quality.   310

The body of this worke is supported by twelue siluer Columnes. At the foure angles of it, foure Pendants play with the Wind; On the top is erected a square Tower, supported by foure golden Columnes. In euery square is presented the Embosd antique head of an Emperour, figuring the foure Monarches of the world, and in them, pointing at foure Kingdomes.

Apollo is the chiefe person; on his head a garland of bayes; In his hand a Lute. Some Hypercriticall Censurer perhaps, will aske, why hauing *Tytan*, I should bring in *Apollo*, sithence they both are names proper to the Sunne. But the yongest Nouice in Poetry can answer 320 for me, that the Sunne when he shines in heauen is called *Tytan*, but being on Earth (as he is here) we call him *Apollo*. Thus therefore *Apollo* tunes his voyce.

Apolloes speech.

Apollo neuer stucke in Admiration till now: My *Delphos* is remouen hither; my Oracles are spoken here: Here the Sages vtter their wisedome, Here the Sybels their diuine verses.

I see Senators this day in Scarlet riding to the Capitoll, and to morrow the same men riding vp and downe the field in Armors. Gowned Citizens, and Warlike Gowne-men. The Gunne here giues 330 place, and the Gowne takes the vpper hand. The Gowne and the Gunne march in one File together.

III

Happy King that has such people, happy Land in such a King! Happy Pretor so grac'd with Honors! Happy Senators so obayed by Citizens. And happy Citizens that can command such Triumphes.

Go on in your full glories: whilst *Apollo*, and these Mistresses of the Learned Sciences, waft you to that Honourable shore, whither Time bids you hasten to arriue.

A speech at Night, at taking leaue of his Lordship at *his Gate, by Oceanus.* 340

After the glorious troubles of this day,
Night bids you welcome home, — Night who does lay
All pompe, all Triumphs, by, — state, now desends,
Here our Officious Trayne their seruice ends.
And yet not all, for see: the golden Sunne,
Albeit he has his dayes worke fully done,
Sits vp aboue his houre, and does his best
To keepe the starres from lighting you to rest.
Him will I take along to lay his head
In Tethys *lape; Peace therefore Guard your bedds:* 350
In your yeeres Zodiacke may you fairely moue,
Shin'd on by Angels, blest with goodnes loue.

Thus much, his owne worth, cryes vp the Workman (Master *Gerard Chrismas*) for his Inuention, that all the peeces were exact, and set forth liuely, with much Cost. And this yeere, giues one Remarkeable Note to after times, that all the Barges followed one another (euery Company in their degree) in a Stately and Maiesticall order. This being the Inuention of a Noble Citizen, one of the Captaines of the Citty.

FINIS.

339 taking] Fairholt; taken Q   340 *Oceanus*] Fairholt; *Oceans* Q
344 *our*] Fairholt; *or* Q

PRESS-VARIANTS IN Q (1629)

[Copies collated: British Museum (C.34.g.11 [wants C1.2]), Huntington Library (CSmH).]

SHEET B (*outer forme*)

Corrected: BM
Uncorrected: CSmH

Sig. B1
  110 *your*] *you*

EMENDATIONS OF ACCIDENTALS

51 Ocean.] ~ ‸
54 Sea-horses] Sea-|horses
67 Speech] Specch
81 *Heightning.*] ~ ,
100 *his*‸] ~ ,
107 *Braueries*] *Brauereis*
123 *Tethys,*] ~ ‸
128 sea-|tyre] sea-tyre
143 angles] angels
164 *pit*] *some mark follows that may be a hyphen*
190 *thwick*] *thick*
199 burning. Who] burning who
219 Ioue] Iove

234 *Allarmes.*] ~ ‸
278 Speech] Specch
280 *Breake.*] ~ ‸
307 Inthro-|ned] *cw;* nd *text*
312 Wind;] *punctuation uncertain*
318 Lute.] ~ ;
324 *Apolloes*] *Apoloes*
335 Citizens.] *punctuation uncertain*
336 on] od
337 shore,] *comma uncertain, possibly a semi-colon*
344 ends.] ~ ,
348 *rest.*] ~ ,
350 Tethys] *Tethys*

Lusts Dominion;

OR, THE

Lascivious Queen,

A

TRAGEDIE.

by Christopher Marloe,

LONDON,

Printed for *F. K.* in the year
1657.

TEXTUAL INTRODUCTION

L U S T ' S   D O M I N I O N (Greg, *Bibliography*, no. 777), a duodecimo, was published in 1657 by Francis Kirkman. The ornaments indicate that Jane Bell was the printer. In its first issue, preserved in a unique copy in the Library of Congress, the preliminaries occupied four leaves and the title, with the neutral imprint 'Printed for *F.K.* in the year | 1657.', did not mention the name of the author. The second issue must have been printed almost simultaneously, since its altered title utilized the standing type of the original. In this form the commendatory poems, which focused the attention on Kirkman, were omitted and the preliminary material was re-imposed in only two leaves, the 'Actors Names' being transferred to the verso of the title-page and the 'Epistle Dedicatorie' occupying sig. A2. In this issue, as in all later forms, a line of type is added on the title-page, 'Written by *Christofer Marloe*, Gent.' The publisher is still Kirkman, but the seller is Robert Pollard.

Subsequently, at least two other issues were contrived, in 1658 and 1661, the new title-pages cancelling the second-issue title, not by excision and substitution, but instead by being pasted over the earlier leaf. The duodecimo was advertised for sale as late as 1670, by William Cademan.

The title-page ascription to Marlowe can have had small authority and is now generally rejected. Instead, with some plausibility *Lust's Dominion* has been associated with *The Spanish Moor's Tragedy*, which Dekker, Day, and Haughton were writing for the Admiral's in February 1600.

The short line of the duodecimo caused the compositors some difficulty, and the extra problems in justification not only affected the spelling characteristics of the workmen but led to so many words being run together or separated only by the thinnest of spaces that in the present edition no attempt has been made to record these anomalies. The text occupies B–G in 12's, with leaf G12 blank, recto and verso. Beginning about one-third of the way down on sig. G7^v (V.ii.167) verse is set as prose except for patches here and there. The last page, sig. G11^v (V.iii.175–183), is lined, and, curiously, all of sig. G8^v and a little text at the top of G9 (V.iii.27–52). Brereton's explanation must be the correct one, that the printer was saving space by compression. The casting-off cannot have been very accurate, for blank G12 gives mute testimony that the compression was overdone. We might perhaps explain the lining on G8^v and G9 by the hypothesis that the compositor was setting sheet G by formes, although such an explanation is not without its difficulties. At any rate, the dislocation of the lining would appear to have a mechanical basis and to be unrelated to any peculiarities in the printer's copy.

Three compositors seem to have worked on this duodecimo. However, the evidence for the presswork afforded by the running-titles shows that these workmen took up their duties in order as the sheets went through the press, and did not compose sections of the book simultaneously. For sheet B two skeleton-formes were constructed, but thereafter the skeleton that had printed outer B was distributed, and starting with C only one skeleton-forme was used to impose the type-pages of both formes of each sheet, this being the skeleton that had imposed inner B. Such a pattern suggests that the compositors were slightly behind the press after sheet B, and it may be that the change in the method of imposing the sheets had something to do with the substitution of another compositor with sheet C.

The compositor of sheet B (I.i.1–I.ii.244) can be identified with some certainty as the compositor *A* in Jane Bell's shop who the year previously had helped to compose *The Sun's Darling*. His use of medial *-i-* or final *-ie* is similar, he also is a 'divell' speller, and he has the same fondness for intrusive apostrophes in verbs like *do's* or *doe's* and *hold's*, or plurals like *Turk's*. In *Lust's Dominion* his work is marked by the use of roman for titles like 'Cardinal', and for 'Moor' as applied to Eleazar.

With the start of Act II on sig. C1 a different, and unidentified, compositor enters, who sets sheets C and D (II.i.1–III.iii.37). With some consistency he puts titles like *Cardinal* in italic, and he distinguishes Eleazar by an italic *Moor*. Beginning with sheet E (III.iii.38) and continuing until the end of the play, a third compositor appears. This workman resembles compositor *B* of *The Sun's Darling*, although the identification is perhaps a little less certain than that of compositor *A*. He is even more free than the compositor of sheets C–D in the use of italic. This compositor of the last three sheets seems to have been assisted from time to time, perhaps while he was distributing, by another compositor, whose spelling characteristics and use of roman instead of italic relate him to compositor *A*, who had set sheet B. In sheet E this workman seems to have composed sigs. E4–4ᵛ (IV.i.1–37 S.D.), and perhaps finished the scene on sig. E5 (IV.i.38–41 S.D.) although there is no evidence one way or another for this short page. Compositor *B* is back again with IV.ii.1 on sig. E5ᵛ and continues to E6ᵛ (IV.ii.41). Sig. E7 was set by compositor *A*, who thereupon continues to E9 (IV.ii.42–116). With the stage-direction before IV.ii.117 compositor *B* resumes, at E9ᵛ and carries on to the end of E12ᵛ (IV.iii.69) or just possibly to the foot of sig. F1 (IV.iii.86).

There is very little evidence on sig. F1, but two small irregularities in the speech-prefixes may argue more for the intervention of compositor *A* here than for continuous setting by compositor *B*. At any rate, compositor *A* is found on F1ᵛ (IV.iii.87) and sets to the end of F4 (IV.iv.72 [quartred, before I'le ‖]) before *B* takes over at F4ᵛ (IV.iv.72 [‖ have my members cut off.]). At sig. F10 (V.i.145) compositor *A* returns. Compositor *B* set sig. F12ᵛ (V.i.227) to the end of the play, and it is likely that he also set F12ʳ (V.i.207–226). The compositor of F10ᵛ–11ᵛ (V.i.160–206) is not certain, but he may have been *A*, at least in part.

Francis Kirkman was an ardent collector of old plays, both in printed and in manuscript form. We have no information how and where he procured the manuscript for *Lust's Dominion*. However, the case seems fairly clear that the printer did not set from a prompt-book. No stage-direction can be given a prompt-book origin with any certainty, whereas a number are obviously descriptive and authorial. Moreover, here and there characteristics of the manuscript peep through the print that indicate that the underlying manuscript was not altogether uniform in its physical characteristics. The evidence, such as it is, supports a hypothesis that the manuscript given to press was non-theatrical and consisted of papers that were in more than one hand. Whether this manuscript was a collection of the original authors' papers (in which case a collaboration is indicated), or of a revision made of the original papers (whether or not by more than one hand), in which scenes or parts of scenes were added to the originals or altered in the reviser's hand, is a question that can be solved only by a searching stylistic analysis that will also take account of various verbal echoes and of some structural anomalies.

For instance, there are a few loose ends that may or may not have resulted from an original collaboration or from revision. Verdugo is a courtier called on by name at III.i.18 but not mentioned as entering in the stage-direction that immediately follows. He is never referred to again in any way, although his fellows Christofero and Roderigo play their parts. It is possible to speculate that this is an economical cut, and that Verdugo's name is preserved only because it appeared within the Queen Mother's speech. Whether or not conjectural cutting of a character has anything to do with what seems to be a false assignment of a speech to Hortenzo in V.i.110 (given in the present text to Roderigo) is uncertain.

At the end of IV.ii, when Eleazar has been beaten in battle, he tells Christofero that he has a stratagem left to win the victory, since he has sent the Queen Mother, who 'hath all this while sate sadly, | Within our tent, expecting to whose bosom, | White winged peace and victory will flie', to disarm the Cardinal. And in the next scene we see her charms operating so successfully that Mendoza deserts Philip and makes a separate peace. This sequence conflicts with a scheme announced at the end of Act III when Eleazar has been first proclaimed. Here in III.iv.36–48 a decision is made to overthrow the Cardinal by sending the Queen Mother to his castle where she will learn his plans. Thereupon 'for your pleasure walk to take the air: | Near to the Castle I'le in ambush lie, | And seem by force to take you prisoner; | This done, I have a practice plotted here, | Shall rid him of his life, and us of fear'. Although the Queen is then urged to start immediately ('About it madam, this is all in all; | We cannot stand unlesse *Mendoza* fall'), she does not do so, and the project is never heard of again, for our next reference is to her in Eleazar's tent awaiting the results of the battle. One cannot say with certainty that such a loose end is the result of collaborative effort never quite reconciled, or of revision, although the subsequent course of the plot would make the former seem somewhat more likely perhaps.

There are some minor discrepancies that might have resulted from revision, as much as from initial collaboration, or from both. Prominent is the variation in indicating the Cardinal Mendoza. His first appearance is in I.ii, where he is Mendoza in stage-direction and speech-prefixes, and again in II.i. Thereafter, he is *Cardinal* in all speech-prefixes throughout the play, although once, in IV.i, he is named *Mendoʒa* in a stage-direction. The shift from *Mendoʒa* in direction and speech-prefix in II.i, to *Cardinal* in II.iii, occurs within sheet C and is, therefore, not likely to be compositorial.

Another interesting case is the variation in form between *Philip* and *Philippo*. Philip is *Philip* exclusively in I.ii. In II.ii (a scene that may have had some revision) he is *Philip* in the initial section ending with the exit of the Queen Mother, then he is *Philippo* once in Eleazar's directions to Baltazar and Zarack (II.ii.85), but *Philip* again in the discussion with the Friars and in Eleazar's final instructions to his slaves. In II.iii he is *Philip* in line 9 but *Philippo* in line 56, a related part of the scene. In III.v he is *Philip*; and thereafter *Philippo* (as well as *Philip*) in IV.ii, iii, iv and V.i, ii, iii. It may be, since even in the *Philippo* scenes the short form is sometimes used, that there is no significance to all the scenes in which only the short form appears.

Curiously, the first time that the spelling is *Philippo* is in sig. E 8 (IV.ii.76). Whether or not the aberration of spelling *Philip* but pronouncing *Philippo* is compositorial or a feature of the underlying manuscript is uncertain. The major instances, in II.ii, iii are all in sheet C in the work of the unidentified compositor. On E 6 compositor *B* set *Philip* at IV.ii.27 where *Philippo* may be required; but since *Philip* would be acceptable if the line is nine syllables with an initial truncated iamb, not much can be proved. The first full form was set by compositor *A* on sig. E 8. Thereafter *B* next sets *Philip* for *Philippo* on E 12^v (IV.iii.54). The *Philippo* on F 1 (IV.iii.77) may be *A*'s. The short form in error is set by *B* again on F 6 (V.i.3). For the first time he sets *Philippo* correctly, on F 7 (V.i.39); but on F 12^v (V.i.244) he falls into error, as he does again on G 7 (V.ii.161), possibly on G 7ᵛ (V.iii.2), but certainly on G 8 (V.iii.14) and G 9ᵛ (V. iii.73, 80). On the other hand, compositor *B* sets *Philippo* correctly in sheet G at V.i.263, V.ii.140 (where the metre does not require it), V.ii.143 (on G 7 where an error appears at the foot), V.ii.167, V.iii.15 (one line below an error), V.iii.28, 32, 93 (this last on the same page as an error). It is difficult to avoid the conjecture that the manuscript was very defective in spelling out the three-syllable form and that in the majority of cases (one hesitates to say in all) the compositor supplied it when he was conscious that the metre required the extra syllable. Possibly one can watch compositor *B* growing aware of this necessity as his stint goes on, and even, perhaps, setting *Philippo* superfluously at V.ii.140. If this is so, and it is very much a conjecture, one could suppose that a copyist had been at work who had misunderstood the form of the name or, perhaps, that an author's foul papers in which an abbreviation was used were the printer's copy.

That the manuscript was not all of a piece in its characteristics, as one would expect if a copyist had intervened for the whole between originals and the printer, may be seen from such variant forms as *Eliaz.* for *Eleazar* in I.i, ii and II.i. Since II.i was set by a different compositor, in sheet C, this anomalous spelling must have derived from the manuscript. Similarly, Alvero's name is thrice spelled *Alvaro*, in III.i, ii and IV.i. The first two times were set by the unknown compositor of sheet D, but the third by compositor *A* on sig. E 4. Both of these spellings should be of some assistance in questions of collaborative authorship or of revision. Also of some assistance, perhaps, may be the use of the phrase 'Mother Queen' for the Queen Mother in II.ii, iii, III.iii, IV.i, ii, V. i, ii. Something might perhaps be made of the use of the name *Mendoza* or of the title *Cardinal*; and perhaps the identification of Eleazar as an Indian (I.ii, III.ii, IV.ii) or as a Negro (III.i, ii, iii, IV.ii, iii) might be of some service.

The device at the end of Act II in which Eleazar tries to induce Maria to poison Fernando seems so feeble and undeveloped as to tempt speculation whether in an early state of the play Maria did not, in fact, poison herself as a sacrifice to escape the King's lustful embraces; but there is no evidence for this guess, and perhaps the author introduced the mention of poison merely to suggest to Maria the use of a sleeping potion instead.

However, there is one line of action where it would seem that bibliographical and structural evidence combine to indicate alteration or unreconciled differences from collaborative effort. In II.ii.1–65 Eleazar persuades the Queen Mother to destroy Philip by declaring him a bastard and securing 'some' friars to proclaim the fact abroad. Philip will be so galled and will so incite the Cardinal that he can be condemned for treason. On her agreement ('Sweet *Moor* it's done'), she leaves to put the plan in action according to Eleazar's order, 'Away then, work with boldness, and with speed'. In this section 'Friers' is in roman and '*Moor*' in italic, the usual practice of the unknown compositor of sheet C in setting the preceding II.i. Scene II.ii then continues with five lines of a soliloquy in which Eleazar congratulates himself on his villainy, and in a sixth line he summons Zarack and Baltazar. In lines 71–81 he informs them that the coming night they are to murder the Cardinal and Philip and orders them not to be seen with him before nightfall. In this section 'Cardinal' is in roman type. In lines 82–90 Eleazar interrupts the slaves' exit to tell them that the Queen Mother is trying to corrupt 'two covetous Friers' to preach abroad Philip's bastardy. They are to search for these friars and to hire them 'to work with you', for 'Their holy callings will approve the fact | Most good and meritorious'. In this passage '*Mo. Qu.*' (abbreviated in order to justify the line) is in italic and 'Friers' in roman.

The exit for Zarack and Baltazar is omitted at line 90, and at line 91 in a line marked as an aside Eleazar announces the arrival of the Queen and the Friers ('*Queen*' in italic and 'Friers' in roman). The 'aside' is perhaps explained by his being at the back of the stage seeing the slaves off by one door, presumably, while the Queen and friars make their entrance at the other, and play their scene alone until Eleazar makes a sudden appearance at line 121. The stage-direction reads '*Enter two Friers, Crab and Cole; and Queen Mother*' and in the lines that follow (92–121), in which they agree to preach against Philip, their speech-prefixes are respectively '*Crab*' and '*Cole*'. Beginning with line 121 Eleazar seconds the Queen, adds a bribe, and at line 140 the friars leave on their mission. In this section 'Frier' is in roman, as is 'Cardinal'. Starting at line 141 the Queen attempts to persuade Eleazar to kill his wife, and he pretends to assent. Baltazar enters to deliver to the Queen Fernando's invitation to attend him, and she makes her exit at line 156. Baltazar then reports that the friars have been won to join them, and the scene ends with the giving of the watchword that will be the signal for Zarack and Baltazar to break open the chamber doors and kill Philip and the Cardinal.

Scene II.iii opens, still in sheet C, showing the escape of Philip and the Cardinal with the connivance of the friars, who deliver the warning of Eleazar's plot, lend their gowns, and permit themselves to be bound and gagged in order to deceive the murderers. The stage-direction begins '*Enter Cole and Crab in Trouses*'. In contrast to the preceding scene, and to the only other scene (II.i) previously set by this compositor, '*Cardinal*' is now in italic, as is '*Frier*' and '*Portugall*', all three earlier in roman. (In italic, as before, are '*Moor*' and '*Mother Queen*'.) In the section of this scene that ends with the flight of Philip and the Cardinal, the only speech-prefix for the friars is the single '*Cole*', except for the unison '2. *Friers*'. In the next section of the scene, beginning with line 35, Eleazar and the rest break in. Eleazar orders Zarack and Baltazar to station themselves in two assigned places, and the other Moors in a third. He is about to station the friars when he misses them and asks 'Where have you plac'd the *Friers*?' When the friars are unbound and tell of the escape, Eleazar in an aside indicates his pleasure at the news (rather curiously), but then turns to the friars and informing them that the Queen wishes to have them proclaim Philip's bastardy he asks whether they will do so. They demur, but after being threatened they agree, and make their exit. In these lines 56–73 no indication is given that this whole matter has been settled, with Eleazar present, in II.ii.121–140, and that the discussion is completely repetitious. This section of the scene closes with Eleazar's instructions to Zarack and Baltazar to kill the friars once they have spread the infection.

We do not see the friars again until III.iii, beginning on sig. D 11ᵛ, a sheet set by the same compositor as in sheet C. After the preparation of Zarack and Baltazar for the murder to follow, the friars enter, the stage-direction repeating the exact words of that in II.ii, '*Enter Crab and Cole, two Friers*'. On sig. D 12ᵛ (III.iii.27–37) the speech-prefixes are different from before, '*Frier Crab*' and '*Frier Cole*'; but when compositor *B* takes over on sig. E 1 in the rest of the scene he sets the prefixes as '*Cole*' and '*Crab*'. Both compositors italicize '*Frier*' in the text; and their practice otherwise does not seem to differ, since on D 12ᵛ we see '*Mother Queen*' italicized, and on E 1ᵛ '*Moor*' is in italics.

When this evidence is surveyed, several points are apparent. The venal friars of II.ii, corrupted by the Queen and Eleazar, bear no resemblance to the friars who abruptly in the next scene save Philip and the Cardinal at great danger to themselves. Also, in this scene the second corruption does not appear to be supplementary to the first, but instead seems like an initial effort on Eleazar's part. Typographically, although set by the same compositor, the two scenes differ: in II.ii '*Cardinal*' and '*Frier*' are set in roman (according to the practice of the preceding scene) but in II.iii the two words are italicized. It may be significant that the order of the friar's names is reversed in the entrance in II.iii from that in II.ii. The repeated corruption of the friars to preach against Philip, one scene seemingly in ignorance of the other, combined with the typographical evidence, suggests that the manuscript papers underlying II.ii and II.iii differed in their origin. Yet there is one very interesting link between the two scenes. In II.ii.87–89 Eleazar orders Zarack and Baltazar to hire the friars to work with them. This is very vague, and might somehow apply to the preaching against Philip, but the real point of the order is seen in II.iii.36–37 when Eleazar inquires of the two Moors where they have placed the friars. Obviously, the hiring was to be in connexion with the assassination of the Cardinal and Philip, and the friars were to be present when the doors were broken open, presumably to attest to some fictitious treason. Whether this is too small a matter to be carried from one collaborator to another in a synopsis, or whether it ought to indicate common authorship of the two scenes (or at least of these sections), can be only a matter of opinion and can perhaps be settled only by an analysis of evidence that is not bibliographical.

All that can be indicated here is that certain characteristics in the printer's copy appear to have differed in II.ii and II.iii and this variation is accompanied by evidence for duplication of action.

When we try to carry forward this conjecture, one or two other matters may be pertinent. The typography of II.ii as it relates to the use of italicized words in the text is the same as that in II.i, which began sheet C. The change in the italicizing of *Cardinal* that took place in sheet C with II.iii is continued in sheet D (III.ii.209), and so with *Frier* (III.iii) in sheet D. Moreover, since this practice is also continued by compositor *B* in sheet E for *Frier*, and for *Cardinal* in the rest of the play, in a sense the change made by the compositor of sheet C between II.ii and II.iii may be confirmed as a reproduction of the manuscript characteristics.

One final point remains. It is interesting that the same phrasing is used in the stage-directions for the friar's entrance in II.ii and in III.iii and that they enter in an order different from that in II.iii, which also does not describe them as '*two Friers*'. It may seem, moreover, that the comic portrayal of the friars in III.iii is closer to the writing in II.ii than in II.iii. Yet in part of III.iii speech-prefixes, which add *Frier* to the names, differ from the plain use of the names alone found in II.ii (and also in II.iii). This form of the speech-prefixes in the lines of III.iii set in sheet D seems to be compositorial, however, since when compositor *B* enters with sig. E1 he sets the form we see in II.ii, iii. However, the italics in the text for *Frier* in III.iii both in sheets D and E differ from the roman setting in II.ii although conforming to the italic setting in II.iii.

The bibliographical evidence, therefore, points to some sort of change in the printer's copy beginning with II.iii, and this hypothesis may be supported by the disappearance of the variant form *Eliaʒar* after II.i. So far as can be told from the typographical conventions used, the copy appears to have been uniform in its characteristics, in general, from II.iii to the end. However, such links as seem to be present between scenes like II.ii and III.iii, or the matter of the hiring of the friars in II.ii to give colour to the assassination of Philip and the Cardinal in II.iii, the use of the phrase 'Mother Queen' as early as II.ii (and also in II.iii) and later, the appearance of the metrical form *Philippo* (even though not the spelling) as early as II.ii, the references to Eleazar as an Indian in I.ii and later in III.ii and IV.ii—such matters do not encourage a hypothesis that in a collaboration a division occurred between II.ii and II.iii. Rather, if one were forced to guess, the partial evidence (pending a fuller linguistic and critical analysis) suggests instead some sort of a revision, with a considerable amount of rewriting, beginning with II.iii systematically. Whether there was touching up in Act I cannot be revealed by similar evidence, for compositor *A* with few exceptions enforced his own treatment on words that the other compositors might set in italic. Whether such revision was by the author of the original, and whether the original was the work of one or of more than one dramatist, is not revealed by the bibliographical evidence investigated.

Lust's Dominion was first reprinted in 1814 in vol. 1 of *Old English Plays*, edited by Charles Wentworth Dilke. Other editions followed, in 1818 by W. Oxberry as no. 4 of Oxberry's *Old English Drama* (collected in 1827 as *The Dramatic Works of Christopher Marlowe*); in 1826 in *The Works of Christopher Marlow*, vol. III, edited by George Robinson [BM 11771.d.4 is interleaved with notes by James Broughton]; in 1875 in *A Select Collection of Old English Plays Originally Published by Robert Dodsley*, 4th ed., ed. W. Carew Hazlitt, vol. XIV. In 1931 J. Le Gay Brereton edited a type facsimile accompanied by extensive historical and critical commentary in *Materials for the Study of the Old English Drama*, New Series, ed. Henry De Vocht, vol. v.

The present text has been edited from the collation of the following seven copies: British Museum, copy 1 (643.a.28), copy 2 (82.c.22 [7], wanting A1); Bodleian Library (Mal. 133[8]), containing Malone's notes; Dyce Collection in the Victoria and Albert Museum; Library of Congress, copy 1 (Longe Collection), copy 2; Harvard University. Of these, only the Library of Congress copy 1 contained the first state of the preliminaries with the commendatory poems.

The classical scene division of the duodecimo has been altered for convenience to the conventional system. It would seem to have nothing to do with Dekker's practice. The system of italicizing titles has been silently made uniform according to the system most generally found in prints. However, *Moor* has been kept in italics (or silently italicized) when it refers to Eleazar, but not otherwise. The cramped measure has caused so many words to be run together in the justifying that these irregularities have not been recorded. The inking of the type in most copies is so poor that the evidence of all collated was necessary to establish the original form of the text. Extensive press-correction was made in sheet C, the first sheet set by the unidentified compositor, but the collated copies reveal no further press-alteration.

Although the correct Spanish spelling *Alvaro* is found three times in setting by two compositors, the usual form—and one that appears in the setting of all three compositors—is *Alvero*. Since this would appear to have been the dominant form in the manuscript immediately underlying the print, it has been adopted in the present text.

To my worthily honored Friend
William Carpenter, Esquire.

SIR!

My Ambition hath long soared so high, as to prompt me to somewhat whereby I might in part render to you my gratitude: and not yet finding any service I can act for you, a sufficient or competent return of any part of those many favours you have still honored me withall; I took on me the resolution (rather then to be thought wholly negligent of you) to lay hold on this means of rendring you my service. SIR! This Piece, which without your favour and command had never past the Presse, I here present to you with this confidence, that as you were instrumental in its production to 10 the world, so your name and favour will be sufficient to protect it from the calumny of this censorious age: In doing of which you will multiply those obligations you have conferred upon

Your devoted servant,

FRA. KIRKMAN *Jun.*

To my honored Friend Mr. *F. K.* on the publishing this Tragedie.

    In this Distemper'd Age where we do finde,
    Nothing more wav'ring then the Peoples minde,
    How they Despise Religion, Break the Laws,
    Deride at all that's Good, with wild Applause
    Cry up what's Bad, and stiffly do Maintain
    All things went wrong, whilst Monarchy did Reign.
    Can'st then Exspect a Pleasing Eye from Them
    Have Trampled on the Sacred Diadem:
    I know thou dost not, But 'tis thy Intent
    To show what Lust and Cruelty invent   10
    To compasse their Designs, Teaching this Age,
    First to Reform, and then Repeal the Stage.
    A Queen is Pictur'd here, whose lustful Flame
    Was so Insatiate, that it wants a Name
    To Speak it forth, Seeking to Bastardize
    Her Royal Issue that a MOOR might Rise.
    He Flatter'd Her, on purpose to Obtain
    His Ends to Sit on th' Royal Throne of Spain.
    Black as his Face his Deeds appear'd at last,
    And What He Climb'd by, Did His Ruine hast.   20
    So may they Fall, that seek for to Betray,
    And Lead the People in an Unknown Way:
    As in a Glasse, thus We may Clearly See,
    All Vanishes That's Built on Tyranny.
                      P. I.

To my Esteemed Friend Mr. F. K. on his publick impression of this
                Tragick Poem.

    What better Subject wings dull time away,
    Then an Ingenious and a well-writ Play;
    It doth Refine our Fancies, Judgments clear,
    And fix our souls, in a sublimer Sphear.
    I'le Vindicate, if any can deny;
    That Plays defect of wit do oft supply.
                JOHN PENRICE, *Esq.*

To my Ingenious Brother Mr. F. K., on his setting forth this Play.

> What strange designe is this I undertake?
> Sure 'tis no Verse that I intend to make.
> And yet me-thinks this Play doth me inspire,
> And all my sences with Poetick fire
> Doe's so inflame, that had I *Johnsons* Quill
> To write its worth, whole Volumes I would fill.
> But I stay you too long; peruse this piece,
> You'l find of language a rich Golden fleece.
> Then thank my freind for publishing this Play
> Which but for him had never seen the day.   10

Joseph Philips, *Gent.*

THE ACTORS NAMES

ELEAZER THE MOOR, Prince of Fesse and Barbary.

PHILIP KING OF SPAIN, Father to Fernando, Philip, and
Isabella.

FERNANDO KING OF SPAIN ⎫
PHILIP PRINCE OF SPAIN ⎭ Sons to Philip.

ALVERO, a Nobleman, and Father in Law to Eleazar, and Father
to Hortenzo and Maria.

MENDOZA, the Cardinal.

CHRISTOFERO ⎫
RODERIGO ⎭ two Noblemen of Spain.   10

[VERDUGO, another Nobleman.]

HORTENZO, Lover to Isabella, and son to Alvero.

ZARACK, ⎫
BALTAZAR ⎭ two Moors, attending Eleazar.

COLE & ⎫
CRAB ⎭ two Friers.

EMMANUEL, King of Portugal.

CAPTAIN, SOULDIERS, cum aliis.

TWO PAGES attending the Queen.

[OBERON and his Fairies.]   20

[EUGENIA] THE QUEEN MOTHER OF SPAIN, and wife to
King Philip.

ISABELLA, the Infanta of Spain.

MARIA, wife to Eleazar, and daughter to Alvero.

The Scene, SPAIN.

Lusts Dominion;
or, The
Lascivious Queen.
A Tragedie.

ACTUS I^{MUS}. SCENA I^{MA}.

Enter Zaracke, Baltazar, *two Moors, taking tobacco; musick*
sounding within: enter Queen Mother of Spain *with two*
Pages, Eleazar *sitting on a chair suddenly draws the curtain.*

Eleazar. On me, do's musick spend this sound on me
That hate all unity:
Hah! *Zarack, Baltazar?*
Qu. Mo.   My gracious Lord.
Eleazar. Are you there with your Beagles? hark you slaves,
Did not I bind you on your lives, to watch
That none disturb'd us.
Qu. Mo.   Gentle *Eleazar.*
Eleazar. There, off: Is't you that deafs me with this noise?
                                        Exeunt two Moors.
Qu. Mo. Why is my love's asspect so grim and horrid?
Look smoothly on me:
Chyme out your softest strains of harmony,   10
And on delicious Musicks silken wings
Send ravishing delight to my loves ears,
That he may be enamored of your tunes.
Come let's kisse.
Eleazar. Away, away.
Qu. Mo. No, no, saies I; and twice away saies stay:
Come, come, I'le have a kiss, but if you strive,
For one denial you shall forfeit five.

3 *Qu. Mo.*] *Here and elsewhere in this scene the speech-prefix is* Queen.
16 I] *i.e.* Ay

Eleazar.   Nay prithee good Queen leave me,
  I am now sick, heavie, and dull as lead.   20
Qu. Mo.   I'le make thee lighter by taking something from thee.
Eleazar.   Do: take from mee
  This Ague: and these fits that hanging on me
  Shake me in pieces, and set all my blood
  A boiling with the fire of rage: away, away;
  Thou believ'st I jeast:
  And laugh'st, to see my wrath wear antick shapes:
  Be gone, be gone.
Qu. Mo.   What means my love?
  Burst all those wyres! burn all those Instruments!   30
  For they displease my *Moor.* Art thou now pleas'd,
  Or wert thou now disturb'd? I'le wage all *Spain*
  To one sweet kisse, this is some new device
  To make me fond and long. Oh! you men
  Have tricks to make poor women die for you.
Eleazar.   What, die for me; away.
Qu. Mo.   Away, what way? I prithee speak more kindly;
  Why do'st thou frown? at whom?
Eleazar.   At thee.
Qu. Mo.   At me?
  Oh why at me? for each contracted frown
  A crooked wrinkle interlines my brow: 40
  Spend but one hour in frowns, and I shal look
  Like to a Beldam of one hundred years:
  I prithee speak to me and chide me not,
  I prithee chide if I have done amisse,
  But let my punishment be this, and this.   *Kiss.*
  I prithee smile on me, if but a while,
  Then frown on me, I'le die: I prithee smile:
  Smile on me, and these two wanton boies,
  These pretty lads that do attend on me,

---

31 *Moor*] *Here and throughout this edition, regardless of the variable practice of* D, *the word* Moor *will be italicized when it refers directly to* Eleazar, *as a name, and printed in roman when it does not.*

45 *Kiss.*] D *places after line* 44, *since there was insufficient room after line* 45.

Shall call thee *Jove*, shall wait upon thy cup   50
And fill thee Nectar: their enticing eies
Shall serve as chrystal, wherein thou maist see
To dresse thy self, if thou wilt smile on me.
Smile on me, and with coronets of pearle,
And bells of gold, circling their pretty arms
In a round Ivorie fount these two shal swim,
And dive to make thee sport:
Bestow one smile, one little little smile,
And in a net of twisted silk and gold
In my all-naked arms, thy self shalt lie,   60
Eleazar.   Why, what to do? Lusts arms do stretch so wide,
That none can fill them! I'le lay there? away.
Qu. Mo.   Where has thou learn'd this language? that can say
No more but two rude words; away, away:
Am I grown ugly now?
Eleazar.   Ugly as hell.
Qu. Mo.   Thou lovd'st me once.
Eleazar.   That can thy bastards tell.
Qu. Mo.   What is my sin? I will amend the same.
Eleazar.   Hence strumpet, use of sin makes thee past shame.
Qu. Mo.   Strumpet.
Eleazar.   I Strumpet.
Qu. Mo.   Too true 'tis, woe is me;
I am a Strumpet, but made so by thee.   70
Eleazar.   By me?
No, no; by these young bauds; fetch thee a glasse
And thou shalt see the bals of both thine eies
Burning in fire of lust; by me? there's here
Within this hollow cistern of thy breast
A spring of hot blood: have not I to cool it
Made an extraction to the quintessence
Even of my soul: melted all my spirits,
Ravish'd my youth, deflour'd my lovely cheeks,
And dried this, this to an anatomy   80
Only to feed your lust, (these boies have ears):

62 there?] Hazlitt; ~ ₐ D   80 an] Dilke; *om.* D

Yet wouldst thou murther me.

Qu. Mo.   I murder thee?

Eleaʒar.   I cannot ride through the Castilian streets
But thousand eies through windows, and through doors
Throw killing looks at me, and every slave
At *Eleaʒar* darts a finger out,
And every hissing tongue cries, There's the *Moor*,
That's he that makes a Cuckold of our King,
There go's the Minion of the Spanish Queen;
That's the black Prince of Divels, there go's hee   90
That on smooth boies, on Masks and Revellings
Spends the Revenues of the King of *Spain*.
Who arms this many headed beast but you,
Murder and Lust are twins, and both are thine;
Being weary of me thou wouldst worry me,
Because some new love makes thee loath thine old.

Qu. Mo.   Eleaʒar!

Eleaʒar.   Harlot! I'le not hear thee speak.

Qu. Mo.   I'le kill my self unless thou hear'st me speak.
My husband King upon his death-bed lies,
Yet have I stolne from him to look on thee: 100
A Queen hath made her self thy Concubine;
Yet do'st thou now abhor me. Hear me speak!
Else shall my sons plague thy adult'rous wrongs,
And tread upon thy heart for murd'ring me,
Thy tongue hath murd'red me (Cry murder boyes.)

2 Boies.   Murder! the Queen's murd'red!

Eleaʒar.   Love! slaves peace!

2 Boies.   Murder! the Queen's murd'red!

Eleaʒar.   Stop your throats!
Hark Hush you Squalls; Dear love look up:
Our Chamber window stares into the Court,
And every wide mouth'd cur, hearing this news   110
Will give Alarum to the cuckold King.
I did dissemble when I chid my love,
And that dissembling was to try my love.

110 cur] Malone's *note*; ear D (*see* Brereton 1800–1 *and* III.ii.210–211)

136

Qu. Mo.   Thou call'dst me strumpet.
Eleazar.   I'le tear out my tongue
From this black temple for blaspheming thee.
Qu. Mo.   And when I woo'd thee but to smile on me,
Thou cri'dst, away, away, and frown'dst upon mee.
Eleazar.   Come now I'le kiss thee, now I'le smile upon thee;
Call to thy ashy cheeks their wonted red:
Come frown not, pout not, smile, smile but upon me,   120
And with my poniard will I stab my flesh,
And quaffe carowses to thee of my blood,
Whil'st in moist Nectar kisses thou do'st pledge me.   *Knock.*

                    Enter Zarack.

How now, why star'st thou thus?
Zarack.   The King is dead.
Eleazar.   Ha! dead!
You hear this, is't true, is't true, the King dead!
Who dare knock thus?
Zarack.   It is the Cardinall,
Making inquiry if the Queen were here.
Eleazar.   See? shee's here, tell him! and yet *Zarack* stay.

                    Enter Baltazar.

Baltazar.   *Don Roderigo*'s come to seek the Queen.   130
Eleazar.   Why should *Roderigo* seek her here?
Baltazar.   The King hath swounded thrice, and being recovered,
Sends up and down the Court, to seek her grace.
Eleazar.   The King was dead with you; Run! and with a voice
Erected high as mine, say thus, thus threaten
To *Roderigo* and the Cardinall.
Seek no Queens here, I'le broach them if they do,
Upon my falchions point. Again more knocking!   *Knock again.*
Zarack.   Your father is at hand, my Gracious Lord.
Eleazar.   Lock all the chambers, bar him out you apes.   140
Hither, a vengeance; stir *Eugenia*,
You know your old walk under ground, away.

      123 Knock. | Enter Zarack.] D *places each one line below.*

                         137

So, down, hye to the King, quick, quick, you Squalls
Crawle with your Dam, i'th dark, dear love farewell,
One day I hope to shutt you up in hell.   Eleazar *shuts them in.*

Enter Alvero.

Alvero.   Son *Eleazar*, saw you not the Queen?
Eleazar.   Hah!
Alvero.   Was not the Queen here with you?
Eleazar.   Queen with mee;
  Because my Lord I'me married to your daughter,
  You (like your daughter) will grow Jealious: 150
  The Queen with me, with me, a Moore, a Devill,
  A slave of *Barbary*, a dog; for so
  Your silken Courtiers christen me, but father
  Although my flesh be tawny, in my veines,
  Runs blood as red, and royal as the best
  And proud'st in *Spain*, there do'es old man:
  My father, who with his Empire, lost his life,
  And left me Captive to a Spanish Tyrant, Oh!
  Go tell him! Spanish Tyrant! tell him, do!
  He that can loose a kingdom and not rave,   160
  He's a tame jade, I am not, tell old *Philip*
  I call him Tyrant: here's a sword and arms,
  A heart, a head, and so pish, 'tis but death:
  Old fellow shee's not here.   But ere I dye,
  Sword I'le bequeath thee a rich legacy.
Alvero.   Watch fitter hours to think on wrongs then now,
  Deaths frozen hand hold's Royal *Philip's* heart,
  Halfe of his body lies within a grave;
  Then do not now by quarrells shake that state,
  Which is already too much ruinate.   170
  Come and take leave of him before he dye.   *Exit.*
Eleazar.   I'le follow you; now purple villany,
  Sit like a Roab imperiall on my back,
  That under thee I closelyer may contrive
  My vengeance; foul deeds hid do sweetly thrive:

145 S.D. *Following*, D *divides*: Act I^{mus}. Scena II^{da}.

Mischief erect thy throne and sit in state
Here, here upon this head; let fools fear fate,
Thus I defie my starrs, I care not I
How low I tumble down, so I mount high.
Old time I'le wait bare-headed at thy heels,   180
And be a foot-boy to thy winged hours;
They shall not tell one Minute out in sands,
But I'le set down the number, I'le stil wake,
And wast these bals of sight by tossing them,
In busie observations upon thee.
Sweet opportunity I'le bind my self
To thee in base apprentice-hood so long,
Till on thy naked scalp grow hair as thick
As mine, and all hands shal lay hold on thee:
If thou wilt lend me but thy rusty sithe,   190
To cut down all that stand within my wrongs,
And my revenge.   Love dance in twenty formes
Upon my beauty, that this Spanish dame
May be bewitch'd, and doat; her amorous flames
Shall blow up the old King, consume his Sons,
And make all *Spain* a bonefire.
This Tragedie beeing acted, hers does begin,
To shed a harlots blood can be no sin.

                                                        Exit.

ACTUS I. SCENA II.

The Courtains being drawn there appears in his bed King Phillip, *with
his Lords, the Princesse* Isabella *at the feet*; [*Cardinal*] Mendoza,
Alvero, Hortensio, Fernando, Roderigo, *and to them Enter Queen*
[*Mother*] *in hast.*

Qu. Mo.   Whose was that Screech-Owls voice, that like the sound
Of a hell-tortur'd soul rung through mine ears

S.D. ACTUS I. Scena II.] Act. I^mus. Scena 3^tia. D
S.D. Isabella_∧ . . . *feet;*] Dilke; ∼ , . . . ∼ _∧ D
1 *Qu. Mo.*] *The speech-prefix for this scene in* D *is* Queen *except* Queen Mo. *lines*
80, 151.

Nothing but horrid shreiks, nothing but death?
Whil'st I, vailing my knees to the cold earth,
Drowning my withered cheeks in my warm tears,
And stretching out my arms to pull from heaven
Health for the Royal Majestie of *Spain*,
All cry'd, The Majestie of *Spain* is dead:
That last word (dead) struck through the ecchoing air,
Rebounded on my heart, and smote me down   10
Breathlesse to the cold earth, and made me leave
My praiers for *Philips* life, but thanks to heaven
I see him live, and lives I hope to see
Unnumbred years to guide this Empery.

K. Phil. The number of my years ends in one day,
E're this Sun's down all a King's glory sets,
For all our lives are but deaths counterfeits.
Father *Mendoza* and you Peers of *Spain*,
Dry your wet eies, for sorrow wanteth force
T'inspire a breathing soul in a dead coarse;   20
Such is your King: Where's *Isabel* our Daughter?

Cardinal. At your beds-feet confounded in her tears.

K. Phil. She of your grief the heaviest burthen bears;
You can but lose a King, but she a Father.

Qu. Mo. She bear the heaviest burthen; Oh say rather
I bear, and am born down, my sorrowing
Is for a husbands losse, losse of a King.

K. Phil. No more, *Alvero* call the Princess hither.

Alvero. Madam, his Majestie doth call for you.

K. Phil. Come hither *Isabella*, reach a hand;   30
Yet now it shall not need, in stead of thine
Death shoving thee back clasps his hands in mine,
And bids me come away; I must, I must;
Though Kings be gods on earth, they turn to dust.
Is not Prince *Philip* come from *Portugal*?

Roderigo. The Prince as yet is not return'd, my Lord.

K. Phil. Commend me to him, if I ne're behold him:
This tells the order of my funeral,

22 *Cardinal.*] *Throughout this scene the* D *speech-prefix is* Mendoza.

Do it as 'tis set down! Embalm my body;
Though worms do make no difference of flesh,   40
Yet Kings are curious here to dig their graves;
Such is man's frailty; when I am embalm'd,
Apparel me in a rich Roial Robe,
According to the custome of the Land;
Then place my bones within that brazen shrine
Which death hath builded for my ancestors:
I cannot name death, but he strait steps in,
And pulls me by the arm.
Fernando.   His Grace doth faint:
Help me my Lords softly to raise him up.

Enter Eleazar, *and stands sadly by.*

K. Phil.   Lift me not up, I shortly must go down;   50
When a few dribling minutes have run out,
Mine hour is ended: King of *Spain* farewell:
You all acknowledg him your Soveraign?
All.   When you are dead we will acknowledg him.
K. Phil.   Govern this kingdom well: to be a King
Is given to many: but to govern well
Granted to few: have care to *Isabel,*
Her virtue was King *Philips* looking-glasse.
Reverence the Queen your mother. Love your sister,
And the young Prince your brother; even that day   60
When *Spain* shall solemnize my Obsequies,
And lay me up in earth; let them crown you.
Where's *Eleazar, Don Alvero's* son?
Fernando.   Yonder with crost arms stands he malecontent.
K. Phil.   I do commend him to thee for a man
Both wise and warlike, yet beware of him,
Ambition wings his spirit, keep him down;
What wil not men attempt to win a crown.
Mendoza is Protector of thy Realm,
I did elect him for his gravity,   70
I trust hee'l be a father to thy youth:
Call help *Fernando,* now I faint indeed.

Fernando. My Lords.

K. Phil. Let none with a distracted voice
Shreik out, and trouble me in my departure:
Heavens hands I see are beckning for my soul;
I come, I come; thus do the proudest die,
Death hath no mercy, life no certainty.

Cardinal. As yet his soul's not from her temple gone,
Therefore forbear loud lamentation.

Qu. Mo. Oh he is dead, hee's dead! lament and die,   80
In her King's end begins *Spains* misery.

Isabella. He shall not end so soon; Father, dear Father!

                                        [*King dies*]

Fernando. Forbear sweet *Isabella*, shreiks are vain.

Isabella. You crie forbear, you by his losse of breath
Have won a kingdom, you may cry forbear:
But I have lost a Father, and a King;
And no tongue shal controul my sorrowing.

Hortenzo. Whither, good *Isabella?*

Isabella. I will go,
Where I will languish in eternal wo.

Hortenzo. Nay, gentle Love.

Isabella. Talk not of love to me.   90
The world and the worlds pride henceforth I'le scorn.   *Exit.*

Hortenzo. My love shall follow thee; if thou deny'st
To live with poor *Hortenzo* as his wife,
I'le never change my love, but change my life.

Enter Philip *Hastily.*

Philip. I know he is not dead, I know proud Death
Durst not behold such sacred majesty.
Why stand you thus distracted? Mother, Brother,
My Lord *Mendoza*, where's my Royal father?

Qu. Mo. Here lyes the temple of his Royall soul.

Fernando. Here's all that's left of *Philips* Majesty.   100
Wash you his tombe with tears; *Fernandoes* mone,
Hating a Partner, shall be spent alone.   *Exit.*

Philip. Oh happy father, miserable Sonne!

142

Philip is gone to Joy; *Philip*'s forlorn:
He dies to live; my life with woe is torn.

Qu. Mo.   Sweet sonne.

Philip.   Sweet mother: oh! how I now do shame
To lay on one so foul so fair a name:
Had you been a true mother, a true wife,
This King had not so soon been robb'd of life.

Qu. Mo.   What means this rage, my sonne?

Philip.   Call not me your sonne: 110
My father whilst he liv'd tyr'd his strong armes
In bearing christian armour, gainst the Turk's,
And spent his brains in warlike stratagems
To bring Confusion on damn'd Infidels;
Whil'st you that snorted here at home betraid
His name to everlasting Infamy;
Whilst you at home suffered his bed-chamber
To be a Brothelry, whilst you at home
Suffered his Queen to be a Concubine,
And wanton red cheekt boy's to be her bawds   120
Whilst shee reeking in that leachers armes —

Eleazar.   Me!

Philip.   Villaine 'tis thee,
Thou hel-begotten fiend at thee I stare.

Qu. Mo.   *Philip* thou art a villain to dishonour me.

Philip.   Mother I am no villain; 'tis this villain
Dishonours you and me, dishonours *Spain*,
Dishonours all these Lords, this Divell is he,
That —

Eleazar.   What! Oh pardon me I must throw off
All chains of duty: wert thou ten Kings sons: 130
Had I as many soules as I have sins,
As this from hence, so they from this should fly;
In just revenge of this Indignity.

                    [*Draws. Lords come between them.*]

Philip.   Give way, or I'le make way upon your bosoms.

Eleazar.   Did my dear Soveraigne live, sirrha that tongue —

Qu. Mo.   Did but King *Philip* live, traytor I'de tell —

Philip.   A tale, that should rid both your soules to hell.
 Tell *Philip's* ghost, that *Philip* tells his Queen,
 That *Philip's* Queen is a Moor's Concubine:
 Did the King live I'de tell him how you two,   140
 Rip't up the entrails of his treasury:
 With Masques and antick Revellings.
Eleaʒar.   Words insupportable; do'st hear me boy?
Qu. Mo.   Stand you all still, and see me thus trod down?
Philip.   Stand you all still, yet let this divell stand here?
Cardinal.   Forbear sweet Prince; *Eleaʒar*, I am now
 Protector to *Fernando* King of *Spain*:
 By that authority and by consent
 Of all these peers, I uterly deprive thee
 Of all those Royalties thou hold'st in *Spain*.   150
Qu. Mo.   Cardinall, who lends thee this Commission?
Eleaʒar.   Cardinall, i'le shorten thee by the head for this.
Philip. Forward my Lord *Mendoʒa*, damne the feind.
Eleaʒar.   Princes of *Spain*, consent you to this pride?
All.   Wee doe.
Qu. Mo.   For what cause? let his faith be try'd.
Cardinall.   His treasons needs no tryal, they're too plain;
 Come not within the Court, for if you do,
 To beg with Indian slaves I'le banish you.
                         Exeunt all, but Alvero, Queen, *and* Eleazar.
Alvero.   Why should my sonne be banished?

                      Enter Maria.

Qu. Mo.   Of that dispute not now *Alvero*,   160
 I'le to the King my sonne, it shall be try'de
 If *Castiles* King can cool a Cardinall's pride.
                              Exeunt Queen *and* Alvero.
Eleaʒar.   If I disgest this Gall; Oh! my *Maria*:
 I am whipt, and rackt, and torn upon the wheel
 Of giddy fortune: She and her Minions
 Have got me down; and treading on my bosome,

                158 S.D. *Following*, D *divides*: Act. I. Scena IV.

They cry, lye still: the Cardinal
(Oh! rare) would bandy me away from *Spain*,
And banish me to beg; I, beg with slaves.
Maria.   Conquer with patience these indignityes.   170
Eleazar.   Patience; ha, ha: yes, yes: an honest Cardinall.
Maria.   Yet smother thy grief and seek revenge.
Eleazar.   Hah! banish me, s'foot, why say they do;
  Ther's *Portugal* a good air, and *France* a fine Country;
  Or *Barbary* rich, and has Moors; the Turke
  Pure Divell, and allowes enough to fat
  The sides of villany; good living there:
  I can live there, and there, and there,
  Troth 'tis, a villain can live any where:
  But say I goe from hence, I leave behind me   180
  A Cardinall, that will laugh, I leave behind me
  A *Philip*, that will clap his hands for joy;
  And dance levaltoes through the *Castile* Court.
  But the deep'st wound of all is this, I leave
  My wrongs, dishonours, and my discontents,
  Oh! unrevenged; my bed-rid enemies
  Shal never be rais'd up by the strong Physic,
  And curing of my sword, therefore stay still;
  Many have hearts to strike, that dare not kil:
  Leave me *Maria*: Cardinall, this disgrace,   190
  Shall dye thy soule, as Inky as my face:
  Pish, hence *Maria*.
                    Enter Alvero.

Maria.   To the King I'le fly.
He shall reveng my Lord's indignity.   *Exit.*
Alvero.   *Mendoza* woo's the King to banish thee;
Startle thy wonted spirits, awake thy soul,
And on thy resolution fasten wings,
Whose golden feathers may out-strip their hate.
Eleazar.   I'le tye no golden fethers to my wings.

---

172 thy] the D
*187–188 Physic, And curing] Physical, | And [*cw*] || Curing D

Alvero. Shall they thus tread thee down, which once were glad,
To Lacquey by thy conquering Chariot wheeles? 200
Eleazar. I care not, I can swallow more sower wrongs.
Alvero. If they triumph o're thee; they'l spurn me down.
Eleazar. Look, spurn again.
Alvero.   What Ice hath coold that fire,
Which sometimes made thy thoughts to heaven aspire;
This patience had not wont to dwell with thee.

Enter Fernando *and* Maria.

Eleazar. 'Tis right, but now the World is chang'd you see;
Though I seem dead to you, here lives a fire,
No more, here comes the King, and my *Maria*;
The Spaniard loves my wife, she swears to me,
Shee's chast as the white Moon, well if she be. 210
Well too if shee be not, I care not, I,
I'le climb up by that love to dignitye.
Fernando. Thou woo'st me to revenge thy husbands wrong,
I woo thy fair self not to wrong thy self;
Swear but to love me, and to thee I'le swear
To crown thy husband with a diadem.
Maria. Such love as I dare yeeld, I'le not deny.
Fernando. When in the golden armes of Majesty —
I am broke off; yonder thy husband stands,
I'le set him free, if thou unite my bands, 220
Soe much for that. Durst then the Cardinall,
Put on such insolence; tell me fair Madam,
Where's your most Valiant Husband?
Eleazar.   He see's me,
And yet inquires for me.
Maria.   Yonder's my Lord.
Fernando. *Eleazar* I have in my brest writ down
From her Report your late receiv'd disgrace:
My father lov'd you dearly, so will I.
Eleazar. True, for my wife's sake.   *Aside.*
Fernando.   This Indignitye

206 World is] World's D

146

Will I have Interest in, for being your King,
You shall perceive I'le curbe my underling: 230
This morning is our Coronation
And father's funerall solemnized,
Be present, step into your wonted place;
Wee'l guild your dim disgraces with our grace.

                              Exeunt. [*Manet* Eleazar.]

Eleazar. I thank my Soveraign that you love my wife;
I thank thee wife that thou wilt lock my head
In such strong armour, to bear off all blows;
Who dare say such wives are their husbands foes:
Let's see now, by her falling I must rise.
Cardinal you die, if the King bid me live;   240
Philip you die for railing at me: proud Lords you die,
That with *Mendoza* cry'd, Banish the *Moor.*
And you my loving Liege, you're best sit fast;
If all these live not, you must die at last.

                                          [*Exit.*]

                The end of the first Act.

ACTUS II. Scena. i.

Enter two Lords, Philip *his brother,* [*Cardinal*] Mendoza, *Eleazar
with him, the King Crown'd, Queen mother,* Alvero, Zarack,
Baltazar, *and attendants.*

Cardinal.   Why stares this Divell thus, as if pale death
Had made his eyes the dreadfull messengers
To carry black destruction to the world.
Was hee not banisht *Spain?*
Philip.   Your sacred mouth,
Pronounc'd the sentence of his banishment:
Then spurn the villain forth.
Eleazar.   Who spurns the *Moor,*

---

1 Cardinal.] *Throughout this scene the* D *speech-prefix is* Mendoza.
2 messengers] D(c); messenger D(u)

Were better set his foot upon the Devill,
Do; spurn me! and this confounding arm of wrath
Shal like a thunderbolt breaking the clouds
Divide his body from his soul. Stand back.   10
Spurn *Eleazar?*
Roderigo.   Shall wee bear his pride.
Alvero. Why not, he underwent much injurie.
Cardinal. What injury have we perform'd proud Lord?
Eleazar. Proud Cardinall; my unjust banishment.
Cardinal. 'Twas wee that did it; and our words are laws.
Fernando. 'Twas wee repeal'd him, and our words are laws.
Zarack & Baltazar. If not, these are.

All the Moors draw.

Philip.   How! threatned and out-dar'd?
Fernando. Shal we give arm to hostile violence?
Sheath your swords, sheath them, it's wee command.
Eleazar. Grant *Eleazar* justice my dread Leige.   20
Cardinal. *Eleazar* hath had justice from our hands,
And he stands banish'd from the Court of *Spain.*
Fernando. Have you done justice? why Lord Cardinall,
From whom do you derive authority,
To banish him the Court without our leav?
Cardinal. From this, the Staffe of our Protectorship;
From this, which the last will of your dear Father
Committed to our trust: from this high place
Which lifts *Mendoza's* spirits beyond the pitch
Of ordinary honour, and from this.   30
Fernando. Which too much over-weening Insolence
Hath quite ta'ne from you, *Eleazar* up,
And from us sway this Staffe of Regency.

Takes the staff from Mendoza *and gives it to* Eleazar.

All. How's this?
Philip. Dare sons presume to break their fathers will?

16 *Fernando.*] *Throughout this scene the* D *speech-prefix is* King.
*18 arm] *stet* D   33 S.D. D *places S.D. in right margin opposite lines* 31–32.

Fernando.   Dare Subjects counter-check their Soveraigns will?
'Tis done, and who gainsaies it is a Traitor.
Philip.   I do *Fernando*, yet I am no Traitor.
Cardinal.   *Fernando* I am wrong'd, by *Peters* Chair
  Mendoça vows revenge. I'le lay aside   40
  My Cardinals hat, and in a wall of steel,
  The glorious livery of a souldier,
  Fight for my late lost honour.
Fernando.   Cardinall.
Cardinal.   King, thou shalt be no King for wronging me.
  The Pope shall send his bulls through all thy Realm,
  And pul obedience from thy Subjects hearts,
  To put on armour of the Mother Church:
  Curses shal fal like lightnings on your heads,
  Bell, book and candle, holy water, praiers,
  Shal all chime vengeance to the Court of *Spain*   50
  Till they have power to conjure down that feind;
  That damned *Moor*, that Devil, that Lucifer,
  That dares aspire the staffe, the Card'nall swaid.
Eleaçar.   Ha ha ha, I laugh yet, that the Cardinall's vext.
Philip.   Laughst thou base slave, the wrinckles of that scorn
  Thine own heart blood shall fill; Brother farewell,
  Since you disprove the will our father left,
  For base lust of a loathed Concubine.
Eleaçar.   Ha, Concubine; who does Prince *Philip* mean?
Philip.   Thy wife, thy daughter, base aspiring Lords,   60
  Who to buy honour, are content to sell,
  Your names to infamy, your souls to hell:
  And stamp you now? do, do, for you shal see,
  I go for vengeance, and she'l com with me.
Eleaçar.   Stay, for she's here already, see proud boy.

                                  They both draw

    39 wrong'd, . . . Chair_∧] Dilke; ~ _∧ . . . ~ _∧
    50 all chime] D(u); allchim D(c)
    50 Court of *Spain*] Dilke; Court Spain D(u), of Court Spain D(c)
    53 Card'nall] D(c); Card'nalls D(u)
    55 Laughst] Dilke; Laughs D(u); Laughts D(c)
    59 Prince] D(c); King D(u)

Qu. Mo.   Hold, stay this fury; if you long for blood,
Murder me first. Dear son you are a King:
Then stay the violent tempest of their wrath.
Fernando.   Shall Kings be overswaid in their desires?
Roderigo.   Shall Subjects be opress'd by tyranny?   70
Qu. Mo.   No State shall suffer wrong, then hear mee speak,
Mendoza, you have sworn you love the Queen,
Then by that love I charge you leave these arms:
Eleazar, for those favours I have given you,
Embrace the Cardinall, and be friends with him.
Eleazar.   And have my wife call'd strumpet to my face.
Qu. Mo.   'Twas rage made his tongue erre, [*aside*] do you not
                    know
The violent love *Mendoza* bears the Queen:
Then speak him fair, for in that honied breath
I'le lay a bait shall train him to his death.   80
Come, come, I see your looks give way to peace;
Lord Cardinall begin, and for reward,
Ere this fair setting Sun behold his bride;
Be bold to challenge love, yet be deni'd.   *Aside.*
Cardinal.   That promise makes me yeild: my gracious Lord;
Although my disgrace hath graven its memory
On every Spaniards eye, yet shall the duty
I owe your sacred Highness; and the love
My Country challengeth, make me lay by
Hostile intendments, and return again   90
To the fair circle of obedience.
Fernando.   Both pardon and our favour bids you welcome,
And for some satisfaction for your wrongs,
We here create you *Salamanka's* Duke;
But first as a true signe all grudges dye,
Shake hands with *Eleazar* and be friends;
This union pleaseth us, now brother *Philip*,
You are included in this league of love,
So is *Roderigo* to forget all wrongs:
Your Castle for a while shall bid us welcom,   100

86 its] D(c); his D(u)

Eleazar shall it not? It is enough,
Lords lead the way, [*aside*] that whil'st you feast your selves,
Fernando may find time all means to prove,
To compasse fair *Maria* for our love.

                                       Exeunt Omnes.

ACTUS II. SCENA II.

Enter Queen Mother, and Eleazar.

Eleazar.   Madam a word now, have you wit or spirit?
Qu. Mo.   Both.
Eleazar.   Set them both to a most gainfull task,
Our enemies are in my Castle-work.
Qu. Mo.   I; but the King's there too, it's dangerous pride,
To strike at those; that couch by a Lyons side.
Eleazar.   Remove them.
Qu. Mo.   How?
Eleazar.   How? a thousand ways;
By poison, or by this, but every groom   [*Dagger.*]
Has skill in such base traffick; no our pollicies
Must look more strange, must flie with loftier wings:
Vengeance the higher it falls, more horror brings: 10
But you are cold, you dare not do.
Qu. Mo.   I dare.
Eleazar.   You have a womans heart, look you this hand,
Oh! 'tis too little to strike home.
Qu. Mo.   At whom?
Eleazar.   Your son.
Qu. Mo.   Which son, the King?
Eleazar.   Angels of heaven,
Stand like his guard about him, how? the King?
Not for so many worlds as here be stars,
Sticking upon th'imbroidred firmament.
The King? he loves my wife and should he die,
I know none else would love her; let him live.
(In heaven.) Good! Lord *Philip* —   *Aside.*

Qu. Mo.   He shall die.   20

Eleaʒar.   How? good good.

Qu. Mo.   By this hand.

Eleaʒar.   When, good good; when?

Qu. Mo.   This night if *Eleaʒer* give consent.

Eleaʒar.   Why then this night. *Philippo* shal not live
To see you kill him! Is he not your son?
A mother be the murd'rer of a brat,
That liv'd within her; hah!

Qu. Mo.   'Tis for thy sake.

Eleaʒar.   Puh! What excuses cannot dam'd sin make
To save it self, I know you love him well,
But that he has an eye, an eye, an eye.
To others our two hearts seem to be lock'd   30
Up in a case of steel, upon our love
Others dare not look, or if they dare, they cast
Squint purblind glances; who care though all see all,
So long as none dare speak, but *Philippo*
Knows that the Iron ribs of our villainies
Are thin: Hee laughs to see them like this hand,
With chinks, and crevises. How! a villanous eye,
A stabbing desperate tongue, the boy dare speak,
A mouth, a villanous mouth, lets muzzle him.

Qu. Mo.   How?

Eleaʒar.   Thus. Go you, and with a face well set   40
Do in good sad colours, such as paint out
The cheek of that fool penitence, and with a tongue
Made clean and glib; Cull from their lazy swarm,
Some honest Friers, whom that damnation gold,
Can tempt to lay their souls to'th stake;
Seek such, they are rank and thick.

Qu. Mo.   What then, I know such, what's the use?

Eleaʒar.   This is excellent.

20 Good! Lord *Philip* —] good Lord *Philip*. D
*23 night. ...live‸] ~ ‸ ... ~ ; D   23 *Philippo*] *Philip* D
34 but,] D(c); but, but D(u)   34 *Philippo*] *Philip* D
35 villainies] Robinson; villains D

Hire these to write books, preach and proclaim abroad,
That your son *Philip* is a bastard.
Qu. Mo.   How?   50
Eleazar.   A bastard; do you know a bastard? doo't;
Say conscience spake with you, and cry'd out; doo't:
By this means shall you thrust him from all hopes
Of wearing *Castiles* diadem, and that spur
Galling his sides, he will flye out, and fling,
And grind the Cardinals heart to a new edg
Of discontent, from discontent grows treason,
And on the stalk of treason death: he's dead
By this blow, and by you; yet no blood shed.
Doo't then; by this trick, he gon!   60
We stand more sure in climbing high;
Care not who fall, 'tis reall policie:
Are you arm'd to do this? hah!
Qu. Mo.   Sweet *Moor* it's done.
Eleazar.   Away then, work with boldness, and with speed;
On greatest actions greatest dangers feed.
                                        Exit Queen Mother.

Ha, ha, I thank thee provident creation,
That seeing in moulding me thou did'st intend,
I should prove villain, thanks to thee and nature
That skilful workman; thanks for my face,
Thanks that I have not wit to blush.
                              What *Zarack?*   70
Ho *Baltazar.*
                  Enter the two Moors.

Both.   My Lord.
Eleazar.   Nearer, so, silence;
Hang both your greedy years upon my lips,
Let them devour my speech, suck in my breath;
And (in) who lets it break prison, here's his death.
This night the Card'nall shall be murd'red.

52 spake] D(c); speake D(u)   52 out;] ~ , D(c); ~ ∧ D(u)
*52 doo't:] D(u); ~ ∧ D(c)   62 reall] *i.e.* regal, royal
72 years] D(u); ears D(c) [*see* II.ii.117]

153

Both.   Where?
Eleazar.   And to fill up a grave *Philippo* dies.
Both.   Where?
Eleazar.   Here.
Both.   By whom?
Eleazar.   By thee; and slave by thee:
  Have you hearts and hands to execute?
Both.   Here's both.
Zarack.   He dies were he my father.
Eleazar.   Ho away!
  Stay, go, go, stay, see me no more till night;   80
  Your cheeks are black, let not your souls look white.
Both.   Till night.
Eleazar.   Till night, a word, the Mother Queene
  Is trying if she can with fire of gold,
  Warpe the green consciences of two covetous Friers,
  To preach abroad *Philippo's* bastardy.
Zarack.   His bastardy, who was his father?
Eleazar.   Who?
  Search for these friers, hire them to work with you;
  Their holy callings will approve the fact
  Most good and meritorious; sin shines clear,
  When her black face Religions masque doth wear.   90
                          [*Exeunt the two Moors.*]
  Here comes the Queen, good; and the Friers.   *Aside.*

      Enter two Friers, Crab *and* Cole; *and Queen Mother.*

Cole.   Your son a bastard, say we do,
  But how then shall we deal with you?
  I tell you as I said before;
  His being a bastard, you are so poor
  In honour and in name, that time
  Can never take away the crime.

76 *Philippo*] *Philip* D   79, 86 *Zarack.*] | *Moor.* D
85 *Philippo's*] *Philip's* D   89 clear] D(c); dear D(u)
91 *Aside.*] D *places to the left of the line like a speech-prefix*
91 *Before the stage-direction* D *prints:* Act. II. Scena. III.

Qu. Mo.   I grant that Frier, yet rather I'le endure
The wound of infamy, to kill my name,
Then to see *Spain* bleeding, with civil swords.   100
The boy is proud, ambitious, he woo's greatnesse,
He takes up Spanish hearts on trust, to pay them
When he shall finger *Castiles* Crown: Oh then
Were it not better my disgrace were known,
Then such a base aspirer fill the Throne.
Cole.   Ha brother *Crab*, what think you?
Crab.   As you dear brother *Cole.*
Cole.   Then wee agree,
Coles Judgment is as *Crabs* you see.
Lady we swear to speak and write,   110
What you please so all go right.
Qu. Mo.   Then as wee gave directions, spread abroad,
In *Cales, Madrid, Granado,* and *Medyna*;
And all the Ryall Cities of the Realm:
Th'ambitious hopes of that proud bastard *Philip*,
And somtimes as you see occasion,
Tickle the years of the Rude multitude,
With *Eleazars* praises; guild his virtues,
Naples recovery and his victories
Atchieved against the Turkish Ottoman: 120
Will you do this for us?
Eleazar.   Say will you?   [*Comes forward.*]
Both Friers.   I.
Eleazar.   Why start you back and stare? ha? are you afraid.
Cole.   Oh! no Sir, no, but truth to tell;
Seeing your face, we thought of hell.
Eleazar.   Hell is a dream.
Cole.   But none do dream in hell.
Eleazar.   Friers stand to her; and me; and by your sin,
I'le shoulder out *Mendoza* from his seat;
And of two Friers create you Cardinalls,

        102 takes] D(c); take D(u)   105 aspirer] D(c); aspier D(u)
        114 Ryall] D(u); Royall D(c)   117 years] D(u) [*i.e.* ears]; ears D(c)
        119 his] D(c); *om.* D(u)   *126 your sin] *stet* D

Oh! how would Cardinalls hats on these heads sit.
Cole.   This face would look most goodly under it: 130
Friers *Crab* and *Cole* do swear,
In those circles still to appear:
In which she, or you, do charge us rise;
For you, our lives wee'l sacrifice.
Valete, Gaudete;
Si pereamus flete;
Orate pro nobis,
Oramus pro vobis.
Cole will be burnt, and *Crab* be prest,
Ere they prove knaves; thus are you crost and blest.   140
                                        Exeunt Friers.
Eleazar.   Away; you know now Madam none shall throw
Their leaden envie in an opposite scale,
To weigh down our true golden happiness.
Qu. Mo.   Yes, there is one.
Eleazar.   One, who? give mee his name
And I will turn it to a magick spell,
To bind him here, here; who?
Qu. Mo.   Your wife *Maria.*
Eleazar.   Hah! my *Maria.*
Qu. Mo.   She's th'Hellespont divides my love and me,
Shee being cut off —
Eleazar.   Stay, stay, cut off; let's think upon't, my wife?   150
Humh! Kill her too!
Qu. Mo.   Do's her love make thee cold?
Eleazar.   Had I a thousand wives, down go they all:
She dies, I'le cut her off:

                    Enter Baltazar.

                    Now *Baltazar.*

Baltazar.   Madam, the King intreats your company.
Qu. Mo.   His pleasure be obey'd, dear love farewell;
Remember your *Maria.*
                                        Exit Queen Mother.

131 Friers₳] Dilke; Frier, D
153 Now *Baltazar.*] D *prints following the first half of the line above the stage-direction.*

156

Eleazar.   Here adieu;
  With this I'le guard her, whil'st it stabs at you.
Baltazar. My Lord! the Friers are won to joine with us.
Eleazar. Be prosperous: about it *Baltazzar.*
Baltazar. The watch word.
Eleazar.   Oh! the word, let it be *treason*;   160
  When we cry *treason*, breake ope chamber doors:
  Kill *Phillip* and the Cardinall. Hence.
Baltazar.   I fly.   *Exit.*
Eleazar. Murder, now ride in triumph; darknesse, horror,
  Thus I invoke your aid, your Act begin;
  Night is a glorious Roab, for th'ugliest sin.
                                                     Exit.

ACTUS II. SCENA III.

Enter Cole *and* Crab *in Trouses, the Cardinall* [Mendoza] *in one
    of their weeds, and* Philip *putting on the other.*

Both Friers. Put on my Lord, and flye, or else you die.
Philip. I will not, I will die first; Cardinall,
  Prithe good Cardinal pluck off, Friers, slave,
  Murder us two, he shall not by this sword.
Cardinal. My Lord, you will endanger both our lives.
Philip. I care not; I'le kill some before I die:
  Away, s'heart; take your raggs; *Moor*, Devill, come.
Both Friers. My Lord put on, or else.
Philip.   Gods foot come help.
Cardinal. Ambitious villain. *Philip*, let us fly
  Into the chamber of the Mother Queen.   10
Philip. Thunder, beat down the lodgings.
Cardinal.   Else let's break
  Into the chamber of the King.
Philip.   Agreed,
  A pox upon those lowzy gaberdines,
  Agreed, I am for you *Moor*; stand side by side,

          S.D. III] IV. D   8 *Both*] 2. D

Come, hands off, leave your ducking, hell cannot fright,
Their spirits that do desperately fight.
Cole.   You are too rash, you are too hot,
Wild desperateness doth valour blot;
The lodging of the Kings beset,
With staring faces black as Jett,   20
And hearts of Iron, your deaths are vow'd
If you fly that way, therefore shrow'd,
Your body in Frier *Coles* gray weed,
For is't not madnesse man to bleed,
When you may scape untouch'd away:
Here's hell, here's heaven, here if you stay
You're gon, you're gon, Frier *Crab* and I,
Will here dance friskin whilst you flie:
Gag us, bind us, come put on;
The Gags too wide, so: gon, gon, gon.   30
Philip.   Oh! well, I'le come again, Lord Cardinall
Take you your Castle, I'le to *Portugall*:
I vow I'le come again, and if I do —
Cardinal.   Nay good my Lord!
Philip.   Black Devill I'le conjure you.
                                                           Exeunt.

To the Friers making a noise, gagg'd and bound, Enter Eleazar,
         Zarack, Baltazar, *and other Moors,*
                all with their Swords drawn.

Eleazar.   Guard all the passages, *Zarack* stand there,
There *Baltazar*, there you, the Friers,
Where have you plac'd the Friers?
All.   My Lord a noise.
Baltazar.   The Friers are gagg'd and bound.
Eleazar.   'Tis *Philip* and the Cardinal: shoot; hah stay!
Unbind them; where's *Mendoza*, and the Prince.   40
Cole.   *Sancta Maria* who can tell:

18 doth] D(c); do D(u)
34 S.D. *Preceding the main direction* D *prints:* Act. II. *S*cena. V.
37 *All.*] Dilke; *Alvero* D   39 shoot] D(c); shoots D(u)

By *Peters* keys they bound us well,
And having crack'd our shaven crowns,
They have escap'd you in our gowns.
*Elea*ʒ*ar.*   Escap'd; escap'd away? [*aside*] I am glad, it's good,
I would their arms may turn to Eagles wings,
To flye as swift as time: sweet air give way,
Winds leave your two and thirty pallaces,
And meeting all in one, join all your might,
To give them speedy and a prosperous flight.   50
Escap'd, Friers? which way?
Both Friers.   This way.
*Elea*ʒ*ar.*   Good:
Alas; what sin is't to shed innocent blood;
For look you holy men, it is the King;
The King, the King, see Friers, sulphury wrath
Having once entred into Royall brests,
Mark how it burns: the Queen, *Philippo's* mother;
Oh! most unnaturall, will have you two
Divulge abroad that hee's a bastard. Oh!
Will you doo't.
Crab.   What says my brother Frier?
Cole.   A Princes love is balm, their wrath a fire.   60
Crab.   'Tis true, but yet I'le publish no such thing;
What fool would lose his soul, to please a King?
*Elea*ʒ*ar.*   Keep there, good there, yet for it wounds my soul,
To see the miserablest wretch to bleed,
I counsell you (in care unto your lives)
T'obey the mother Queen, for by my life
I thinke shee has been prick'd, her conscience,
Oh! it has stung her, for some fact mis-don,
She would not else disgrace her selfe and son.
Doo't therefore, harke, shee'l work your deaths else, hate   70
Bred in a woman is insatiate.
Doo't Friers.

47 as] us D
51 *Both Friers.*] *Both.* D   56 *Philippo's*] *Philip's* D
66 T'obey] D(c) *and* cw; To obey D(u)

159

Crab.   Brother *Cole?* Zeal sets me in a flame,
I'le doo't.
Cole.   And I.
                 His basenesse wee'l proclaim.

                                    Exeunt Friers.

Eleaȝar.   Do, and be damn'd; *Zarack* and *Baltaȝar,*
  Dog them at th' hee'ls, and when their poisonous breath
  Hath scattered this infection, on the hearts
  Of credulous Spaniards, here reward them thus,
  Slaves too much trusted do grow dangerous;
  Why this shall feed,
  And fat suspition, and my pollicy.   80
  I'le ring through all the Court, this loud alarum:
  That they contriv'd the murder of the King,
  The Queen and me; and being undermin'd,
  To scape the blowing up, they fled. Oh good!
  There, there, thou there, cry treason; each one take
  A severall door, your cries my musick make.
Baltaȝar.   Where's the King? treason persues him.

          Enter Alvero *in his shirt, his sword drawn.*

Eleaȝar.   Where's the sleepy Queen?
  Rise, rise, and arm, against the hand of treason.
Alvero.   Whence comes this sound of treason?   90

          Enter King in his shirt, his sword drawn.

Fernando.   Who frights our quiet slumbers, with this heavy noise?

          Enter Queen [Mother] in her night attire.

Qu. Mo.   Was it a dream? or did the sound
  Of monster treason call me from my rest.
Fernando.   Who rais'd this rumour *Eleaȝar,* you?
Eleaȝar.   I did my Liege, and still continue it,
  Both for your safety, and mine own discharge.
Fernando.   Whence coms the ground then?

          75 th'] D(c); *om.* D(u)   78 Slaves] D(c); Slave D(u)
          91 Fernando.] *Throughout this scene the* D *speech-prefix is* King.

                             160

Eleazar.   From the Cardinall,
And the young Prince, who bearing in his mind
The true Idea of his late disgrace,
In putting him from the Protectorship,   100
And envying the advancement of the *Moor*,
Determined this night to murder you;
And for your Highnesse lodg'd within my Castle,
They would have laid the murder on my head.
Fernando.   The Cardinall, and my Brother, bring them forth:
Their lives shall answer this ambitious practice.
Eleazar.   Alas my Lord it is impossible,
For when they saw I had discovered them,
They train'd two harmlesse Friers to their lodgings;
Disrob'd them, gagg'd them, bound 'em to two posts,   110
And in their habits did escape the Castle.
Fernando.   That Cardinall, is all ambition,
And from him doth our Brother gather heart.
Qu. Mo.   Th'ambition of the one infects the other,
And in a word they both are dangerous;
But might your mothers counsell stand in force,
I would advise you send the trusty *Moor*
To fetch them back, before they had seduc'd
The squint ey'd multitude from true allegiance,
And drawn them to their dangerous faction.   120
Fernando.   It shall be so, therefore my States best prop,
Within whose bosome I durst trust my life,
Both for my safety and thine own discharge,
Fetch back those traitors, and till your return
Our self will keep your Castle.
Eleazar.   My Leige; the tongue of true obedience
Must not gainsay his Soveraigns impose;
By heaven, I will not kiss the cheek of sleep,
Till I have fetch'd those traitors to the Court.
Fernando.   Why; this sorts right; he gon, his beauteous wife   130
                                                    [*Aside*]
Shall sail into the naked arms of love.
Qu. Mo.   Why, this is as it should bee, he once gon,   [*Aside.*]

His wife that keeps me from his marriage bed,
Shall by this hand of mine be murthered.
Fernando.   This storm is well nigh past, the swelling clouds
That hang so full of treason, by the wind
In awfull Majestie are scattered.
Then each man to his rest; good night sweet friend.
Whil'st thou persu'st the traitors that are fled,   [*Aside.*]
Fernando means to warm thy marriage bed.   140

                              Exeunt. [*Manet* Eleazar.]

Eleazar.   Many good nights, [*aside*] consume and dam your souls.
I know he means to Cuckold mee this night;
Yet do I know no means to hinder it.
Besides, who knows whether the lustful King,
Having my wife and Castle at command,
Will ever make surrender back again:
But if he do not, with my falchions point
I'le lance those swelling veins in which hot lust
Does keep his Revels, and with that warm blood
Where *Venus's* bastard coold his sweltring spleen,   150
Wash the disgrace from *Eleazars* brows.

                         Enter Maria.

Maria.   Dear *Eleazar* —
Eleazar.   If they lock the gates
I'le tosse a ball of wild-fire o're the walls.
Maria.   Husband, sweet husband —
Eleazar.   Or else swim o're the moat,
And make a breach through the flinty sides
Of the rebellious walls —
Maria.   Hear me, dear heart.
Eleazar.   Or undermine the chamber where they lie,
And by the violent strength of gunpowder,
Blow up the Castle, and th'incestuous couch,
In which lust wallows; but my labouring thoughts,   160

---

140 *Exeunt*] Dilke; *Exit* D   144 knows‸] Dilke; know‸ D(u); know, D(c)
149 his] D(c); the D(u)   151 *Following*, D *prints*: Act. II. Scena. VI.
155 through] *i.e.* thorough

Wading too deep in bottomless extreams;
Do drown themselvs in their own stratagems.
Maria.   Sweet husband! dwell not upon circumstance,
When weeping sorrow like an Advocate
Importunes you for aid; look in mine eyes,
There you shall see dim grief swimming in tears,
Invocating succor. Oh succor!
Eleazar.   Succor. Zounds for what?
Maria.   To shield me from *Fernando's* unchast love,   170
Who with uncessant praiers importun'd me.
Eleazar.   To lie with you; I know't.
Maria.   Then seek some means
How to prevent it.
Eleazar.   'Tis impossible;
For to the end that his unbridled lust
Might have more free accesse unto thy bed,
This night he hath enjoined me
To fetch back *Philip* and the Cardinall.
Maria.   Then this ensuing night shall give an end
To all my sorrows, for before foul lust
Shall soil the fair complexion of mine honour,
This hand shall rob *Maria* of her life.   180
Eleazar.   Not so dear soul, for in extremities
Choose out the least, and ere the hand of death
Should suck this Ivorie pallace of thy life,
Imbrace my counsell, and receive this poison:
Which in the instant he attempts thy love,
Then give it him: do, do,
Do; poison him, he gon, thou'rt next;   [*Aside.*]
Be sound in resolution; and farewell;
By one, and one, I'le ship you all to hell.   [*Aside.*]
Spain I will drown thee with thine own proud blood,   190
Then make an ark of carcasses: farewell.
Revenge and I will sail in blood to hell.   *Exit.*
Maria.   Poison the King, Alas my trembling hand
Would let the poison fall, and through my cheeks

172 impossible] Hazlitt; possible D

Fear suted in a bloodless livery,
Would make the world acquainted with my guilt,
But thanks prevention, I have found a means
Both to preserve my Royall Soveraignes life,
And keep my self a true and Loyall wife.

Exit.

The end of the second Act.

ACTUS III. Scena i.

Enter Queen Mother, with a Torch, solus.

Qu. Mo.   Fair eldest child of love, thou spotlesse night,
Empresse of silence, and the Queen of sleep;
Who with thy black cheeks pure complexion,
Mak'st lovers eyes enamour'd of thy beauty:
Thou art like my *Moor*, therefore will I adore thee,
For lending me this opportunity,
Oh with the soft skin'd Negro! heavens keep back
The saucy staring day from the worlds eye,
Untill my *Eleaʒar* make return;
Then in his Castle shall he find his wife,   10
Transform'd into a strumpet by my son;
Then shall he hate her whom he would not kill!
Then shall I kill her whom I cannot love!
The King is sporting with his Concubine.
Blush not my boy, be bold like me thy mother,
But their delights torture my soul like Devills,
Except her shame be seen: Wherefore awake
Christophero, *Verdugo*, raise the Court,
Arise you Peers of *Spain*, *Alvero* rise,
Preserve your country from base infamies.   20

164

Enter severally at severall doors, with lights and Rapiers drawn,
Alvero, Roderigo, [Verdugo,] *and* Christophero, *with others.*

All.   Who rais'd these exclamations through the Court?
Qu. Mo.   Sheath up your Swords, you need not swords, but eyes
  To intercept this treason.
Alvero.   What's the treason?
  Who are traitors? ring the larum bell;
  Cry arm through all the City; once before
  The horrid sound of treason did affright
  Our sleeping spirits.
Qu. Mo.   Stay,
  You need not cry arm, arm, for this black deed
  Works treason to your King, to me; to you,   30
  To *Spain*, and all that shall in *Spain* ensue.
  This night *Maria* (*Eleaʒars* wife)
  Hath drawn the King by her Lascivious looks
  Privately to a banquet, I unseen
  Stood and beheld him in her lustfull arms.
  Oh God! shall bastards wear *Spains* Diadem?
  If you can kneel to basenesse, vex them not;
  If you disdain to kneel, wash of this blot.
Roderigo.   Lets break into the chamber and surprize her!
Alvero.   Oh miserable me! do, do, break in,   40
  My Country shall not blush at my childs sin.
Qu. Mo.   Delay is nurse to danger, follow me,
  Come you and witnesse to her villany.
Alvero.   Haplesse *Alvero*, how art thou undone,
  In a light daughter, and a stubborn son.

                                                Exeunt omnes.

              35 in her] Dilke; in him in her D

ACTUS III. SCENA II.

Enter King with his Rapier drawn in one hand, leading
Maria *seeming affrighted in th'other.*

Maria.   Oh! kill me ere you stain my chastity.
Fernando.   My hand holds death, but love sits in mine eye,
Exclaim not dear *Maria*, do but hear me;
Though thus in dead of night as I do now
The lustfull *Tarquin* stole to the chast bed
Of *Collatines* fair wife, yet shalt thou be
No *Lucrece*, nor thy King a Romane slave,
To make rude villanie thine honours grave.
Maria.   Why from my bed have you thus frighted me?
Fernando.   To let thee view a bloody horrid Tragedy.   10
Maria.   Begin it then, I'le gladly loose my life,
Rather then be an Emperours Concubine.
Fernando.   By my high birth I swear thou shalt be none,
The Tragedy I'le write with my own hand,
A King shall act it, and a King shall dye;
Except sweet mercies beam shine from thine eye.
If this affright thee it shall sleep for ever,
If still thou hate me, thus this Noble blade,
This Royall purple temple shall invade.
Maria.   My husband is from hence, for his sake spare me.   20
Fernando.   Thy husband is no Spaniard, thou art one,
So is *Fernando*, then for countries sake
Let mee not spare thee: on thy husbands face
Eternall night in gloomy shades doth dwel;
But I'le look on thee like the guilded Sun,
When to the west his fiery horses run.
Maria.   True, true, you look on me with Sun-set eyes,
For by beholding you my glory dies.
Fernando.   Call me thy morning then, for like the morn,
In pride *Maria* shall through *Spain* be born.   *Music plays within.* 30

2 *Fernando.*] *Throughout this scene the* D *speech-prefix is* King.

166

This musick I prepar'd to please thine ears,
Love mee and thou shalt hear no other sounds,
Lo here's a banquet set with mine own hands;

A banquet brought in.

Love me, and thus I'le feast thee like a Queen:
I might command thee being thy Soveraign;
But love me and I'le kneel and sue to thee,
And circle this white forehead with the Crown
Of *Castile*, *Portugall*, and *Arragon*,
And all those petty Kingdoms which do bow
Their tributarie knees to *Philip's* heir.   40
Maria.   I cannot love you whilst my husband lives.
Fernando.   I'le send him to the wars, and in the front
Of some maine army shall he nobly dye.
Maria.   I cannot love you if you murder him.
Fernando.   For thy sake then, I'le call a Parlament
And banish by a law all Moors from *Spain*.
Maria.   I'le wander with him into banishment.
Fernando.   It shall be death for any Negroes hand,
To touch the beauty of a Spanish dame.
Come, come, what needs such cavells with a King?   50
Night blinds all Jealous eyes, and we may play,
Carowse that bole to me, I'le pledg all this,
Being down, we'l make it more sweet with a kiss.
Begin, I'le lock all doors, begin *Spains* Queen,
Love's banquet is most sweet, when 'tis least seen.

Locks the doors.

Maria.   Oh thou conserver of my honours life!

[*Pours sleeping potion in Kings drink.*]

Instead of poisoning him, drown him in sleep.
Because I'le quench the flames of wild desire,
I'le drink this off, let fire conquer loves fire.
Fernando.   Were love himselfe in reall substance here,   60
Thus would I drink him down, let your sweet strings,
Speak lowder (pleasure is but a slave to Kings)

31 to please] Dilke; *om.* D
*57 Instead of poisoning him...] *stet* D (sleep.] ~ , D)

167

In which love swims. *Maria* kiss thy King,
Circle me in this ring of Ivory.
Oh! I grow dull, and the cold hand of sleep
Hath thrust his Icie fingers in my brest,
And made a frost within me; sweet, one kiss
To thaw this deadnesse that congeales my soul.
Maria.   Your Majestie hath overwatch'd your self;
He sleeps already, not the sleep of death,   70
But a sweet slumber, which the powerfull drugg
Instill'd through all his spirits. Oh! bright day
Bring home my dear Lord, ere his King awake,
Else of his unstain'd bed he'l shipwrack make.   *Offers to go.*

> *Enter* Oberon, *and Fairyes dancing before him,*
> *and musick with them.*

Maria.   Oh me! what shapes are these?
Oberon.   Stay, stay, *Maria.*
Maria.   My Soveraign Lord awake, save poor *Maria.*
Oberon.   He cannot save thee, save that pain,
Before he wake thou shalt be slain;
His mothers hand shall stop thy breath,   80
Thinking her own son is done to death:
And she that takes away thy life,
Does it to be thy husbands wife.
Adieu *Maria*, we must hence,
Imbrace thine end with patience;
Elves and *Fairyes* make no stand,
Till you come in Fairy Land.   *Exeunt dancing and singing.*
Maria.   Fairyes or Divels, whatsoe're you be,
Thus will I hide me from your company.   *Offers to be gone.*

> *To her, Enter Queen Mother suddainly, with* Alvero,
> *and* Roderigo, *with Rapiers.*

Qu Mo.   Lay hold upon the strumpet, where's the King?   90
Fernando, son; ah me your King is dead!
Lay hand upon the murdresse.

89 *Following,* D *prints*: Act. III. Scena. III.

168

Maria.   Imperious Queen,
  I am as free from murder as thy self,
  Which I will prove, if you will hear me speak:
  The King is living.
Roderigo.   If he liv'd his breath
  Would beat within his breast.
Qu. Mo.   The life he leads,
  Maria thou shalt soon participate.
Maria.   O father save me!
Alvero.   Thou'rt no child of mine,
  Had'st thou been owner of *Alvero's* spirit,
  Thy heart would not have entertain'd a thought   100
  That had converst with murder: yet mine eyes
  (Howe're my tongue want words) brim full with tears,
  Intreat her further tryall.
Verdugo.   To what end:
  Here lies her tryall: from this royall brest
  Hath she stolen all comfort, all the life
  Of every bosom in the Realm of *Spain.*
Roderigo.   She's both a trayter and a murderess.
Qu Mo.   I'le have her forthwith strangled.
Alvero.   Hear her speak.
Qu. Mo.   To heaven let her complain if she have wrong,
                                    [*Stab her.*]
  I murder but the murdresse of my son.   110
All.   We murder the murdresse of our King.
Alvero.   Ah me my child oh! Oh cease your torturing!
Maria.   Heaven ope the windows, that my spotlesse soul,
  Riding upon the wings of innocence,
  May enter Paradice, Fairyes farewell;
  Fernandoes death in mine you did foretell.
                          She dyes, King wakes.
Fernando.   Who calls *Fernando?* love, *Maria,* speak:
  Oh! whither art thou fled? whence flow these waters
  That fall like winter storms, from thy drown'd eyes.

107 and a] Hazlitt; and D   111 *All.*] Dilke; *Alv.* D
116 S.D. *wakes.*] wake, D   119 thy] the D

Alvero.   From my *Maria's* death!

Fernando.   My *Maria* dead?   120
  Damn'd be the soul to hell that stop'd her breath;
  Maria, Oh me who durst murder her?

Qu. Mo.   I thought my dear *Fernando* had been dead,
  And in my indignation murdred her.

Fernando.   I was not dead untill you murdred me
  By killing fair *Maria.*

Qu. Mo.   Gentle son.

Fernando.   Ungentle mother, you a deed have done,
  Of so much ruth that no succeeding age
  Can ever clear you of; Oh my dear love,
  Yet heavens can witnesse thou wert never mine: 130
  Spains wonder was *Maria.*

Qu. Mo.   Sweet have done.

Fernando.   Have done! for what, for shedding zealous tears
  Over the tomb of virtuous chastitie;
  You cry have done, now I am doing good,
  But cri'd do on, when you were shedding blood:
  Have you done mother; yes, yes, you have done,
  That which will undo your unhappy son.

Roderigo.   These words become you not my gracious Lord.

Fernando.   These words become not me, no more it did
  Become you Lords to be mute standers by,   140
  When lustfull fury ravish'd chastity.
  It ill becoms mee to lament her death,
  But it became you well to stop her breath:
  Had she been fair and not so virtuous,
  This deed had not been halfe so impious.

Alvero.   But she was fair in virtue, virtuous fair,
  Oh me!

Fernando.   Oh me! she was true honours heir.
  Hence beldame from my presence, all flye hence,
  You are all murderers, com poor innocence,
  Clasp thy cold hand in mine, for here I'le lye,   150
  And since I liv'd for her, for her I'l die.

133 virtuous] Dilke; virtues D   151 *Following*, D *prints*: Act. III. Scena IV.

Enter Eleazar *with a Torch and Rapier drawn.*

Eleazar.　Bar up my Castle Gates; fire and confusion
　Shall girt these Spanish Currs; was I for this,
　Sent to raise power against a fugitive:
　To have my wife deflowr'd. Zounds where's my wife,
　My slaves cry out, she's dallying with the King!
　Stand by, where is your King? *Eleazars* bed
　Shall scorn to be an Emperours brothelrie.
Qu. Mo.　Be patient *Eleazar*, here's the King.
Eleazar.　Patience and I am foes, where's my *Maria*?　　　160
Alvero.　Here is her haplesse coarse that was *Maria*.
Fernando.　Here lies *Maria's* body, here her grave,
　Her dead heart in my breast a tomb shal have.
Eleazar.　Now by the proud complexion of my cheeks,
　Tan'e from the kisses of the amorous sun;
　Were he ten thousand Kings that slew my love,
　Thus shou'd my hand (plum'd with revenges wings)
　Requite mine own dishonour, and her death.

　　　　　　　　　　　　　　　　Stabs the King.

Qu. Mo.　Ah me! my son.
All.　　　　　　　　　　The King is murdered,
　Lay hold on the damn'd traitor.
Eleazar.　　　　　　　　　In his brest　　　170
　That dares but dart a finger at the *Moor*,
　I'le bury this Sharp steel yet reeking warm,
　With the unchast blood of that lecher King,
　That threw my wife in an untimely grave.
Alvero.　She was my daughter, and her timelesse grave
　Did swallow down my joies as deep as yours:
　But thus —
Eleazar.　　　　　But what? bear injuries that can,
　I'le wear no forked crest.
Roderigo.　　　　　　　Damn this black feind,
　Crie treason through the Court. The King is murdred.
Eleazar.　He that first opes his lips, I'le drive his words　　　180
　Down his wide throat upon my rapiers point.

The King is murdred and I'le answer it;
I am dishonour'd, and I will revenge it.
Bend not your dangerous weapons at my brest:
Thinke where you are, this Castle is the *Moors*,
You are inviron'd with a wall of flint.
The Gates are lock'd, Purcullesses let down.
If *Eleazar* spend one drop of blood,

      Zarack and Baltazar *above with Calivers.*

On those high turret tops my slaves stand arm'd,
And shall confound your souls with murdring shot.   190
Or if your murder me, yet under ground
A villain that for me will dig to hell,
Stands with a burning limstock in his fist,
Who firing gunpowder, up in the air
Shall fling your torn and mangled carcasses.
Qu. Mo. Oh! sheath your weapons, though my son be slain,
Yet save your selvs, choose a new Soveraign.
All. Prince *Philip* is our Soveraign, choose him King.
Eleazar. Prince *Philip* shall not be my Soveraign,
Philip's a bastard, and *Fernando*'s dead;   200
Mendoza sweats to wear *Spains* Diadem,
Philip hath sworn confusion to this Realm,
They both are up in arms, warrs flames do shine
Like lightning in the air, wherefore my Lords
Look well on *Eleazar*; value me
Not by my sun-burnt cheek, but by my birth;
Nor by my birth, but by my losse of blood,
Which I have sacrificed in *Spains* defence.
Then look on *Philip*, and the Cardinall:
Look on those gaping currs, whose wide throats   210
Stand stretch'd wide open like the gates of death,
To swallow you, your country, children, wives.
Philip cries fire and blood, the Cardinall
Cries likewise fire and blood, I'le quench those flames;
The *Moor* cries blood and fire, and that shall burn
Till *Castile* like proud *Troy* to Cinders turn.   [*Aside.*]
Roderigo. Lay by these Ambages, what seeks the *Moor*?

Eleaʒar.   A Kingdom, *Castiles* crown.
Alvero.   Peace divell for shame.
Qu. Mo.   Peace doting Lord for shame, Oh miserie!
  When Indian slaves thirst after Empery;   220
  Princes and Peers of *Spain* wee are beset,
  With horror on each side; you deny him,
  Death stands at all our backs, we cannot flye him.
  Crown *Philip* King, The Crown upon his head,
  Will prove a fiery Meteor, Warr and vengeance
  And desolation will invade our land,
  Besides Prince *Philip* is a bastard born.
  Oh! give mee leave to blush at mine own shame;
  But I for love to you, love to fair *Spain*,
  Choose rather to rip up a Queens disgrace,   230
  Then by concealing it to set the Crown
  Upon a bastards head. Wherefore my Lords
  By my consent crown that proud Blackamore;
  Since *Spains* bright glory must so soon grow dim,
  Since it must end, let it end all in him.
All.   *Eleaʒar* shall be King.
Alvero.   Oh treachery!
  Have you so soon rac't out *Fernando's* love;
  So soon forgot the duty of true Peers;
  So soon, so soon buried a mothers name,
  That you will crown him King that slew your King.   240
Eleaʒar.   Will you hear him or me, who shall be King?
All.   *Eleaʒar* shall be *Castiles* Sovereign.
Alvero.   Do, do; make hast to crown him! Lords adieu.
  Here hell must be when the Divel governs you.   *Exit.*
Eleaʒar.   By heavens great Star, which Indians do adore,
  But that I hate to hear the giddy world
  Shame that I waded to a Crown through blood,
  I'de not disgest his pills, but since my Lords
  You have chosen *Eleaʒar* for your King?
  Invest me with a generall applause.   250
All.   Live *Eleaʒar*, *Castiles* Royall King.
Roderigo.   A villain and a base born fugitive.   *Aside.*

Christofero.   A bloody tyrant, an usurping slave.   *Aside.*

Eleazar.   Thanks to you all, 'tis not the Spanish Crown
That *Eleazar* strives for, but *Spains* peace.
Amongst you I'le divide her Empery;
Christofero shall wear *Granado's* Crown;
To *Roderigo* I'le give *Arragon*:
Naples, Navar and fair *Jerusalem,*
I'le give to other three, and then our vice-Roys,   260
Shall Shine about our bright Castilian crown,
As stars about the Sun. Cry all, arm, arm;
Prince *Philip* and the Cardinall do ride;
Like *Jove* in thunder, in a storme we'l meet them;
Go levy powers, if any man must fall,
My death shall first begin the funerall.

                                        Exeunt.

ACTUS III. Scena III.

Enter Zarack *and* Baltazar *with Calivers.*

Baltazar.   Is thy cock ready, and thy powder dry.

Zarack.   My cock stands pearching, like a cock o'the game, with
a red cole for his crest instead of a colme; and for my powder,
'tis but touch and take.

Baltazar.   I have tickling geer too, anon I'le cry here I have it,
and yonder I see it; But *Zarack* is't policie for us to kill these
bald-pates.

Zarack.   Is't pollicy for us to save our selves? If they live, we die.
Is't not wisdom then to send them to heaven, rather then be sent
our selves? Come you black slave, be resolute. This way they come,   10
here they will stand, and yonder wil I stand.

Baltazar.   And in yonder hole I.

Zarack.   Our amiable faces cannot be seen, if we keep close:
therefore hide your cocks head, lest his burning cocks-comb
betray us. But soft, which of the two shall be thy white.

Baltazar.   That black villain Frier *Cole.*

263 ride;] ~ ‸ D   S.D. III] V D

Zarack.   I shall have a sharp piece of service.   Frier *Crab* shall be
my man.   Farewell and be resolute.
Baltaȝar.   Zounds *Zarack* I shall never have the heart to doo't.
Zarack.   You rogue; think who commands, *Eleaȝar.*   20
Who shall rise, *Baltaȝar?*
Who shall die, a louzy Frier?
Who shall live our good Lord and Master?
The Negro King of *Spain.*
Baltaȝar.   *Cole,* thou art but a dead man, and shall turn to ashes.
                                                          Exit.
Zarack. Crab, here's that shall make vinegar of thy carcasse. *Exit.*

> *Enter* Crab *and* Cole, *two Friers, with a rout of*
> *Stinkards following them.*

Crab.   I brother 'tis best so, now we have drawn them to a head,
we'l begin here i'th market place.   Tut so long as we be commanded
by the Mother Queen, we'l say her son is a bastard, and he were
ten *Philips.*   30
Cole.   Take you one market form, I'le take another.
Crab.   No, Gods so; we must both keep one form.
Cole.   I in oration, but not in station; mount, mount!
1.   Well my masters, you know him not so well as I; on my word
Frier *Crab* is a sowr fellow.
2.   Yet he may utter sweet doctrine by your leave; but what think
you of Frier *Cole?*
1.   He's all fire, and he be kindled once — a hot Catholick.
3.   And you mark him, he has a zealous nose, and richly inflam'd.
1.   Peace you Rogues, now they begin.   40
Crab.   *Incipe Frater?*
Cole.   *Non ego Domine.*
Crab.   *Nec ego.*
Cole.   *Quare?*
Crab.   *Quia?*
Cole.   *Quæso.*
All.   Here's a queazy beginning me thinks; silence, silence.

27 *Crab.*] *The speech-prefixes in* D *are* Frier Crab *and* Frier Cole *up to line* 33.
38 He's] He D   38 once —] ~ ˄ D

175

Crab. Brethren, Citizens, and market-folks of *Sivell*.

Cole. Well beloved and honoured Castilians.

Crab. It is not unknown to you!   50

Cole. I am sure you are not ignorant.

Crab. How villanous and strong!

Cole. How monstruous and huge!

Crab. The faction of Prince *Philip* is.

Cole. *Philip* that is a bastard.

Crab. *Philip* that is a dastard.

Cole. *Philip* that kill'd your King.

Crab. Onely to make himself King.

Cole. And by Gads blessed Lady you are all damn'd, and you
suffer it.   60

1. Frier *Cole* says true, he speaks out of the heat of his zeal;
look how he glows.

2. Well Frier *Crab* for my money, he has set my teeth an edge
against this bastard.

1. Oh! his words are like Vergis, to whet a mans stomach.

All. Silence, silence.

Crab. Now contrariwise.

Cole. Your Noble King the *Moor*.

Crab. Is a valiant Gentleman.

Cole. A Noble Gentleman.   70

Crab. An honourable Gentleman.

Cole. A fair black Gentleman.

Crab. A friend to Castilians.

Cole. A Champion for Castilians.

Crab. A man fit to be King.

Cole. If he were not born down by him that would be King, who
(as I said before) is a bastard, and no King.

1. What think you my masters? do you mark his words well.

Crab. Further compare them together.

All. S'blood, there's no comparison between them.   80

Cole. Nay, but hear us good Countrymen.

All. Hear Frier *Cole*, hear Frier *Cole*.

Cole. Set that bastard and *Eleaȝar* together.

1. How? mean you, by the ears.

Crab. No, but compare them.
Cole. Do but compare them.
2. Zounds, we say again comparisons are odious.
1. But say on, say on.
>   *Pieces go of, Friers dye.*
All.   Treason, treason, every man shift for himself. This is *Philips*
treason. Arm, Arm, Arm.   90
>   *Exeunt.*

ACTUS III. SCENA IV.

Enter Eleazar, Zarack, *and* Baltazar.

Eleazar. *Zarack* and *Baltazar*, are they dispatch'd?
Zarack. We saw 'em sprawl, and turn up the white of the eye.
Eleazar. So shall they perish, that lay countermines;
To crosse our high designments: by their habits,
The Cardinall and *Philip* scap'd our nets.
And by your hands they tasted our revenge.

Enter Queen Mother.

Here coms the Queen, away! under our wings,
You shall stand safe, and brave the proudest Kings.   *Exeunt.*
Qu. Mo.   Oh! flie my *Eleazar*, save thy life.
Else point a guard about thee, the mad people   10
Tempestuous like the Sea run up and down
Some crying kill the bastard, some the *Moor*;
Some cry, God save King *Philip*; and some cry,
God save the *Moor*; some others, he shall die.
Eleazar.   Are these your fears, thus blow them into air.
I rusht amongst the thickest of their crowds,
And with a countenance Majestical,
Like the Imperious Sun disperst their clouds;
I have perfum'd the rankness of their breath,
And by the magick of true eloquence,   20
Transform'd this many headed *Cerberus*,

S.D. iv] VI D

This py'd Camelion, this beast multitude,
Whose power consists in number, pride in threats;
Yet melt like snow when Majestie shines forth.
This heap of fools, who crowding in huge swarms,
Stood at our Court gates like a heap of dung,
Reeking and shouting out contagious breath
Of power to poison all the elements;
This Wolf I held by'th ears, and made him tame,
And made him tremble at the *Moors* great name. 30
No, we must combate with a grimmer foe,
That damn'd *Mendoza* over-turns our hopes.
He loves you dearly.

Qu. Mo. By his secret Letters
He hath intreated me in some disguise
To leave the Court, and fly into his arms.

Eleazar. The world cannot devize a stratagem
Sooner to throw confusion on his pride:
Subscribe to his desires, and in dead night
Steal to his Castle, swear to him his love
Hath drawn you thither; undermine his soul, 40
And learn what villanies are there laid up,
Then for your pleasure walk to take the air:
Near to the Castle I'le in ambush lie,
And seem by force to take you prisoner;
This done, I have a practice plotted here,
Shall rid him of his life, and us of fear:
About it madam, this is all in all;
We cannot stand unlesse *Mendoza* fall.

[*Exeunt.*]

ACTUS IV. Scena. I.

Enter Emanuel *King of* Portugal, *Prince* Philip, [*Cardinal*]
Mendoza, Alvero, *with Drums and Souldiers marching.*

K. Port. Poor *Spain,* how is the body of thy peace
Mangled and torn by an ambitious Moor!

How is thy Prince and Counsellors abus'd,
And trodden under the base foot of scorn:
Wrong'd Lords, *Emanuel* of *Portugal* partakes
A feeling share in all your miseries:
And though the tardy-hand of slow delay
With-held us from preventing your mishaps;
Yet shall revenge dart black confusion
Into the bosom of that damned fiend.   10
Philip.   But is it possible our Mother Queen
Should countenance his ambition.
Alvero.   Her advice
Is as a Steers-man to direct his course.
Besides, as we by circumstance have learnt,
She means to marry him.
Philip.   Then here upon my knees
I pluck allegiance from her; all that love
Which by innative duty I did owe her,
Shall henceforth be converted into hate.
This will confirm the worlds opinion
That I am base born, and the damned *Moor*   20
Had interest in my birth, this wrong alone
Gives new fire to the cinders of my rage:
I may be well transformed from what I am,
When a black divel is husband to my dam.
K. Port.   Prince, let thy rage give way to patience,
And set a velvet brow upon the face
Of wrinkled anger, our keen swords,
Must right these wrongs, and not light airy words.
Philip.   Yet words may make the edge of rage more sharp,
And whet a blunted courage with revenge.   30
Alvero.   Here's none wants whetting, for our keen resolves
Are steel'd unto the back with double wrongs;
Wrongs that would make a handlesse man take arms;
Wrongs that would make a coward resolute.
Cardinal.   Why then join all our severall wrongs in one,
And from these wrongs assume a firm resolv,

6 feeling] falling D

To send this divell to damnation.

Drums afar off.

Philip.   I hear the sound of his approaching march,
Stand fair; Saint *Jaques* for the right of *Spain*.

To them, Enter the Moor, Roderigo, Christofero, *with drums,
colours, and souldiers, marching bravely.*

Eleazar.   Bastard of *Spain*?
Philip.   Thou true stamp'd son of hell,   40
Thy pedigree is written in thy face.

Alarum, and a Battail, the Moor *prevails: All Exeunt.*

ACTUS IV. SCENA II.

Enter Philip *and Cardinall.*

Philip.   Move forward, with your main battalion,
Or else all is lost.
Cardinal.   I will not move a foot.
Philip.   S'heart, wil you lose the day.
Cardinal.   You lose your witts,
You're mad, it is no pollicy.
Philip.   You lye.
Cardinal.   Lye?
Philip.   Lye, a pox upon't, Cardinall com on,
Second the desperate vanguard which is mine,
And where I'le dye or win, follow my sword
The bloody way I lead it, or by heaven
I'le play the Devill, and mar all, we'l turn our backs
Upon the Moors, and set on thee; I thee,   10
Thee Cardinall, s'heart thee.
Cardinal.   Your desperate arm
Hath almost thrust quite through the heart of hope;
Our fortunes lye a bleeding by your rash
And violent on set.

10 the] Dilke; thee D

180

Philip. Oh! oh! s'life, s'foot, will you fight?
Cardinal. We will not hazard all upon one cast.
Philip. You will not?
Cardinal.   No.
Philip.   Coward.
Cardinal.   By deeds I'le try,
Whether your venemous tongue says true, farewell.
Courage shines both in this, and policy.   *Exit.*
Philip. To save thy skin whole, that's thy policy;   20
You whorson fat-chopt guts. I'le melt away
That larded body by the heat of fight,
Which I'le compel thee to, or else by flying;
To work which I'le give way to the proud foe,
Whilst I stand laughing to behold thee run.
Cardinall I'le do't, I'le do't, a *Moor*, a *Moor*,
Philippo cries a *Moor*, holla! ha! whoo!

Enter King of Portugal.

K. Port. Prince *Philip*, *Philip*.
Philip.   Here, plague where's the *Moor*.
K. Port. The *Moor*'s a Devill, never did horrid feind
Compel'd by som Magicians mighty charm,   30
Break through the prisons of the solid earth,
With more strange horror, then this Prince of hell,
This damned Negro Lyon-like doth rush,
Through all, and spite of all knit opposition.
Philip. Puh! puh! where? Where? I'le meet him, where? you
              mad me.
'Tis not his arm,
That acts such wonders, but our cowardise,
This Cardinall, oh! this Cardinall is a slave.

Enter Captain.

Captain. Sound a retreat, or else the day is lost.
Philip. I'le beat that dog to death, that sounds retreat.   40
K. Port. *Philip.*

27 *Philippo*] *Philip* D   28 Prince_∧] Dilke; *Prince*, D

181

Philip.   I'le tear his heart out, that dares name but *Sound*.
K. Port.   Sound a retreat.
Philip.   Who's that? you tempt my sword Sir.
 Continue this alarum, fight pell mell!
 Fight, kill, be damn'd! this fat-back Coward Cardinal,
 Lies heavie on my shoulders; this, I this
 Shall fling him off: Sound a retreat! Zounds, you mad me.
 Ambition plumes the *Moor*, whilst black despair
 Offering to tear from him the Diadem
 Which he usurps, makes him to cry at all,   50
 And to act deeds beyond astonishment;
 But *Philip* is the night that darks his glories,
 This sword yet reeking with his Negro's blood,
 Being grasp't by equity, and this strong arm,
 Shall through and through.
All.   Away then.
Philip.   From before mee;
 Stay, stand, stand fast, fight! A *Moor*, a *Moor*.

> *To them enter* Eleazar, Zarack, Baltazar, Roderigo, Christo-
> fero, *and others, they fight, Moors are all beat in, Exeunt*
> *omnes, manet* Eleazar *weary; staies, a Moor lies slain.*

Eleazar.   Oh for more work, more souls to post to hell;
 That I might pile up *Charons* boat so full,
 Untill it topple o're, Oh 'twould be sport
 To see them sprawl through the black slimy lake.   60
 Ha, ha; there's one going thither, sirrah, you,
 You slave, who kill'd thee? how he grins! this breast,
 Had it been tempered, and made proof like mine,
 It never would have been a mark for fools
 To hit afar off with their dastard bullets.
 But thou didst well, thou knew'st I was thy Lord;
 And out of love and duty to me here,
 Where I fell weary, thou laidst down thy self
 To bear me up, thus: God a-mercy slave.
 A King for this shall give thee a rich grave.   70

53 sword] Dilke; swords D   56 *Following*, D *prints*: Act. IV. Scena. III.

As he sits down, enter Philip *with a broken sword.*

Philip.   I'le wear thee to the pommel, but I'le finde
 The subject of mine honour and revenge.
 Moor 'tis for thee I seek; Come now, now take me
 At good advantage: speak, where art thou?
Eleazar.   Here.
Philip.   Fate and revenge I thank you; rise.
Eleazar.   Leave and live.
Philip.   Villain, it is *Philippo* that bids rise.
Eleazar.   It had been good for thee to have hid thy name.
 For the discovery, like to a dangerous charm,
 Hurts him that finds it, wherefore do's those blood-hounds,
 Thy rage and valour chase me?
Philip.   Why to kill thee.   80
Eleazar.   With that! what, a blunt axe? think'st thou I'le let
 Thy fury take a full blow at this head,
 Having these arms; be wise, go change thy weapon.
Philip.   Oh, Sir!
Eleazar.   I'le stay thy coming.
Philip.   Thou't be damn'd first.
Eleazar.   By all our Indian gods.
Philip.   Puh, never swear;
 Thou know'st 'tis for a kingdome which we fight;
 And for that who'l not venture to hell-gates.
 Come *Moor*, I am arm'd with more then compleat steel,
 The justice of my quarrel: when I look
 Upon my Fathers wrongs, my brothers wounds,   90
 My mothers infamie, *Spains* miserie,
 And lay my finger here, Oh! 'tis too dull,
 To let out blood enough to quench them all.
 But when I see your face, and know what fears
 Hang on thy troubled soul, like leaden weights,
 To make it sink; I know this fingers touch
 Has strength to throw thee down, I know this iron
 Is sharp and long enough to reach that head.
 Fly not divel, if thou do —

Eleazar.   How, fly; Oh base!
Philip.   Come then.
Eleazar.   Stay *Philip*, whosoe're begat thee —   100
Philip.   Why slave, a King begat me.
Eleazar.   May be so.
  But I'le be sworn thy mother was a Queen;
  For her sake will I kill thee nobly:
  Fling me thy sword, there's mine, I scorn to strike
  A man disarm'd.
Philip.   For this dishonoring me
  I'le give thee one stab more.
Eleazar.   I'le run away,
  Unlesse thou change that weapon, or take mine.
Philip.   Neither.
Eleazar.   Farewel.
Philip.   S'heart, stay, and if you dare,
  Do as I do, oppose thy naked breast
  Against this poniard; see, here's this for thine.   110
Eleazar.   I am for thee *Philip.*
Philip.   Come, nay take more ground,
  That with a full career thou maist strike home.
Eleazar.   Thou't run away then.
Philip.   Hah!
Eleazar.   Thou't run away then.
Philip.   Faith, I will, but first on this I'le bear
  Thy panting heart, thy head upon my spear.
Eleazar.   Come.

Enter on both sides, Cardinall, and King of Portugal, *on the one
        side, and Moors on the other side.*

Cardinals Side.   Upon the Moors.
Moors Side.   Upon the Cardinall.
Philip.   Hold Cardinall, strike not any of our side —
Eleazar.   Hold Moors, strike not any of our side —

    115 my] thy D
    117 *Cardinals Side.* Upon] Brereton *suggestion; Card.* Side upon D
    117 *Moors Side.* Upon] Brereton *suggestion; Moor.* Side upon D

Philip.　Wee two will close this battail.

Eleaʒar.　　　　　　　　　　　Come, agreed.　　　　120
Stand armies and give aim, whil'st wee two bleed.

Cardinal.　With poniards; 'tis too desperate, dear *Philip.*

Philip.　Away, have at the *Moor*, s'heart let me come!

K. Port.　Be arm'd with manly weapons, 'tis for slaves,
To dig their own and such unworthy graves.

Eleaʒar.　I am for thee any way, thus, or see thus,
Here try the vigour of thy sinewy arm,
The day is ours already, brainless heads
And bleeding bodyes like a crown do stand,
About the temples of our victory.　　　　　　130
Yet Spaniards if you dare we'l fight it out,
Thus man to man alone, I'le first begin,
And conquer, or in blood wade up to th' chin.

Philip.　Let not a weapon stir, but his and mine.

Eleaʒar.　Nor on this side, conquest in blood shall shine.

*Alarum. They fight a Combate, The Moor is struck down, which his
side seeing, step all in and rescue him; The rest joine and drive in the
Moors. Alarum continuing, Spaniards and Moors with drums and
colours flye over the stage, persued by* Philip, Cardinall, King of
Portugall, *And others. Enter* Zarack, Christofero, *and* Eleazar
at severall doors.

Christofero.　Where is my Lord?

Zarack.　　　　　　　　　　　Where is our Soveraign?

Eleaʒar.　What news brings *Zarack* and *Christofero?*

Zarack.　Oh flye my Lord! flye; for the day is lost.

Eleaʒar.　There are three hundred and odd days in a year,
And cannot we lose one of them, com fight.　　　140

Christofero.　The Lords have left us, and the souldiers faint,
You are round beset with proud fierce enemies;
Death cannot be prevented but by flight!

Eleaʒar.　He shall *Christofero*, I have yet left
One stratagem that in despite of fate,
Shal turn the wheel of war about once more.
The Mother Queen hath all this while sate sadly,

Within our tent, expecting to whose bosom,
White winged peace and victory will flie,
Her have I us'd as a fit property,   150
To stop this dangerous current; her have I sent,
Arm'd with loves magick to inchant the Cardinall;
And bind revenge down with resistlesse charms.
By this time does she hang about his neck,
And by the witchcraft of a cunning kiss,
Has she disarm'd him, hark, they sound Retreat.
She has prevail'd, a womans tongue and eye,
Are weapons stronger then Artillery.

Exeunt.

ACTUS IV. SCENA III.

Enter Cardinall, Queen Mother. Souldiers, drums, and colours.

Qu. Mo.   By all those sighs which thou (like passionate tunes)
Hast often to my dull ears offered,
By all thy hopes to injoy my roial Bed;
By all those mourning lines which thou hast sent,
Weeping in black to tell thy languishment:
By loves best richest treasure, which I swear,
I wil bestow, and which none else shal wear,
As the most prised Jewell, but thy selfe,
By that bright fire which flaming through thine eyes,
From thy love scorched bosom does arise;   10
I do conjure thee, let no churlish sound,
With wars lewd horror my desires confound;
Dear, dear *Mendoza*, thus I do intreat,
That stil thou would'st continue this retreat;
I'le hang upon thee till I hear thee say,
Woman prevail; or chiding, cri'st away.
Cardinal.   Is there no trick in this, forg'd by the *Moor?*

156 Retreat] Dilke; *Retreat* D (*in separate line, as S.D., at right*)
S.D. iii] IV D

Qu. Mo.   I would the *Moors* damnation were the ransom,
Of all that innocent blood, that has been shed
In this black day; I care not for the *Moor*,   20
Love to my kingdoms peace makes me put on
This habit of a suppliant; shall I speed?
Cardinal.   You shall, were it to have my bosom bleed:
I have no power to spare the Negroes head,
When I behold the wounds which his black hand
Has given mine honour: but when I look on you,
I have no power to hate him, since your breath
Disolves my frozen heart, being spent for him;
In you my life must drown it self or swim.
You have prevail'd: Drum swiftly hence! cal back   30
Our fierce pursuing troops, that run to catch
The lawrel wreath of conquest: Let it stand
A while untouch'd by any souldiers hand.

Exit drum.

Away! stay you and guard us, where's the *Moor?*
I'le lose what I have got, a victors prize,
Yielding my self a prisoner to your eyes.
Qu. Mo.   Mine eyes shall quickly grant you liberty,
The *Moor* stays my return, I'le put on wings,
And fetch him, to make peace belongs to Kings.

*As she goes out, Enter Eleazar, Zarack, Baltazar, and souldiers
well arm'd, at sight of each other all draw.*

Cardinal.   Souldiers call back the drum, wee are betraid.   40
Eleazar.   Moors stand upon your guard, avoid, look back.
Qu. Mo.   What means this jealousie? *Mendoza, Moor,*
Lay by your weapons, and imbrace, the sight
Of this, and this, begets suspition;
Eleazar by my birth, he coms in peace,
Mendoza by mine honour so coms he.
Cardinal.   Discharge these souldiers then.
Eleazar.   And these.
Cardinal.   Away.

187

Eleazar.   Go.

                                                  Souldiers stand a loof.
Qu. Mo.   Soul, rejoice to see this glorious day.

                    She joins them together, they imbrace.

Cardinal.   Your virtues work this wonder: I have met,
  At her most dear command, whats your desires?   50
Eleazar.   Peace and your honour'd arms: how loathingly
  I sounded the alarums, witnesse heaven.
  'Twas not to strike your breast, but to let out,
  The rank blood of ambition: That *Philippo*
  Makes you his ladder, and being climb'd so high
  As he may reach a diadem, there you lie.
  He's base begotten, that's his mothers sin
Qu. Mo.   God pardon it.
Eleazar.   I, amen, but he's a bastard,
  And rather then I'le kneel to him, I'le saw
  My leggs off by the thighs, because I'le stand   60
  In spite of reverence: he's a bastard, he's,
  And to beat down his usurpation,
  I have thrown about this thunder, but *Mendoza,*
  The people hate him for his birth,
  He only leans on you, you are his pillar;
  You gon, he walks on crutches, or else falls;
  Then shrink from under him, are not they fools,
  That bearing others up themselvs seem low,
  Because they above sit high? Why, you do so.
Cardinal.   'Tis true.
Qu. Mo.   Behold this error with fixt eies.   70
Cardinal.   'Tis true, well.
Eleazar.   Oh! have you found it, have you smelt
  The train of powder that must blow you up,
  Up into air, what air? why this, a breath,
  Look you, in this time may a King meet death;
  An eye to't, check it, check it.

48 S.D. *Souldiers*...] D *places below* And these *in line* 47.
54 *Philippo*] *Philip* D

188

Cardinal.   How?

Eleazar.   How! thus:
Steal from the heat of that incestuous blood,
Where ravisht honor, and *Philippo* lies;
Leave him, divide this huge and monstrous body
Of armed Spanyards into limbs thus big;
Part man from man, send every souldier home,   80
I'le do the like; Peace with an Olive branch
Shall flie with Dove-like wings about all *Spain*:
The crown which I as a good husband keep,
I will lay down upon the empty chair;
Marry you the Queen and fill it, for my part
These knees are yours, Sir.

Cardinal.   Is this sound?

Eleazar.   From my heart.

Cardinal.   If you prove false —

Eleazar.   If I do, let fire fall —

Cardinal.   Amen.

Eleazar.   Upon thy head, and so it shall.   [*Aside.*]

Cardinal.   All of my self is yours; souldiers be gone.

Eleazar.   And that way you.

Cardinal.   The rest I will divide: 90
The Lords shall be convented.

Eleazar.   Good.

Cardinal.   Let's meet.

Qu. Mo.   Where.

Eleazar.   Here anon, [*aside*] this is thy winding-sheet.
                              Exit Cardinal.

          The Moor *walks up and down musing.*

Qu. Mo.   What shape will this prodigious womb bring forth,
Which groans with such strange labour.

Eleazar.   Excellent.

Qu. Mo.   Why, *Eleazar*, art thou wrap't with joyes,
Or does thy sinking policy make to shore.

Eleazar.   Ha!

Qu. Mo.   *Eleazar*, mad man! hear'st thou *Moor*.

Eleazar. Well, so; you turn my brains, you mar the face
  Of my attempts i'th making: for this *chaos*,
  This lump of projects, ere it be lick't over,   100
  'Tis like a Bears conception; stratagems
  Being but begot, and not got out, are like
  Charg'd Cannons not discharg'd, they do no harm,
  Nor good: true policy breeding in the brain
  Is like a bar of Iron, whose ribs being broken,
  And softned in the fire, you then may forge it
  Into a sword to kill, or to a helmet,
  To defend life: 'tis therefore wit to try
  All fashions, ere you apparel villany;
  But, but I ha suited him, fit, fit, Oh fit!   110
Qu. Mo. How? prethee how?
Eleazar.   Why thus; yet no, let's hence,
  My heart is nearest of my counsel, yet
  I scarce dare trust my heart with't, what I do,
  It shall look old, the hour wherein 'tis born,
  Wonders twice seen are garments over-worn.

                      Exeunt.

ACTUS IV. Scena IV.

Enter Cardinal at one door, Philippo *half arm'd, and two*
souldiers following him with the rest of the armour: the
Cardinal seeing him, turns back again.

Philip. Sirrah, you Cardinal, coward, runaway:
  So ho ho, what Cardinal.
Cardinal.   I am not for your lure.   *Exit.*
Philip. For that then, Oh! that it had nail'd thy heart
  Up to the pommel to the earth; come, arm me,
  Ha! s'foot,
  When all our swords were royally guilt with blood,
  When with red sweat that trickled from our wounds,
  Wee had dearly earn'd a victory! when hell

          S.D. iv] V D

Had from their hinges heav'd off her iron gates
To bid the damn'd *Moor* and the divels enter;   10
Then to lose all, then to sound base retreat;
Why souldiers, hah!

1. Sould.   I am glad of it my Lord.

Philip.   Hah! glad; art glad I am dishonored?
That thou and he dishonored.

1. Sould.   Why? my Lord;
I am glad, that you so cleanly did come off.

Philip.   Thou hast a lean face, and a carrion heart:
A plague on him and thee too: then, s'heart then,
To crack the very heart-strings of our Army,
To quarter it in pieces, I could tear my hair,
And in cursing spend my soul.   20
Cardinal; what *Judas*! come, wee'l fight,
Till there be left but one, if I be hee,
I'le die a glorious death.

1. Sould.   So will I, I hope in my bed.

2. Sould.   Till there be but one left, my Lord, why that's now;
for all our fellows are crawl'd home; some with one leg, some with
ne're an arm, some with their brains beaten out, and glad they
scap't so.

Philip.   But my dear Countrymen, you'l stick to me.

1. Sould.   Stick! I my Lord, stick like Bandogs, till wee be 30
pull'd off.

Philip.   That's nobly said, I'le lead you but to death,
Where I'le have greatest share, we shall win fame
For life, and that doth crown a souldiers name.

1. Sould.   How! to death my Lord? not I by gadsled: I have a
poor wife and children at home, and if I die they beg; and do you
think I'le see her go up and down the wide universal world.

Philip.   For every drop of blood which thou shalt lose,
Coward I'le give thy wife a wedge of gold.

2. Sould.   Hang him meacock, my Lord, arm your self, I'le fight 40
for you, till I have not an eye to see the fire in my touch-hole.

18 heart-strings] Dilke; hearts-strings D
33-34 fame⌄ For life,] Dilke; ~ , ~ ~ ⌄ D [For *equals* in exchange for]

Philip.   Be thou a King's companion, thou and I
Will dare the Cardinal, and the *Moor* to fight,
In single combate, shall we? hah!
2. Sould.   Agreed.
Philip.   Wee'l beat 'em to hell gate, shall we? hah!
2. Sould.   Hell gate's somwhat too hot, somewhat too hot; the
Porter's a knave: I'de be loath to be damn'd for my conscience;
I'le knock any bodies costard, so I knock not there, my Lord;
hell gates!   50
Philip.   A pox upon such slaves.
1. Sould.   Hang him, a peasant, my Lord; you see I am but a scrag,
my Lord; my legs are not of the biggest, nor the least, nor the
best that e're were stood upon, nor the worst, but they are of God's
making; And for your sake, if ever we put our enemies to flight
again, by Gad's lid if I run not after them like a Tiger, hoffe me.
Philip.   But wilt thou stand to't e're they flye? ha! wilt thou?
1. Sould.   Will I quoth a? by this hand, and the honour of a
souldier.
Philip.   And by a souldiers honour I will load thee   60
With Spanish pistolets: to have this head,
Thy face, and all thy body, stuck with scars,
Why 'tis a sight more glorious, then to see
A Lady hung with Diamonds: If thou lose
A hand, I'le send this after, if an arm,
I'le lend thee one of mine, com then lets fight.
A mangled Lame true souldier is a jem,
Worth *Cesars* Empire, though fools spurn at them.
1. Sould.   Yet my Lord I ha seen lame souldiers, not worth the
crutches they leant upon, hands and arms quotha? Zounds not I, 70
I'le double my files, or stand centry, or so; But I'le be hang'd and
quartred, before I'le have my members cut off.
2. Sould.   And I too, hold thee there.
Philip.   Hold you both there, away you rogues, you durt,

                                                    Beats 'em both in.

Thus do I tread upon you, out, begon!
One valiant is an host, fight then alone.

                    74 S.D. D *places after line* 73.

                              192

Enter Cardinall, Alvero, Christofero, *and Souldiers.*

Cardinal.   Prince *Philip.*
Philip.   For the Crown of *Spain,* come all.
Cardinal.   We come in love and peace.
Philip.   But come in warr:
  Bring naked swords, not lawrell boughs. In peace?
  Plague on your rank peace, will you fight and cry   80
  Down with the *Moor,* and then I'm yours: I'le dye,
  I have a heart, two arms, a soul, a head,
  I'le lay that down, I'le venture all; s'foot, all.
  Come tread upon me, so that *Moor* may fal.
Cardinal.   By heaven that *Moor* shall fall.
Philip.   Thy hand, and thine.
                              Flings down his weapons.
  Give me but halfe your hearts, you have all mine,
  By heaven, shall he fall?
Cardinal.   Yes, upon thee
  Like to the ruines of a tower, to grind
  Thy body into dust: traitor, and bastard,
  I do arrest thee of High treason.
Philip.   Hah!   90
  Traitor? and bastard? and by thee? my weapons!
Cardinal.   Lay hands upon him.
Philip.   I, you're best do so.
Cardinal.   *Alvero* there's the warrant, to your hands
  The prisoner is committed, Lords lets part,
  Look to him on your life.
                              Exeunt Cardinall &c.

              Manent, Philip *and* Alvero.

Philip.   Hart, hart, hart, hart,
                              Tears the warrant.
  The Devill, and his dam, the *Moor,* and my Mother,
  Their warrant? I will not obey. Old gray beard,
  Thou shalt not bee my Jayler, there's no prison,
  No dungeon deep enough, no grates so strong,

That can keep in a man so mad with wrong. 100
What do'st thou weep?
Alvero. I would fain shed a tear,
But from mine eyes so many showrs are gon,
Grief drinks my tears so fast, that here's not one,
You must to prison.
Philip. Do'st thou speak to me?
Alvero. You must to prison.
Philip. And from thence to death;
I thought I should have had a tomb hung round,
With tottred colours, broken spears, I thought
My body should have fallen down, full of wounds.
But one can kill an Emperor, fool then why
Would'st thou have many? curse, be mad, and dye. *Exeunt.* 110

The end of the fourth Act.

ACTUS V. SCENA I.

Enter Roderigo, *and* Christofero, *two bare-headed before them*;
Alvero, *Cardinall alone*, Zarack, *and* Baltazar *bearing the Crown
on a cushion*, Eleazar *next*, Queen Mother *after him*, *other Lords
after her.* Alvero *sad*, *meets them.*

Cardinal. Alvero, 'tis the pleasure of the King,
Of the Queen Mother, and these honoured States,
To ease you of *Philippo*, there's a warrant
Sent to remove him to a stronger guard.
Alvero. I thank you, you shall rid me of much care.
Eleaʒar. Sit down, and take your place!
Alvero. If I might have
The place I like best, it should be my grave. *Sits down.*

The Moors stand aside with the Crown, Eleazar *rising*, *takes it.*

Eleaʒar. Stand in voice, reach, away!
Both Moors. Wee are gon. *Exeunt.*

3 *Philippo*] Hazlitt; *Philip* D

194

Eleazar. Princes of *Spain* if in this royall Court,
  There sit a man, that having laid his hold,   10
  So fast on such a jewel, and dare wear it,
  In the contempt of envie as I dare,
  Yet uncompell'd (as freely as poor pilgrims,
  Bestow their praiers) would give such wealth away;
  Let such a man step forth; what, do none rise?
  No, no, for Kings indeed are deities.
  And who'd not (as the sun) in brightnesse shine?
  To be the greatest, is to be divine:
  Who among millions would not be the mightiest?
  To sit in God-like state, to have all eyes,   20
  Dazled with admiration, and all tongues
  Showting lowd Praiers, to rob every heart
  Of love, to have the strength of every arm.
  A Soveraigns name, why 'tis a Soveraign charm.
  This glory round about me hath thrown beams,
  I have stood upon the top of fortunes wheel,
  And backward turn'd the Iron screw of fate,
  The destinies have spun a silken thread
  About my life, yet Noble Spaniards see?
  Hoc tantum tanti, thus I cast aside   30
  The shape of Majestie and on my knee,

   Kneels: the Cardinall fetches the Crown and sets it on the chair.

To this Imperiall State, lowly resigne
This usurpation, wiping off your fears,
Which stuck so hard upon me, let a hand,
A right, and royall hand take up this wreath,
And guard it, right is of it self most strong,
No kingdom got by cunning can stand long.
Cardinal.   Proceed to new election of a King.
All. Agreed.
Eleazar.   Stay Peers of *Spain*, if young *Philippo*,
  Be *Philips* son, then is he *Philips* heir,   40
  Then must his Royall name be set in gold,
  Philip is then the Diamond to that ring;

But if he be a bastard, here's his seat,
For basenesse has no gall, till it grow great.
First therefore let him blood, if he must bleed,
Yet in what vein you strike him, best take heed:
The *Portugall*'s his friend, you saw he came
At holding up a finger, arm'd; this peace
Rid hence his dangerous friendship, he's at home,
But when he hears, that *Philip* is ty'd up,   50
Yet hears not why, he'l catch occasions lock,
And on that narrow bridg make shift to lead
A scrambling army through the heart of *Spain*:
Look to't, being in, he'l hardly out again.
Therefore first prove, and then proclaim him bastard.
Alvero.   How shall we prove it?
Eleaʒar.   He that put him out
To making, I am sure can tell, if not,
Then she that shap'd him can, here's the Queen Mother
Being prick'd in conscience, and preferring *Spain*,
Before her own respect, will name the man.   60
If he be noble and a Spaniard born,
Hee'l hide the apparent scarrs of their infamies
With the white hand of marriage; that and time,
Will eat the blemish off, say? shall it?
All.   No.
Cardinal.   Spaniard or Moor, the saucy slave shall dye.
Hortenʒo.   Death is too easie for such villany.
Eleaʒar.   Spaniard or Moor, the saucy slave shall dye.
I would he might, I know my self am clear
As is the new born Infant. Madam stand forth,
Be bold to speak, shame in the grave wants sence: 70
Heaven with sins greatest, forfeits can dispence.
Qu. Mo.   Would I were covered with the vail of night,
You might not see red shame sit on my cheecke;
But being *Spains* common safety stands for truth,
Hiding my weeping eyes, I blush, and say;
Philippo's father sits here.
Roderigo.   Here! name him!

196

Qu. Mo.   The Lord *Mendoza* did beget that son,
  Oh! let not this dishonour further run!
Alvero.   What, Cardinall *Mendoza?*
Qu. Mo.   Yes, yes, even hee.
Eleazar.   Spaniard or Moor, the saucy slave shall die.   80
Cardinal.   I *Philips* father?   *Coms down, the rest talk.*
Qu. Mo.   Nay! deny me not!   [*Aside, to him.*]
  Now may a kingdom and my love be got.
Cardinal.   Those eyes and tongue bewitch me, shame lie here;
  That love has sweetest tast that is bought dear.
Christofero.   What answers Lord *Mendoza* to the Queen?
Cardinal.   I confesse guilty, *Philip* is my son,
  Her Majestie hath nam'd the time and place.
Alvero.   To you, but not to us, go forward Madam.
Qu. Mo.   Within the circle of twice ten years since,
  Your deceast King made warr in *Barbarie*,   90
  Won *Tunis*, conquered *Fesse*, and hand to hand,
  Slew great *Abdela*, King of *Fesse*, and father
  To that Barbarian Prince.
Eleazar.   I was but young,
  But now methinks I see my fathers wounds,
  Poor *Barbaria!* No more.
Qu. Mo.   In absence of my Lord, mourning his want,
  To me alone, being in my private walk,
  I think at *Salamanca*; I, 'twas there;
  Enters *Mendoza* under shew of shrift,
  Threatens my death if I deni'd his lust,   100
  In fine by force he won me to his will,
  I wept, and cri'd for help, but all in vain;
  Mendoza there abus'd the bed of *Spain*.
Eleazar.   Spaniard or Moor, that saucy slave shall die.
Alvero.   Why did not you complain of this vile act?
Qu. Mo.   Alas! I was alone, young, full of fear;
  Bashful, and doubtfull of my own defame;
  Knowing King *Philip* rash and jealious,
  I hid his sin, thinking to hide my shame.

109 sin] sins D

197

Roderigo.   What says the Cardinall?

Cardinal.   Such a time there was;   110
'Tis past, I'le make amends with marriage,
And satisfie with Trentalls, dirges, praiers,
The offended spirit of the wronged King.
                              Queen and they talk.

Eleaʒar.   Spaniard or Moor, that saucy slave shall die;
                              [*Aside to Cardinall.*]
Oh! 'twould seem best, it should be thus *Mendoʒa*:
She to accuse, I urge, and both conclude,
Your marriage like a comick interlude.
Lords will you hear this hatefull sin confest?
And not impose upon the ravisher death,
The due punishment, oh! it must be so.   120

Alvero.   What does the Queen desire?

Qu. Mo.   Justice, revenge,
On vile *Mendoʒa* for my ravishment:
I kiss the cold earth with my humbl'd knees,
From whence I will not rise, till some just hand,
Cast to the ground the Traitor Cardinall.

All.   Stand forth *Mendoʒa*.

Eleaʒar.   Swells your heart so high?
Down *Lecher*; if you wil not stand, then lie.

Cardinal.   You have betrai'd me, by my too much trust,
I never did this deed of Rape and Lust.

Roderigo.   Your tongue confest it.

Cardinal.   True, I was intic'd.   130

Eleaʒar.   Intic'd? do you beleeve that?

Qu. Mo.   Justice Lords!
Sentence the Cardinall for his hatefull sin.

Alvero.   We will assemble all the States of *Spain*,
And as they Judge, so Justice shall be done.

Eleaʒar.   A guard! to prison with the Cardinall.

                    Enter Zarack, Baltazar *and others.*

Cardinal.   Dam'd slave my tongue shall go at liberty
To curse thee, ban that strumpet; Doggs keep off.

                    *110 *Roderigo.*] *Horten.* D

                    198

Eleazar.   Hist, hist, on, on.
Qu. Mo.   I cannot brook his sight.
Alvero.   You must to prison, and bee patient.
Cardinal.   Weep'st thou *Alvero?* all struck dumb? my fears,   140
Are that those drops will change to bloody teares.
This woman, and this Serpent —
Qu. Mo.   Drag him hence.
Cardinal.   Who dares lay hands upon me, Lords of *Spain*
Let your swords bail me, this false Queen did lye.
Eleazar.   Spaniard or Moor, the saucy slave shall die.
Cardinal.   I'le fight with thee, damn'd hell-hound for my life.
Eleazar.   Spaniard or Moor, the saucy slave shall die.
Cardinal.   I'le prove upon thy head.
Eleazar.   The slave shall die.
Cardinal.   Lords stop this villains throat.
Eleazar.   Shal die, shall die.
Cardinal.   Hear me but speak.
Eleazar.   Away.
Alvero.   Words are ill spent,   150
Where wrong sits Judg, you'r arm'd if innocent.
Cardinal.   Well then, I must to prison: *Moor*, no more:
Heavens thou art just, Prince *Philip* I betraid,
And now my self fall: Guile with guile is paid.
                         Exit [with Zarack, Baltazar, *and others].*
Qu. Mo.   *Philip* being prov'd a bastard; who shall sit
Upon this empty throne?
Eleazar.   Strumpet, not you.
Qu. Mo.   Strumpet! and I not sit there! who then?
Eleazar.   Down;
Back; if she touch it shee'l bewitch the chair;
This throne belongs to *Isabel* the fair,
Bring forth the Princess drest in royal robes,   160
The true affecter of *Alvero's* son,
Virtuous *Hortenzo.* Lords, behold your Queen.

          160 Princess] Dilke; Princes D
          162 *Following,* D *prints:* Act. V. Scena II.

Enter Isabella *led in, in royal robes.* Hortenzo.

Qu. Mo.   Thou villain! what intendst thou, savage slave?

Eleazar.   To advance virtue thus, and thus to tread
On lust, on murther, on adulteries head.
Look Lords upon your Sovereign *Isabel*,
Though all may doubt the fruits of such a Womb,
Is she not like King *Philip?* let her rule.

Qu. Mo.   She rule?

Eleazar.   She rule? I shee.

Qu. Mo.   A child to sway
An empire? I am her Protectress;   170
I'le pour black curses on thy damned head,
If thou wrongst me. Lords, Lords!

Eleazar.   Princes of *Spain*,
Be deaf, be blind, hear not, behold her not,
She kill'd my virtuous wife.

Qu. Mo.   He kill'd your King.

Eleazar.   'Twas in my just wrath.

Qu. Mo.   'Twas to get his Crown.

Eleazar.   His Crown! why here 'tis: thou slewst my *Maria*,
To have accesse to my unstained bed.

Qu. Mo.   Oh heaven!

Eleazar.   'Tis true, how often have I stopt
Thy unchast songs from passing through mine ears?
How oft, when thy luxurious arms have twin'd   180
About my jetty neck, have I cry'd out
Away, those scalding veins burn me, 'tis true.

Qu. Mo.   Divel, 'tis a lie.

Eleazar.   Thou slewst my sweet *Maria*;
Alvero, 'twas thy daughter, 'twas: *Hortenzo*,
She was thy sister; Justice *Isabella*!
This Serpent poison'ed thy dear fathers bed,
Setting large horns on his Imperial head.

Qu. Mo.   Hear me.

Eleazar.   Hah! why?

Alvero.   Madam you shall be heard,

200

Before the Courts, before the Courts of *Spain*.
Eleazar.   A guard, a guard.   190

      Enter two Moors [Zarack *and* Baltazar], *and others.*

Qu. Mo.   A guard; for what? for whom?
Hortenzo.   To wait on you,
So many great sins must not wait with few.
Qu. Mo.   Keep me in prison! dare you Lords?
Alvero.   Oh no!
Were your cause strong, we would not arm you so;
But honor fainting needeth many hands,
Kingdoms stand safe, when mischief lies in bands:
You must to prison.   *Exeunt.*
Qu. Mo.   Must I? must I, slave!
I'le dam thee, ere thou triumph'st o're my grave.
                       Exit with a guard.
        Manet Eleazar.

Eleazar.   Do, do! my jocund spleen;
It does, it will, it shall, I have at one throw,   200
Rifled away the Diademe of *Spain*;
'Tis gone, and there's no more to set but this
At all, then at this last cast I'le sweep up
My former petty losses, or lose all,
Like to a desperate Gamester; hah! how? fast?

        Enter Zarack.

Zarack.   Except their bodies turn to airy spirits,
And fly through windows, they are fast my Lord:
If they can eat through locks and barrs of Iron,
They may escape, if not? then not.
Eleazar.   Ho! *Zarack*!
Wit is a thief, there's pick-lock policie,   210
To whom all doors flye open: therefore go,
In our name charge the Keeper to resign
His office; and if he have tricks of cruelty,

      198 *Following*, D *prints*: Act. V. Scena III.

           201

Let him bequeath 'em at his death, for kill him;
Turn all thy body into eyes,
And watch them, let those eyes like fiery comets
Sparkle out nothing but the death of Kings.
And — ah! now thus thou know'st I did invent,
A torturing Iron chain.
Zarack.　　　　　　Oh! for necks my Lord.
Eleazar.　I that, that, that, away and yoak them, stay,　　220

Enter Baltazar.

Here's *Baltazar*, go both, teach them to preach,
Through an Iron Pillory: I'le spread a net,
To catch *Alvero*, oh! he is old and wise,
They are unfit to live, that have sharp eyes,
Hortenzo, Roderigo, to't, to't all:
They have supple knees, sleack'd brows, but hearts of gall:
The bitterness shall be wash'd off with blood,
Tyrants swim safest in a crimson flood.
Baltazar.　I com to tel your grace that *Isabella,*
Is with *Hortenzo* arm in arm at hand,　　230
Zarack and I may kill them, now with ease
Is't done, and then 'tis done.
Zarack.　　　　　　Murther thou the man.
And I'le stab her.
Eleazar.　　　　No, I'le speed her my selfe,
Arm in arm, so, so, look upon this Ring,
Who ever brings this token to your hands
Regard not for what purpose, seiz on them,
And chain them to the rest, they com, away,
Murder be proud, and Tragedy laugh on,
I'le seek a stage for thee to jett upon.

[*Exeunt* Zarack *and* Baltazar.]

Enter Isabella, Hortenzo, *seeing the* Moor *turn back.*

Eleazar.　My Lord! my Lord *Hortenzo.*
Hortenzo.　　　　　　Hah! is't you,　　240
Trust me I saw you not.

223 he is] Dilke; he's is D　　　　231 ease₎] ~ , D

Eleazar.　What makes your grace so sad?
Hortenzo.　She grievs for the imprisoned Queen her Mother,
　And for *Philippo*; in the sandy heap,
　That wait upon an hour, there are not found
　So many little bodies as those sighs
　And tears, which she hath every Minute spent,
　Since her lov'd Brother felt Imprisonment.
Eleazar.　Pity, great pity, would it lay in mee,
　To give him liberty.
Isabella.　　　　　　It does.
Eleazar.　　　　　　　In me?　　　　　　　　　250
　Free him, your Mother Queen, and Cardinall too.
　In me? alas! not me, no, no, in you;
　Yet for I'le have my conscience, white and pure,
　Here Madam take this Ring, and if my name
　Can break down Castle walls, and open Gates,
　Take it, and do't, fetch them all forth: and yet,
　'Tis unfit you should go.
Hortenzo.　　　　　　That happy office
　I'le execute my selfe.
Eleazar.　　　　　　Will you? would I
　Stood gracious in their sight: well, go,
　Do what you will *Hortenzo*, if this charm　　　　　260
　Unbinds them, here 'tis; Lady, you and I
　Aloof will follow him, and when we meet,
　Speak for me, for I'le kisse *Philippo's* feet.
Hortenzo.　I shall be proud to see all reconcil'd.
Eleazar.　Alas! my Lord, why true, go, go.
Isabella.　Make hast dear love.　　　　　*Exit* [Hortenzo].
Eleazar.　　　　　　*Hortenzo* is a man
　Compos'd of sweet proportion, ha's a foot,
　A leg, a hand, a face, an eye, a wit,
　The best. *Hortenzo* in the Spanish Court,
　Oh! he's the Nonpareil.

　　　　244 *Philippo*] Hazlitt; *Philip* D
　　　　266 *Exit*] Dilke; D *places after line* 264.
　　　　269 best. *Hortenzo*...Court,] best‸ *Hortenzo*...Court. D

Isabella.   Your tongue had wont,   270
To be more sparing in *Hortenzo's* praise.
Eleazar.   I, I may curse his praises, rather ban
Mine own nativity, why did this colour,
Dart in my flesh so far? oh! would my face,
Were of *Hortenzo's* fashion, else would yours
Were as black as mine is.
Isabella.   Mine like yours, why?
Eleazar.   Hark!
I love you, yes faith, I said this, I love you,
I do, leave him.
Isabella.   Damnation vanish from me.
Eleazar.   Coy? were you as hard as flint, Oh! you shou'd yield
Like softned wax, were you as pure as fire,   280
I'le touch you, yes, I'le taint you, see you this,
I'le bring you to this lure.
Isabella.   If I want hands
To kill my self, before thou do'st it; do.
Eleazar.   I'le cut away your hands: well, my desire
Is raging as the Sea, and mad as fire,
Will you?
Isabella.   Torment me not good Devill.
Eleazar.   Will you?
Isabella.   I'le tear mine eyes out if they tempt thy lust.
Eleazar.   Do.
Isabella.   Touch me not, these knives —
Eleazar.   I, I, kill your selfe,
Because I jest with you: I wrong *Hortenzo*?
Settle your thoughts, 'twas but a trick to try,   290
That which few women have, true constancy.
Isabella.   If then my speeches tast of gall —
Eleazar.   Nay faith,
You are not bitter, no, you should have rail'd,
Have spit upon me, spurn'd me, you are not bitter;
Why, do you think that I would nurse a thought,
To hurt your honour? If that thought had brains,

295 I would] Hazlitt; I'de D

204

I'de beat them out, but come, by this, *Hortenʒo*
Is fast.
Isabella.   Hah! fast?
Eleaʒar.   I fast in *Philip's* arms.
Wrestling together for the price of love;
By this, they're on the way, I'le be your guard,   300
Come follow me, I'le lead you in the van,
Where thou shalt see four chins upon one chain.

                                                    Exeunt.

ACTUS V. Scena ii.

Enter Hortenzo, *Queen Mother, Cardinall, and* Philip *chain'd
by the necks,* Zarack, *and* Baltazar *busie about fastning*
Hortenzo.

Hortenʒo.   You damned Ministers of villany,
Sworn to damnation by the book of hell;
You maps of night, you element of Devills,
Why do you yoak my neck with Iron chains?
Baltaʒar.   Many do borrow chains, but you have this *gratis*, for
nothing.
Cardinal.   Slaves unbind us.
Both Moors.   No ——   *Exeunt two Moors.*
Philip.   I am impatient, veins why crack you not?
And tilt your blood into the face of heaven,   10
To make red clouds like Ensignes in the sky,
Displaying a damn'd tyrants cruelty;
Yet can I laugh in my extreamest pangs,
Of blood, and spirit, to see the Cardinall,
Keep ranck with me, and my vile Mother Queen,
To see her self, where she would have mee seen.
Good fellowship I'faith.
Hortenʒo.   And I can tell,
True misery, loves a companion wel.

                197   price] *i.e.* prize   S.D. ii] IV D
                8 *Both Moors.*] *Both.* D

Philip.   Thou left'st me to the mercy of a Moor,
That hath damnation dy'd upon his flesh;   20
'Twas well: thou Mother did'st unmotherly
Betray thy true son to false bastardy:
Thou left'st me then, now thou art found, and staid,
And thou who did'st betray me, art betraid.
A plague upon you all.
Cardinal.   Thou cursest them,
Whom I may curse; first may I curse my self,
Too credulous of Loyalty and love;
Next may I curse the *Moor*, more then a Devill.
And last thy Mother, mother of all evill.
Qu. Mo.   All curses, and all crosses light on thee,   30
What need I curse my selfe, when all curse mee.
I have been deadly impious I confesse,
Forgive mee, and my sin will seem the less:
This heavie chain which now my neck assaults,
Weighs ten times lighter then my heavie faults.
Philip.   *Hortenzo*, I commend my self to thee,
Thou that art near'st, stand'st furthest off from mee.
Hortenzo.   That mold of Hell, that *Moor* has chain'd me here.
'Tis not my self, but *Isabel* I fear.

                Enter Eleazar, [Isabella,] Zarack, *and* Baltazar.

Eleazar.   It's strange! will not Prince *Philip* come with *Hortenzo.* 40
Zarack.   He swears he'l live and die there.
Eleazar.   Marry, and shall;
I pray perswade him you, to leave the place,
A prison? why its hell; Alas here they be,
Hah! they are they i'faith, see, see, see, see.
All.   Moor, Devill, toad, serpent.
Eleazar.   Oh sweet airs, sweet voices.
Isabella.   Oh my *Hortenzo*!
Eleazar.   Do not these birds sing sweetly *Isabella*?
Oh! how their spirits would leap aloft and spring,
Had they their throats at liberty to sing.

                39 *Following,* D *prints*: Act. V. Scena V.

                206

Philip.　Damnation dog thee.
Cardinal.　　　　　Furies follow thee.　　　　　50
Qu. Mo.　Cometts confound thee.
Hortenʒo.　　　　　And hell swallow thee.
Eleaʒar.　Sweeter and sweeter still, Oh! harmony,
Why there's no musick like to miserie.
Isabella.　Hast thou betrai'd me thus?
Eleaʒar.　　　　　Not I, not I.
Philip.　Sirrah, hedge-hog.
Eleaʒar.　　　　　Hah! I'le hear thee presently.
Isabella.　Hear me then, Hell-hound; slaves, Unchain my love,
Or by — —
Eleaʒar.　　　By what? is't not rare walking here.
Me thinks this stage shews like a Tennis Court;
Do's it not *Isabell?* I'le shew thee how:
Suppose that Iron chain to be the line,　　　　　60
The prison doors the hazard, and their heads
Scarce peeping ore the line suppose the bals;
Had I a racket now of burnish'd steel,
How smoothly could I bandy every ball,
Over this Globe of earth, win sett and all.
Philip.　How brisk the villain jetts in villany!
Eleaʒar.　Prating? he's proud because he wears a chain:
Take it off *Baltaʒar,* and take him hence.
　　　　　　　　　　　They unbind him.
Philip.　And whither then you dog?
Isabella.　　　　　Pity my brother.
Eleaʒar.　Pity him, no; away; I, come, do, come.　　　　　70
Philip.　I pray thee kill me: come.
Eleaʒar.　　　　　I hope to see
Thy own hands do that office, down with him.
Philip.　Is there another hell?
Both Moors.　　　　　Try, try, he's gone.
　　　　　　　　　　　[*Thrust him down trap.*]
Eleaʒar.　So; him next, her next, and next him; and then?

　　　*70 I, come, do, come.] *stet* D　　　73 *Both*] 2. D
　　　74 her] Robinson; he D

　　　　　　　　　　207

All. Worse then damnation, feind, monster of men.

Eleaȝar. Why, when? down, down.

Cardinal.   Slave, as thou thrusts me down,
Into this dungeon, so sink thou to hell.   [*Down Cardinal.*]

Qu. Mo. Amen, Amen.   [*Down Queen Mother.*]

Eleaȝar.   Together so, and you.

Isabella. O pity my *Hortenȝo*!

Hortenȝo. Farewel sweet *Isabel*, my life adieu.   80
                                  [*Down Hortenȝo.*]

All. Mischief and horror let the *Moor* pursue.   [*Under stage.*]

Eleaȝar. A consort, that amain, play that amain.
Amain, Amain. No; so soon fallen asleep,
Nay I'le not loose this musick, sirrah! sirrah!
Take thou a drum, a Trumpet thou, and Hark;
Mad them with villanous sounds.

Zarack.   Rare sport, let's go.
                              Exeunt Zarack, Baltazar.

Eleaȝar. About it.   Musick will doe well, in woe;
How like you this?

Isabella.   Set my *Hortenȝo* free,
And I'le like any thing.

Eleaȝar.   A fool, a fool!

Hortenȝo free, why look you, hee free? no;   90
Then must he marry you, you must be Queen,
Hee in a manner King, these dignities
Like poyson make men swell, this Ratsbane honour
O 'tis so sweet, they'le lick it till all burst.
Hee will be proud, and pride you know must fall.
Come, come, he shall not; no, no; 'tis more meet,
To keep him down, safe standing on his feet.

Isabella. *Eleaȝar?*

Eleaȝar.   Mark: the imperial chair of *Spain*,
Is now as empty as a Misers Alms;
Be wise, I yet dare sit in't; it's for you,   100
If you will be for me, there's room for two.
Do, meditate, muse on't: it's best for thee
To love me, live with me, and lye with me.

208

Isabella.　Thou knowst I'le first lye in the arms of death,
My meditations are how to revenge,
Thy bloody tyrannies; I fear thee not
Inhumane slave, but to thy face defie
Thy lust, thy love, thy barbarours villany.
Eleaʒar.　Zarack.
　　　　　　Enter Zarack.

Zarack.　　　My Lord!
Eleaʒar.　　　　　　Where's *Baltaʒar?*
Zarack.　　　　　　　　　　A drumming.
Eleaʒar.　I have made them rave, and curse, and so: guard her:　110
Your Court shall be this prison, guard her, slaves,
With open eyes; defie me? see my veins,
Stuck't out, being over heated with my blood,
Boyling in wrath: I'le tame you.
Isabella.　　　　　　Do, do.
Eleaʒar.　　　　　　　　Hah!
I wil, and once more fil a kingdoms Throne.
Spain I'le new-mould thee, I will have a chair
Made all of dead mens bones, and the ascents
Shall be the heads of Spaniards set in ranks;
I will have *Philip's* head, *Hortenʒo's* head,
Mendoʒa's head, thy Mothers head, and this,　120
This head that is so crosse, I'le have't:
The Scene wants Actors, I'le fetch more, and cloth it
In rich Cothurnall pompe. A Tragedy
Ought to be grave, graves this shall beautifie.
Moor, execute to'th life my dread commands,
Vengeance awake, thou hast much work in hand.　　　*Exit.*
Zarack.　I'm weary of this office, and this life,
It is too thirsty, and I would your blood,
Might scape the spilling out: By heaven I swear,
I scorn these blows, and his rebukes to bear.　130
Isabella.　Oh! *Zarack* pity me, I love thee well,
Love deserves pity, pity *Isabel.*

　　　　*110 I have…curse, and] *stet* D　　113 Stuck't] Struck't D
　　　　129 spilling] filling D

Zarack. What would you have me do?
Isabella. To kill this *Moor.*
Zarack. I'le cast an eye of death upon my face.
I'le be no more his slave; swear to advance me,
And by yo'n setting sun, this hand, and this
Shall rid you of a tyrant.
Isabella. By my birth;
No Spaniards honour'd place shall equall thine.
Zarack. I'le kill him then.
Isabella. And *Baltazar.*
Zarack. And hee.
Isabella. I pray thee first, fetch *Philippo* and *Hortenzo*   140
Out of that Hell; they two will be most glad
To ayd thee in this Execution.
Zarack. My Lord *Philippo*; and *Hortenzo*; rise;

[*Up* Philip *and* Hortenzo.]

Your hands; so, talk to her; at my return
This sword shall reek with blood of *Baltazar.*   *Exit.*
Philip. Three curses (like three comendations
To their three soules) I send; thy tortur'd brother
Does curse the Cardinall, the *Moor*, thy Mother.
Isabella. Curse not at all dear soules; revenge is hot,
And boyles in *Zaracks* brains; the plot is cast,   150
Into the mold of Hell: You freemen are;
Zarack will kill the *Moor*; and *Baltazar.*
Hortenzo. How can that relish?
Isabella. Why? I'le tell you how!
I did profess; I, and protested too,
I lov'd him well, what will not sorrow do?
Then he profest; I, and protested too,
To kill them both, what will not devils do?
Philip. Then I profess; I, and protest it too,
That here's for him, what will not *Philip* do?
Hortenzo. See where hee coms.

Enter the two Moors.

Baltazar.   *Zarack*, what do I see?   160
  Hortenzo and *Philippo*! who did this?
Zarack.   I *Baltazar.*
Baltazar.   Thou art halfe damn'd for it,
  I'le to my lord.
Zarack.   I'le stop you on your way,
  Lie there; thy tongue shal tel no tales today.   *Stubs him.*
Philip.   Nor thine to morrow. This revenge was well,   *Stabs him.*
  By this time both the slaves shake hands in hell.
Isabella.   *Philippo* and *Hortenzo* stand you still?
  What; doat you both? cannot you see your play?
  Well fare a woman then, to lead the way.
  Once rob the dead, put the Moors habits on,   170
  And paint your faces with the oil of hell,
  So waiting on the Tyrant —
Philip.   Come no more,
  'Tis here, and here; room there below, stand wide,
  Bury them well since they so godly di'd.
                    [*Cast* Zarack *and* Baltazar *down trap.*]
Hortenzo.   Away then, fate now let revenge be plac'd —
Philip.   Here.
Hortenzo.   And here, a tyrants blood doth sweetly tast.
                                   Exeunt [*omnes*].

ACTUS V. SCENA III.

Enter Eleazar, Alvero, Roderigo, Christofero, *and other Lords.*

Eleazar.   What, I imprison, who?
All.   *Philip* and *Hortenzo.*
Eleazar.   *Philip* and *Hortenzo*, Ha, ha, ha.
Roderigo.   Why laughs the *Moor*?
Eleazar.   I laugh because you jest.
  Laugh at a jest; who I imprison them?

I prize their lives with weights, their necks with chains,
Their hands with Manacles? do I all this?
Because my face is in nights colour dy'd,
Think you my conscience and my soul is so,
Black faces may have hearts as white as snow;
And 'tis a generall rule in morall rowls,   10
The whitest faces have the blackest souls.
Alvero.   But touching my *Hortenƶo.*
Eleaƶar.   Good old man,
I never touch'd him, do not touch me then
With thy *Hortenƶo.*
Christofero.   Where's *Philippo* too?
Eleaƶar.   And where's *Philippo* too? I pray, I pray,
Is *Philip* a tame Spaniard? what, can I
Philip him hither, hither make him flye.
First where's *Hortenƶo*, where's *Philippo* too?
Roderigo.   And where is *Isabel*, she was with you.
Eleaƶar.   And where is *Isabel*, she was with me,   20
And so are you, yet are you well you see,

Enter Philip *and* Hortenzo *like Moors.*

But in good time, see where their keepers come.
Come hither *Zarack, Baltaƶar,* come hither;
Zarack, old Lord *Alvero* asks of thee,
Where young *Hortenƶo* is.
Hortenƶo.   My Lord! set free.
Eleaƶar.   Oh! is he so; come hither *Baltaƶar,*
Lord *Christofero* here would ask of thee
Where Prince *Philippo* is.
Philip.   My Lord set free.
Eleaƶar.   Oh is he so! *Roderigo* asketh mee
For *Isabel.*
Philip.   I say my Lord shee's free.   30
Eleaƶar.   Oh! is she so.
Philip.   Believe me Lords.
Hortenƶo.   And mee.

14 *Philippo*] *Philip* D

212

Philip.   I set *Philippo.*
Hortenzo.   I *Hortenzo* free.
Eleazar.   My Lords because you shal believe me too,
Go to the Castle, I will follow you.
Alvero.   Thanks to the mighty *Moor*, and for his fame,
Be more in honour, then thou art in name;
But let me wish the other prisoners well,
The Queen and Cardinall, let all have right,
Let law absolve them or disolve them quite.
Eleazar.   Grave man, thy gray hairs paint out gravity,   40
Thy counsells wisedom, thy wit pollicie.
There let us meet, and with a general brain,
Erect the peace of spirit and of *Spain*.
Alvero.   Then will *Spain* flourish.
Eleazar.   I, when it is mine.   [*Aside.*]
Roderigo.   O heavenly meeting!
Eleazar.   We must part in hell.   [*Aside.*]
Christofero.   True peace of joy.

        Exeunt, manent Eleazar, Philip, Hortenzo.

Eleazar.   'Tis a dissembling knel. [*Aside.*]
Farewell my Lords, meet there; so, ha, ha, ha.
                        Draws his Rapier.
Now Tragedy thou Minion of the night,
Rhamnusias pew-fellow; to thee I'le sing
Upon an harp made of dead Spanish bones,   50
The proudest instrument the world affords;
When thou in Crimson jollitie shalt Bath,
Thy limbs as black as mine, in springs of blood;
Still gushing from the Conduit-head of *Spain*:
To thee that never blushest, thou thy cheeks
Are full of blood. O! Saint revenge: to thee
I consecrate my Murders, all my stabs,
My bloody labours, tortures, stratagems:
The volume of all wounds, that wound from me;
Mine is the stage, thine is the Tragedy.   60
Where am I now? oh at the prison? true,

        213

Zarack and *Baltazar* come hither, see,
Survey my Library. I study, I,
Whil'st you two sleep, marry 'tis villany.
Here's a good book, *Zarack* behold it well,
It's deeply written for 'twas made in hell.
Now *Baltazar*, a better book for thee,
But for my selfe, this, this, the best of all;
And therefore do I chain it every day,
For fear the Readers steal the art away.   70
Where thou stand'st now, there must *Hortenzo* hang,
Like *Tantalus* in a maw-eating pang:
There *Baltazar* must Prince *Philippo* stand,
Like damn'd *Prometheus*; and to act his part,
Shal have a dagger sticking at his heart.
But in my room I'le set the Cardinall,
And he shal preach Repentance to them all.
Ha, ha, ha.
Philip.   Damnation tickles him, he laughs again,   [*Aside.*]
Philippo must stand there and bleed to death: 80
Well villain I onely laugh to see,
That we shal live to out-laugh him and thee.
Eleazar.   Oh! sit, sit, sit, stay a rare jest, rare jest.
Zarack, suppose thou art *Hortenzo* now?
I pray thee stand in passion of a pang,
To see by thee how quaintly he would hang.
Hortenzo.   I am *Hortenzo*, [*aside*] tut, tut, fear not man,
Thou lookest like *Zarack*.
Eleazar.   I *Hortenzo*, here;
Hee shall hang here, I'faith, come *Zarack*, come,
And *Baltazar*, take thou *Philippo's* room.   90
First let me see you plac'd.
Philip.   We're plac'd.
Eleazar.   Slaves, ha, ha, ha,
You are but players, they must end the play:
How like *Hortenzo* and *Philippo* ha,
Stand my two slaves, were they as black as you.

73 *Philippo*] *Philip* D   80 *Philippo*] *Philip* D

Well *Zarack* I'le unfix thee first of all,
Thou shalt help me to play the Cardinall;
This Iron engine on his head I'le clap,
Like a Popes Miter, or a Cardinalls Cap.
Then Manacle his hands as thou dost mine:
So, so, I pray thee *Zarack*, set him free,　　　　　100
That both of you may stand and laugh at mee.
Philip.　'Tis fine I'faith, cal in more company,
Alvero, Roderigo, and the rest,
Who will not laugh at *Eleazars* jest?
Eleazar.　What? *Zarack, Baltazar.*
Philip.　　　　　　　　I, anon, anon,
We have not laught enough, it's but begun.
Who knocks.
Eleazar.　　　Unmanacle my hands I say.
Philip.　Then shall we mar our mirth and spoil the play.
Who knocks.
Alvero.　　*Alvero.*　　　　　　　*Within.*
Philip.　　　　　Let *Alvero* in.
Eleazar.　And let me out.

　Enter all [and Queen Mother and Cardinall from] below.

Philip.　　　　　　I thank you for that flout,　　　110
To let *Alvero* in, and let you out.
Eleazar.　Villains, slaves, am I not your Lord the *Moor,*
And *Eleazar.*
Qu. Mo.　　　And the Devill of hell,
And more then that, and *Eleazar* too.
Eleazar.　And Devills dam, what do I here with you.
Qu. Mo.　My tongue shall torture thee.
Eleazar.　　　　　　　I know thee then,
All womens tongues are tortures unto men.
Qu. Mo.　Spaniards this was the villain, this is he
Who through enticements of alluring lust,
And glory which makes silly women proud,　　　120
And men malicious, did incense my spirit

　　107, 109 Who knocks.] Dilke; D *prints in right margin as a stage-direction.*

Beyond the limits of a womans mind,
To wrong my self and that Lord Cardinall;
And that which sticks more near unto my blood,
He that was nearest to my blood, my son;
To dispossesse him of his right by wrong.
Oh! that I might embrace him on this brest,
Which did enclose him when he first was born.
No greater happinesse can heaven showre upon me;
Then to circle in these arms of mine,   130
That son whose Royall blood I did defame,
To Crown with honour an ambitious Moor.
Philip.   Thus then thy happinesse is compleat: *Embraces her.*
Behold thy *Philip* ransom'd from that prison
In which the *Moor* had cloistered him.
Hortenʒo.   And here's *Hortenʒo.*
Eleaʒar.   Then am I betray'd
And cozen'd in my own designs: I did
Contrive their ruine, but their subtil policie
Hath blasted my ambitious thoughts:
Villains! where's *Zarack?* Where is *Baltaʒar?*   140
What have you done with them.
Philip.   They're gon to *Pluto's* kingdom to provide
A place for thee, and to attend thee there;
But least they should be tyred with too long
Expecting hopes, come brave spirits of *Spain,*
This is the *Moor,* the actor of these evills:
Thus thrust him down to act amongst the devills.   *Stabs him.*
Eleaʒar.   And am I thus dispatch'd;
Had I but breath'd the space of one hour longer,
I would have fully acted my revenge.   150
But oh! now pallid death bids me prepare,
And hast to *Charon* for to be his fare.
I com, I com, but ere my glasse is run,
I'le curse you all, and cursing end my life.
Maist thou *Lascivious Queen* whose damned charms,
Bewitch'd me to the circle of thy arms,

140 Where is] Where's D

216

Unpitied dye, consumed with loathed lust,
Which thy venereous mind hath basely nurst.
And for you *Philip*, may your days be long,
But clouded with perpetuall misery.   160
May thou *Hortenʒo* and thy *Isabell*,
Be fetch'd alive by Furies into hell,
There to be damn'd for ever, oh! I faint;
Devills com claim your right, and when I am
Confin'd within your kingdom then shall I
Out-act you all in perfect villany.   *Dyes.*
Philip.   Take down his body while his blood streams forth,
His acts are past, and our last act is done.
Now do I challenge my Hereditary right,
To th' Royall Spanish throne usurp'd by him.   170
In which,
In all your sights I thus do plant my self.
Lord Cardinall, and you the Queen my mother,
I pardon all those crimes you have committed.
Qu. Mo.   I'le now repose my self in peacefull rest,
And flye unto some solitary residence;
Where I'le spin out the remnant of my life,
In true contrition for my past offences.
Philip.   And now *Hortenʒo* to close up your wound,
I here contract my sister unto thee,   180
With Comick joy to end a Tragedie.
And for this Barbarous *Moor*, and his black train,
Let all the Moors be banished from *Spain*.

                                                  Exeunt.

                 The end of the fifth Act.

                    F I N I S

TEXTUAL NOTES

I.ii

187–188 Physic, And curing] D reads as the last line of sig. B11 recto, 'Shal never be rais'd up by the strong Physical,' followed by the catchword 'And'. Sig. B11 verso begins, 'Curing of my sword, therefore stay still;'. All editors read 'Physical | Curing', but the line limps and the anomalous catchword is unexplained, as is the comma after 'Physical' that is anomalous standing between an adjective and its noun. Brereton conjectures that there has been rearrangement of type and that line 182 originally ended sig. B11 recto; but this is idle speculation in default of evidence. It seems simpler to believe that *Physical* (but not its comma) is in error, and that the compositor skipped a word (whether or not through improper marking of his copy) between setting the recto and verso pages. *Physical curing* is an odd phrase, whereas *physic and curing* is quite natural.

II.i

18 give arm] The D phrase perhaps means 'to give my arm to'; that is, to assist hostile violence, as a companion. See V.i.194: 'Were your cause strong, we would not arm you so', spoken to the Queen Mother, who is being forcibly conveyed to prison. In the Bodleian copy Malone placed a dot above the letter *r*, presumably to emend to 'give aim'. This is tempting, as in the *O.E.D.* sense of 'To guide one in his aim, by informing him of the result of a preceding shot'. Nevertheless, the text's *arm* makes perfectly acceptable sense without emendation. Brereton's (p. 174) cited parallel for Malone's emendation is not pertinent: 'Stand armies and give aim, whil'st wee two bleed' (IV.ii.121). Here 'give aim' seems to mean 'keep the enemy within your sights but do not fire'.

II.ii

23 this night.] D reads: 'Why then this night *Philip* shall not live;'. (The semi-colon at the end of the line is uncertain; possibly it is a colon.) If D's punctuation is right, then Eleazar after pretending to agree makes his turn with 'To see you kill him.', which would need to be exclamatory. It is tempting to read a vicious play in the whole sentence, such as 'Do it tonight, and in the dark *Philip* will not live to see you murder him.' But this would seem to be unlikely, for 'To see you kill him' must at least in part introduce such phrases as 'Is he not your son?'. The simplest way of dealing with the crux is to assume that there has been transposition of the

punctuation, one of the commonest kinds of error in the play. Thus if the strong stop after 'live' is transferred (here in the shape of a full stop) to appear after 'night', and no stop appears at the end of the line, we have a sense such as this. Eleazar agrees in a brief phrase: 'Why then this night.' This is a natural reply, and the rhythm is right. Then in an exclamation of disbelief he reverses the course of the agreement. No, he says in effect, no matter how long Philip lives he will never see you kill him, for you will never do so. Is he not your son, etc.

52 cry'd out; doo't:]   Oddly, the press-corrector removed the colon present in the original setting after *doo't* as part of an extensive repunctuation of lines 51–52. I take it, *contra* other editors, that *doo't* is a simple repetition of the phrase in line 51, and not a quotation of what conscience cried out. Hence, it has seemed best to strengthen the corrector's added comma after *cry'd out*.

126 your sin]   This is presumably addressed to the Queen Mother and not to the Friars.

III.ii

57 Instead of poisoning him. . . .]   These lines offer a difficulty that might perhaps go back to a reworking of the scene in case the original version had Maria saving her chastity by drinking the poison herself. However, strained as they are, some sense can be forced into them. We may take it (with other editors) that a stronger stop than the D comma should be placed after *sleep*. The first two lines are addressed to the potion and are spoken as the King is down stage locking the doors. Then in the following couplet Maria explains to the audience that she is drinking from her own bowl in order to encourage the King to drink from his so that the flames of his desire will be quenched. (Fernando has left with the command for her to *begin* the feast with the drink.) Fernando sees her drink (although it is unlikely that *I'le drink this off* is addressed to him, interrupting her aside), and is satisfied that she has capitulated. Thus on his return he drinks from his own cup, containing the potion, without further discussion. If this is the interpretation, *let fire conquer loves fire* must mean that the fire of the liquor she is unwillingly drinking will, paradoxically, be the means of conquering Fernando's passion, since her act has encouraged him to drink the potion. We may perhaps blame the couplet form for the contorted expression.

V.i

110 *Roderigo*.]   D assigns this speech to Hortenzo. The whole question turns on when Hortenzo enters. Between lines 162 and 163 is the direction for Isabella's entrance followed by a full stop and then the name 'Hortenzo.' Ordinarily one would take this as representing the entrance of Hortenzo

with Isabella, the future husband and consort perhaps a little behind Isabella in her royal robes. Otherwise, we should need to take the placing of Hortenzo's name in this direction as indicating that he has been among the group of lords interrogating the Cardinal, and on Isabella's entrance that he detaches himself and comes forward 'to her'. This is to strain the direction. Since Roderigo is concerned with the questioning in line 130, he is an appropriate character to speak line 110. See the Textual Introduction for a query whether Verdugo may not have been the original speaker.

V.ii

70 I, come, do, come.] Hazlitt, with Brereton's approval, would transfer these words from Eleazar to Philip, presumably as a prelude to line 71: '*Philip*. I pray thee kill me: come.' Although Philip often speaks in just such a series of ejaculations, so does Eleazar, and it is not inappropriate here for him to be impatient with Philip, who is resisting Zarack and Baltazar's efforts to remove him.

110 I have...curse, and] D *mislines here:* '*Elea.* I have...and | So: guard her:'. This may have tempted Brereton, who suggests that 'I have...and' should be assigned to Zarack, with Eleazar cutting him short with 'So'. But there is nothing uncharacteristic here in Eleazar's description of what he has made his prisoners feel by reason of his orders.

PRESS-VARIANTS IN D

[Copies collated: BM¹ (British Museum 643.a.28), BM² (82.c.22[7]); Bodl (Bodleian Library Mal. 133[8]), Dyce (Victoria and Albert Museum); DLC¹ (Library of Congress, copy 1 [Greg, *A*1]), DLC² (Library of Congress, Greg *A*1v); MH (Harvard University).]

SHEET C (*outer forme*)

Corrected: BM¹⁻², Bodl, Dyce, DLC¹, MH
Uncorrected: DLC¹

Sig. C1.

II.i.2 messengers] messenger
    8 Do;] Do

Sig. C2ᵛ

II.i.49 candle,] candle
    49 water,] water
    49 praiers,] praiers
    50 allchim] all chime
    50 the of Court] the Court
    51 conjure] conjre
    53 Card'nall] Card'nalls
    55 Laughts] Laughs
    57 our] onr
    59 Prince] King
    62 names] names,
    62 infamy,] infamy
    66 blood,] blood.

Sig. C3.

II.i.81 looks] looks,
    86 its] his
    86 memory] memory.

Sig. C4ᵛ

II.ii.19 els] else
    19 live] liv
    22 *Qu. M.*] *Qu. Ns*
    28 self,] self
    28 well] wel
    30 two] too
    34 but,] but, but

221

Sig. C5.

II.ii.38 tongue,] tongue
42 penitence,] penitence
44 Friers,] Friers
46 such,] such
47 the] ye
51 bastard;] bastard,
51 you;] you
51 bastard?] bastard,
52 conscience] conscience,
52 spake] speake
52 out,] out
52 doo't] doo't:

Sig. C6ᵛ.

II.ii.89 clear,] dear
96 name,] name
96 time] time;
101 ambitious,] ambitious
101 woo's] woos
102 takes] take

Sig. C7.

II.ii.105 aspirer] aspier
112 directions,] directions
114 Royall] Ryall
117 ears] years
119 his] *omit*
124 face,] face

Sig. C8ᵛ.

II.ii.162 Cardinall;] Cardinall.
165 th'] the
II.iii.2 first;] first
7 raggs;] raggs
7 *Moor,*] *Moor*
7 Devill,] Devill
7 come.] come,
8 on,] on

Sig. C9.

II.iii.16 desperately] desparately
17 too...too] to...to
18 doth] do

222

20 Jett,] Jett.
23 *Coles*] *Cole*
28 here] hee
30 too] to
32*cw* I vow] I now

Sig. C 10^v

II.iii.66 T'obey] To obey
72 *Friers*] *Eriers*
74 *Baltazar.*] *Baltaz.*
75 th'] *omit*
75 poi-|sonous breath] poison-|breath
78 Slaves] Slave
78 dangerous;] dangerous,
80 suspition,] suspition
80 pollicy] pollicy,

Sig. C 11.

II.iii.90 treason] trason
99 Idea] idea

Sig. C 12^v.

II.iii.142 Cuckolc] Cuckcold
144 know,] know
147 falchions] falcshions
149 his] the
150 coold] cold

SHEET C (*inner forme*)

Corrected: Bodl, Dyce, DLC², MH
Uncorrected: BM¹⁻², DLC¹

Sig. C 6.

II.ii.72 ears] years

Sig. C 9^v.

II.iii.39 shoot] shoots

EMENDATIONS OF ACCIDENTALS

Dedication

2 some-|what] somewhat

P. I.

2 minde,] ~ .   18 Spain.] *punctuation uncertain*

Persons

6 Alvero,] ~ ∧   19 Pages] pages
8 Mendoza,] ~ ∧   23 Isabella,] ~ ∧
12 Hortenzo,] ~ ∧   24 Maria,] ~ ∧
17 Emmanuel,] ~ ∧

I.i

S.D. *Moors,*] ~ ∧   100 thee:] ~ ;
2–3 That...*Baltaʒar?*] *one line in*   101 Concubine;] ~ :
  D   102 me. Hear] me, hear
2 *Zarack,*] ~ ∧   105 boyes.] ~ ∧
5–6 Did...us.] *one line in* D 106 Love! ...peace!] ~ ? ... ~ ?
17 strive,] ~ ∧   107 throats!] ~ ?
22–23 *one line in* D   108 Squalls] Squales
26–27 *one line in* D   120 smile∧ ...me,] ~ , ... ~ ∧
29–30 *one line in* D   125–126 *one line in* D
29 love?] ~ ,   127–128 It...here.] *one line in* D
30 wyres! ...Instruments!] ~ ? 128 Queen] Qeen
  ... ~ ?   129 him!] ~ ?
36 What,] ~ ∧   134 Run! ...voice∧] ~ ? ... ~ .
38–39 At...frown] *one line in* D   143 so, down,] ~ ∧ ~ ∧
49 These] these   148–149 Queen...daughter] *one line*
52 Shall] D *cw;* Shal *text*   *in* D
61 wide,] ~ .   149 daughter,] ~ :
62 them!] ~ ?   150 Jealous:] Jealous,
69 *Eleaʒar.*] *Eliaʒ.*   156–157 D *lines:* And...father, |
71–72 *one line in* D   Who...life,
71 me?] ~ ;   159 Tyrant! ...do!] ~ ? ... ~ ?
79 cheeks,] ~ .   162 Tyrant:] ~ ∧
89 There] there   172 you; ...villany,] ~ , ... ~ ;

224

177 fate,] ~ .
181 And] and
187 To] to
189 mine, . . . thee:] ~ : . . . ~ ,

194 doat;] ~ ,
195 King, consume] King. Consume
197 acted,] ~ ⌄

I.ii

9 (dead)] [~]
33 away;] *point may be comma*
39 down!] ~ ?
40 flesh,] ~ ;
41 graves;] ~ ,
48–49 His. . .up.] *one line in* D
50 down;] ~ ,
53 Soveraign?] ~ .
92 thee;] ~ ,
93 wife,] ~ ;
104 Joy;] ~ ⌄
112 Turk's,] ~ ⌄
121 armes —] ~ .
123–124 *one line in* D
129 That —] *concludes line* 128 *in* D
130 sons:] ~ ,
131 sins,] ~ :

135 tongue —] ~ .
136 tell⌄ —] ~ , —
144 down?] ~ .
145 here?] ~ .
152 *Eleaȝar*] *Ele.* text; *Eli.* cw
155 Wee] wee
163 Oh] *Oh*
200 wheeles?] ~ .
203 What] what
205 S.D. *Enter*⌄] ~ .
218 Majesty —] ~ .
221 Cardinall] Card'nall
223 Where's] Wher'es
223–224 He. . .me.] *one line in* D
228–229 This. . .King,] *one line in* D
229 in,] ~ ⌄
234 Wee'l] wee'l

II.i

4–5 Your. . .banishment:] *one line in* D
6–7 Who. . .Devill,] *one line in* D
8 me!] ~ ?
17 &] *om.* D
17 not,] ~ ⌄
41 steel,] ~ ⌄
42–43 *one line in* D
42 souldier,] ~ ;
47 Church:] ~ ,

48 heads,] ~ :
65 *Eleaȝar.*] *Eliaȝ.*
66 fury;] ~ ,
72 *Mendoȝa,*] *Mendo,*
74 *Eleaȝar,*] *Eliaȝ.*
76 *Eleaȝar.*] *Eliaȝ.*
85 yeild: . . .Lord;] ~ ; . . . ~ :
94 Duke;] ~ ,
95 dye,] ~ ;

II.ii

14–15 Angels. . .King?] *one line in* D
15 like] likə
15 King?] ~ ⌄
18 he] BMᵗ *clear* h
18 die,] ~ ;

19 else] D(u); els D(c)
19 her;] ~ ,
19 live.] *point uncertain*
20 In] in
20 heaven.)] ~ ⌄)
24 him!] ~ .

28 well] D(u); wel D(c)
29 eye.] ~ ,
31–32 D *lines*: Up...others |
Dare...cast
37 crevises. How!] crevises, how ∧
40–41 D *lines*: Thus. | Go...do |
In...out
41 colours,] ~ ;
43 glib; ...swarm,] ~ , ... ~ ;
51 you∧] D(u); ~ ; D(c)
62 fall,] ~ ∧
65 S.D. *Exit*] *Eʒit*
70–71 What...*Baltaʒar*.] *one line in D*
71 My] my
71 so,] ~ ∧
74 (in)] ∧ ~ ∧
74 death.] ~ ,
79 away!] ~ ?

88 fact∧] ~ .
100 swords.] ~ ∧
120 Turkish] Tutkish
123 Oh!] ~ ?
139 prest,] ~ ;
140 knaves;] ~ ,
144–145 D *lines*: One...will |
Turn...spell,
146 here;] ~ ,
149 off —] ~ .
153 Now] now
156 adieu] a dieu
159 prosperous:] ~ ∧
160 word,] ~ ∧
161 *treason*] treason
162 Cardinall.] D(u); ~ ; D(c)
163 triumph; ...horror,] ~ ,
... ~ ;

II.iii

6 before] bfeore
7 s'heart;] ~ |
11–12 Else...King.] *one line in D*
24 bleed,] ~ :
25 away:] ~ ,
29 on;] ~ ∧
30 so:] ~ ∧
33 do —] ~ :
39 Cardinal:] ~ ,
47 time:] ~ ∧
50 flight.] ~ ,
51 Escap'd, Friers?] ~ ∧ ~ ,
51–52 Good...blood;] *one line in*
D
54 Friers,] ~ ∧
55 brests,] ~ :
56 burns:] ~ ,
61 yet] yer
62 King] *perhaps* Klng
64 bleed,] ~ .
67 conscience,] ~ ∧
68 mis-don] mis-|don
69 son.] ~ ∧

73 I.] ~ ,
74 *Baltaʒar*,] ~ .
80 pollicy.] ~ , D(u); ~ ∧ D(c)
88 Queen?] *Qu.*
91 Who...noise?] D *lines:* Who
...slumbers, | With...noise:
91 noise?] ~ :
94 *Eleaʒar*,] *Eleaʒ.*
97 From] from
101 advancement] advancment
105 forth:] ~ ∧
114 of the] of th'
127 impose;] ~ ,
128 heaven,] ~ ;
130 right; ...gon,] ~ , ... ~ ;
134 murthered] muthered
135 past, ...clouds∧] ~ ∧ ... ~ ,
136 treason, ...wind∧] ~ ∧ ... ~ ,
137 scattered] scatt'red
138 friend.] ~ ,
152 *Eleaʒar* —] ~ ;
154 husband —] ~ :
156 walls —] ~ :

226

165 eyes,] ~ ∧
171 you;] ~ ∧
171–172 Then...it.] *one line in D*
172–173 'Tis...lust] *one line in D*

183 life,] ~ :
184 poison:] ~ ∧
187 Do;] ~ ∧
191 carcasses:] ~ ∧

III.i

12 kill!] ~ ?
13 love!] ~ ?
19 *Alvero*] *Alvaro*

28–29 Stay...deed] D *lines:* Stay
  ...arm | Arm...deed
29 cry arm,] ~ ~ ∧
39 her!] ~ ?

III.ii

10 thee] the
11 gladly] glaldly
23 thee:] ~ ,
32 Love] Loue
48 Negroes] *Negroes*
69 self;] ~ ,
70 death,] ~ ;
89 S.D. Alvero] Alvaro
92–93 Imperious...self,] *one line in* D
94 hear] here
95–96 If...breast.] *one line in* D
96–97 The...participate.] *one line in* D
98–99 Thou'rt...spirit,] *one line in* D
98 Thou'rt] thou'rt
100 entertain'd] enterain'd
103–104 To...brest] *one line in* D
105 stolen] stolne
107 murderess] murdress
146–147 But...me!] *one line in* D
156 King!] ~ ?

157–158 Stand...brothelrie.] D
  lines: Stand...shall | Scorn...
  brothelrie.
169–170 The...traitor.] *one line in*
  D
169 murdered] murdred
170–171 In...Moor,] *one line in* D
177 thus —] ~ .
178–179 Damn...murdred.] D
  lines: Damn...Court. | The...
  murdred.
187 down.] ~ ∧
194 gunpowder,   ...air∧] ~ ∧
  ... ~ ,
205–207 D *lines:* Look...sun-burnt
  | Cheek...by | My...blood,
233 Blackamore;] ~ ,
234 dim,] ~ ;
236–237 Oh...love;] *one line in* D
241 King?] ~ .
246 world∧] ~ ;
247 through ∧] ~ ;
260 vice-Roys] vice Roys

III.iii

2–4 D *lines:* My...game; | With
  ...colme; | And...take.
2 game,] ~ ;
5–7 D *lines:* I...it, | And...us |
  To...-pates.

8–11 D *lines:* Is't...selves, | If...
  then | To...selves; | Come...
  come, | Here...stand.
8 selves?] ~ ,
10 selves?] ~ ;

13–15 D *lines:* Our...close: |
   Therefore...us. | But...white.
17–18 D *lines:* I...service. | *Frier*
   ...man. | Farewell...resolute.
20 rogue;] ~ ∧
21 rise,] ~ ∧
25 D *lines:* Cole...man, | And...
   ashes.
26 *Exit*] *Exit*
27–30 D *lines:* I...head, | We'l
   ...place. | Tut...*Queen.* |
   We'l...*Philips.*
27 best∧ so,] ~ , ~ ∧
29 Queen,] ~ .
33 mount!] ~ ?
34–35 D *lines:* Well...word |
   Frier...fellow.

36–37 D *lines:* Yet...what | Think
   ...*Cole?*
39 D *lines:* And...nose, | And...
   inflam'd.
48 market-folks] market-|folks
52 strong!] ~ ?
53 huge!] ~ ?
61–62 D *lines:* *Frier*...zeal; |
   Look...glows.
63–64 D *lines:* Well...edge |
   Against...bastard.
76–77 D *lines:* If...King, | Who
   ...King.
81 Countrymen] Country-|men
89–90 D *lines:* Treason...himself.
   | This...Arm.

III.iv

4 crosse] erosse
24 like] llke
24 forth.] ~ ∧

25 huge∧] ~ .
28 Of] of
33–35 By...arms.] *one line in* D

IV.i

S.D. Alvero] Alvaro
12–13 Her...course.] *one line in* D

17 innative] t *barely inks*

IV.ii

5 upon't,] ~ ∧
13–14 D *lines:* Our...violent | On
   set.
44 mell!] ~ ?
45 damn'd!] ~ ?
54 arm,] ~ ∧
56 fight!] ~ ?
75 you;] ~ ∧
79 -hounds,] ~ ∧
81 what,] ~ ∧
83 arms; ...wise,] ~ , ... ~ ;
87 hell-gates] hell-|gates
98 head.] ~ ∧

99 do —] ~ ?
100 thee —] ~ .
118 side —] ~ ,
119 side —] ~ ,
120 Wee] wee
123 come!] ~ ?
135 S.D. Portugall,] *Port.*
135 S.D. Zarack,] ~ ∧
143 flight!] ~ ?
144 left∧] ~ ,
146 more.] ~ ,
155 kiss,] ~ ;

IV.iii

9 eyes,] ~ ;
10 arise;] ~ .
29 swim.] ~ ,
30 hence!] ~ ?
34 Away!] ~ ?
43 imbrace, ...sight∧] ~ ∧ ... ~ ,
44 and this, ...suspition;] ~ ~ ;
...~ ,
52 heaven.] ~ ∧

67–68 D *lines:* Then...they |
Fools...low,
69 high? Why,] high, why∧
87 false —] ~ .
92 winding-sheet] winding-|sheet
107–108 D *lines:* Into...life: | 'Tis
...try
112 yet∧] ~ ,
115 over-worn] over-|worn

IV.iv

1 runaway] run-|away
5–6 Ha...blood,] *one line in* D
20 soul.] ~ ,
61 With] Whith
70 quotha] qnotha
75 begon!] ~ ?
79 boughs. In] boughs, in

83 all.] ~ ∧
85 thine.] ~ ,
89 dust:] ~ ,
91 weapons!] ~ ?
93 warrant, ...hands∧] ~ ∧ ... ~ ,
97 obey.] ~ ,

V.i

S.D. Roderigo] Ronerigo
S.D. Christofero, ...*them;*] ~ ;
...~ ,
S.D. *bare-headed*] *bare-|headed*
S.D. *her.*] ~ ,
1 *Alvero,*] ~ ∧
6–7 If...grave.] *one line in* D
7 S.D. *it.*] ~ !
15 what,] ~ ∧
29 About] about
32 State, ...resigne∧] ~ ∧ ... ~ ,
34 hand,] ~ ∧
53 *Spain:*] ~ ,
54 to't,] ~ ∧
56–57 D *lines:* He...making, |
I...not,
60 man.] ~ ,
61–62 D *lines:* If...hide, | The...
infamies
62 hide∧] ~ ,
70 Be bold] Behold

71 greatest,] ~ ∧
76 him!] ~ ?
78 run!] ~ ?
79 What,] ~ ∧
81 not!] ~ ?
88 you] y ou
93–95 D *lines:* I...methinks | I...
Barbaria! | No more.
96 Lord,] ~ ∧
108 jealious] jealous
128 betraid] bretraid
131–132 Justice...sin.] D *lines:*
Justice...for | His...sin.
142 Serpent —] ~ .
146 hell-hound] hell-|hound
152 Well∧ then,] ~ , ~ ∧
158 Back;] ~ ,
169–170 A...Protectress] *one line in* D
182 me,] ~ ∧
184 *Alvero,*] ~ ∧
204 all,] ~ .

218 And —] ~ .
221 *Baltazar,*] Balt.
224–225 *one line in* D
226 knees,] ~ ∧
227 shall be] shallbe
244 *Philippo;*] ~ ,
246 little] lit tle
251 too] *too*

257–258 D *lines:* That...execute |
    My selfe.
258 I∧] ~ ,
288 knives —] ~ .
292 gall —] ~ .
295 Why,] ~ ∧
301 Come] Com *cw*

V.ii

S.D. *chain'd*] chaind'
5–6 D *lines:* Many...this | *Gratis*
    ...nothing.
16 seen.] *full stop not always inked*
21 well:] ~ ,
28 Devill.] *point uncertain*
66 villany !] ~ ?
70 away; I,] ~ ∧ ~ ∧
74 So;] ~ ∧
88 Set] set
89 fool !] ~ ?
100 in't;] ~ ,
102 Do,] ~ ∧
110 D *lines:* I...and | So...her:
111 her,] ~ ∧
115 Throne.] ~ ∧

125 Moor,] ~ ∧
135 slave; ...me,] ~ , ... ~ ;
142 thee∧] ~ ;
153 how !] ~ ?
154 too,] ~ :
156 too,] ~ ∧
161 *Philippo* !] ~ ,
162–163 Thou...lord.] *one line in* D
163–164 I'le...today.] *prose in* D
165 morrow. This] morrow, this
165 well,] ~ .
167–174 *prose in* D
167 still?] ~ ,
172 Tyrant —] ~ .
175 plac'd —] ~ ∧

V.iii

3–7 *prose in* D
3 jest.] ~ ;
4 jest;] ~ ,
6 this?] ~ ,
7 dy'd,] ~ .
9 snow;] ~ ∧
12–30 *prose in* D
15 I pray, I] ~ ~ ∧ ~
16 Spaniard?] ~ ,
16 what,] ~ ∧
45 We] we
47 there; so,] ~ ∧ ~ ∧
53–101 *prose in* D
56 revenge: ...thee∧] ~ ∧ ... ~ :
62 hither,] ~ ∧
74 *Prometheus*; ...part,] ~ ,
    ... ~ ;

88 here;] ~ ∧
89 *Zarack,*] ~ ∧
90 *Philippo's*] Phiyippo's
105–106 I...begun.] *one line in* D
112–113 Villains...*Eleazar.*] *one*
    line in D
116–117 I...men.] *one line in* D
118–132 *prose in* D
125 blood, ...son;] ~ ; ... ~ ∧
136–174 *prose in* D
144 tyred] tyr'd
145 hopes, come] hopes. Come
146 *Moor,*] ~ ∧
146 evills] D *cw*; evils *text*
164 am∧] ~ ,
165 I∧] ~ ,

THE NOBLE
SOVLDIER.
OR,
A CONTRACT
BROKEN, JUSTLY
REVENG'D.

A TRAGEDY.

Written by S. ROWLEY

Non eſt, Lex Iuſtior Ulla,
Quam Neſcis Artifices, Arte perire Sua.

LONDON:
Printed for *Nicholas Vavasour*, and are to be
ſold at his ſhop in the *Temple*, neere the
Church. 1 6 3 4.

TEXTUAL INTRODUCTION

THE NOBLE SPANISH SOLDIER (Greg, *Bibliography*, no. 490) was printed in 1634, probably by John Beale, for Nicholas Vavasour, who initialled the address of the Printer to the Reader. The first entry in the Stationers' Register is dated 16 May 1631, combined with Dekker's *Wonder of a Kingdom*: 'Iohn Iackman. Entred for his Copie vnder the hands of Sr Henry Herbert & Mr Kingston Warden a Comedy called The Wonder of a Kingdome by Tho: Decker. vj^d | Idem. Entred for his Copy vnder the same hands a Tragedy called The Noble Spanish Souldier by Tho: Deckar. vj$^{d'}$. In 9 December 1633 there is the following entry: 'Nich: Vavasour. Entred for his Copy vnder the hands of Sr Henry Herbert & Mr Kingston warden A^o. dñi 1631. a Tragedy called The Noble Spanish soldior written by m^r Decker vj$^{d'}$. Greg points out that this latter must be a re-entrance of the same manuscript, since Felix Kingston, who was warden in 1630–1, was not warden in 1633. He adds that Jackman is not heard of after 1631.

In his account of the play, Bentley (*Jacobean and Caroline Stage*, III, 257–260) argues for the accuracy of the ascription of authorship in the Register for plays licensed by Herbert and notes that Fleay, Chambers, Lloyd, Adams, and Golding have accepted the attribution at least in part. The 1634 title-page listing of the author as 'S. R.' is puzzling. These initials are generally conjectured to stand for Samuel Rowley (although there is no evidence that they do), but no critic has assigned any specific lines in the play to Rowley.

Extraordinary parallels exist between II.i and Character 4 of John Day's *Parliament of Bees*, which contains dialogue between Armiger and a Don who seems to be named Cocadillio (and who is also the King's Barber), with further parallels between III.ii and Character 5. S. R. Golding, 'The Parliament of Bees', *R.E.S.* III (1927), 280–304, surveys these, and also the parallels between the *Bees* and Dekker's *Wonder of a Kingdom*. His conclusions are, briefly, the following. Despite the opinions of other critics, it is likely that the preserved manuscript version of the *Bees* is to be dated 1633–4 and that the first printed version was the quarto of 1641. The parallels are not evidence for Day's collaboration in either play, but 'Chars. 4 and 5 and Chars. 2, 3, 7, 9, and 10 seem to have been lifted almost bodily—in some cases with only slight modification—from *The Noble Soldier* and *The Wonder of a Kingdom* respectively. Where the quarto of the *Bees* corresponds to passages in these plays, Dekker's craftsmanship is nearly always distinguishable; where it deviates, Day's hand is equally well marked.'

Bentley has no patience with those critics who follow Fleay in conjecturing that *The Noble Spanish Soldier* is a reworking of an anonymous play called *The Spanish Fig* for which Henslowe made a partial payment on 6 January 1601/2.

At II.ii.29–30 Baltazar inquires, 'Shall I bee that Germane Fencer, and beat all the knocking boyes before me?'. In his edition, p. 286, Bullen very plausibly calls attention to the *Nares* quotation from *The Owles Almanacke* of 1618, p. 6, 'Since the German fencer cudgell'd most of our English fencers, now about 5 moneths past'. Bentley elaborates an allusion noticed by Fleay at IV.ii.54–56:

> Balta*z*ar. Woo't not trust an Almanacke?
> Cornego. Nor a Coranta neither, tho it were seal'd with Butter; and yet
> I know where they both lye passing well.

In his view 'this is another of the many allusions—even if the expression is proverbial—to the series of courantes or corantos issued by Nathaniel Butter and uniformly castigated for their lies by late Jacobean and Caroline dramatists, most familiarly by Jonson in *The Staple of News* (1625), a series which seems to have got properly under way in 1622'. The allusion seems clear, and would date the composition of the play between 1622 and 16 May 1631 (the entry in the Stationers' Register) unless we are to believe that the play has been revised, in which case only the date of revision might be secured.

Critics from Fleay to Bentley have agreed that the omission of the characters Signor No, Carlo, Alanzo, Cornego, and Juanna from the quarto's dramatis personae is significant. Bentley writes: 'though character lists in seventeenth-century quartos are often incomplete, this list of omissions seems unusually large and includes Cornego, which is a fat part. These facts, coupled with other characteristics of the play like loose ends and vague connexions, make it likely enough that *The Noble Soldier* is a revision of an earlier play.' In my opinion the omissions in the dramatis personae have no significance whatever as signs of a revision. If they were significant, we should need to imagine that Dekker copied out the list from the earlier play and then proceeded to write his revision on succeeding leaves. This is not a hypothesis to be seriously contemplated. Fortunately, it is clear that the publisher or the printer made up this particular list, for the inclusion of the Fryer as a separate character, who is really Sebastian in disguise, discloses that the compiler was automatically noting characters without reading the play very carefully. It would seem that he missed a fair number, or, more likely, did not bother with listing what he considered to be minor persons of no importance to the plot.

The question of revision, therefore, must be tackled from other evidence than that appropriate for a textual editor to consider. However, one or two remarks may be made here. This is a relatively short play with an uncomplicated single plot. The most obvious vague connexion is at IV.ii.191–192 in which (without our prior information) the Cardinal reveals that he has been privy to Medina's disguise and is sympathetic to the faction. Secondly, not until V.i.34 is Alanzo identified as the Captain of the Guard and, thirdly, not until V.iv is Onælia's maid Juanna introduced and named. A first impression might well be that *if* these anomalies arose from revision, they would have come about at least in some part from extensive cutting, a hypothesis that might be encouraged by the shortness of the play.

However, there are problems. One ordinarily associates cutting with the preparation of copy for acting, that is, with a prompt-book. Yet in contrast to the number of descriptive directions that are patently authorial there is no single direction anywhere that can be isolated as coming from copy prepared for acting. Thus if the manuscript used for the quarto had had a theatrical origin, it must have been an intermediate transcript, already cut, from which the prompt-copy was to be prepared. From the remarkably good text offered by the quarto one would suppose that the printer's copy was a clean and legible manuscript in good condition, certainly not foul papers. Hence the need for transcription from such a copy to form a prompt-book is not obvious, unless we are dealing with a private transcript. However, we can scarcely know all the circumstances. Juanna, who does not have a speaking role, may have been cut to reduce the size of the cast and the mention of her in the direction to V.iv may have been an oversight. Possibly Alanzo, who at first seems to be a courtier, has been merged with the Captain of the Guard, whose title, only, is given at his entrance, although his speech-prefix is *Alanzo*. But this is not very much evidence for the rather special kind of manuscript that would have been given to the printer if the present text is a revision of an earlier play. I am inclined to feel that the odds favour a fair copy of a manuscript that has been cut and perhaps slightly altered with staging in view. But whether the manuscript that was behind the fair copy was a revision of an earlier play (for which no evidence exists) or a revision of the original form of the present text is scarcely to be decided without further evidence.

The proper title is the full one, *The Noble Spanish Soldier*. This is demonstrated by the wording of the entry in the Stationers' Register and by the head-title (from which the running-titles were drawn). The title-page form can have no authority.

Starting with the text on sig. B 1 the printer used only one skeleton to impose the type-pages of both formes of sheets B–D. For sheet E a new outer-forme skeleton was constructed and printing thereafter proceeded with two formes to the sheet. There is no evidence for any change in compositors after sheet D; hence it is likely that the same compositor set the play throughout but found after three sheets that he had reached a favourable adjustment with the press and could switch over to a more efficient system of imposition once he had the time to prepare a forme in advance.

The play has been edited before only by A. H. Bullen, who offered a modified old-spelling text in *A Collection of Old English Plays* (1882), vol. 1. In 1913 J. S. Farmer produced a photographic facsimile in the series of *Tudor Facsimile Texts*. The copy he used was BM 664.c.15, which had been robbed by T. J. Wise of sigs. C4, E2.3, F4, and G1. These leaves Farmer supplied from photographs of the Dyce copy. D. F. Foxon has traced the original C4 and F 4 to the Ashley copy. Sigs. E 3 and G 1 in the Wrenn copy at the University of Texas are not homogeneous but only G 1 can be positively identified as the BM leaf. The fate of E 2 (possibly of E 2.3) is unknown.[1]

The following eleven copies have been collated in the preparation of the present text: British Museum, copy 1 (C.12.f.2[2]), copy 2 (Ashley 1452), copy 3 (644.c.15), wants C 4, E 2.3, F 4, G 1; Bodleian Library, copy 1 (Mal. 831), copy 2 (Mal. 167[3]), copy 3 (Douce R. 130); Eton College; Library of Congress, wants E 2.3; University of Chicago, Newberry Library, and Princeton University.

No press-variants were observed in these copies.

---

[1] *Thomas Wise and the Pre-Restoration Drama* (1959), pp. 26–27.

DRAMMATIS PERSONAE.

KING OF SPAINE

CARDINALL

DUKE OF MEDINA

MARQUESSE DÆNIA

ALBA
RODERIGO
VALASCO } Dons of Spayne
LOPEZ

QUEENE [PAULINA], A Florentine

ONÆLIA, Neece to Medina, the Contracted Lady   10

SEBASTIAN, Her Sonne

[COUNT] MALATESTE, A Florentine

BALTAZAR, The Souldier

A POET

COCKADILLIO, A foolish Courtier

[SIGNEOR NO, A Courtier inclining to Medina

ALANZO, Captain of the King's Guard

CARLO, Of Medina's Faction

CORNEGO, Servant of Onælia

JUANNA, Maid to Onælia]   20

15 Cockadillio] *below this line and ending the original list is:* A Fryer

238

The Printer *to the* Reader

Understanding Reader, I present this to your view, which has received applause in Action. The Poet might conceive a compleat satisfaction upon the Stages approbation: But the Printer rests not there, knowing that that which was acted and approved upon the Stage, might bee no lesse acceptable in Print. It is now communicated to you whose leisure and knowledge admits of reading and reason: Your Iudgement now this *Posthumus* assures himselfe will well attest his predecessors endevours to give content to men of the ablest quality, such as intelligent readers are here conceived to be. I could have troubled you with a longer Epistle, but I feare to stay 10 you from the booke, which affords better words and matter than I can. So the work modestly depending in the skale of your Iudgement, the Printer for his part craves your pardon, hoping by his promptnesse to doe you greater service, as conveniency shall enable him to give you more or better testimony of his entirenesse towards you.

N.V.

The
Noble Spanish
Souldier

ACTUS PRIMUS. Scæna Prima.

Enter in Magnificent state, to the sound of lowd musicke, the King and Queene, as from Church, attended by the Cardinall, Count Malateste, Dænia, Roderigo, Valasco, Alba, Carlo, and some waiting Ladies. The King and Queene with Courtly Complements salute and part; she with one halfe attending her: King, Cardinall, and th'other halfe stay, the King seeming angry and desirous to be rid of them too. — King, Cardinall, Dænia, &c.

King.   Give us what no man here is master of,
(Breath:) leave us pray, my father Cardinall
Can by the Physicke of Philosophy
Set al agen in order. Leave us, pray.   *Exeunt.*
Cardinal.   How is it with you, Sir?
Kinge.   As with a Shippe
Now beat with stormes, now safe, the stormes are vanisht,
And having you my Pylot, I not onely
See shore, but harbour; I, to you will open
The booke of a blacke sinne, deepe-printed in me:
Oh father! my disease lyes in my soule.   10
Cardinal.   The old wound, Sir?
King.   Yes that, it festers inward:
For though I have a beauty to my bed
That even Creation envies at, as wanting
Stuffe to make such another, yet on her pillow
I lye by her, but an Adulterer,
And she as an Adulteresse. Shee's my Queene
And wife, yet but my strumpet, tho the Church
Set on the seale of Mariage; good *Onælia,*

Neece to our Lord high Constable of *Spaine*,
Was precontracted mine.
Cardinal.   Yet when I stung   20
Your Conscience with remembrance of the Act,
Your eares were deafe to counsell.
King.   I confesse it.
Cardinal.   Now to unty the knot with your new Queene
Would shake your Crowne halfe from your head.
King.   Even *Troy*
(Tho she hath wept her eyes out) wud find teares
To wayle my kingdomes ruines.
Cardinal.   What will you doe then?
King.   She has that Contract written, seal'd by you,
And other Churchmen (witnesses untoo't)
A kingdome should be given for that paper.
Cardinal.   I wud not, for what lyes beneath the Moone,   30
Be made a wicked Engine to breake in pieces
That holy Contract.
King.   'Tis my soules ayme to tye it
Vpon a faster knot.
Cardinal.   I doe not see
How you can with safe conscience get it from her.
King.   Oh! I know
I wrastle with a Lyonesse: to imprison her,
And force her too't, I dare not: death! what King
Did ever say I dare not? I must have it:
A Bastard have I by her, and that Cocke
Will have (I feare) sharpe spurres, if he crow after   40
Him that trod for him: something must be done
Both to the Henne and Chicken; haste you therefore
To sad *Onælia*, tell her I'me resolv'd
To give my new Hawke bells, and let her flye;
My Queene I'me weary of, and her will marry:
To this our Text adde you what glosse you please,
The secret drifts of Kings are depthlesse Seas.

                                        Exeunt.

[ACT I, SCENE ii]

A Table set out cover'd with blacke: two waxen Tapers: the Kings Picture at one end [a dagger stuck in it], a Crucifix at the other, Onælia walking discontentedly weeping to the Crucifix, her Mayd with her, to them Cornego.

Song.

Question. *Oh sorrow, sorrow, say where dost thou dwell?*
Answer.   *In the lowest roome of Hell.*
Question. *Art thou borne of Humane Race?*
Answer.   *No, no, I have a furies face.*
Question. *Art thou in City, Towne or Court?*
Answer.   *I to every place resort.*
Question. *Oh why into the world is sorrow sent?*
Answer.   *Men afflicted, best repent.*
Question. *What dost thou feed on?*
Answer.   *Broken sleepe.*   10
Question. *What tak'st thou pleasure in?*
Answer.   *To weepe,*
           To sigh, to sob, to pine, to groane,
           To wring my hands, to sit alone.
Question. *Oh when? oh when shall sorrow quiet have?*
Answer.   *Never, never, never, never,*
           Never till she finds a Grave.

Enter Cornego.

Cornego. No lesson, Madam, but Lacrymae's? if you had buried
nine husbands, so much water as you might squeeze out of an
Onyon had beene teares enow to cast away upon fellowes that 20
cannot thanke you, come be Ioviall.
Onælia. Sorrow becomes me best.
Cornego. A suit of laugh and lye downe would weare better.
Onælia. What should I doe to be merry, *Cornego?*
Cornego. Be not sad.

S.D. [*a dagger stuck in it*]] stet   4 *furies*] Bullen *query; furier* Q

Onælia.   But what's the best mirth in the world?
Cornego.   Marry this, to see much, say little, doe little, get little, spend little, and want nothing.
Onælia.   Oh but there is a mirth beyond all these:
This Picture has so vex'd me, I'me halfe mad,   30
To spite it therefore I'le sing any song
Thy selfe shalt tune; say then what mirth is best?
Cornego.   Why then, Madam, what I knocke out now is the very
Maribone of mirth, and this it is.
Onælia.   Say on.
Cornego.   The best mirth for a Lawyer is to have fooles to his
Clients: for Citizens, to have Noblemen pay their debts: for Taylors
to have store of Sattin brought in, for then how little soere their
houses are, they'll bee sure to have large yards: the best mirth for
bawds is to have fresh handsome whores, and for whores to have 40
rich guls come aboard their pinnaces, for then they are sure to build
Galley-Asses.
Onælia.   These to such soules are mirth, but to mine none:
Away.   *Exit* [Cornego].
              Enter Cardinall.

Cardinal.   Peace to you, Lady.
Onælia.   I will not sinne so much as hope for peace,
And tis a mocke ill suits your gravity.
Cardinal.   I come to knit the nerves of your lost strength,
To build your ruines up, to set you free
From this your voluntary banishment,   50
And give new being to your murdred fame.
Onælia.   What *Æsculapius* can doe this?
Cardinal.   The King —
Tis from the King I come.
Onælia.   A name I hate;
Oh I am deafe now to your Embassie.
Cardinal.   Heare what I speake.
Onælia.   Your language breath'd from him
Is deaths sad doome upon a wretch condemn'd.
Cardinal.   Is it such poyson?

Onælia.   Yes, and were you christall,
What the King fills you with, wud make you breake:
You should (my Lord) be like these robes you weare,
(Pure as the Dye) and like that reverend shape,   60
Nurse thoughts as full of honour, zeale, and purity;
You should be the Court-Diall, and direct
The King with constant motion, be ever beating
(Like to Clocke-Hammers) on his Iron heart
To make it sound cleere, and to feele remorse:
You should unlocke his soule, wake his dead conscience,
Which like a drowsie Centinell gives leave
For sinnes vast army to beleaguer him;
His ruines will be ask'd for at your hands.
Cardinal.   I have rais'd up a scaffolding to save   70
Both him and you from falling, doe but heare me.
Onælia.   Be dumbe for ever.
Cardinal.   Let your feares thus dye:
By all the sacred relliques of the Church,
And by my holy Orders, what I minister
Is even the spirit of health.
Onælia.   I'le drinke it downe
Into my soule at once.
Cardinal.   You shall.
Onælia.   But sweare.
Cardinal.   What Conjurations can more bind mine oath?
Onælia.   But did you sweare in earnest?
Cardinal.   Come, you trifle.
Onælia.   No marvell, for my hopes have bin so drown'd,
I still despaire: Say on.
Cardinal.   The King repents.   80
Onælia.   Pray that agen, my Lord.
Cardinal.   The King repents.
Onælia.   His wrongs to me?
Cardinal.   His wrongs to you: the sense
Of sinne has pierc'd his soule.
Onælia.   Blest penitence!

65 remorse:] Bullen; ~ ᴀ Q

Cardinal. 'Has turnd his eyes into his leprous bosome,
And like a King vowes execution
On all his traiterous passions.
Onælia.   God-like Iustice!
Cardinal. Intends in person presently to begge
Forgivenesse for his Acts of heaven and you.
Onælia. Heaven pardon him, I shall.
Cardinal.   Will marry you.
Onælia. Vmh! marry me? will he turne Bigamist?   90
When, when?
Cardinal.   Before the morrow Sunne hath rode
Halfe his dayes journey; will send home his Queene
As one that staines his bed, and can produce
Nothing but bastard Issue to his Crowne:
Why how now? lost in wonder and amazement?
Onælia. I am so stor'd with joy that I can now
Strongly weare out more yeares of misery
Then I have liv'd.

Enter King.

Cardinal.   You need not: here's the King.
King. Leave us.   *Exit Cardinal.*
Onælia.   With pardon, Sir, I will prevent you,
And charge upon you first.
King.   'Tis granted, doe: 100
But stay, what meane these Embleames of distresse?
My Picture so defac'd! oppos'd against
A holy Crosse! roome hung in blacke! and you
Drest like chiefe Mourner at a Funerall?
Onælia. Looke backe upon your guilt (deare Sir) and then
The cause that now seemes strange, explaines it selfe:
This, and the Image of my living wrongs
Is still confronted by me to beget
Griefe like my shame, whose length may outlive Time:
This Crosse, the object of my wounded soule,   110
To which I pray to keepe me from despaire;

That ever as the sight of one throwes up
Mountaines of sorrowes on my accursed head:
Turning to that, Mercy may checke despaire,
And bind my hands from wilfull violence.
King.   But who hath plaid the Tyrant with me thus?
And with such dangerous spite abus'd my picture?
Onælia.   The guilt of that layes claime, Sir, to your selfe,
For being by you ransack'd of all my fame,
Rob'd of mine honour, and deare chastity,   120
Made by your act the shame of all my house,
The hate of good men, and the scorne of bad,
The song of Broome-men, and the murdering vulgar,
And left alone to beare up all these ills
By you begun, my brest was fill'd with fire,
And wrap'd in just disdaine, and like a woman
On that dumb picture wreak'd I my passions.
King.   And wish'd it had beene I.
Onælia.   Pardon me, Sir,
My wrongs were great, and my revenge swell'd high.
King.   I will descend, and cease to be a King,   130
To leave my judging part, freely confessing
Thou canst not give thy wrongs too ill a name.
And here to make thy apprehension full,
And seat thy reason in a sound beleefe,
I vow to morrow (e're the rising Sunne
Begin his journey) with all Ceremonies
Due to the Church, to seale our nuptials,
To prive thy sonne with full consent of State,
Spaines heire Apparant, borne in wedlocke vowes.
Onælia.   And will you sweare to this?
King.   By this I sweare.   140
Onælia.   Oh you have sworne false oathes upon that booke.
King.   Why then by this.
Onælia.   Take heed you print it deeply:
How for your Concubine (Bride I cannot say)
She staines your bed with blacke Adultery:

121 your] Bullen; you Q

And though her fame maskes in a fairer shape
Then mine to the worlds eye, yet (King) you know
Mine honour is lesse strumpetted than hers,
How-ever butcher'd in opinion.

King.   This way for her, the Contract which thou hast,
By best advice of all our Cardinals   150
To day shall be enlarg'd, till it be made
Past all dissolving: then to our Counsell-Table
Shall she be call'd, that read aloud, she told
The Church commands her quicke returne for *Florence*,
With such a dower as *Spaine* received with her,
And that they will not hazard heavens dire curse
To yeeld to a match unlawfull, which shall taint
The issue of the King with Bastardy:
This done, in state Majesticke come you forth
(Our new crown'd Queene) in sight of all our Peeres: 160
Are you resolv'd?

Onælia.   To doubt of this were Treason,
Because the King has sworne it.

King.   And will keepe it:
Deliver up the Contract then, that I
May make this day end with thy misery.

Onælia.   Here, as the dearest Iewell of my fame,
Lock'd I this parchment from all viewing eyes,
This your Indenture held alone the life
Of my suppos'd dead honour; yet (behold)
Into your hands I redeliver it.
Oh keepe it, Sir, as you should keepe that vow,   170
To which (being sign'd by heaven) even Angels bowe.

King.   Tis in the Lions paw, and who dares snatch it?
Now to your Beads and Crucifix agen.

Onælia.   Defend me heaven!

King.   Pray there may come Embassadors from *France*,
Their followers are good Customers.

Onælia.   Save me from madnesse!

King.   'Twill raise the price, being the Kings Mistris.

Onælia.   You doe but counterfeit to mocke my joyes.

247

King.   Away bold strumpet.   180
Onælia.   Are there eyes in heaven to see this?
King.   Call and try, here's a whores curse,
    To fall in that beleefe which her sinnes nurse.   *Exit.*

Enter Cornego.

Cornego.   How now? what quarter of the Moone has she cut out
now? my Lord puts me into a wise office, to be a mad womans
keeper: why madam!
Onælia.   Ha! where is the King, thou slave?
Cornego.   Let go your hold, or I'le fall upon you as I am a man.
Onælia.   Thou treacherous caitiffe, where's the King?
Cornego.   Hee's gone, but not so farre gone as you are.   190
Onælia.   Cracke all in sunder, oh you Battlements,
    And grind me into powder.
Cornego.   What powder? come, what powder? when did you ever
    see a woman grinded into powder? I am sure some of your sex
    powder men and pepper 'em too.
Onælia.   Is there a vengeance yet lacking to my ruine?
    Let it fall, now let it fall upon me!
Cornego.   No, there has too much falne upon you already.
Onælia.   Thou villaine, leave thy hold, I'le follow him:
    Like a rais'd ghost I'le haunt him, breake his sleepe,   200
    Fright him as hee's embracing his new Leman,
    Till want of rest bids him runne mad and dye,
    For making oathes Bawds to his perjury.
Cornego.   Pray be more season'd, if he made any Bawds he did ill,
    for there is enough of that flye-blowne flesh already.
Onælia.   I'me now left naked quite:
                                        All's gone, all all.
Cornego.   No Madam, not all, for you cannot be rid of mee:
    Here comes your Vncle.

Enter Medina.

Onælia.   Attir'd in robes of vengeance, Are you, Vncle?
Medina.   More horrors yet?
Onælia.   Twas never full till now;   210
    And in this torrent all my hopes lye drown'd.

248

Medina.   Instruct me in the cause.
Onælia.   The King, the Contract! *Exit.*
Cornego.   There's cud enough for you to chew upon.   *Exit.*
Medina.   What's this? a riddle! how? the King, the Contract!
  The mischiefe I divine, which proving true,
  Shall kindle fires in *Spaine* to melt his Crowne
  Even from his head: here's the decree of Fate,
  A blacke deed must a blacke deed expiate.
                                                            Exit.

ACTUS SECUNDUS, Scæna Prima.

Enter Baltazar *slighted by Dons.*

Baltazar.   Thou god of good Apparell, what strange fellowes
  Are bound to doe thee honour! Mercers books
  Shew mens devotions to thee; heaven cannot hold
  A Saint so stately: Doe not my Dons know me
  Because I'me poore in clothes? stood my beaten Taylor
  Playting my rich hose, my silke stocking-man
  Drawing upon my Lordships Courtly calfe
  Payres of Imbroydred things, whose golden clockes
  Strike deeper to the faithfull shop-keepers heart
  Than into mine to pay him. — Had my Barbour   10
  Perfum'd my louzy thatch here, and poak'd out
  Me Tuskes more stiffe than are a Cats muschatoes,
  These pide-wing'd Butterflyes had knowne me then:
  Another flye-boat! save thee, Illustrious Don.

Enter Don Roderigo.

  Sir is the King at leisure to speake Spanish
  With a poore Souldier?
Roderigo.   No.   *Exit.*
Baltazar.   No, sirrah, you, no!
  You Don with th'oaker face, I wish to ha thee
  But on a Breach, stifling with smoke and fire,
  And for thy No, but whiffing Gunpowder

Out of an Iron pipe, I woo'd but aske thee   20
If thou wood'st on, and if thou didst cry No,
Thou shudst read Canon-Law, I'd make thee roare,
And weare cut-beaten-sattyn; I woo'd pay thee
Though thou payst not thy Mercer: meere Spanish Iennets.

Enter Cockadillio.

Signeor is the King at leisure?
Cockadillio.   To doe what?
Baltazar.   To heare a Souldier speake.
Cockadillio.   I am no eare-picker
  To sound his hearing that way.
Baltazar.   Are you of Court, Sir?
Cockadillio.   Yes, the Kings Barber.
Baltazar.   That's his eare-picker:
  Your name, I pray.
Cockadillio.   Don *Cockadilio*:
  If, Souldier, thou hast suits to begge at Court,   30
  I shall descend so low as to betray
  Thy paper to the hand Royall.
Baltazar.   I begge, you whorson muscod! my petition
  Is written on my bosome in red wounds.
Cockadillio.   I am no Barbar-Surgeon.   *Exit.*
Baltazar.   You yellow hammer; why, shaver:
  That such poore things as these, onely made up
  Of Taylors shreds and Merchants silken rags,
  And Pothecary drugs to lend their breath
  Sophisticated smells, when their ranke guts   40
  Stinke worse than cowards in the heate of battaile;
  Such whalebon'd-doublet-rascals, that owe more
  To Landresses and Sempsters for laced Linnen
  Then all their race from their great grand-father
  To this their reigne, in clothes were ever worth:
  These excrements of Silke-wormes! oh that such flyes
  Doe buzze about the beames of Majesty!
  Like earwigs, tickling a Kings yeelding eare
  With that Court-Organ (Flattery) when a souldier

Must not come neere the Court gates twenty score,   50
But stand for want of clothes, (tho he win Townes)
Amongst the Almesbasket-men! his best reward
Being scorn'd to be a fellow to the blacke gard:
Why shud a Souldier (being the worlds right arme)
Be cut thus by the left? (a Courtier?)
Is the world all Ruffe and Feather, and nothing else?
Shall I never see a Taylor give his coat
With a difference from a Gentleman?

Enter King, Alanzo, Carlo, Cockadilio.

King. My *Balta*ʒ*ar*!
Let us make haste to meet thee: how art thou alter'd?   60
Doe you not know him?
Alanʒo.   Yes, Sir, the brave Souldier
Employed against the Moores.
King.   Halfe turned Moore!
I'le honour thee, reach him a chaire, that Table,
And now *Æneas*-like let thine owne Trumpet
Sound forth thy battell with those slavish Moores.
Baltaʒar. My musicke is a Canon; a pitcht field my stage; Furies
the Actors, blood and vengeance the scæne; death the story;
a sword imbrued with blood, the pen that writes, and the Poet
a terrible buskind Tragicall fellow, with a wreath about his head
of burning match instead of Bayes.   70
King. On to the Battaile.
Baltaʒar. 'Tis here without bloud-shed: This our maine Battalia,
that the Van, this the Vaw, these the wings, here we fight, there
they flye, here they insconce, and here our sconces lay seventeene
Moones on the cold earth.
King. This satisfies mine eye, but now mine eare
Must have his musicke too; describe the battaile.
Baltaʒar. The Battaile? Am I come from doing to talking? The
hardest part for a Souldier to play is to prate well; our Tongues
are Fifes, Drums, Petronels, Muskets, Culverin and Canon, these 80

*73 Vaw] *stet* Q

251

are our Roarers; the Clockes which wee goe by, are our hands;
thus wee reckon tenne, our swords strike eleven, and when steele
targets of proofe clatter one against another, then 'tis noone, that's
the height and the heat of the day of battaile.

King. So.

Baltaȝar. To that heat we came, our Drums beat, Pikes were
shaken and shiver'd, swords and Targets clash'd and clatter'd,
Muskets ratled, Canons roar'd, men dyed groaning, brave laced
Ierkings and Feathers looked pale, totter'd rascals fought pell mell;
here fell a wing, there heads were tost like foot-balls; legs and 90
armes quarrell'd in the ayre, and yet lay quietly on the earth;
horses trampled upon heaps of Carkasses, Troopes of Carbines
tumbled wounded from their horses; we besiege Moores, and
famine us, Mutinies bluster and are calme; I vow'd not to doff
mine Armour, tho my flesh were frozen too't and turn'd into Iron,
nor to cut head nor beard till they yeelded; my hayres and oath
are of one length, for (with *Cæsar*) thus write I mine owne story,
Veni, vidi, vici.

King. A pitch'd field quickly fought: our hand is thine;
And 'cause thou shalt not murmure that thy bloud 100
Was lavish'd forth for an ingratefull man,
Demand what we can give thee, and 'tis thine.

Baltaȝar. Onely your love.

King. 'Tis thine, rise, Souldiers best accord
When wounds of wrongs are heal'd up by the sword.

Onælia beats at the doore.

Onælia. Let me come in, I'le kill that treacherous King,
The murderer of mine honour, let me come in.

King. What womans voyce is that?

Omnes.   *Medina's* Neece.

King. Bar out that fiend.

Onælia.   I'le teare him with my nayles,
Let me come in, let me come in, helpe, helpe me. 110

King. Keepe her from following me; a gard.

*109 teare] stet Q

Alanҙo.   They are ready, Sir.

King.   Let a quicke summons call our Lords together;
This disease kils me.

Baltaҙar.   Sir I would be private with you.

King.   Forbeare us, but see the dores well guarded.   *Exeunt.*

Baltaҙar.   Will you, Sir, promise to give mee freedome of speech?

King.   Yes I will, take it, speake any thing, 'tis pardon'd.

Baltaҙar.   You are a whoremaster; doe you send me to winne
townes for you abroad, and you lose a kingdome at home?   120

King.   What kingdome?

Baltaҙar.   The fayrest in the world, the kingdome of your fame,
your honour.

King.   Wherein?

Baltaҙar.   I'le be plaine with you; much mischiefe is done by the
mouth of a Canon, but the fire begins at a little touch-hole; you
heard what Nightingale sung to you even now.

King.   Ha, ha, ha.

Baltaҙar.   Angels err'd but once and fell, but you, Sir, spit in
heavens face every minute, and laugh at it: laugh still; follow your   130
courses; doe; let your vices runne like your Kennels of hounds
yelping after you, till they plucke downe the fayrest head in the
heard, everlasting blisse.

King.   Any more?

Baltaҙar.   Take sinne as the English snuffe Tobacco, and scorn-
fully blow the smoake in the eyes of heaven, the vapour flyes up
in clowds of bravery; but when 'tis out, the coale is blacke (your
conscience,) and the pipe stinkes; a sea of Rose-water cannot
sweeten your corrupted bosome.

King.   Nay, spit thy venome.   140

Baltaҙar.   'Tis *Aqua Cœlestis,* no venome; for when you shall
claspe up those two books, never to be open'd againe, when by
letting fall that Anchor, which can never more bee weighed up,
your mortall Navigation ends: then there's no playing at spurne-
point with thunderbolts. A Vintner then for unconscionable
reckoning, or a Taylor for unmeasurable *Items* shall not answer
in halfe that feare you must.

King.   No more.

Baltaʒar. I will follow Truth at the heeles, tho her foot beat
my gums in peeces. 150
King. The Barber that drawes out a Lions tooth
Curseth his Trade; and so shalt thou.
Baltaʒar. I care not.
King. Because you have beaten a few base-borne Moores,
Me think'st thou to chastise? what's past I pardon,
Because I made the key to unlocke thy railing;
But if thou dar'st once more be so untun'd,
I'le send thee to the Gallies: who are without there,
How now?

Enter Lords drawne.

Omnes. In danger, Sir? 160
King. Yes, yes, I am; but 'tis no point of weapon
Can rescue me; goe presently and summon
All our chiefe Grandoes, Cardinals, and Lords
Of *Spaine* to meet in Counsell instantly:
We call'd you forth to execute a businesse
Of another straine, — but 'tis no matter now;
Thou dyest, when next thou furrowest up our brow.
Baltaʒar. So: dye! *Exit.*

Enter Cardinall, Roderigo, Alba, Dænia, Valasco.

King. I find my Scepter shaken by enchantments
Charactred in this parchment, which to unloose, 170
I'le practise onely counter-charmes of fire,
And blow the spells of lightning into smoake:
Fetch burning Tapers. *Exeunt [Servants and return].*
Cardinal. Give me Audience, Sir;
My apprehension opens me a way
To a close fatall mischiefe, worse then this
You strive to murder; O this Act of yours
Alone shall give your dangers life, which else
Can never grow to height; doe, Sir, but read
A booke here claspt up, which too late you open'd,
Now blotted by you with foule marginall notes. 180

254

King.   Art franticke?
Cardinal.   You are so, Sir.
King.   If I be,
  Then here's my first mad fit.
Cardinal.   For Honours sake,
  For love you beare to conscience —
King.   Reach the flames:
  Grandoes and Lords of *Spaine* be witnesse all
  What here I cancell; read, doe you know this bond?
Omnes.   Our hands are too't.
Dænia.   'Tis your confirmed Contract
  With my sad kinswoman: but wherefore, Sir,
  Now is your rage on fire, in such a presence
  To have it mourne in Ashes?
King.   Marquesse *Dænia*,
  Wee'll lend That tongue, when this no more can speake.   190
Cardinal.   Deare Sir!
King.   I am deafe,
  Playd the full consort of the Spheares unto me
  Vpon their lowdest strings. — so burne that witch
  Who would dry up the tree of all *Spaines* Glories,
  But that I purge her sorceries by fire: [*Burnes contract.*]
  Troy lyes in Cinders; let your Oracles
  Now laugh at me if I have beene deceiv'd
  By their ridiculous riddles: why (good father)
  (Now you may freely chide) why was your zeale   200
  Ready to burst in showres to quench our fury?
Cardinal.   Fury indeed, you give it proper name:
  What have you done? clos'd up a festering wound
  Which rots the heart: like a bad Surgeon,
  Labouring to plucke out from your eye a moate,
  You thrust the eye cleane out.
King.   Th'art mad *ex tempore*:
  What eye? which is that wound?
Cardinal.   That Scrowle, which now
  You make the blacke Indenture of your lust,
  Altho eat up in flames, is printed here,

In me, in him, in these, in all that saw it, 210
In all that ever did but heare 'twas yours:
That scold of the whole world (Fame) will anon
Raile with her thousand tongues at this poore shift
Which gives your sinne a flame greater than that
You lent the paper; you to quench a wild fire,
Cast oyle upon it.
King.   Oyle to blood shall turne,
I'le lose a limbe before the heart shall mourne.   *Exeunt.*

Manent Dænia, Alba.

Dænia.   Hee's mad with rage or joy.
Alba.   With both; with rage
To see his follies check'd, with fruitlesse joy
Because he hopes his Contract is cut off   220
Which Divine Iustice more exemplifies.

Enter Medina.

Medina.   Where's the King?
Dænia.   Wrapt up in clouds of lightning
Medina.   What has he done? saw you the Contract torne?
As I did heare a minion sweare he threatned.
Alba.   He tore it not, but burnt it.
Medina.   Openly!
Dænia.   And heaven with us to witnesse.
Medina.   Well, that fire
Will prove a catching flame to burne his kingdome.
Alba.   Meet and consult.
Medina.   No more, trust not the ayre
With our projections, let us all revenge
Wrongs done to our most noble kinswoman;   230
Action is honours language, swords are tongues,
Which both speake best, and best do right our wrongs.
                                        Exeunt.

232 *Exeunt*] Bullen; *Exit* Q

[ACT II, Scene ii]

Enter Onælia *one way,* Cornego *another.*

Cornego.   Madam, theres a beare without to speak with you.
Onælia.   A Beare.
Cornego.   Its a Man all hairye, and thats as bad.
Onælia.   Who ist?
Cornego.   Tis one Master Captaine *Baltazar.*
Onælia.   I doe not know that *Baltazar.*
Cornego.   He desires to see you: and if you love a water-spaniel
before he be shorne, see him.
Onælia.   Let him come in.

Enter Baltazar.

Cornego.   Hist; a ducke, a ducke; there she is, Sir.   10
Baltazar.   A Souldiers good wish blesse you Lady.
Onælia.   Good wishes are most welcome (Sir) to me,
So many bad ones blast me.
Baltazar.   Doe you not know me?
Onælia.   I scarce know my selfe.
Baltazar.   I ha beene at Tennis, Madam, with the King: I gave
him fifteene and all his faults, which is much, and now I come to
tosse a ball with you.
Onælia.   I am bandyed too much up and downe already.
Cornego.   Yes, shee has beene strucke under line, master Souldier.   20
Baltazar.   I conceit you, dare you trust your selfe alone with me?
Onælia.   I have beene laden with such weights of wrong,
That heavier cannot presse me: hence *Cornego.*
Cornego.   Hence *Cornego?* stay Captaine? when man and woman
are put together, some egge of villany is sure to be sate upon.
                                                        Exit.
Baltazar.   What would you say to him should kill this man
That hath you so dishonoured?
Onælia.   Oh I woo'd crowne him
With thanks, praise, gold, and tender of my life.

Baltazar. Shall I bee that Germane Fencer, and beat all the
knocking boyes before me? shall I kill him? 30

Onælia. There's musick in the tongue that dares but speak it.

Baltazar. That Fiddle then is in me, this arme can doo't, by
ponyard, poyson, or pistoll: but shall I doo't indeed?

Onælia. One step to humane blisse is sweet revenge.

Baltazar. Stay; what made you love him?

Onælia. His most goodly shape
Marryed to royall vertues of his mind.

Baltazar. Yet now you would divorce all that goodnesse; and
why? For a little lechery of revenge? it's a lye: the Burre that
stickes in your throat is a throane; let him out of his messe of 40
kingdomes cut out but one, and lay *Sicilia, Arragon, Naples,* or
any else upon your trencher, and you'll prayse Bastard for the
sweetest wine in the world, and call for another quart of it: 'Tis
not because the man has left you, but because you are not the
woman you would be, that mads you: A shee-cuckold is an un-
tameable monster.

Onælia. Monster of men thou art; thou bloudy villaine,
Traytor to him who never injur'd thee;
Dost thou professe Armes? and art bound in honour
To stand up like a brazen wall to guard 50
Thy King and Country, and wood'st thou ruine both?

Baltazar. You spurre me on too't.

Onælia. True;
Worse am I then the horrid'st fiend in hell
To murder him whom once I lou'd too well:
For tho I could runne mad, and teare my haire,
And kill that godlesse man that turn'd me vile,
Though I am cheated by a perjurous Prince
Who has done wickednesse, at which even heaven
Shakes when the Sunne beholds it, O yet I'de rather 60
Ten thousand poyson'd ponyards stab'd my brest
Than one should touch his: bloudy slave! I'le play
My selfe the Hangman, and will Butcher thee
If thou but prick'st his finger.

Baltazar. Saist thou me so! give me thy goll, thou art a noble

258

girle; I did play the Devils part, and roare in a feigned voyce, but
I am the honestest Devill that ever spet fire: I would not drinke
that infernall draught of a Kings blood, to goe reeling to damnation,
for the weight of the world in Diamonds.

Onælia.   Art thou not counterfeit?   70

Baltazar.   Now by my skarres I am not.

Onælia.   I'le call thee honest Souldier then, and woo thee
To be an often Visitant.

Baltazar.   Your servant;
Yet must I be a stone upon a hill,
For tho I doe no good, I'le not lye still.

Exeunt.

ACTUS TERTIUS. Scæna Prima.

Enter Malateste *and the Queene.*

Malateste.   When first you came from *Florence*, wud the world
Had with an universal dire ecclipse
Bin ouerwhelm'd, no more to gaze on day,
That you to *Spaine* had never found the way,
Here to be lost for ever.

Queen.   We from one Climate
Drew suspiration: as thou then hast eyes
To read my wrongs, so be thy head an Engine
To raise up ponderous mischiefe to the height,
And then thy hands the Executioners:
A true Italian Spirit is a ball   10
Of Wild-fire, hurting most when it seemes spent;
Great ships on small rockes beating oft, are rent;
And so let *Spaine* by us: but (*Malateste*)
Why from the Presence did you single me
Into this Gallery?

Malateste.   To shew you, Madam,
The picture of your selfe, but so defac'd,
And mangled by proud Spanyards, it woo'd whet

A sword to arme the poorest Florentine
In your just wrongs.
Queen. As how? let's see that picture.
Malateste. Here 'tis then: Time is not scarce foure dayes old,   20
Since I, and certaine Dons (sharp-witted fellowes,
And of good ranke) were with two Iesuits
(Grave profound Schollers) in deepe argument
Of various propositions; at the last,
Question was mov'd touching your marriage,
And the Kings precontract.
Queen. So; and what followed?
Malateste. Whether it were a question mov'd by chance,
Or spitefully of purpose (I being there,
And your owne Country-man) I cannot tell,
But when much tossing   30
Had bandyed both the King and you, as pleas'd
Those that tooke up the Rackets; in conclusion,
The Father Iesuits (to whose subtile Musicke
Every eare there was tyed) stood with their lives
In stiffe defence of this opinion —
Oh pardon me if I must speake their language.
Queen. Say on.
Malateste. That the most Catholike King in marrying you,
Keepes you but as his whore.
Queen. Are we their Theames?
Malateste. And that *Medina's* Neece (*Onælia*)   40
Is his true wife: her bastard sonne they said
(The King being dead) should claim and weare the Crown;
And whatsoever children you shall beare,
To be but bastards in the highest degree,
As being begotten in Adultery.
Queen. We will not grieve at this, but with hot vengeance
Beat downe this armed mischiefe: *Malateste*!
What whirlwinds can we raise to blow this storme
Backe in their faces who thus shoot at me?
Malateste. If I were fit to be your Counsellor,   50
Thus would I speake: Feigne that you are with childe;

260

The mother of the Maids, and some worne Ladies,
Who oft have guilty beene to court great bellies,
May, tho it be not so, get you with childe
With swearing that 'tis true.
Queen.   Say 'tis beleev'd,
  Or that it so doth prove?
Malateste.   The joy thereof,
  Together with these earth-quakes, which will shake
  All *Spaine*, if they their Prince doe dis-inherit,
  So borne, of such a Queene; being onely daughter
  To such a brave spirit as the Duke of *Florence*,   60
  All this buzz'd into the King, he cannot chuse
  But charge that all the Bels in *Spaine* eccho up
  This Joy to heaven; that Bone-fires change the night
  To a high Noone, with beames of sparkling flames;
  And that in Churches, Organs (charm'd with prayers)
  Speake lowd for your most safe delivery.
Queen.   What fruits grow out of these?
Malateste.   These; you must sticke
  (As here and there spring weeds in banks of flowers)
  Spyes amongst the people, who shall lay their eares
  To every mouth, and steale to you their whisperings.   70
Queen.   So.
Malateste.   'Tis a plummet to sound Spanish hearts
  How deeply they are yours: besides, a ghesse
  Is hereby made of any faction
  That shall combine against you; which the King seeing,
  If then he will not rouze him like a Dragon
  To guard his golden fleece, and rid his Harlot
  And her base bastard hence, either by death,
  Or in some traps of state, insnare them both,
  Let his owne ruines crush him.
Queen.   This goes to tryall:
  Be thou my Magicke booke, which reading o're   80
  Their counterspels wee'll breake; or if the King

74 combine] Bullen; combide Q

Will not by strong hand fix me in his Throne,
But that I must be held *Spaines* blazing Starre,
Be it an ominous charme to call up warre.

Exeunt.

[ACT III, Scene ii]

Enter, Cornego, Onælia.

Cornego.   Here's a parcell of mans flesh has beene hanging up and
downe all this morning to speake with you.
Onælia.   Is't not some executioner?
Cornego.   I see nothing about him to hang in but's garters.
Onælia.   Sent from the King to warne me of my death:
I prethe bid him welcome.
Cornego.   He sayes he is a Poet.
Onælia.   Then bid him better welcome:
Belike he's come to write my Epitaph,
Some scurvy thing I warrant; welcome Sir.   10

Enter Poet

Poet.   Madam, my love presents this booke unto you.
Onælia.   To me? I am not worthy of a line,
Vnlesse at that line hang some hooke to choake me:
To the Most honour'd Lady — *Onælia.*   *Reads.*
Fellow thou lyest, I'me most dishonoured:
Thou shouldst have writ to the most wronged Lady.
The Title of this booke is not to me,
I teare it therefore as mine Honour's torne.
Cornego.   Your Verses are lam'd in some of their feet, Master Poet.
Onælia.   What does it treat of?
Poet.   Of the sollemne Triumphs   20
Set forth at Coronation of the Queene
Onælia.   Hissing (the Poets whirle-wind) blast thy lines:
Com'st thou to mocke my Tortures with her Triumphs?
Poet.   'Las Madam!
Onælia.   When her funerals are past,

Crowne thou a Dedication to my joyes,
And thou shalt sweare each line a golden verse:
Cornego, burne this Idoll.
Cornego.   Your booke shall come to light, Sir.   *Exit.*
Onælia.   I have read legends of disastrous Dames;
Will none set pen to paper for poore me?   30
Canst write a bitter Satyre? brainlesse people
Doe call 'em Libels: dar'st thou write a Libell?
Poet.   I dare mix gall and poyson with my Inke.
Onælia.   Doe it then for me.
Poet.   And every line must be
A whip to draw blood.
Onælia.   Better.
Poet.   And to dare
The stab from him it touches: he that writes
Such Libels (as you call 'em) must lanch wide
The sores of mens corruptions, and even search
To'th quicke for dead flesh, or for rotten cores:
A Poets Inke can better cure some sores   40
Then Surgeons Balsum.
Onælia.   Vndertake that Cure,
And Crowne thy verse with Bayes.
Poet.   Madam I'le doo't:
But I must haue the parties Character.
Onælia.   The King.
Poet.   I doe not love to plucke the quils
With which I make pens, out of a Lions claw:
The King! shoo'd I be bitter 'gainst the King,
I shall have scurvy ballads made of me,
Sung to the Hanging Tune. I dare not, Madam.
Onælia.   This basenesse followes your profession:
You are like common Beadles, apt to lash   50
Almost to death poore wretches not worth striking,
But fawne with slavish flattery on damn'd vices,
So great men act them: you clap hands at those,
Where the true Poet indeed doth scorne to guild
A gawdy Tombe with glory of his Verse,

Which coffins stinking Carrion: no, his lines
Are free as his Invention; no base feare
Can shake his penne to Temporize even with Kings,
The blacker are their crimes, he lowder sings.
Goe, goe, thou canst not write: 'tis but my calling   60
The Muses helpe, that I may be inspir'd:
Cannot a woman be a Poet, Sir?
Poet.   Yes, Madam, best of all; for Poesie
Is but a feigning, feigning is to lye,
And women practise lying more than men.
Onælia.   Nay, but if I shoo'd write, I woo'd tell truth:
How might I reach a lofty straine?
Poet.   Thus, Madam:
Bookes, Musicke, Wine, brave Company, and good Cheere,
Make Poets to soare high, and sing most cleare.
Onælia.   Are they borne Poets?
Poet.   Yes.
Onælia.   Dye they?
Poet.   Oh never dye. 70
Onælia.   My misery is then a Poet sure,
For Time has given it an Eternity:
What sorts of Poets are there?
Poet.   Two sorts, Lady:
The great Poets, and the small Poets.
Onælia.   Great and small!
Which doe you call the great? the fat ones?
Poet.   No:
But such as have great heads, which emptied forth,
Fill all the world with wonder at their lines;
Fellowes which swell bigge with the wind of praise:
The small ones are but shrimpes of Poesie.
Onælia.   Which in the kingdome now is the best Poet?   80
Poet.   Emulation.
Onælia.   Which the next?
Poet.   Necessity.
Onælia.   And which the worst?
Poet.   Selfe-love.

Onælia.   Say I turne Poet, what should I get?
Poet.   Opinion.
Onælia.   'Las I have got too much of that already;
  Opinion is my Evidence, Iudge, and Iury;
  Mine owne guilt, and opinion, now condemne me;   90
  I'le therefore be no Poet; no, nor make
  Ten Muses of your nine; I sweare for this;
  Verses, tho freely borne, like slaves are sold,
  I Crowne thy lines with Bayes, thy love with gold:
  So fare thou well.
Poet.   Our pen shall honour you.   *Exit.*

Enter Cornego.

Cornego.   The Poets booke, Madam, has got the Inflammation of
  the Livor, it dyed of a burning Feaver.
Onælia.   What shall I doe, *Cornego?* for this Poet
  Has fill'd me with a fury: I could write
  Strange Satyrs now against Adulterers,   100
  And Marriage-breakers.
Cornego.   I beleeve you, Madam; — but here comes your Vncle.

Enter Medina, Alanzo, Carlo, Alba, Sebastian, Dænia.

Medina.   Where's our Neece?
  Turne your braines round, and recollect your spirits,
  And see your Noble friends and kinsmen ready
  To pay revenge his due.
Onælia.   That word Revenge
  Startles my sleepy Soule, now throughly wakend
  By the fresh Object of my haplesse childe,
  Whose wrongs reach beyond mine.
Sebastian.   How doth my sweet mother?   110
Onælia.   How doth my prettiest boy?
Alanzo.   Wrongs, like great whirlewinds,
  Shake highest Battlements; few for heaven woo'd care,
  Shoo'd they be ever happy: they are halfe gods
  Who both in good dayes, and good fortune share.
Onælia.   I have no part in either.

Carlo.   You shall in both,
Can Swords but cut the way.

Onælia. I care not much, so you but gently strike him,
And that my Child escape the lightening.

Medina. For that our Nerves are knit; is there not here
A promising face of manly princely vertues,   120
And shall so sweet a plant be rooted out
By him that ought to fix it fast i'th ground?
Sebastian, what will you doe to him
That hurts your mother?

Sebastian. The King my father shall kill him I trow.

Dænia. But, sweet Coozen, the King loves not your mother.

Sebastian. I'le make him love her when I am a King.

Medina. La you, there's in him a Kings heart already:
As therefore we before together vow'd,
Lay all your warlike hands upon my Sword,   130
And sweare.

Sebastian. Will you sweare to kill me, Vncle?

Medina. Oh not for twenty worlds.

Sebastian. Nay then draw and spare not, for I love fighting.

Medina. Stand in the midst (sweet Cooz) we are your guard;
These Hammers shall for thee beat out a Crowne
If all hit right; sweare therefore (Noble friends)
By your high bloods, by true Nobility,
By what you owe Religion, owe to your Country,
Owe to the raising your posterity,   140
By love you beare to vertue, and to Armes,
(The shield of Innocence) sweare not to sheath
Your Swords, when once drawne forth.

Onælia.   Oh not to kill him
For twenty thousand worlds.

Medina.   (Will you be quiet?)
Your Swords when once drawne forth, till they ha forc'd
Yon godlesse, perjurous, perfidious man, —

Onælia. Pray raile not at him so.

Medina.   Art mad? y'are idle: —
Till they ha forc'd him

266

To cancell his late lawlesse bond he seal'd
At the high Altar to his Florentine Strumpet,   150
And in his bed lay this his troth-plight wife.
Onælia.   I, I, that's well; pray sweare.
Omnes.   To this we sweare.
Sebastian.   Vncle, I sweare too.
Medina.   Our forces let's unite, be bold and secret,
And Lion-like with open eyes let's sleepe,
Streames smooth and slowly running, are most deepe.

                                             Exeunt.

[ACT III, Scene iii]

Enter King, Queene, Malateste, [Roderigo,] Valasco, Lopez.

King.   The Presence doore be guarded; let none enter
On forfeit of your lives, without our knowledge:
Oh you are false Physitians all unto me,
You bring me poyson, but no Antidotes.
Queen.   Your selfe that poyson brewes.
King.   Prethe no more.
Queen.   I will, I must speake more.
King.   Thunder aloud.
Queen.   My child, yet newly quickned in my wombe,
Is blasted with the fires of Bastardy.
King.   Who! who dares once but thinke so in his dreame?
Malateste.   *Medina's* faction preach'd it openly.   10
King.   Be curst he and his Faction: oh how I labour
For these preventions! but so crosse is Fate,
My ills are ne're hid from me, but their Cures:
What's to be done?
Queen.   That which being left undone,
Your life lyes at the stake: let 'em be breathlesse
Both brat and mother.
King.   Ha!
Malateste.   She playes true Musicke, Sir:
The mischiefes you are drench'd in are so full,

You need not feare to adde to 'em; since now
No way is left to guard thy rest secure,
But by a meanes like this.

Lopez.   All *Spaine* rings forth   20
Medina's name, and his Confederates.

Roderigo.   All his Allyes and friends rush into troopes
Like raging Torrents.

Valasco.   And lowd Trumpet forth
Your perjuries: seducing the wild people,
And with rebellious faces threatning all.

King.   I shall be massacred in this their spleene,
E're I have time to guard my selfe; I feele
The fire already falling: where's our guard?

Malateste.   Planted at Garden gate, with a strict charge
That none shall enter but by your command.   30

King.   Let 'em be doubled: I am full of thoughts,
A thousand wheeles tosse my incertaine feares,
There is a storme in my hot boyling braines,
Which rises without wind, a horrid one:
What clamor's that?

Queen.   Some treason: guard the King.

Enter Baltazar *drawne; one of the Guard fals.*

Baltazar.   Not in?

Malateste.   One of your guard's slaine, keepe off the murderer.

Baltazar.   I am none, Sir.

Valasco.   There's a man drop'd downe by thee.

King.   Thou desperate fellow, thus presse in upon us!   40
Is murder all the story we shall read?
What King can stand, when thus his Subjects bleed?
What has thou done?

Baltazar.   No hurt.

King.   Plaid even the Wolfe,
And from a fold committed to my charge,
Stolne and devour'd one of the flocke.

Baltazar.   Y'ave sheepe enow for all that, Sir; I have kill'd none

tho; or if I have, mine owne blood shed in your quarrels, may
begge my pardon; my businesse was in haste to you.   50
King.   I woo'd not have thy sinne scoar'd on my head
For all the Indian Treasury: I prethe tell me,
Suppose thou hadst our pardon, O can that cure
Thy wounded conscience, can there my pardon helpe thee?
Yet having deserv'd well both of *Spaine* and us,
We will not pay thy worth with losse of life,
But banish thee for ever.
Baltazar.   For a Groomes death?
King.   No more: we banish thee our Court and kingdome:
A King that fosters men so dipt in blood,   60
May be call'd mercifull, but never good:
Be gone upon thy life.
Baltazar.   Well: farewell.   *Exit.*
Valasco.   The fellow is not dead but wounded, Sir.
Queen.   After him, *Malateste*; in our lodging
Stay that rough fellow, hee's the man shall doo't:
Haste, or my hopes are lost.   *Exit* Malateste.
                    Why are you sad, Sir?
King.   For thee, *Paulina*, swell my troubled thoughts,
Like billowes beaten by two warring winds.
Queen.   Be you but rul'd by me, I'le make a calme   70
Smooth as the brest of heaven.
King.   Instruct me how.
Queen.   You (as your fortunes tye you) are inclin'd
To have the blow given.
King.   Where's the Instrument?
Queen.   'Tis found in *Baltazar.*
King.   Hee's banish'd.
Queen.   True,
But staid by me for this.
King.   His spirit is hot
And rugged, but so honest, that his soule
Will ne're turne devill to doe it.
Queen.   Put it to tryall:

48 mine] Bullen; thine Q

269

Retire a little, hither I'le send for him,
Offer repeale and favours if he doe it;
But if deny, you have no finger in't, 80
And then his doome of banishment stands good.
King. Be happy in thy workings; I obey. *Exit.*
Queen. Stay *Lopez.*
Lopez. Madam.
Queen. Step to our Lodging (*Lopez*)
And instantly bid *Malateste* bring
The banish'd *Baltazar* to us.
Lopez. I shall. *Exit.*
Queen. Thrive my blacke plots, the mischiefes I have set
Must not so dye; Ills must new Ills beget.

Enter Malateste *and* Baltazar.

Baltazar. Now! what hot poyson'd Custard must I put my
Spoone into now?
Queen. None, for mine honour now is thy protection. 90
Malateste. Which, Noble Souldier, shee will pawne for thee,
But never forfeit.
Baltazar. 'Tis a faire gage, keepe it.
Queen. Oh *Baltazar*! I am thy friend, and mark'd thee;
When the King sentenc'd thee to banishment
Fire sparkled from thine eyes of rage and griefe;
Rage to be doom'd so for a Groome so base,
And griefe to lose thy Country: thou hast kill'd none,
The Milke-sop is but wounded, thou art not banish'd.
Baltazar. If I were, I lose nothing, I can make any Country mine: 100
I have a private Coat for Italian Steeletto's, I can be treacherous
with the Wallowne, drunke with the Dutch, a Chimney-sweeper
with the Irish, a Gentleman with the Welsh, and turne arrant
theefe with the English, what then is my Country to me?
Queen. The King (who rap'd with fury) banish'd thee,
Shall give thee favours, yeeld but to destroy
What him distempers.
Baltazar. So: And what's the dish I must dresse?

98 Country] Bullen: County Q

Queen.   Onely the cutting off a paire of lives.
Baltaȝar.   I love no Red-wine healths.   110
Malateste.   The King commands it, you are but Executioner.
Baltaȝar.   The Hang-man? An office that will hold so long as
hempe lasts, why doe not you begge the office, Sir?
Queen.   Thy victories in field did never crowne thee
As this one Act shall.
Baltaȝar.   Prove but that, 'tis done.
Queen.   Follow him close, hee's yeelding.
Malateste.   Thou shalt be call'd thy Countries Patriot,
For quenching out a fire now newly kindling
In factious bosomes, and shalt thereby save   120
More Noble Spanyards lives, than thou slew'st Moores.
Queen.   Art thou not yet converted?
Baltaȝar.   No point.
Queen.   Read me then:
Medina's Neece (by a Contract from the King)
Layes clayme to all that's mine, my Crowne, my bed;
A sonne she has by him must fill the Throne,
If her great faction can but worke that wonder:
Now heare me —
Baltaȝar.   I doe with gaping eares.   130
Queen.   I swell with hopefull issue to the King.
Baltaȝar.   A brave Don call you mother.
Malateste.   Of this danger the feare afflicts the King.
Baltaȝar.   Cannot much blame him.
Queen.   If therefore by the riddance of this Dame —
Baltaȝar.   Riddance? oh! the meaning on't is murder.
Malateste.   Stab her, or so, that's all.
Queen.   That *Spaine* be free from frights, the King from feares,
And I, now held his Infamy, be called Queene,
The Treasure of the kingdome shall lye open   140
To pay thy Noble darings.
Baltaȝar.   Come, I'le doo't, provided I heare *Jove* call to me, tho
he rores; I must have the Kings hand to this warrant, else I dare
not serve it upon my Conscience.
Queen.   Be firme then; behold the King is come.

271

Enter King.

Baltaʒar. Acquaint him.

Queen. I found the mettall hard, but with oft beating
Hee's now so softned, he shall take impression
From any seale you give him.

King.   *Baltaʒar,*   150
Come hither, listen; whatsoe're our Queene
Has importun'd thee to touching *Onælia,*
Neece to the Constable, and her young sonne,
My voyce shall second it, and signe her promise.

Baltaʒar. Their riddance?

King.   That.

Baltaʒar.   What way? by poyson?

King.   So.

Baltaʒar. Starving? or strangling, stabbing, smothering?

Queen.   Good.

King. Any way so 'tis done.

Baltaʒar.   But I will have, Sir,
This under your owne hand, that you desire it,
You plot it, set me on too't.

King.   Penne, Inke, and paper.

Baltaʒar. And then as large a pardon as law and wit
Can engrosse for me.

King.   Thou shalt ha my pardon.   160

Baltaʒar. A word more, Sir, pray will you tell me one thing?

King. Yes any thing, deare *Baltaʒar.*

Baltaʒar.   Suppose
I have your strongest pardon, can that cure
My wounded Conscience? can there your pardon help me?
You not onely knocke the Ewe a'th head, but cut the Innocent
Lambes throat too, yet you are no Butcher.

Queen. Is this thy promis'd yeelding to an Act
So wholesome for thy Country?

King.   Chide him not.

Baltaʒar. I woo'd not have this sinne scor'd on my head
For all the Indæan Treasury.

King.   That song no more: 170
Doe this and I will make thee a great man.
Baltazar. Is there no farther tricke in't, but my blow, your purse,
and my pardon?
Malateste. No nets upon my life to entrap thee.
Baltazar. Then trust me: these knuckles worke it.
King. Farewell, be confident and sudden.
Baltazar.   Yes:
Subjects may stumble, when Kings walke astray;
Thine Acts shall be a new Apocrypha.
                                        Exeunt.

ACTUS QUARTUS. Scæna Prima.

Enter Medina, Alba, [Carlo,] *and* Dænia, *met by* Baltazar
with a Ponyard and a Pistoll.

Baltazar. You meet a *Hydra*; see, if one head failes
Another with a sulphurous beake stands yawning.
Medina. What hath rais'd up this Devill?
Baltazar. A great mans vices, that can raise all hell.
What woo'd you call that man, who under-saile,
In a most goodly ship, wherein hee ventures
His life, fortunes, and honours, yet in a fury
Should hew the Mast downe, cast Sayles over-boord,
Fire all the Tacklings, and to crowne this madnesse,
Shoo'd blow up all the Deckes, burne th'oaken ribbes,   10
And in that Combat 'twixt two Elements
Leape desperately, and drowne himselfe i'th Seas,
What were so brave a fellow?
Omnes.   A brave blacke villaine.
Baltazar. That's I; all that brave blacke villaine dwels in me,
If I be that blacke villaine; but I am not,
A Nobler Character prints out my brow,
Which you may thus read, I was banish'd *Spaine*
For emptying a Court-Hogshead, but repeal'd,
So I woo'd (e're my reeking Iron was cold)

Promise to give it a deepe crimson dye   20
In — none heare, — stay — no, none heare.
Medina.   Whom then?
Baltazar.   Basely to stab a woman, your wrong'd Neece,
And her most innocent sonne *Sebastian.*
Alba.   The Boare now foames with whetting.
Dænia.   What has blunted
Thy weapons point at these?
Baltazar.   My honesty;
A signe at which few dwell: (pure honesty!)
I am a vassaile to *Medina's* house,
He taught me first the A, B, C, of warre:
E're I was Truncheon-high, I had the stile
Of beardlesse Captaine, writing then but boy,   30
And shall I now turne slave to him that fed me
With Cannon-bullets! and taught me, Estridge-like,
To digest Iron and Steele! no: yet I yeelded
With willow-bendings to commanding breaths.
Medina.   Of whom?
Baltazar.   Of King and Queene: with supple Hams,
And an ill-boading looke, I vow'd to doo't:
Yet, lest some choake-peare of State-policy
Shoo'd stop my throat, and spoyle my drinking-pipe,
See (like his cloake) I hung at the Kings elbow,
Till I had got his hand to signe my life.   40
Dænia.   Shall we see this and sleepe?
Alba.   No, whilst these wake.
Medina.   'Tis the Kings hand.
Baltazar.   Thinke you me a quoyner?
Medina.   No, no,
Thou art thy selfe still, Noble *Baltazar.*
I ever knew thee honest, and the marke
Stands still upon thy fore-head.
Baltazar.   Else flea the skin off.
Medina.   I ever knew thee valiant, and to scorne
All acts of baseness: I have seene this man
Write in the field such stories with his sword,

274

That our best Chiefetaines swore there was in him
As 'twere a new Philosophy of fighting,   50
His deeds were so Puntillious: In one battell,
When death so nearely mist my ribs, he strucke
Three horses stone-dead under me: This man,
Three times that day (even through the jawes of danger)
Redeem'd me up, and (I shall print it ever)
Stood o're my body with *Collossus* thighes,
Whilst all the Thunder-bolts which warre could throw,
Fell on his head: And *Baltazar*, thou canst not
Be now but honest still, and valiant still,
Not to kill boyes and women.   60
Baltazar.   My byter here, eats no such meat.
Medina.   Goe fetch the mark'd-out Lambe for slaughter hither,
Good fellow-souldier ayd him, — and stay — marke,
Give this false fire to the beleeving King,
That the child's sent to heaven, but that the mother
Stands rock'd so strong with friends, ten thousand billowes
Cannot once shake her.
Baltazar.   This I'le doe.
Medina.   Away:
Yet one word more; your Counsell, Noble friends;
Harke *Baltazar*, because nor eyes nor tongues,
Shall by lowd Larums, that the poore boy liues,   70
Question thy false report, the child shall closely
Mantled in darknesse, forthwith be conveyed
To the Monastery of Saint *Paul.*
Omnes.   Good.
Medina.   Dispatch then, be quicke.
Baltazar.   As Lightening.   *Exit.*
Alba.   This fellow is some Angell drop'd from heauen
To preserve Innocence.
Medina.   He is a wheele
Of swift and turbulent motion; I have trusted him,
Yet will not hang on him too many plummets,
Lest with a headlong Gyre he ruines all:

79 Gyre] Bullen *query*; Cyre Q

In these State-consternations, when a kingdome   80
Stands tottering at the Center, out of suspition
Safety growes often; let us suspect this fellow,
And that albeit he shew us the Kings hand,
It may be but a Tricke.
Dænia.   Your Lordship hits
A poyson'd nayle i'th head: this waxen fellow
(By the Kings hand so bribing him with gold)
Is set on skrews, perhaps is made his Creature,
To turne round every way.
Medina.   Out of that feare
Will I beget truth: for my selfe in person
Will sound the Kings brest.
Carlo.   How! your selfe in person?   90
Alba.   That's halfe the prize he gapes for.
Medina.   I'le venture it,
And come off well I warrant you, and rip up
His very entrailes, cut in two his heart,
And search each corner in't, yet shall not he
Know who it is cuts up th'Anatomy.
Dænia.   'Tis an exploit worth wonder.
Carlo.   Put the worst,
Say some Infernall voyce shoo'd rore from hell,
The Infant's cloystering up.
Alba.   'Tis not our danger,
Nor the imprison'd Prince's, for what Theefe
Dares by base sacrilege rob the Church of him?   100
Carlo.   At worst none can be lost but this slight fellow!
Medina.   All build on this as on a stable Cube;
If we our footing keepe, we fetch him forth,
And Crowne him King; if up we flye i'th ayre,
We for his soules health a broad way prepare.
Dænia.   They come.

Enter Baltazar *and* Sebastian.

Medina.   Thou knowst where to bestow him, *Baltazar.*
Baltazar.   Come Noble Boy.

Alba.   Hide him from being discovered.

Baltaʒar.   Discover'd? woo'd there stood a troope of Moores
Thrusting the pawes of hungry Lions forth,   110
To seize this prey, and this but in my hand,
I should doe something.

Sebastian.   Must I goe with this blacke fellow, Vncle?

Medina.   Yes, pretty Coz, hence with him, *Baltaʒar.*

Baltaʒar.   Sweet child, within few minutes I'le change thy fate
And take thee hence, but set thee at heavens gate.   *Exeunt.*

Medina.   Some keepe aloofe and watch this Souldier.

Carlo.   I'le doo't.
                                              [*Exit.*]

Dænia.   What's to be done now?

Medina.   First to plant strong guard
About the mother, then into some snare
To hunt this spotted Panther, and there kill him.   120

Dænia.   What snares have we can hold him?

Medina.   Be that care mine;
Dangers (like Starres) in darke attempts best shine.

                                              Exeunt.

[ACT IV, SCENE ii]

Enter Cornego, Baltazar.

Cornego.   The Lady *Onælia* dresseth the stead of her commendations in the most Courtly Attire that words can be cloth'd with,
from her selfe to you, by me.

Baltaʒar.   So Sir; and what disease troubles her now?

Cornego.   The Kings Evill; and here she hath sent something
to you wrap'd up in a white sheet, you need not feare to open it,
tis no coarse.

Baltaʒar.   What's here? a letter minc'd into five morsels?
What was she doing when thou camst from her?

Cornego.   At her pricke-song.   10

Baltaʒar.   So me thinks, for here's nothing but sol-Re-me-fa-mi:
What Crotchet fils her head now, canst tell?

Cornego.   No Crotchets, 'tis onely the Cliffe has made her mad.

Baltazar.   What Instrument playd she upon?

Cornego.   A wind instrument, she did nothing but sigh.

Baltazar.   Sol, Re, me, Fa, Mi.

Cornego.   My wit has alwayes had a singing head, I have found out her Note Captaine.

Baltazar.   The tune? come.

Cornego.   Sol, my soule; re, is all rent and torne like a raggamuffin; me, mend it good Captaine; fa, fa, whats fa Captaine? 20

Baltazar.   Fa, why farewell and be hang'd.

Cornego.   Mi, Captaine, with all my heart; haue I tickled my Ladies Fiddle well?

Baltazar.   Oh but your sticke wants Rozen to make the strings sound clearly: no, this double Virginall, being cunningly touch'd, another manner of Iacke leaps up then is now in mine eye: Sol, Re, me, fa, mi, I have it now, *Solus Rex me facit miseram*: Alas poore Lady, tell her no Pothecary in *Spaine* has any of that *Assa fetida* she writes for. 30

Cornego.   *Assa fetida?* what's that?

Baltazar.   A thing to be taken in a glister-pipe.

Cornego.   Why what ayles my Lady?

Baltazar.   What ayles she? why when she cryes out, *Solus Rex me facit miseram*, she sayes in the Hypercronicall language, that she is so miserably tormented with the wind-Chollicke that it rackes her very soule.

Cornego.   I said somewhat cut her soule in peeces.

Baltazar.   But goe to her, and say the Oven is heating.

Cornego.   And what shall be bak'd in't? 40

Baltazar.   Carpe pyes: and besides, tell her the hole in her Coat shall be mended: and tell her if the Dyall of good dayes goe true, why then bounce Buckrum.

Cornego.   The Divell lyes sicke of the Mulligrubs.

Baltazar.   Or the Cony is dub'd, and three sheepskins —

Cornego.   With the wrong side outward —

Baltazar.   Shall make the Fox a Night-cap.

Cornego.   So the Goose talkes French to the Buzzard.

35 Hypercronicall] Hypocronicall Q

Baltazar.   But, Sir, if evill dayes justle our prognostication to the
wall, then say there's a fire in a Whore-masters Cod-peece.   50
Cornego.   And a poyson'd Bagge-pudding in Tom Thumbes belly.
Baltazar.   The first cut be thine: farewell.
Cornego.   Is this all?
Baltazar.   Woo't not trust an Almanacke?
Cornego.   Nor a Coranta neither, tho it were seal'd with Butter;
and yet I know where they both lye passing well.

Enter Lopez.

Lopez.   The King sends round about the Court to seek you.
Baltazar.   Away Otterhound.
Cornego.   Dancing Beare, I'me gone.   *Exit.*

Enter King attended.

King.   A private roome,   *Exeunt omnes.* 60
Is't done? hast drawne thy two-edg'd sword out yet?
Baltazar.   No, I was striking at the two Iron Barres that hinder
your passage, and see Sir.   *Drawes.*
King.   What meanst thou?
Baltazar.   The edge abated, feele.
King.   No, no, I see it.
Baltazar.   As blunt as Ignorance.
King.   How? put up — So — how?
Baltazar.   I saw by chance hanging in Cardinall *Alvarez* Gallery
a picture of hell.   70
King.   So, what of that?
Baltazar.   There lay upon burnt straw ten thousand brave fellowes
all starke naked, some leaning upon Crownes, some on Miters,
some on bags of gold: Glory in another Corner lay like a feather
beaten in the raine; Beauty was turn'd into a watching Candle,
that went out stinking: Ambition went upon a huge high paire of
stilts, but horribly rotten; some in another nooke were killing
Kings, and some having their elbowes shov'd forward by Kings to
murther others; I was (me thought) halfe in hell my selfe whilst
I stood to view this peece.   80
King.   Was this all?

279

Baltazar.   Was't not enough to see that a man is more healthfull
that eats dirty puddings, than he that feeds on a corrupted
Conscience.

King.   Conscience! what's that? a Conjuring booke ne're open'd
Without the readers danger: 'tis indeed
A scare-crow set i'th world to fright weake fooles:
Hast thou seene fields pav'd o're with carkasses,
Now to be tender-footed, not to tread
On a boyes mangled quarters, and a womans!   90

Baltazar.   Nay, Sir, I have search'd the records of the Low-
Countries, and finde that by your pardon I need not care a pinne
for Goblins, and therefore I will doo't Sir. I did but recoyle because I was double charg'd.

King.   No more, here comes a Satyre with sharpe hornes.

Enter Cardinall, and Medina *like a French Doctor.*

Cardinal.   Sir here's a Frenchman charg'd with some strange
                              businesse
Which to your close eare onely hee'll deliver,
Or else to none.

King.   A Frenchman?   100

Medina.   We Mounsire.

King.   Cannot he speake the Spanish?

Medina.   Si Signior, un Poco: — Monsir Acontez in de Corner,
me come for offer to your Bon grace mi trezhumbla service, by
gar no Iohn fidleco shall put into your neare braver Melody dan
dis un petite pipe shall play upon to your great bon Grace.

King.   What is the tune you'll strike up, touch the string.

Medina.   Dis; me ha run up and downe mane Countrie, and
learne many fine ting, and mush knavery, now more and all dis,
me know you ha jumbla de fine vench and fill her belly wid a 110
Garsoone, her name is le Madame —

King.   Onælia.

Medina.   She by gar: Now Monsire, dis Madam send for me to
helpe her Malady, being very naught of her corpes (her body)
me know you no point lovea dis vensh; but royall Monsire donne

103 un] vr Q

Moye ten towsand Frensh Croownes she shall kicke up her taile
by gar, and beshide lye dead as dog in de shannell.

Kinge.   Speake low.

Medina.   As de bagge-pipe when de winde is puff, Gar beigh.

King.   Thou nam'st ten thousand Crownes, I'le treble them   120
Rid me but of this leprosie: thy name?

Medina.   Monsire Doctor *Devile.*

King.   Shall I a second wheele adde to this mischiefe
To set it faster going? if one breake,
Th'other may keepe his motion.

Medina.   Esselent fort boone.

King.   Baltazar.
To give thy Sword an edge againe, this French-man
Shall whet thee on, that if thy pistoll faile,
Or ponyard, this can send the poyson home.   130

Baltazar. Brother *Cain* wee'll shake hands.

Medina.   In de bowle of de bloody busher: tis very fine wholesome.

King.   And more to arme your resolution,
I'le tune this Churchman so, that he shall chime
In sounds harmonious, Merit to that man
Whose hand has but a finger in that act.

Baltazar.   That musicke were worth hearing.

King.   Holy Father,
You must give pardon to me in unlocking.
A Cave stuft full with Serpents, which my State   140
Threaten to poyson, and it lyes in you
To breake their bed with thunder of your voyce.

Cardinal.   How Princely sonne?

King.   Suppose an universall
Hot Pestilence beat her mortiferous wings
O're all my kingdome, am not I bound in soule,
To empty all our Achademes of Doctors,
And Æsculapian spirits to charme this plague?

Cardinal.   You are.

King.   Or had the Canon made a breach
Into our rich Escuriall, downe to beat it
About our eares, shoo'd I to stop this breach   150

Spare even our richest Ornaments, nay, our Crowne,
Could it keepe bullets off.
Cardinal.   No Sir, you should not.
King.   This Linstocke gives you fire: shall then that strumpet
And bastard breathe quicke vengeance in my face;
Making my kingdome reele, my subjects stagger
In their obedience, and yet live?
Cardinal.   How? live!
Shed not their bloods to gaine a kingdome greater
Then ten times this.
Medina.   Pishe, not mattera how Red-cap and his wit run.
King.   As I am Catholike King, I'le have their hearts,   160
Panting in these two hands.
Cardinal.   Dare you turne Hang-man?
Is this Religion Catholike to kill
What even bruit beasts abhorre to doe, (your owne!)
To cut in sunder wedlockes sacred knot
Tyed by heavens fingers! to make *Spaine* a Bonfire,
To quench which must a second Deluge raine
In showres of blood, no water; If you doe this,
There is an Arme Armipotent that can fling you
Into a base grave, and your Pallaces
With Lightning strike, and of their Ruines make   170
A Tombe for you (unpitied, and abhorr'd:)
Beare witnesse all you Lamps Cœlestiall
I wash my hands of this.   *Kneeling.*
King.   Rise my good Angell,
Whose holy tunes beat from me that evill spirit
Which jogs mine Elbow, hence thou dog of hell.
Medina.   Baw wawghe.
King.   Barke out no more thou Mastiffe, get you all gone,
And let my soule sleepe: [*aside*] there's gold, peace, see it done.
                                                                    Exit.
          Manent Medina, Baltazar, *Cardinall.*

Baltazar.   Sirra, you Salsa-Perilla Rascall, Toads-guts, you
whorson pockey French Spawne of a bursten-bellyed Spyder, doe 180
you heare, Monsire.

                              282

Medina. Why doe you barke and snap at my Narcissus, as if
I were de Frenshe doag?
Baltazar. You Curre of *Cerberus* litter,   *Strikes him.*
You'll poyson the honest Lady? doe but once toot into her
Chamber-pot, and I'le make thee looke worse then a witch does
upon a close-stoole.
Cardinal. You shall not dare to touch him, stood he here
Single before thee.
Baltazar. I'le cut the Rat into Anchovies.   190
Cardinal. I'le make thee kisse his hand, imbrace him, love him
And call him —   *Medina discovers.*
Baltazar. The perfection of all Spanyards, *Mars* in little, the best
booke of the art of Warre printed in these Times: as a French
Doctor I woo'd have given you pellets for pills, but as my noblest
Lord, rip my heart out in your service.
Medina. Thou art the truest Clocke
That e're to time paidst tribute, (honest Souldier)
I lost mine owne shape, and put on a French,
Onely to try thy truth, and the Kings falshood,   200
Both which I find: now this great Spanish volume
Is open'd to me, I read him o're and o're,
Oh what blacke Characters are printed in him.
Cardinal. Nothing but certaine ruine threats your Neece,
Without prevention: well, this plot was laid
In such disguise to sound him, they that know
How to meet dangers, are the lesse afraid;
Yet let me counsell you not to text downe
These wrongs in red lines.
Medina.   No, I will not, father;
Now that I have Anatomiz'd his thoughts,   210
I'le read a lecture on 'em that shall save
Many mens lives, and to the kingdome minister
Most wholesome Surgery; here's our Aphorisme;
These letters from us in our Neeces name,
You know treat of a marriage.

204 threats] threat Q

Cardinal   There's the strong Anchor
To stay all in this tempest.
Medina.   Holy Sir,
With these worke you the King, and so prevaile,
That all these mischiefes *Hull* with Flagging saile.
Cardinal.   My best in this I'le doe.
Medina.   Souldier, thy brest
I must locke better things in.
Baltazar.   'Tis your chest,   220
With three good keyes to keep it from opening, an honest hart,
a daring hand, and a pocket which scornes mony.
                                        Exeunt.

ACTUS QUINTUS, SCÆNA PRIMA

Enter King, Cardinall with letters[, Valasco, Lopez].

King.   Commend us to *Medina*, say his letters
Right pleasing are, and that (except himselfe)
Nothing could be more welcome: counsell him
(To blot the opinion out of factious numbers)
Onely to have his ordinary traine
Waiting upon him: for, to quit all feares
Vpon his side of us, our very Court
Shall even but dimly shine with some few Dons,
Freely to prove our longings great to peace.
Cardinal.   The Constable expects some pawne from you,   10
That in this Fairy circle shall rise up
No Fury to confound his Neece nor him.
King.   A Kings word is engag'd.
Cardinal.   It shall be taken.   [*Exit.*]
King.   *Valasco*, call the Captaine of our Guard,
Bid him attend us instantly.
Valasco.   I shall.   *Exit.*
King.   *Lopez* come hither: see,
Letters from Duke *Medina*, both in the name
Of him and all his Faction, offering peace,

And our old love (his Neece) *Onælia*
In marriage with her free and faire consent   20
To *Cockadillio*, a Don of *Spaine*.
Lopez.   Will you refuse this?
King.   My Crowne as soone: they feele their sinowy plots
  Belike to shrinke i'th joynts; and fearing Ruine,
  Have found this Cement out to piece up all,
  Which more endangers all.
Lopez.   How Sir! endangers!
King.   Lyons may hunted be into the snare,
  But if they once breake loose, woe be to him
  That first seiz'd on 'em. A poore prisoner scornes
  To kisse his Iaylor; and shall a King be choak'd   30
  With sweet-meats, by false Traytors! no, I will fawne
  On them, as they stroake me, till they are fast
  But in this paw: And then —
Lopez.   A brave revenge!
  The Captaine of your Guard.

Enter Captaine [Alanzo].

King.   Vpon thy life
  Double our Guard this day: let every man
  Beare a charg'd Pistoll, hid; and at a watch-word
  Given by a Musket, when our selfe sees Time,
  Rush in; and if *Medina's* Faction wrastle
  Against your forces, kill; but if yeeld, save:
  Be secret.
Alanzo.   I am charm'd, Sir.   *Exit.*
King.   Watch, *Valasco*;   40
  If any weare a Crosse, Feather, or Glove,
  Or such prodigious signes of a knit Faction,
  Table their names up: at our Court-gate plant
  Good strength to barre them out, if once they swarme:
  Doe this upon thy life.
Valasco.   Not death shall fright me.
                           Exeunt [Valasco *and* Lopez].

Enter Baltazar.

Baltazar.   'Tis done, Sir.

King.   Death! what's done?

Baltazar.   Young Cub's flayd, but the shee-Fox shifting her hole
is fled; the little Iackanapes the boy's braind.

King.   *Sebastian?*   50

Baltazar.   He shall ne're speake more Spanish.

King.   Thou teachest me to curse thee.

Baltazar.   For a bargaine you set your hand to.

King.   Halfe my Crowne I'de lose, were it undone.

Baltazar.   But halfe a Crowne! that's nothing:
His braines sticke in my conscience more than yours.

King.   How lost I the French Doctor?

Baltazar.   As French-men lose their haire: here was too hot
staying for him.

King.   Get thou too from my sight, the Queen wu'd see thee.   60

Baltazar.   Your gold, Sir.

King.   Goe with *Judas* and repent.

Baltazar.   So men hate whores after lusts heat is spent:
I'me gone, Sir.

King.   Tell me true, is he dead?

Baltazar.   Dead.

King.   No matter; tis but morning of revenge,
The Sun-set shall be red and Tragicall.   *Exit.*

Baltazar.   Sinne is a Raven croaking her owne fall.

                                                             Exit.

[ACT V, Scene ii.]

Enter Medina, Dænia, Alba, Carlo, *and the Faction with
Rosemary in their hats.*

Medina.   Keepe lock'd the doore, and let none enter to us
But who shares in our fortunes.

Dænia.   Locke the dores.

Alba.   What entertainment did the King bestow

59 croaking] Bullen; creaking Q

286

Vpon your letters and the Cardinals?
Medina.   With a devouring eye he read 'em o're,
Swallowing our offers into his empty bosome,
As gladly as the parched earth drinks healths
Out of the cup of heaven.
Carlo.   Little suspecting
What dangers closely lye enambushed.
Dænia.   Let us not trust to that; there's in his brest   10
Both Fox and Lion, and both those beasts can bite:
We must not now behold the narrowest loope-hole,
But presently suspect a winged bullet
Flyes whizzing by our eares.
Medina.   For when I let
The plummet fall to sound his very soule
In his close-chamber, being French-Doctor like,
He to the Cardinals eare sung sorcerous notes,
The burthen of his song, to mine, was death,
Onælia's murder, and *Sebastians*;
And thinke you his voyce alters now? 'tis strange,   20
To see how brave this Tyrant shewes in Court,
Throan'd like a god: great men are petty starres,
Where his rayes shine, wonder fills up all eyes
By sight of him, let him but once checke sinne,
About him round all cry, oh excellent King!
Oh Saint-like man! but let this King retire
Into his Closet to put off his robes,
He like a Player leaves his part off too;
Open his brest, and with a Sunne-beame search it,
There's no such man; this King of gilded clay,   30
Within is ugliness, lust, treachery,
And a base soule, tho reard *Collossus*-high.
                            Baltazar *beats to come in.*
Dænia.   None till he speakes, and that we know his voyce:
Who are you?
Within Baltazar.   An honest house-keeper in Rosemary-lane too,
if you dwell in the same parish.
Medina.   Oh tis our honest Souldier, give him entrance.

Enter Baltazar.

Baltazar. Men show like coarses, for I meet few but are stuck
with Rosemary: every one ask'd mee who was married to day,
and I told 'em Adultery and Repentance, and that Shame and 40
a Hangman followed 'em to Church.

Medina. There's but two parts to play, shame has done hers,
But execution must close up the Scæne,
And for that cause these sprigs are worne by all,
Badges of Marriage, now of Funerall,
For death this day turnes Courtier.

Baltazar. Who must dance with him?

Medina. The King, and all that are our opposites:
That dart or This must flye into the Court
Either to shoot this blazing starre from *Spaine*,   50
Or else so long to wrap him up in clouds,
Till all the fatall fires in him burne out,
Leaving his State and conscience cleere from doubt
Of following uprores.

Alba. Kill not, but surprize him.

Carlo.   Thats my voyce still.

Medina. Thine, Souldier?

Baltazar. Oh this Collicke of a kingdome, when the wind of
treason gets amongst the small guts, what a rumbling and a roaring
it keepes: and yet make the best of it you can, it goes out stinking:
kill a King?   60

Dænia. Why?

Baltazar. If men should pull the Sun out of heaven every time
'tis ecclips'd, not all the Wax nor Tallow in *Spaine* woo'd serve
to make us Candles for one yeare.

Medina. No way to purge
The sicke State, but by opening a vaine.

Baltazar. Is that your French Physicke? if every one of us shoo'd
be whip'd according to our faults, to be lasht at a carts taile would
be held but a flea-biting.

288

Enter Signeor No: *whispers* Medina.

Medina.   What are you? come you from the King?   70
No.   No.
Baltazar.   No? more no's? I know him, let him enter.
Medina.   Signeor, I thanke your kind Intelligence,
  The newes long since was sent into our eares,
  Yet we embrace your love, so fare you well.
Carlo.   Will you smell to a sprig of Rosemary?
No.   No.
Baltazar.   Will you be hang'd?
No.   No.
Baltazar.   This is either Signeor *No*, or no Signeor.   80
Medina.   He makes his love to us a warning-peece
  To arme our selves against we come to Court,
  Because the guard is doubled.
Omnes.   Tush, we care not.
Baltazar.   If any here armes his hand to cut off the head, let him
  first plucke out my throat: in any Noble Act I'le wade chin-deepe
  with you: but to kill a King?
Medina.   No, heare me —
Baltazar.   You were better, my lord, saile five hundred times to
  Bantam in the West-Indies, than once to *Barathrum* in the Low-
  Countries: It's hot going under the line there, the Callenture of 90
  the soule is a most miserable madnesse.
Medina.   Turne then this wheele of Fate from shedding blood
  Till with her owne hand Iustice weyes all.
Baltazar.   Good.

                                        Exeunt.

[ACT V, SCENE iii]

Enter Queene, Malateste.

Queen.   Must then his Trul be once more sphear'd in Court
  To triumph in my spoyles, in my ecclipses?
  And I like moaping *Juno* sit, whilst *Jove*

Varies his lust into five hundred shapes
To steale to his whores bed! no, *Malateste*,
Italian fires of Iealousie burne my marrow;
For to delude my hopes, the leacherous King
Cuts out this robe of cunning marriage,
To cover his Incontinence, which flames
Hot (as my fury) in his blacke desires: 10
I am swolne big with child of vengeance now,
And till deliver'd, feele the throws of hell.

Malateste.   Iust is your Indignation, high, and Noble,
And the brave heat of a true Florentine;
For *Spaine* Trumpets abroad her Interest
In the Kings heart, and with a blacke cole drawes
On every wall your scoff'd at injuries,
As one that has the refuse of her sheets,
And the sicke Autumne of the weakned King,
Where she drunke pleasures up in the full spring.   20

Queen.   That (*Malateste*) That, That Torrent wracks me:
But *Hymens* Torch (held downe-ward) shall drop out,
And for it, the mad Furies swing their brands
About the Bride-chamber.

Malateste.   The Priest that joynes them,
Our Twin-borne malediction.

Queen.   Lowd may it speake.

Malateste.   The herbs and flowers to strew the wedding way,
Be Cypresse, Eugh, cold Colliquintida.

Queen.   Henbane and Poppey, and that magicall weed
Which Hags at midnight watch to catch the seed.

Malateste.   To these our execrations, and what mischiefe   30
Hell can but hatch in a distracted braine,
I'le be the Executioner, tho it looke
So horrid it can fright e'ne murder backe.

Queen.   Poyson his whore to day, for thou shalt wait
On the Kings Cup, and when heated with wine
He cals to drinke the Brides health, Marry her
Aliue to a gaping grave.

Malateste.   At board?

Queen.   At board.
Malateste.   When she being guarded round about with friends,
Like a faire Iland, hem'd with Rockes and Seas,
What rescue shall I find?
Queen.   Mine armes: dost faint?   40
Stood all the Pyrenæan hills that part
Spaine and our Country, on each others shoulders,
Burning with Ætnean flame, yet thou shouldst on,
As being my steele of resolution,
First striking sparkles from my flinty brest:
Wert thou to catch the horses of the Sunne
Fast by their bridles, and to turne backe day,
Wood'st thou not doo't (base coward) to make way
To the Italians second blisse (revenge.)
Malateste.   Were my bones threatned to the wheele of torture   50
I'le doo't.
                    Enter Lopez.

Queen.   A Ravens voyce, and it likes me well.
Lopez.   The King expects your presence.
Malateste.   So, so, we come —
To turne this Brides day to a day of doome.
                                                            Exeunt.

[ACT V, Scene iv]

A Banquet set out, Cornets sounding; Enter at one dore Lopez,
Valasco, Alanzo, No: *after them* King, Cardinall, *with* Don
Cockadillio *Bridegroome,* Queene *and* Malateste *after. At the other
dore* Alba, Carlo, Roderigo, Medina *and* Dænia *leading* Onælia
as Bride, Cornego *and* Juanna *after,* Baltazar *alone, Bride and
Bridegroome kisse, and by the Cardinall are joyn'd hand in hand:
King is very merry, hugging* Medina *very lovingly.*

King.   For halfe *Spaines* weight in Ingots I'de not lose
This little man to day.
Medina.   Nor for so much
Twice told, Sir, would I misse your kingly presence;

Mine eyes have lost th'acquaintance of your face
So long, and I so (little) late read o're
That Index of the royall booke your mind,
That scarce (without your Comment) can I tell
When in those leaves you turne o're smiles or frownes.

King. 'Tis dimnesse of your sight, no fault i'th letter;
  Medina, you shall find that free from Errata's: 10
And for a proofe,
If I could breath my heart in welcomes forth,
This Hall should ring naught else; welcome *Medina,*
Good Marquesse *Dænia,* Dons of *Spaine* all welcome:
My dearest love and Queene, be it your place
To entertaine the Bride, and doe her grace.

Queen. With all the love I can, whose fire is such,
To give her heat, I cannot burne too much.

King. Contracted Bride, and Bridegroome sit,
Sweet flowres not pluck'd in season, lose their scent,   20
So will our pleasures; Father Cardinall,
Me thinkes this morning new-begins our reigne.

Cardinal. Peace had her Sabbath ne're till now in *Spaine.*

King. Where is our Noble Souldier *Baltazar?*
So close in conference with that Signior?

No.   No.

King. What think'st thou of this great day, *Baltazar?*

Baltazar. Of this day? why as of a new play, if it ends well, all's
  well; all men are but Actors, now if you being the King, should be
  out of your part, or the Queene out of hers, or your Dons out of
  theirs, here's *No* wil never be out of his.   30

No. No.

Baltazar. 'Twere a lamentable peece of stuffe to see great States-
  men have vile Exits; but I hope there are nothing but plaudities
  in all your eyes.

King. Mine I protest are free.

Queen.   And mine by heaven.

Malateste. Free from one good looke till the blow be given.
                                              [*Aside.*]

King. Wine; a full Cup crown'd to *Medina's* health.

Medina.   Your Highnesse this day so much honors me,
  That I to pay you what I truly owe,
  My life shall venture for it.
Dænia.   So shall mine.   40
King.   Onælia, you are sad: why frownes your brow?
Onælia.   A foolish memory of my past ills
  Folds up my looke in furrowes of old care,
  But my heart's merry, Sir.
King.   Which mirth to heighten,
  Your Bridegroome and your selfe first pledge this health
  Which we begin to our high Constable.

> *Three Cups fild: 1. to the King. 2. to the Bridegroome.*
> *3. to* Onælia, *with whom the King complements.*

Queen.   Is't speeding?
Malateste.   As all our Spanish figs are.
King.   Here's to *Medina's* heart with all my heart.
Medina.   My hart shal pledge your hart i'th deepest draught   50
  That ever Spanyard dranke.
King.   *Medina* mockes me,
  Because I wrong her with the largest Bowle:
  I'le change with thee, *Onælia.*   *Malateste rages.*
Queen.   Sir you shall not.
King.   Feare you I cannot fetch it off?
Queen.   *Malateste*!
King.   This is your scorne to her, because I am doing
  This poorest honour to her: Musicke sound,
  It goes were it ten fadoms to the ground.

> *Cornets. King drinkes, Queen and* Malateste *storms.*

Malateste.   Fate strikes with the wrong weapon.
Queen.   Sweet royall Sir no more, it is too deepe.
Malateste.   Twill hurt your health sir.   60
King.   Interrupt me in my drinke? tis off.
Malateste.   Alas sir;
  You have drunke your last, that poyson'd bowle I fill'd
  Not to be put into your hand, but hers.

King.   Poyson'd?

Omnes.   Descend blacke speckled soule to hell.

                                              Kil Malateste.

Malateste.   The Queene has sent me thither.   *Dyes.*

Cardinal.   What new furie shakes now her snakes locks.

Queen.   I, I, tis I;
  Whose soule is torne in peeces, till I send
  This Harlot home.

Cardinal.   More murders! save the Lady.

Balta̠ar.   Rampant? let the Constable make a mittimus.   70

Medina.   Keepe 'em a sunder.

Cardinal.   How is it, royall sonne?

King.   I feele no poyson yet, onely mine eyes
  Are putting out their lights: me thinks I feele
  Deaths Icy fingers stroking downe my face;
  And now I'me in a mortall cold sweat.

Queen.   Deare my Lord.

King.   Hence, call in my Physicians.

Medina.   Thy Physician, Tyrant,
  Dwels yonder, call on him or none.

King.   Bloody *Medina*, stab'st thou *Brutus* too?

Dænia.   As hee is, so are we all.

King.   I burne,   80
  My braines boyle in a Caldron, O one drop
  Of water now to coole me.

Onælia.   Oh let him have Physicians.

Medina.   Keepe her backe.

King.   Physicians for my soule, I need none else;
  You'll not deny me those: oh holy Father,
  Is there no mercy hovering in a cloud
  For me a miserable King so drench'd
  In perjury and murder?

Cardinal.   Oh Sir great store.

King.   Come downe, come quickly downe.

Cardinal.   I'le forthwith send
  For a grave Fryer to be your Confessor.   90

King.   Doe, doe.

Cardinal.   And he shall cure your wounded soule:
Fetch him good Souldier.
Baltazar.   So good a worke I'le hasten.   [*Exit.*]
King.   *Onælia*! oh shee's drown'd in teares! *Onælia*,
Let me not dye unpardoned at thy hands.

          Enter Baltazar, Sebastian *as a Fryer, with others.*

Cardinal.   Here comes a better Surgeon.
Sebastian.   Haile my good Sonne
I come to be thy ghostly Father.
King.   Ha?
My child! 'tis my *Sebastian*, or some spirit
Sent in his shape to fright me.
Baltazar.   'Tis no gobling, Sir, feele; your owne flesh and blood,
and much younger than you tho he be bald, and cals you son; had 100
I bin as ready to ha cut his sheeps throat, as you were to send him
to the shambles, he had bleated no more; there's lesse chalke
upon your score of sinnes by these round o'es.
King.   Oh my dul soule looke up, thou art somwhat lighter.
Noble *Medina*, see *Sebastian* lives:
Onælia cease to weepe, *Sebastian* lives;
Fetch me my Crowne: my sweetest pretty Fryer,
Can my hands doo't, I'le raise thee one step higher:
Th'ast beene in heavens house all this while sweet boy?
Sebastian.   I had but course cheere.
King.   Thou couldst ne're fare better: 110
Religious houses are those hyves, where Bees
Make honey for mens soules: I tell thee, Boy,
A Fryery is a Cube, which strongly stands,
Fashioned by men, supported by heavens hands:
Orders of holy Priest-hood are as high
I'th eyes of Angels, as a Kings dignity:
Both these unto a Crowne give the full weight,
And both are thine: you tha :our Contract know,
See how I seale it with this Marriage;
My blessing and *Spaines* kingdome both be thine.   120

          103 your] Bullen; you Q

Omnes.   Long live *Sebastian.*

Onælia.   Doff that Fryers course gray;
And since hee's crown'd a King, clothe him like one.

King.   Oh no: those are right Soveraigne Ornaments:
Had I beene cloth'd so, I had never fill'd
Spaines Chronicle with my blacke Calumny:
My worke is almost finish'd: where's my Queene?

Queen.   Here peece-meale torne by Furies.

King.   *Onælia!*
Your hand *Paulina* too, *Onælia* yours:
This hand (the pledge of my twice broken faith)
By you usurp'd is her Inheritance;   130
My love is turn'd, see as my fate is turn'd,
Thus they to day laugh, yesterday which mourn'd:
I pardon thee my death; let her be sent
Backe into *Florence* with a trebled dowry;
Death comes: oh now I see what late I fear'd!
A Contract broke, tho piec'd up ne're so well,
Heaven sees, earth suffers, but it ends in hell.   *Moritur.*

Onælia.   Oh I could dye with him.

Queen.   Since the bright spheare
I mov'd in falls, alas what make I here?   *Exit.*

Medina.   The hammers of black mischiefe now cease beating,   140
Yet some Irons still are heating: you, Sir Bridegroome,
(Set all this while up as a marke to shoot at)
We here discharge you of your bed-fellow,
Shee loves no Barbars washing.

Cockadillio.   My Balls are sav'd then.

Medina.   Be it your charge, so please you reverend Sir,
To see the late Queene safely sent to *Florence*:
My Neece *Onælia*, and that trusty Souldier,
We doe appoint to guard the Infant King:
Other distractions, Time must reconcile:
The State is poyson'd like a Crocodile.   150

                                                          Exeunt.

FINIS.

296

TEXTUAL NOTES

I.ii

S.D. [*A dagger stuck in it*]] For this tragic convention, see Bowers, 'The Stabbing of a Portrait in Elizabethan Tragedy', *Modern Language Notes*, XLVII (1932), 378–385.

92 journey;] This Q stop is correct, and the time does not refer to his dismissal of the Queen. On the evidence of lines 135–137 the marriage is to take place in the morning, although the King promises an earlier hour than the Cardinal. See also *The Welsh Embassador* I.iii.52–55: 'I vow to morrow e're the god of daie | Has putt a golden ringe about bright noone, | Thou shalt bee myne, as fast in nuptiall band | As I am thine by contract....'

II.i

73 Vaw] Although *vaward* as another form of *vanguard* is common, the word *vaw* for *van* is not listed in *O.E.D.* Bullen's emendation *rear* best suits the context. Nevertheless, the odds are that *vaw* is what the author wrote (despite its parallel to *van* in the same narrative). Precisely what he thought he meant by it is the question, however.

109 teare] The type for the 'r' is broken, but the letter can be clearly determined in Bodleian, copy 3.

EMENDATIONS OF ACCIDENTALS

Persons

11 Sebastian,] ~ ^   13 Baltazar,] ~ ^
12 Malateste,] ~ ^   15 Cockadillio,] ~ ^

To Reader

12 your] yonr

I.i

head-title Souldier ^] Sovldier: 16 Adulteresse.] ~ ,
2 Breath:] ~ ^

I.ii

heading Song.] ~ ,   150 Cardinals ^] ~ ,
    52–53 The King — Tis...come]   154 *Florence*] *Florenee*
    one line in Q [— tis]   188 *Cornego.*] *Car.*
52 *Æsculapius*] *Æseulapius*   190 gone, but] gcne, but
60 shape,] ~ ;   196–197 Q *lines:* Is...vengeance |
75–76 I'll drinke...once.] *one line*   Yet...fall, | Now...me?
    in Q   196 vengeance] vengegnce
84 'Has] Has   197 me!] ~ ?
122 bad,] *punctuation uncertain*   209 vengeance] veneeance
149 hast,] ~ ^

II.i

S.D. SCÆNA SCŒNA   123 your] | Your
    28–29 That's...pray] *one line in* Q   126 touch-hole] touch-|hole
    36 -hammer; why,] ~ , ~ ^   144 spurne-|point] spurne-point
    42 whalebon'd] whalebond   158 Gallies: ...there,] ~ , ... ~ :
    57–58 Shall...Gentleman?] *prose*   166 now;] ~ ^
    in Q   168 S.D. Alba] Albia
62 turned] turn'd   183 conscience ^] ~ .
81 which] whieh   194 strings.] ~ ^
106 King,] ~ ^   222 lightning] linghtning
120 townes] | Townes   230 noble] hoble

298

II.ii

S.D. Cornego] Cornogo
24 Captaine?] ~ :
41 kingdomes ‸] ~ ;

44 are not] are uot
59 heaven] heauen

III.i

S.D. Malateste] Malattste
38 you] yon
59 daughter] danghter

63 This] Tſiis
63 Joy] Ioy
69 Spyes] *cw*; Spies *text*

III.ii

19 feet] fect
25 Dedication] Dedieation
44 love] lovc
75–76 No...forth] *one line in* Q
102 S.D. Dænia] Denia

112 care,] ~ .
118 lightening] lightning
123–124 Sebastian...mother?]   *one*
    line in Q
147–148 Art...him] *one line in* Q

III.iii

69 two] too
101–104 Italian...English] *Italian*
    ...English
133 Q *lines:* Of...danger | The...
    King.

149–150 *Baltaʒar*...Queene]   *one*
    line in Q
165 You] | you

IV.i

42–43 No...*Baltaʒar*] *one line in* Q
43 *Baltaʒar.*] ~ ,
74 Lightening] Lightning
86–87 (By...Creature,] Q *lines:*
    (By...skrews, | Perhaps...
    Creature

101 fellow!] ~ ?
107 Q *lines:* Thou...where | To...
    Baltaʒar.
108 Noble] Moble

IV.ii

20 raggamuffin] ragga-|muffin
45 sheepskins —] ~ ‸
46 outward —] ~ ‸
50 Cod-peece] Cod-|peece
106 un] vn

115 lovea] love a
122 *Devile*] *Deuile*
158 Then ten] Thenten
191 imbrace] imbraee
193 Spanyards,] ~ .

V.i

16 see,] ~ ‸
21 *Cockadillio*] *Cockadillia*
33 then —] ~ .
33 revenge!] ~ .

40 *Valasco;*] ~ ,
48–49 Q *lines:* Young...flayd, |
    But...fled; | The...braind.

V.ii

36 if] | If
40 Shame] shame
56 Souldier?] ~ .

65–66 No...vaine.] *prose in* Q
89 *Bantam*] *Bantom*

V.iii

3 *Juno...Jove*] *Iuno...Iove*
33 horrid] harrid

34 whore] whor e
52 come —] ~ ∧

V.iv

S.D. Juanna] Iuanna
18 burne] burue
18 much] mnch
29 Queene] Queenc
30] out] eut
32 States-|men] Statesmen
61 drinke?] ~ :
69 Harlot] Hatlot
74–75 Q *lines:* Deaths...now |
    I'me...sweat.

89 downe.] dowue.
92 Souldier] Sovldier
96–97 Ha...spirit] *one line in* Q
104 lighter.] ~ ,
106 lives] livea
109 boy?] ~ .
113 strongly] stiongly
148 guard] guarp (*turned* d)

THE WELSH EMBASSADOR

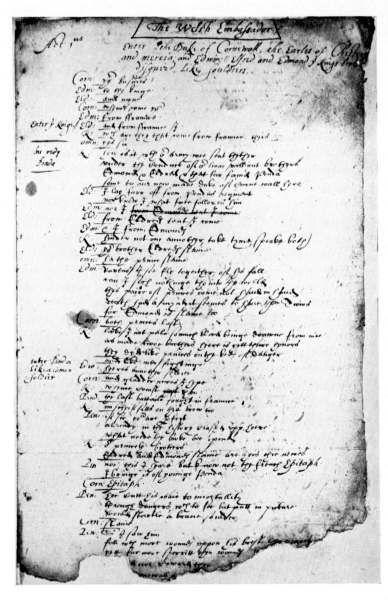

The first MS. page of *The Welsh Embassador*

TEXTUAL INTRODUCTION

THE WELSH EMBASSADOR (Bentley, *Jacobean and Caroline Stage*, III, 267–268) is a manuscript play now preserved in the Cardiff Public Library. The physical details of the manuscript and its known history are described in Greg, *Dramatic Documents from the Elizabethan Playhouses* (1931), pp. 279–282, but more particularly in the Malone Society Reprint edition edited in 1920 by Professor H. Littledale of University College, Cardiff.

The Welsh Embassador is the title of a manuscript in a list found among the papers of Abraham Hill that seems to represent an account of some bookseller's stock set down between 1677 and 1703. The exact entry is 'the Welch Embassador or a Comedy in disguises Tho Dekker'. There can be no doubt that Hill's entry refers to the present play,[1] even though the earliest identifiable owner of the Cardiff manuscript was Joseph Haslewood, who may have come into possession of the manuscript as early as 1821.

The source of the attribution to Dekker in Hill's list is unknown, but as Bertram Lloyd has shown[2] it was certainly a sound one. Lloyd was also of the opinion that marked parallels in situation and in language between the *Embassador* and *The Noble Spanish Soldier* developed from borrowing by the later *Embassador*.[3] My impression is that this is the correct view.

The hand in the *Embassador* is that of the scribe who also prepared the Dyce manuscript of Massinger's *Parliament of Love*. As Bentley remarks, 'Since that play was licensed by Sir Henry Herbert 3 November 1624 for the Cockpit company, i.e. Lady Elizabeth's men, there is some reason to think *The Welsh Embassador* was of approximately the same date and perhaps prepared for the same

[1] See especially II.ii.136–137: 'For a comedy of disguises letts then Arme, | Which tho it doe no good, can doe no harme.' We must also assume that the Cardiff manuscript is that listed by Hill, in which case the form of the entry giving the sub-title and authorship comes in question. Since the first leaf of the manuscript is missing, perhaps the information was jotted there.
[2] 'The Authorship of *The Welsh Embassador*', *R.E.S.* XXI (1945), 192–201.
[3] '*The Noble Soldier* and *The Welsh Embassador*', *R.E.S.* III (1927), 304–307.

company'. All critics have noticed the Clown's prophetic reference (V.iii.95–97): 'But now in [the raigne of this kinge heere in the] yeares 1621:22 and 23 such a wooden fashion will come vpp that hee whoe walkes not with a *Battoone* shalbee held noe gallant.' Generally 1623, the latter date, has been suggested but in fact any one of the three years would serve as a topical reference.[1] However, the rotting at the foot of the leaves of the *Embassador* and the *Parliament of Love* (though more extensive in the *Parliament*) leads Greg to conjecture that 'they once lay together in a damp receptacle'.[2] If so, it is likely that both were inscribed within a short time of each other in 1624. The scribe's hand is not otherwise known.

After the manuscript for *The Welsh Embassador* had been written it was evidently reread and the same scribe added the marginal warning notices and the directions for flourishes. Perhaps at the same time some corrections were made in the text. The excisions at the end in the Clown's prophecies may well, as critics believe, be accounted for as normal theatrical cuts of somewhat dull material. On the other hand even though there is no evidence to connect these cuts with censorship, it cannot be ignored that if the deletions were made unofficially the responsible agent felt progressively uneasier as the time of the prophecies drew towards the present, and the cuts were made in the late and not the early prophecies. Moreover, only a desire to remove all emphasis would account for the deletion of the reference to 'the raigne of this kinge heere' in the 1621–3 prophecy. No evidence exists whether, after all the preparation, the manuscript was actually put to use as a prompt-book for a production. There is, of course, no evidence that it was not.

In the inscription of the manuscript a number of false starts and memorial lapses were repaired by the scribe *currente calamo*. These are recorded in the 'Emendations of Accidentals' list and are mostly trifling. Mere slips of the pen comprise a common group, like *which if you dare convay* (I.i.85) in which the scribe first started to write *ar* after *you* before he stopped, deleted it, and continued with the correct *dare*. Or *tho her soule and shee* (I.ii.54) where the scribe wrote and then excised *see* before writing *shee*. Very common are memorial

---

[1] Just possibly the scribe wrote 1620 and mended it to 1621.
[2] *Dramatic Documents*, p. 282.

lapses. One word may suggest another, as *you cannot at the layings out repent* (I.ii.13) in which the scribe wrote the letter *p* after *at the* before deleting it and continuing with *layings*. Or else a different idiom or some change in the trend of the meaning may come into the scribe's head under the influence of the context. For example, *I take you to bee none of my landlord* (I.iii.8–9) was started as *I take it* before the scribe recovered, deleted *it*, and continued with *you*.

An occasional false start might be explained conjecturally by the scribe's eye having fallen on the wrong word when he returned to his copy after coming to the end of some memorized series of words. Thus at I.i.42 in *tho it doe noe good but wash them*, after *noe* the scribe wrote *d* (perhaps as the start of repeated *doe*) before crossing it out and continuing with *good*. In the nature of the case we cannot be sure whether, as suggested, this *d* came by reference back to *doe* in the copy, or whether the nonsense word *dood* had started to form in the scribe's memory; but the former is at least possible. Similarly, at II.iii.76 we have *end heere then* before the excision of *then* followed by *all rights then of this funerall*. Whether this was memorial transposition of *then*, the accidental omission of *all rights*, or a wrong consultation may well seem doubtful. Somewhat clearer, perhaps, is *and your af* in which *af* is lined through before the continuation with *gates* (*after* (III.i.87).

Memory will play strange tricks. At I.i.23 we have *whence comst thost*, before the scribe recognized his error and wrote the correct *thou*. More usual memorial transpositions are represented by II.ii.84, which was first *you allow vs noe sawce to o* before the scribe recollected himself, lined through *sawce to o* and added *meate to our sawce*, an inversion of the usual phrase.

What any editor, and reader, is most concerned with, however, is the evidence for the scribe's accuracy, and any indication whether the inscriber was or was not the author. That the writer of this manuscript was prone to false starts and memorial error of different kinds is clear from the records of his misadventures. Yet the number of times in which he immediately recognized an error and altered it before continuing with the inscription is very encouraging. For instance, at V.i.200 he copied the Prince's speech *blesse mee what does this villaine* but then instantly stopped and corrected *villaine* to *fellow* before continuing with the final word, *talke*. Moreover, the King's following words *a villaines language* show that the first *villaine* was a memorial error of anticipation; hence *fellow* cannot be regarded as a sophistication. In this and other similar instances what is worth remarking is the speed with which the scribe realized that something was wrong and took steps to correct his mistake.

More dangerous than anticipation was the scribe's tendency to be led into other words than those in his copy, for ordinarily we have no means of identifying such lapses except when he himself caught them. But his ear seems to have been very good. For example, at II.ii.33 Armante remarks *blesse mee this grim fellow sh* before the scribe paused, deleted *sh*, and continued with *frights mee*. Possibly *sh* was the start of his misreading of copy *frights*, but it could easily have represented some different word that had formed in his mind. At any rate, he knew he had deviated from copy before more than two letters had been written. Correspondingly, in I.iii.76 he was led to write *this your Indenture holds in it* before recognizing (presumably) his departure from copy, which led him to delete *in it* and to substitute *alone*.

One cannot always be sure that what appears to be deletion *currente calamo* and substitution was not, instead, simple deletion made at the time of the later rereading, such as the excision of *I* before *I prithee* at II.i.29. On the whole, however, the number of times that departure from copy was currently mended gives one some confidence in the general accuracy of the transcription. One very small example may be mentioned. It may be true that care for copy-spelling and for copy-reading is not necessarily identical. But at II.iii.80 it would seem that the *a* that was written and deleted before *embassador* was inscribed may represent the start of a scribal spelling that was altered to conform to copy. If this is so, it gives us a useful hint that the scribe had his mind on his business.

Nevertheless, there is one particular place where the odds are that the scribe has deliberately sophisticated his copy. At V.ii.10 part of Eldred's Welsh talk is found as follows, the two deleted words being placed in square brackets: 'there is a greate teale of [prapples &] quarrells and high vrds | goe vpp & towne to yon rascalls'. At first sight it might be argued that *prapples &* could have been excised at a later time; but I believe, instead, that it was crossed out before *quarrells* was written and that *quarrells* is a real scribal alteration for *prapples*, a word (in the form of *prabbles*) found elsewhere in Dekker's Welsh dialect. That the scribe could have invented *prapples* from his copy *quarrells* is far from likely, and it may be significant that *quarrells* is not given a dialect spelling. But more important is the fact that *and* before *high vrds* is an interlineation and so was not made currently. It would seem that the copy read *prapples & high vrds*, and that the *and* (now interlined) was inadvertently omitted when *prapples &* was deleted and the scribe continued, *quarrels high vrds*.

If this is an example of scribal intervention, then other possibilities must be surveyed. Anticipation (or real error) like the *villaine* at V.i.200 already remarked may account for some substitutions. Others are slightly doubtful. At V.i.158 the error *learne to bee good & reconcile my poule*, with *poule* deleted and *peace* substituted, might seem suspicious as if a slip of the pen for *soule* had been wrongly altered. But the next line *to hirs, alas poore soule* shows that *poule* is only a confused anticipation. Ordinarily one might be inclined to query III.i.28 *a wise puddinge without*, changed to *a wise puddinge has it noe eggs*. But the odds are that it merely represents the scribe going off on his own tack momentarily (*a wise puddinge without eggs*) and rescuing himself forthwith. So when at III.ii.53 the disguised Penda speaks of 'o^r Bardhes play on twincklinge' and then the scribe starts to write 'we' (doubtless for 'welse') before stopping and carrying on with 'harpes', it is more likely that he was being faithful to copy in refusing to complete *welse* from his own train of thought than that he was suppressing a manuscript word. The curious case of *prapples* seems to be the only sure indication of a deliberate departure from copy, as against a number of indications of faithfulness.

With some confidence it may be said that not enough of the alterations represent what we might fairly expect from a copying author, who would—of course—need to be a collaborator of Dekker if he were to exist. Moreover, the existence of *The Parliament of Love* manuscript in the same hand seems to point very firmly in the direction of a scribe.

A very common error with this scribe was the omission of words. He left out a whole line by eyeskip after II.i.32, but most cases take in only a word or two, as at V.i.159 *alas poore soule how haue I wrongd hir* in which the scribe started to write *haue* after *soule* before recognizing his mistake, deleting the *ha* already formed, and following with *how haue*. A certain number of currently overlooked omissions, although not all, were rectified by interlineation when the manuscript was reread, possibly at the time that the prompt markings were made. It may well be that someone read from the original copy while the scribe followed his transcription. At V.iii.187, for instance, the interlineation of *hart* above deleted *head* would not necessarily suggest itself to a simple reader; but the example at II.ii.37 seems conclusive. Here the originally inscribed *tother quart* was altered by interlineation to *another quart*. (*Another quart*, incidentally, is the reading of *The Noble Spanish Soldier* in a closely parallel speech.) A change of this minute kind one would scarcely suppose to concern an independent reader; instead, it must have resulted from a careful comparison with copy. That the Cardiff manuscript was reread against copy is also suggested by some of the interlined words that are additions and not substitutions but are far from strictly necessary if the reading had been made only for sense.

It would seem, then, that we have to do with a scribal transcript that was copied originally with some care. Subsequently, it would seem, the transcript—perhaps in the course of preparation as a prompt-book—was reread against the original and a number of the scribe's omissions, together with a few of his unauthoritative substitutions, were recognized and corrected. Thus it would seem that the text itself, as preserved, is on the whole a particularly trustworthy one.

It is idle to attempt to conjecture from the transcript very much about the nature of the manuscript that served as its copy. The scribal spelling characteristics are remarkably uniform and on the whole resemble those also found in *The Parliament of Love*. The variant spellings of Cornwall's name (Cornwall, Cornewall, Cornewalle) seem to have no significance. On the other hand, Eldred in his disguise as a Welsh servingman is known as *Reese* in III.ii and IV.ii but as *Reece* in V.ii and V.iii. Since it is difficult to detect any difference in the authorship of these scenes, it is likely that one spelling represents the copy and the other the scribe's.

The opening stage-direction includes Edwin, presumably another of the King's brothers, and the Earl of Mercia. Nothing more is heard of the Earl. At I.i.21 the speech-prefix *Edw* is assigned to a single line but thereafter Edwin drops out. Both are associated in the opening direction with the lords who are of the King's side. In the nature of the case one cannot know whether the two were planned in the original foul-papers version but then in the course of the scene found to be superfluous, or whether they were characters throughout the manuscript used as copy but were cut to reduce the number of actors, and their speeches distributed among Chester and Cornwall as part of the preparation of the copy for transcription as a prompt-book. It may be that the slight evidence favours the first hypothesis. Certainly it is odd that these fossil characters were permitted to make an initial appearance if they had been cut throughout. Moreover, the speeches of Chester and of Cornwall are so few and brief as not readily to contain amplification from other persons. A loyal brother Edwin, finally, might be expected to have something more of a part than could be hacked out without trace. But this is mere guesswork.

The existence of a Malone Society Reprint edition materially eases the task of an editor, since with a completely clear conscience he can engage himself to the preparation of a critical reading edition, aware that the scholar who has need of an exact transcript at every point can find what he wants elsewhere.

The present text has been printed from an independent transcript of the photographed manuscript. This transcript has been checked against the Malone Society edition and the photographs carefully scrutinized when the two transcripts differed. In some cases the lightness of the strokes used for punctuation marks has caused the editor to rely on the Malone reprint when the punctuation in the photographs was in legitimate doubt. A list of the MSR mistranscriptions of other features concludes the apparatus at the end of the present text. Happily these are mostly venial although a few substantive errors appear. Since differences of opinion about word division may easily arise and are difficult to resolve with any certainty, the relatively few occasions in which the two editions differ in this respect have not been recorded.

The spelling of the manuscript has been exactly transcribed, and all alterations are recorded in the 'Emendations of Accidentals' in the apparatus appendix or else in the footnotes. However, all abbreviations like w^th, y^r, ꝑ have been silently expanded. The final ſ character has not been reproduced as it is in MSR, but instead has been transcribed simply as 's'. The scribe used two forms of initial secretary 'c', one the standard minuscule and the other the standard majuscule. However, the appearance of one or other form seems to be quite without significance, and the majuscule is used frequently where no intention to capitalize could possibly exist. Under these conditions, the present editor has taken the responsibility (since this is not a facsimile edition) of transcribing most of the majuscule forms of this letter in lower case, and has capitalized very conservatively. Otherwise, the capitalizations in the manuscript have been reproduced. Finally, all lines of verse have been silently capitalized, and proper names have been silently capitalized and set in italics.

The punctuation has presented something of a problem since it is very erratic in the manuscript. The scribe never used a query or exclamation and only rarely introduced commas, semi-colons, and colons. The few slants have been removed from the text but recorded in the apparatus. As remarked by the MSR editor, how many full stops there are in the manuscript is very much in doubt. I have added a full stop silently at the end of speeches, but otherwise editorial addition has been recorded. In general, editorial punctuation reproduces a conservative early seventeenth-century punctuation system such as might be found in the usual printed quarto made from such a manuscript.

In the accompaniments of the text all speech-prefixes have been silently expanded. Entrance stage-directions are centred, but are recorded in the Accidentals List if they are marginally inscribed in the manuscript. (Whether placed in the margin or across the page, the entrances seem all to have been written at the time the text was inscribed.) The italic and roman type conventions found in print have been silently imposed on the prefixes and directions. As usual, square brackets enclose editorially added stage-directions.

In the text the mutilation of the foot of the leaves (and sometimes of their side-edges) has caused some of the text to be lost. Known missing text is indicated by pointed brackets ⟨ ⟩, and letters found within these pointed brackets have been guessed at from partial indications in the manuscript. When no evidence exists to identify the missing letters or words but they have been supplied by editorial conjecture, square brackets enclose the guessed-at material within the pointed brackets indicating the mutilated areas. In some cases the text can be reconstructed with certainty (as at I.ii.99–102) from corresponding lines in *The Noble Spanish Soldier*. Since the transcript for the MSR edition was made at a time when the mutilation was slightly less extensive, the present editor has relied heavily on Professor Littledale's opinions about the reconstruction of letters for which some evidence exists.

The footnotes record not only editorial emendation, but also the prompt-warnings added in the left margin of the manuscript. All other details, such as deletions, additions, and substitutions, are found in the 'Emendations of Accidentals' list, since they are almost wholly scribal corrections and of no independent authority. The marginal additions of flourishes made for prompt purposes have been added to the appropriate stage-directions in the text but are also noted in the Accidentals list.

Throughout, an attempt has been made to apply to this text the various editorial conventions adopted for the presentation of the texts from printed quartos.

[PERSONS]

⟨[ATHEL]⟩STANE Kinge of England

EDMOND ⎱ his Brothers
ELDRED ⎰

THE DUKE OF CORNEWALL

PENDA his sonne

CARINTHA his wife

DUKE [OF] COLCHESTER

ARMANTE his Daughter

THE PRINCE hir sonne

THE EARLE OF KENT

THE EARLE OF CHESTER

THE BISHOP OF WINCHESTER

A SERUANT

THE CLOWNE

VOLTIMAR A Captaine

1 Above Athelstane is the underlined title *The Welch Embassador* in which the false start *Ems* has been deleted.

The Welsh Embassador

ACT^{us} I^{us} [SCENE i]

Enter [at one door] the Duke of Cornewall, *the Earle of* Chester;
[*at the other door*] Eldred *and* Edmond *the Kings* broth⟨[ers]⟩
disguiz̧d like souldiers.

Cornewall.	Your busines?
Edmond.	To the kinge.
Eldred.	And myne.
Cornewall.	Whence come you?
Edmond.	From *Fraunce.*
Eldred.	And from *Fraunce* I.

Enter the Kinge.

Kinge. Which are they that come from *Fraunce* — theis?
Omnes.   Yes sir.
Kinge. How is it with our army wee sent thether
Vnder the conduct of our twoe valliant brothers
Edmond and *Eldred*, and that far fam'd *Penda*,
Sonne to our new made duke of *Cornewall* here.
Eldred. I lay farr off from *Pendas* regiment
Nor know I what fate followes him.
Edmond.   Nor I.
Eldred. From *Eldreds* tent I come.
Edmond.   And I from *Edmonds*.   10
Kinge. Hinder not one annother, take tyme, speake both.
Eldred. Your brother *Eldred*'s slaine.
Omnes.   Ha, the prince slaine?
Edmond. Ravens I see fly togeither; of his fall
Can I sigh nothinge; tho into the world

S.D. *Earle of* Chester;] *Earles of Chester and mercia; and Edwin;* // MS
S.D. Eldred] Elfred MS
4 In left margin: *bee redy* | *Penda*   7 Sonne] MSR; some MS

313

This paire of princes came not hand in hand,
Death had a mynd it seemes to haue them Twins,
For *Edmond* is slaine too.
Cornewall.   Both princes lost?
Kinge.   Looke I not pale, so much blood beinge drawne from mee
As made twoe brothers? Heere is yett theire honors:
They dy'd like princes on the beds of danger   20
And like men fightinge.

Enter Penda *like a Comon soldier.*

Chester.   Heeres annother soldier.
Cornewall.   And gladder newes I hope.
Kinge.   Whence comst thou?
Penda.   The last battaile fought in *Fraunce.*
Kinge.   Mischeif sitts on thie brow too.
Penda.   If sir you are perfect
Already in the history claspd vpp heere,
What neede the booke bee opend.
Kinge.   Our princely brothers
Eldred and *Edmond*'s slaine, are theis thie newes?
Penda.   No; this I heare but know not, the french *Epitaph*
I bringe is of younge *Penda.*
Cornewall.   *Epitaph?*
Penda.   Hee cutt his waie to imortallity   30
Through dangers, which to see but putt in picture
Would startle a braue soulder.
Cornewall.   Slaine?
Penda.   Sir I saw him
Fall with more wounds vppon his brest than ⟨y⟩eares,
Yett far more sperritt then wounds.
⟨[*Cornewall.*   He dy]e⟩d noe coward then.
⟨[*Kinge.*]   [*Co*]⟩*rnewall* a⟨   ld   ⟩
Cornewall.   Sir had I stood but by to see my boy
Acted what hee speakes, I would have clap'd my hands,
And tho I will not mourne for him in black,
I cannot for my hart hinder myne eyes   40

21 *Chester.*] *Edw:* MS

314

From droppinge this warme balsame into's wounds
Tho it doe noe good but wash them; now I ha done,
His funerall is past by, to his sad wife
Ile goe and tell the newes.   *Exit.*
Kinge.   And comfort her.
Hee will bee drownd too, pray goe and comfort him.
Chester.   I shall.   *Exit.*
Kinge.   Soldiers your names.
Eldred.   Myne *Vffa.*
Edmond.   And myne *Gildas.*
Kinge.   See vs anon.   *Exeunt they twoe.*
                    And how art thou calld.
Penda.   *Conon.*
Kinge.   A saxon?
Penda.   Yes.
Kinge.   And sawst thou *Penda* fall?
Penda.   I did, and help'd to teare the scaffoldings downe   50
That did support his life; please you read this.
Kinge.   Whoes.
Penda.   Captaine *Voltimars.*
Kinge.   Oh *Voltimars.*
Penda.   When hottest weare the fyers, and that the battaile
Flamd in wild uprores, *Voltimar* (and I
Sett on by him) struck both our well aymd swords
Through *Pendas* back.
Kinge.   Heers all hee writes; *tis done.*
Penda.   Tis done, and 'twas your will to haue it Done;
Your oathes too flew to *Fraunce* when it was done
To pay vs gold.
Kinge.   Did *Voltimar* tell thee that too?
Thou canst not sure but bee an honest man,   60
A wonderous honest man, whome *Voltimar*
Would turne into a cabinett to lock
A tresure of this vallue in't. My brothers —
Heaven speed e'm on theire voyage, ambitious boyes!
Hard feathers shall noe more now stuff my pillow,

                53 In left margin: *bee redy* | *Edmond &* | *Eldred*

                              315

But *Penda* stood betwene mee and a prize
Worth a whole masse of kingdomes.
Penda.   I vnderstand you not.
Kinge.   I would not haue thee yett; thou shalt hereafter
Vnderstand this; the whilst, with thie best speed
Aske to the duke of *Cornewalls*, the old fellow   70
That cry'd heere for that *Penda* (twas his sonne),
And lett his daughter heare it from thie lipps
Her husbands dead, shee'l not beleeue yt ells.
Penda.   But sir — yf to this duke you in some fitt
Should tell what I haue done —
Kinge.   I tell? — hange padlocks
Best on your owne lipps, you and *Voltimar*;
Should you blabb all, this can outface you both.
Looke toot.
Penda.   I am lessond.   *Exit.*

                    Enter Edmond *and* Eldred.

Kinge.   *Vffa* and *Gildas*, ha,
Hit I your names right?
Bot⟨h.   [Ye]s⟩ sir.
⟨[*Kinge.*]   ⟩ers, leaue mee,
⟨   1   ⟩ *Pendas* losse too, a noble fel⟨[low]   ⟩   80
⟨   d   ⟩ly   ⟨   ⟩
Edmond.   Vnles your maiestie
Comaund my service I will or'e againe.
Eldred.   And I.
Kinge.   Your service staie; wee shall imploy you
In trobled streames; which if you dare convay —
Eldred.   Dare!
Edmond.   Try vs.
Kinge.   So: you shall haue golden paie.
                                    Exeunt.

[ACT I, Scene ii]

Enter Carintha; Cornwall *and* Chester.

Carintha.   Where is his body, lett mee see but that.
Cornewall.   Now as wee came alonge, wee hard his bodie
   (After the french had seizd it) could by noe force,
   Gold or intreaties bee rescud, for in triumph
   Awaie the spoyle they hurryd.
Chester.   And you must lady
   Make vpp your greate losse by sweete patience
   To keepe your hart from breakinge. His noble father
   You see plaies the phisitian to restore you
   When his owne sicknes is more desperate;
   Nor must it bee your torment now to looke o're   10
   Th'accompts of *Pendas* vallor, youth or Virtues,
   For hees runne out of all, but so well spent
   You cannot at the layings out repent.
Carintha.   I doe not.
Chester.   Please you lady heare the souldier
   That tells the perfect story of his death.
   T'will so delight you that hee out went man
   In's doings; you'l scarce wish him heere agen.
Carintha.   That soldior sunge to mee the funerall Anthem
   Er'e you or the kinge hard it. I thanck your loues
   For theis your tracts of consolation,   20
   But sir methincks I weare best comfort you,
   You haue a manly waie to fight with greefe,
   Yett I that am a woman can ward off
   The blowes better then you. I ha lost a husband,
   A sonne you; if you will make our wracks euen,
   And heeres the ballance — hee's gon well to heauen.
   Penda (my noblest loue) for's cuntry dy'd,
   And is not so much mourn'd for as envyd

11 In left margin: *Bee redy* | *Penda*
16 man] men MS

For the braue end hee made; three tymes hee flew
(Like an armd thunder) into the thickest French, 30
And with the lighteninge of his sword made waie
As greate winds doe through woods, rootinge vpp oakes;
So reel'd the armies buildings at his stroakes.
Must not I proudlier heare this then behold him
Breake twenty staves ith Tilt yard? tis more honor.
Could I wed twenty husbands I would wish
Theire glories in this world to bee noe greater,
Theire fate noe worse, and theire farwell noe better.
Cornewall. Thou art a noble girle.
Chester. And teachest all of vs
To putt on the best armor; heere comes the soldier. 40

Enter Penda [*disguiȝd as* Conon.]

Penda. The kinge for feare theis lords, as loath to wound you,
Should faile in some poynts of your husbands story,
Sends mee to speake it fully, that your sorrowes
May know what they must trust to, and not stagger
In hope that hees alive, — for theis eyes ⟨s⟩aw⟨[—]⟩
Carintha. ⟨[Ho]l⟩d.
⟨*P*[*enda.*]⟩ ⟨[Lady]⟩ I sunge this not to you be⟨fo[re.]⟩
⟨[*Carintha.*]⟩ ⟩ a bad suite t⟨ ⟩

Enter King⟨[e.]⟩

Kinge. By this his cominge
To drye the widdowes teares vpp, 'tis a signe
Hee would not haue her kill her self with weepinge.
Carintha. My cheekes haue not been wett sir.
Kinge. Pitty to drowne 50
Such a rich land of bewtie in salt water.
Pray lett her bee my patient, I haue phisick
Weare shee eaten vpp with anguish shall agen
Putt life into her, tho her soule and shee
Weare shakinge hands.
Cornewalle. Applie your phisick sir.
Chester. Wee shalbee proud of her recouery.
Exeunt [Cornewall *and* Chester.]

318

Kinge.   Whoe now shall pluck *Carintha* from myne Armes?
Before a fatall matrimoniall chaine
Lay crosse our waies, myne to a wisht for bed,
Thine to a crowne. Both rocks are now remoud,   60
Wee both haue sea roome, sitt thou at helme alone,
The ship my kingdome, and the sailes my throwne.
Carintha.   Braue voyage,
Whoe would not venture; are the *Destinies*
Your spinsters that when you cry cutt that thred,
Tis done?
Kinge.   I am puzzell'd, a riddle?
Carintha.   Tis heere resolvd;
I know (at least a spirrit within mee prompts it)
Penda was shipt for *Fraunce* that *Athelstane*
Might without danger both beseige this fort —
Kinge.   Tis true.
Carintha.   And win it if hee could.
Kinge.   Ile practize   70
What engines a whole kingdome can invent
But I will enter it.
Carintha.   You shall never force it.
Tis yeilded sir on composition —
Kinge.   Name it.
Carintha.   To bee your *Queene.*
Kinge.   Wee'le to Church instantly.
Carintha.   Weare I a lady lock't in a brazen tower
And that a prince but spy'd mee, passinge by,
I'de leape (weart neare so high) into his armes,
Becon'd hee for mee; the name of prince should beare it.
I'de spurne at Indian hills of new tryd gold
To come to his embraces, but to a kings —   80
Kinge.   Never such musique, tis some Angell sings;
To morrow weel bee married.
Carintha.   Not for ten kingdomes.
I must a while in mourninge maske myne eyes

67 In left margin: *Bee redy* | *winchester*
80 kings —] ~ ∧ MS

319

To stop the worlds tongue and to temporize
With *Pendas* father.
Kinge.   Doe so then.
Carintha.   Besides
Theres a dukes daughter, whome men call *Armante*,
Contracted to you vnder your owne hand
And has by you a sonne; vntye that knott,
Vnwind that bottome, I'me yours, otherwise —   *Exit.*
Kinge.   Not;
Ile doo't with my little finger, —   90

Enter Winchester.

My lord of *Winchester*, in happy tyme
You come to bee my good phisitian.
Winchester.   First lett me know your sicknes.
Kinge.   There is you know
A contract written vnder myne owne hand,
Seald by your self and other witnesses —
Winchester.   Betwene the lady *Armante* and your highnes.
Kinge.   Right my sperituall surgion, step you to her
And cure her e're I come of that wild phrenzie
⟨[T]h⟩at s⟨[e]⟩tts her tongue a raylinge, bid her make ready
⟨[The contrac]⟩t, for by all my hopes deere father   100
⟨[Tomorrow wee shall] be⟩e married, and wipe off
⟨[The stain of bastard from]⟩ the princly bo⟨y⟩
I gott vppon her body. Shee shall change
Her name of a kings concubin to a *Queene*.
Winchester.   I would not for what lyes beneath the moone
Bee made a wicked engine to breake in peices
That holy contract.
Kinge.   Tis my ayme to tye it
Vppon a knott never to bee vndone.
Goe to my deere *Armante*, tell her I am hirs
At first by oath and now by conscience.   110
Winchester.   I am happy in the message.   *Exit.*

*89 Not;] *stet* MS
92 In left margin: *bee redy* | *Colchester*

Enter Colchester

Kinge.   My lord of *Colchester*, the man I looke for.

Colchester.   And you the man I looke for my deere leige.

Kinge.   Thou hast a buxome cheeke, a Iouiall front.

Colchester.   Haue I not cause when the blood royall roones
In to some parte of myne? my girle, kings mistris;
My grandchild (one of Iupiters scapes) your sonne.

Kinge.   Ha ha.

Colchester.   Hee was gott laughinge, hee laughes so too,
Hee has your owne eyes, ther's his nose, his lipp,   120
His gayte iust yours, a legg and foote like yours,
But yours is some what more calf, kinge hee's thine owne,
For when hee plaies at trap, of all the boyes
Hee must bee kinge too, all call him the younge prince.

Kinge.   They doe?

Colchester.   Hee struttinge some tymes, to his companions
In a maiesticke tone, will saie, my lads
I at my coronation will make you all
Greate men, tho now you are boyes, as I am a prince.

Kinge.   Is hee so forward?

Colchester.   Forward, whie sir, kings bastards   130
Are made of lighteninge — oh!

Kinge.   How does his mother?

Colchester.   Shee, las poore whore.

Kinge.   How sir, my loue a whore?

Colchester.   I cry thee mercy, a kings concubine,
But the true antient english is plaine whore.

Kinge.   Shee lost sir nothinge by beinge myne.

Colchester.   Tis true shee gott a child by it.

Kinge.   And you gott somthinge sir.

Colchester.   Right sir, a duke dome,
And wud I had twoe daughters more to play em
Awaie at twoe such casts.

Kinge.   A braue old boy.

Colchester.   Some haue by daughters falne, whie should not others 140

120 In left margin: *bee redy* | *winchester &* | *Armante*

Bee raizd by daughters, but in sooth my leige
Would thou couldst coyt her off; bandy this white ball
Into some gallants bed, there are enow
Would take her at rebound.
Kinge. Her at rebound?
Noe, in few daies my self will call thee father.
Colchester. Ile call you sonne then.
Kinge. To *Armante* haue I sent good *Winchester*
And my self am goinge to her.
Colchester. Are you;
My howse shall bid you welcome; some busines ended,
Ile there waite on your grace.
Kinge. Doe so. *Exit.*
Colchester. Thie grace? 150
Would thou hadst anie. I will smooth my for head,
Bee the kings foole, and calld the good old man,
The silly duke; and tho a barbed horse,
The shakinge of his wand makes mee stand still,
I wilbee rid and spurd, but kinge take heede;
Head longe I flinge thee when to much I ble⟨[e]d.

E⟩xit.

[ACT I, Scene iii]

Enter Winchester *and* Armante.

Armante. Did the kinge speake this?
Winchester. Did both speake and sweare it,
⟨[Int])en⟨[ds in]⟩ person present⟨[ly] t[o begg]⟩
⟨[Forgivnes for his acts of heaven and you.]⟩
Armante. Heaven pardon him, I doe not.
Winchester. Lett not wild rage
Beare you beyond your self.
Armante. I thanck your counsell.
Winchester. Bee not ore flowne with gall.
Armante. Noe, I'le talke nothinge.

Enter Clowne.

Winchester. Fellow avoyd the roome.

Clowne. The roome? weare it Quarter daie, I take you to bee none of my landlord. Avoyd without warninge?

Winchester. I ha busines for the Kinge heere.   10

Clowne. And I ha busines for the kinge heere too, that is to haue a care to this lady my mistris, whoe is the kings game.

Armante. Game?

Clowne. Yes game, Ime sure his hawck with the longe winge has flowne at you. [*To* Winchester] I haue as much to doe heere as you, and therefore avoyd you the roome.

Armante. My lord, the fellow is silly.

Clowne. For ought I know hees as silly as I am.

Armante. Sett not your witt to his.

Clowne. I doe not meane hee shall, if hee would give mee a 20 benifice to boote Ile not change my witt for his. My lord the duke of *Colchester* (vnder whome I haue an office about oysters) bids mee haue an eye to his daughter; now sir will I haue twoe eyes.

Winchester. A good servant.

Clowne. Nay more, if I fetch my suspective glasse (in which, standinge at queene hive dock, I can tell to a kernell how farr dover peere is) I will then cast three eyes at her.

Winchester. I, doe so, doe so.

Clowne. Nay more, when I'me at age to weare wofull spectacles, my four eyes shall not haue an eye to see, but Ile looke to her 30 water —

Winchester. Thou art too care full, prithee leaue vs now — Stay, whats thie name?

Clowne. My name is *Lapland,* my mother was a witch, my father a broaker, myne Aunt cryd ends of gold and silver, my grandsire went vpp and downe with an Ape; my lord of *Landosses* fine Awpe, heers a iolly kindred.

Winchester. Borne in *London*?

Clowne. Yes on the back side of billinsgate, there are of my name ith Citty, young gentlemen know the laplands, theres a cozen 40

20 In left margin: *bee redy* | *Kinge*

a scrivener (that can looke through an inch bourd his eyes are so
sharpe) has lapd more lands in sheepe skin then all our backs
can carry.

Enter Kinge.

Winchester.   Peace, heers the kinge.

Kinge.   Leave vs.

Clowne.   Avoyd the roome.   *Exeunt* [Winchester *and Clowne.*]

Kinge.   Oh my *Armante.*

Armante.   This is strange that I
 Whoe haue so long been nip'd euen dead with could,
 Should now haue sunne beames warme mee, oh Sir my wrongs —

Kinge.   Come dreame not of them, I will fan them off   50
 As if they nere had been, for heere *Armante*
 I vow to morrow e're the god of daie
 Has putt a golden ringe about bright noone,
 Thou shalt bee myne, as fast in nuptiall band
 As I am thine by contract, and thy sonne
 With full consent of state freely proclaymd
 Myne and my kingdomes heire, which to effect
 That contract which thou hast shall bee inlarg'd.

Armante.   Tis well enough already.

Kinge.   But now it shalbee made past all dissolvinge.   60
 ⟨[The]⟩ Bisshop did not see the Contract did hee?

⟨[*Armante.*   Nor he]⟩ nor anie shall.

⟨[*Kinge.*   I must.]⟩

⟨[*Armante.*   You shall not.]⟩

Kinge.   Keepe it and marry that then, lye with that,
 Call that your husband, if that paper kinge
 Can gett younge paper princes of you, lett him.
 Come I with all my drossy scales fyld off,
 Pollisht, and smoothd, and doe you vse mee still
 As if I weare base mettall? raile noe more at mee,
 Remember thus I came to you, thus leaue you.

Armante.   Royall sir the Contracts heere.

---

56 In left margin: *bee redy* | *Clowne*
62 The mutilated words supplied according to the suggestions of *MLR.*

Kinge.   I will not touch it,   70
Not see it, lett mee goe, pray.
Armante.   Las, beinge before
Ith faulcons gripe, I would bee pincht noe more.
Kinge.   The faulcon would flye from you.
Armante.   Hee shall not, see sir,
Heere as the deerest Iewell of my fame
Lockt I this parchment from all couetous eyes.
This your Indenture holds alone the life
Of my sick wasted honor, yett behold,
Into your hands I redeliver it.
Kinge.   So, it is ith lyons paw and whoe dares snatch it?
Armante.   Ha, you doe but counterfeit to mock my ioyes.   80
Kinge.   Awaie bould strumpit.   *Exit.*

Enter Clowne.

Armante.   Are there eyes in heaven to see this?
Clowne.   Mad maudlin are you goeinge to bedlam?
Armante.   Yes, lett mee haue fresh straw, I am mad.
Clowne.   So am I, lett goe your catts nayles, or I'le fall vppon
you as I'me a man.
Armante.   Is the kinge gon, thou slaue?
Clowne.   Hees gon but not so farr gon as you.
Armante.   Rocks leape out of the sea to fall vppon mee
And grinde mee into powder.   90
Clowne.   What powder, come what powder, when did you see anie
woman grinded into powder, I'me sure some of you powder men,
and pepper em too.
Armante.   Awaie, Ile bee a ghost and haunt this kinge
Till want of sleep bids him runne mad and dye
For makinge oathes bawds to his periury.   *Exit.*

Enter Colchester.

Colchester.   How now, whers my daughter.
Clowne.   Troath my lord I know not, the kinge was heere, out
they fell about a writinge, which hee gott from her; through
a crevis I saw all.   100

97 *Colchester.*] *omit* MS

325

Colchester.   A writinge?

Clowne.   Yes Sir and her nayles in her rage weare currycombes
in my haire, for shee lookes as wild as a gentleman frighted by
a seriant.

Colchester.   A writinge? I devine the mischeif.   *Is goinge.*

Clowne.   My lord I would faine give vpp my cloake, this livery
of waitinge on my lady your daughter. I haue some learninge,
and am loath to grubb my penn wholly in a womans busines,
there's a goose quill sticks in my stomach, I haue a mighty desire
to bee bound to a cronicler, or some such lyinge trade.   110

Colchester.   Leaue her not yett I prithee; one storme blowne ore,
Take thine owne course.

Clowne.   And then my muse shall rore.

Exeunt.

Finis Actus Primi

ACT 2^{DUS} [SCENE i]

Enter Eldred, Edmond, Penda, *and Captaine* Voltimar.

Eldred.   Alls well, our dice runne faire, Fortune her self
Lends vs a lucky hand.

Edmond.   The kinge throwes on vs
Bownties in such aboundance they come rowlinge
Like waues on waues, wee know not for what service
Vnles because wee brought him like french foote posts
Newes of the twoe slaine princes; but wee hope
His kinglie largesse is a goulden hooke
At which some high attempt hangs, and on vs
Hee meanes to putt the execution.

Voltimar.   Will not you meete his offers?

Omnes.   Oh by all meanes.   10

Penda.   As eagerly as an old *Regiment*
Of totterd soldiers (whoe amon⟨g [them all]⟩
⟨C⟩arri⟨[e]⟩s not so much ⟨   [as]⟩
A shirts half sleeue) runne on your fresh blowne troopes

326

Of gallants that come briske into the feild,
Of scarlett larded thick with glitteringe lace
And feathers that plumed estriges out face.
Voltimar.   I am glad since all of you are come afishinge,
Your netts are cast so well.
Eldred.   Pshew beyond fate,
And this superfluous dandlinges of the kinge   20
Teach all the court to daunce vs on theire knees.
Edmond.   Theres not a morninge but wee breake our fast
Vppon the salutation of some duke,
Some earle, greate lord or so, and passinge by,
Good morrow to captaine *Gildas.*
Eldred.   The good daie
To noble captaine *Vffa.*
Penda.   Oh captaine *Conon,*
Myne Armes are proud to reach you.
Eldred.   Saies Duke *Cornewalle* —
Vffa pray dyne with mee. — I thanck your grace.
Penda.   Saies th'Earle of *Chester* — *Conon* prithee see mee
So soone as I ha dyn'd — I come — discourse   30
How heere our maine battailia came vpp prowdlie,
Heere the right wings flew hotly vpp: left heere,
Pell mell, all heere togeither by the eares:
Heere wheele a troope of horse, the pikes chardge there,
The bow men yonder with theire showers of Arrowes
Gall the braue French chevalls, as they discend
That hill there, heere our Saxons are at poynt
To flye, our Captaines sweare 'em into courage;
Heere they turne head agen, and heere my mounsiers
Are malld, and cry *Mort Dieu*; then sir I tell him   40
That in this quarter braue prince *Eldred* fell,
Hackt in a thowsand peices.
Voltimar.   So
Penda.   Prince *Edmond*
(His body beinge nothinge but a signe
Hung at a surgions dore) in yonder Quarter.
Voltimar.   Good.

Penda.   And afarr off in yon regiment
Penda was cutt in mammocks. I talke high,
Some truth, some lyes, which ended my earle dropps
Twentie half peeces for more noyse and number
Into my hand, I pockett em.
Edmond.   Soldiers weare never
Blest with such daies as theis.
Voltimar.   Troath so thinck I too —   50
How shall I gett accesse now to the kinge,
For I'me so ouer growne with haire, the guard
Will take mee for a savage —
Edmond.   I'le in and tell him.
Eldred. You shall not, the labors savd.

   Florish. Enter Kinge: Cornewall *and* Chester. *The three
step to the Kinge.*

Kinge.   My *Voltimar,*
I will make haste to meete thee, rise; of all,
Of all those fyrie sperrits that flew to *Fraunce,*
Are all to cinders turnd, but *Voltimar?*
Voltimar. Noe sir, heeres a Messe of vs, sett by for a second
service.
Kinge. You weare a vollume of Arithmetique   60
And now foure figures are the some of all.
I wilbee thrifty, and the rest beinge spent
Make much of whats heere left mee, art well *Capten?*
Voltimar. Sir my sword and I haue tane phisick in *Fraunce.*
Kinge. Ar't full of French crownes honest *Voltimar?*
Voltimar. Wee had our hands full of so many crackt one's, they
weare not worth ⟨[the] c⟩arryinge.
Kinge. ⟨[Saw y]o⟩u my brother *Eldred* when hee dy'd?
⟨[*Voltimar.* I saw]⟩ him.
⟨[*Kinge.*]⟩   ⟩es.   70
Cornewall. And when my *Penda* fell?
Voltimar. Yes at my foote hee fell.
Kinge. Weare my brothers forward in the battaile?

   53 In left margin: *bee redy Kinge | Cornewall & | Chester*

Voltimar.   As any.

Chester.   The French did come vpp brauely; did they?

Voltimar.   Like the French.

Chester.   Wee hard the fight lasted some seuen howers.

Voltimar.   T'was a pritty longe breakefast.

Cornewall.   Was the French kinge ith feild in person?

Kinge.   With draw —   80

Voltimar.   Make much of theis three men sir.

                                        Exeunt. [*Manent Kinge and* Voltimar.]

Kinge.   I weare them soldier

As Iewells on my boosome, I had thie Letter.

Voltimar.   'Twas short.

Kinge.   Only twoe words: *Tis Done.*

Voltimar.   And tis done, and almost as quickly done as those
words weare read; would tweare to doe agen.

Kinge.   Whie?

Voltimar.   I would then forsweare writinge that court hand;
'tis done.   90

Kinge.   Dost repent?

Voltimar.   Doe not you? Would you and I stood vppon equall
basses, would I weare your fellow but for half an howers talke,
freely to ease my mynd, my hart swells, it's ready to burst.

Kinge.   Vnbutton then thie hart, for one half hower

Wee are fellowes, come, be couerd and talke bouldly.

Whate're it bee tis pardon'd.

Voltimar.   If it bee not I care not, it's but your yea and my nay,
yf you sweare I'le sweare as fast as you.

Kinge.   Well said, letts fall too't, come.   100

Voltimar.   Did not you send mee a letter, which did cry out that
Penda was a pernitious traytor, that you saw earth quakes ins
eyes to shake your kingdome, to tosse you out of your throwne,
that if hee stood you must fa⟨[ll;]⟩ did not you chardge mee vppon
my loyalty to rid him awaie, and in him your feares; ha?

Kinge.   Tis true I wrott so.

Voltimar.   Tis falce what you wrott so; *Penda* was noe traytor,
Penda was honest, honorable in all his actions, a souldier the
world has noe better, a man mortallytie has none so good, yett

him, would you ruin, him; all this heape of admirable buildinge 110
haue I for you demollisht, you haue made mee both your butcher
and your bawd.

Kinge. Bawd?

Voltimar. Yes bawd, I never was a carpenter till now, I haue
made a bridge of the husbands body for you to goe to his wife.

King. Ha.

Voltimar. Y'are a whoremaster.

Kinge. How?

Voltimar. A most horrible whoremaster, the divills master poynt
lyes in the codpeice, and that poynt you haue untyd, doe you send 120
mee to win townes for you, and you loose a kingdome at home?

Kinge. What kingdome.

Voltimar. The fairest in the world, the kingdome of your fame,
your honor, your soule.

Kinge. Wherein.

Voltimar. I must bee plaine with you.

Kinge. So methincks you are.

Voltimar. Angells er'd once and fell, but you sir spitt in heavens
face euery minute, and laugh at it: laugh still, follow your courses,
doe, lett your vices runne like your kennell of hounds yealpinge 130
after you till they pluck downe the fairest head ith heard, your
euerlastinge blisse.

Kinge. Spitt thie vennon.

Voltimar. Tis Aqua Cælestis, noe vennon.

Kinge. Thie half hower is out.

Voltimar Turne vpp the glasse agen, I will follow tr⟨[uth at]
h⟩er heele⟨[s tho her foote]⟩ beate my gumms in peices.

Kinge. The barber that drawes out a lyons tooth
Curses his trade, and ⟨s[o shalt thou.]⟩

Voltimar. I care not.   140

Kinge. Because you ha beaten a few base french peasants,
Mee thinckst thou to chastize; whats past I pardon,
But if thou darst once more bee so vntund
Ile send thee to the gallies.

119 In left margin: *bee redy* | *Cornewall* | *& Chester*
137 gumms] gumm MS (doubtfully)

330

Voltimar. Noe to'th gallowes, vppon a ladder a man may talke
freely, and never bee sent to prison; I had a raw stomach before,
and now tis eas'd hange mee, draw mee, quarter mee, cutt mee,
carbonado mee, this, pish.

Kinge. Is your half hower runne out now?

Voltimar. Yes, yes, I am quiett.　　　　　　　　　　　　　　　150

Kinge. Prithee noe more of this, thou shalt not aske
The thinge which Ile deny thee, and since thast waded
For mee thus vpp to'th middle, on now deere *Voltimar.*

Voltimar. I, I, ouer shoes, ouer bootes, anie thinge, anie more
throates to cutt?

Kinge. None, only at her fathers winde thie self
Into this ladies companie (sad *Armante.*)
Shees mad with rage, and in her desperate vengeance
May plott against my life, sound her for that.

Voltimar. That all? I am both your lyne and plomett.　　　　160

Enter Cornwall *and* Chester.

Kinge. I'me haunted with a fury, yon younge witch
Whoe with her bastard both laies clayme to mee
And to my crowne, I haue no waie to scape
From beinge still blasted by her, but to marry,
And marry out of hand.

Chester.　　　　　　　　But wheres a lady,
Fitt for your royall bed?

Kinge.　　　　　　　　A kinswoman
To euery one of you, *Pendas* noble wife
Whoe dy'd in *Fraunce.*

Cornewall. I would shee weare so happie
To haue her losse in him, repaird so fairely.　　　　　　　　170

Chester. Theres not a man heere whoe to see his familie
Crownd with such royall honors, but would spend
Half his estate to grace the nuptialls.

Kinge. It is the voyce of all of you that I
Should call you noble kinsmen?

161 *Kinge.*] MSR; *omit* MS
163 In left margin: *bee redy* | *winchester*

Omnes.   Sir, of all.
Kinge.   Wee all must bandy, with that faction then
Her father and her frenzie shall give fyer to.
One blow they haue alreadie, see I haue gott
My contract from her.
Omnes.   Keepe it.
Kinge.   Keepe it, noe;
In paper I'le noe longer wrapp my feares.   180

Enter Winchester.

Winchester.   Had you none else but mee to brand ith forhead
With infamy, with treachery, with periury?
Kinge.   Art frantick?
Winchester.   You are so sir.
Kinge.   Raue thie fill,
Kings subiects are to none but theire owne will.

Exeunt: manet Winchester.

Enter Colchester *and* Kent.

Both.   Wheres the kinge.
Winchester.   Wrap'd vpp in clowds of lightninge.
Kent.   What, is hee turnd *Ioue?*
Lett him, wee'l thunder too.
Colchester.   Wee hard my lord of *Winchester* hee changd
You to a stalkinge horse, you weare his hooke
And your sweete words the fly at which my poore girle   190
Armante niblinge, you strangled her, gott from her
The contract hee was ty'd in.
Kent.   Whats done with it?
Winchester.   I know not, in sight of *Cornewall,*
Chester and others, when hee had baffled mee,
Made mee his property to wronge the lady,
And speakinge home, hee bad mee raue my fill,
Sayinge kings must stoope to none but theire owne will.
Kent.   Whie then in sight of *Colchester* her father,

185 *Both.*] *omit* MS
192 In left margin: *bee redy* | *Voltimar &* | *Armante*

332

Winchester and *Kent*, (men high in blood as they)
His periurie shalbee his ruin.
Winchester.   Or ours.   200
Thus I fall from the duty hee has blasted,
To ⟨[bee]⟩ revengd with you.
Kent.   ⟨[Thus I em]⟩brace you,
Meete and consult.
⟨[*Winchester*.   No more, trust] n⟩ot the ayre
⟨[With our proie]⟩ctio⟨[n]s,⟩ lett v⟨s⟩ all revenge
⟨[Wrongs done to our most noble]⟩ ki⟨ns[w]⟩oman.
Kent.   Action is honors language, swords are tongues
Which both speake best, and best doe write our wrongs.
Colchester.   Those tongues shall scould then.

                                              Exeunt.

[ACT II, Scene ii]

Enter Voltimar: *and* Armante.

Voltimar.   The Kinge has done you infinitt wronge.
Armante.   Infinite.
Voltimar.   And noe question you ha done him some.
Armante.   Never any.
Voltimar.   Noe? yes sure, for had not those twoe balls of wild fire
in your head burnt him into dotage, had you not embrothered
your face with wanton glaunces, hee had been quiet, your self not
tormented; a lady of your birth, fortunes, freinds, and sperri⟨t,⟩
yett lett him scape so —
Armante.   Hee must not.   10
Voltimar.   Ieere at you —
Armante.   Hee dares not.
Voltimar.   Baffle you and your noble familie —
Armante.   Hee cannot.
Voltimar.   What would you say to him should kill this man
that hath you so dishonord.

                    *201 Thus I fall] *stet* MS

                              333

Armante.   Oh I would crowne him
With thancks, praise, gold, and tender of my life.
Voltimar.   This is hee shall doot.
Armante.   Theres musique in the tongue that dares but speake it.   20
Voltimar.   Your fidler then am I, lett mee see, poniard, poyson,
any revenge.
Armante.   One step to human blisse is sweete revenge.
Voltimar.   *Revenge*; tis milke, tis honny, tis balme, delicate in
the mouth, pretious in the hand, nourishinge to the stomach, life
to the soule, so shed is an elixar, so drunck a Iulip, it fattens, it
battens, revenge, oh! stay, stay, one question, what made you
loue him?
Armante.   His most goodly shape,
Married to royall virtues of his mynd.   30
Voltimar.   Did it so, and now you would divorse all that goodnes,
but whie? for liquorishnes of revenge? tis a lye.
Armante.   Blesse mee this grim fellow frights mee.
Voltimar.   Ile not hurt you. For revenge? noe the burr that
sticks in your throate is a throwne: had hee a messe of kingdomes
and laid but one vppon your trencher, you'd praise bastard for the
sweetest wine ith world and call for another quart; 'tis not because
the man has left you, but because you are not the woman you would
bee. I shoote my boult now to our market, whats my wages when
I ha done?   40
Armante.   The wages of a slaue (dispaire and death)
Monster of men thou art, thou bloody villaine,
Trator to him whoe never iniurd thee,
Dost thou professe Arms and art bound by honor
To stand vpp like a brazen wall to guard
Thie kinge and cuntry, and wouldst ruin both?
Voltimar.   For gold anie, you, him, noe matter whome, doe you
clapp spurrs to my sides yett raine mee hard in, am I ridd with a
martingall?
Armante.   Hence, tho I could runne mad and teare my haire   50
And kill that godles man that turnd mee strompitt,

35 In left margin: *bee redy K:* | *Cornewall* | *Chester: Edm:* | *Eldred & Penda*
*35 throwne] thorne MS

334

Tho I am cheated by a periurous prince
Whoe has done wickednes at which even heaven
Shakes when the sunne beholds it, oh yet I'de rather
Ten thowsand poysond poniards struck my brest
Then one should touch his.
Voltimar.   Are you in earnest?
Armante.   Leaue mee or I shall doe my best to mischeif thee.
Voltimar.   Live wretched still then.
Armante.   Out of myne eye I prithee.   60
Voltimar.   Your eye — I'me gon — give me thie goll, thou art
a noble girle; I did bu⟨t [play]⟩ the divills parte, and rore in a
feign'd voyce, but I am the honestest divi⟨[ll that ever]⟩ spitt fyer,
nor would I drinck that draught ⟨[of a]⟩ kings bl⟨[ood to goe
reelinge]⟩ downe wards for the waight of the world i⟨n [diam]o⟩nds.
Armante.   Art thou in earnest?
Voltimar.   As you are lady.
Armante.   Are not you one of the kings ⟨q⟩ua⟨[ile]⟩ pi⟨[pers?]⟩
Voltimar.   I am not, crack mee, tho my shell bee rough theres
a wholesome meate within mee.   70
Armante.   Ile call thee honest soldier then, and woe thee
To bee an often visitant.
Voltimar.   Your servant.
Armante.   Come like a gentle gale to coole my wrongs
And call my roofe thine owne.   *Exit.*
Voltimar.   Ile bee nothinge else.

> *Florish.* **Enter** *Kinge*: Cornewall, Chester. Edmond,
> Eldred, *and* Penda *followinge.*

Kinge.   Step you before, my lord, tell her wee are cominge.
                                          Exit Cornewall.
Pray troble mee not, I'me busy.
All 3.   You promist vs imployment.
Kinge.   Wee ha noe warrs; when the drome beates, call to vs.   80
Edmond.   May bee sir you stop your eares with woole and can
hardlie heare a soldiers call.
Chester.   Y'are sawcy.

335

Eldred.   Sawcy; you allow vs noe meate to our sawce.

Penda.   Wee are restiff for want of exercise.

Edmond.   And pursie at hart for want of ridinge.

Eldred.   Good spurrs clapt to our sides would shew our mettle.

Kinge.   *Voltimar*: rid mee of theis flyes; tis a sommer of peace, and wee neede more sickles then swords.

Exeunt Kinge and Chester.

Penda.   Flyes, marry buzz.   90

Voltimar.   Ha ha, did not I tell you?

Edmond.   More sickles then swords, hee would haue vs turne reapers.

Eldred.   Noe, noe, weel fall to thrashinge.

Voltimar.   Tis a sommer of peace, and soldiers you may take a purse in winter and bee hangd ere next springe.

Penda.   The best is tho hee plucks vs on like straight bootes, hee does not yett complayne where wee pinch him.

Voltimar.   Did not I steere your course well at our cominge out of *Fraunce* to land you in *Wales*, tho t'weare the fardest waie about.   100

Edmond.   A witch could not haue fore tould the weather better.

Voltimar.   Will you gentre then to the twincklinge of that welsh harpe I tun'd for you in Shropsheire or noe?

Omnes.   By anie meanes.

Penda.   Whie else haue I theis Lettres of Credence from the welsh kinge (*Howell* by name) to bringe only a message of loue vnto *Athelstane* till the tribute of *Wales* bee sent, of so many Runts, so many hawkes, so many hounds, so many pounds of gold and so many of silver, and that wilbee about a moneth hence.

Edmond.   Your welsh mountaine of aucthority wilbee digd downe   110 to a mole hill before that tyme.

Eldred.   Walke vppon noe lower stilts then those of an embasador.

Voltimar.   Ile fitt you followers, cuttinge boyes, roringe soldadoes, that if neede bee shall eate fyer.

Eldred.   At the end of the last battaile in *Wales*, I drunck healthes in metheglin amonge 'em, never mett nobler companions, and

84 meate] meale MS   89 neede] MSR; *omit* MS
102 gentre] gent' MS
108 In left margin: *bee redy | Cornewall & | Carintha*

staid so longe, I could gabble very handsomly, so that for a sentill
man of *Wales*, one of my lord embassadors followers, if I faile
flea mee.

Edmond.   What must I doe, Ile bee a bowle in your Ally too, but 120
not of your byas, noe welsh I; weart in *Ireland* with the Kernes
and galloglasses could I haue good sport. You talke of metheglin:
Morrogh mac Breean the kinge of *Leinstar*, *Dermot* kinge of *Vlster*,
with *Mac Dermond* kinge of *Connacht* whoe weare all three in thatt
battaile against vs, when the fight was done and all freinds, so
souct mee in *Vsquebagh* my very braines burnt blew, so that
ifaatla for an Irishman gett but a taylor to fitt mee, and pluck my
tongue out if I runne not glibb awaie with it.

Penda.   Runne, whie will you not come as some greate Irish lord?

Edmond.   Pshew theres noe pleasure in state, I had rather haue 130
a scramblinge hunters breakfast, then a Cardinalls dynner. Lord,
noe, only a footman to ⟨y[ou]r [e]m⟩bassadorship, I shall not
laugh else.

Voltimar.   W⟨[hatev]⟩er oares wee must row with leave mee to
furnish.

Penda.   For a comedy of disguises letts then Arme,
Which tho it doe noe good, can doe noe harme.

                                                  Exeunt.

[ACT II, Scene iii]

Enter Cornwall; *and* Carintha, *vaild in black.*

Cornewall.   The kinge in person comes to drye your teares
And will I thinck pull you to his royall bed;
If hee does, fasten him; tho your former husband,
Penda my sonne, was deere to mee as life
Hee cannot bee calld back, yett for his sake
I shalbee glad to see your fortunes raizd.
A Queene is a braue name, bee wise and catch
Tymes lock if it bee given you — see hee comes.

Enter Kinge and Chester.

Kinge.   A pious deede my lord, comfort the sick,
Shees sick at soule (poore hart) pray dare you trust   10
The widdow and mee togeither?
Chester.   And wish that you Sir
May haue the skill to make those clowds cleire vpp
Which darken so her bewty.
Kinge.   *Chester* Ile try it.
Chester.   A lucky hand may you haue.
                                    Exeunt Cornewall *and* Chester.
Kinge.   Dost mourne in sadnes?
Carintha.   Doe anie mourne in iest?
Kinge.   Shine like thie self and drive awaie theis mists
In which I cannot see thee.
Carintha.   Tis for your sake,
I counterfeit this sorrow that the court
(Espetially old *Cornwall, Pendas* father)
Might not reproue mee for a carelesse lady   20
To loose so braue a husband and not weepe
Myne eyes out for him.
Kinge.   But I hope thou dost not.
Carintha.   Never wett thus much of a handkercher.
Kinge.   I gott my contract from yon scouldinge creature
And that thine eyes may witnes I speake truth
Doe with it what thie self wilt.
Carintha.   Ile read it ore, and teare it then in peices.
Kinge.   Please thie self in it.
Tis to the lords thie noble freinds made knowne
That I wish you my Queene, they are prowd of it.   30
Carintha.   They are?
Kinge.   And give consent; come, prithee noe longer
Lock thie self vpp thus in a tragique roome.
Carintha.   I am now so vsd toot, I could bee content
To lyve and dye heere.
Kinge.   Out vppon't, what pleasure

17 In left margin: *bee redy* | *Penda and* | *Voltimar aboue*

338

Can dwell betwene twoe mellancholly walls,
What obiects hast thou heere to feede the eye.
Carintha.   Yes, rare ones.
Kinge.   Rare ones —
Carintha.   See else.

Shews Penda [*above*] *with a leadinge staff.* Voltimar
at his back: his sword in him.

Kinge.   Ha, what's this.
Carintha.   By *Pendas* picture I a workman hird
  To carve that statue for mee, oh sir I pleasd
  His father highly in it.
Kinge.   But whats hee   40
  That stands behind him in that dangerous posture?
Carintha.   I know not what hee is.
Kinge.   Noe? tis the shape
  Of a most honest soldier, his name *Voltimar.*
Carintha.   I now remember, when I had desire
  To figure out that divell which slew my *Penda,*
  By chaunce a fellow fashiond iust like this
  Past by, my workman eyed him, and cutt this,
  A more illfavord slaue I nere beheld,
  And such a one methought was that ro⟨[gue, sur]⟩e,
  That killd my lord, and so this stands fo⟨[r him.]⟩   50
Kinge.   Alter it prithee, hee whome it resembles
  Is a most honest man.
Carintha.   Is hee; I am sorry,
  Ile then shew him — noe, I ha funerall masques too
  Of fyer drakes, ghosts and witches, and oft tymes
  At midnight daunce they round about the roome
  To nuzzle mee in melancholly, and so please you
  Ile call in one of those masques —   [*Close scene above.*]
Kinge.   Oh by noe meanes,
  I haue enough of this, one night to live thus
  Would turne mee madd; for sake thie charnell howse

45 In left margin: *bee redy Chester* | *Cornewall &* | *Voltimar*
59 mee] MSR; *omit* MS   59 charnell] carnell MS

And change it to a Court, the name of widdow   60
Into a wife and Queene.
Carintha.   I shalbee haunted with your old sweete hart.
Kinge.   For her head shee dares not.
Carintha.   I am at your disposure.
Kinge.   In that word thou dost include thie coronation.
My lords you may come in now, wee ha done.

> *Enter* Chester, Cornwall *and* Voltimar.

Chester.   Are the fates gentle to you,
To spin you golden threds of happines
By marriage with this lady; haue you brought her
To handle *Cupids* bow?
Kinge.   And to shoote *Chester*
His arrowes too; so you vppon hir lay   70
Noe black aspertion of neglect or lightnes
For hir so suddaine castinge of her sorrow
For a most noble husband, shee is content
To fill my court with gladnes by her presence.
Cornewall.   It is a day I wish for.
Chester.   So doe wee all,
End heere all rights then of this funerall.
Kinge.   And for them *Hymen* shall by his pure fyers
Purge th'aire, and ad new flames to our desires.
Accompanie the lady — *Voltimar:* —

> *Exeunt omnes, manent Kinge and* Voltimar.

Voltimar.   Thers a welsh embassador sir a cominge.   80
Kinge.   I care not whoe is cominge; how didst find her.
Voltimar.   Full of mischeif, her spittle poyson, breath a whirlwind,
words thunder, and voyce lightninge.
Kinge.   The furies at my weddinge of this ladie then
Will daunce about our court.
Voltimar.   Furies; alas poore doue, shee has noe gall, loues you
too well to heare you ill nam'd; shee sees you slight her, and shee
cares not for you. Tho shee bee not full waight, in my conscience

79 S.D. *manent*] *manet* MS

340

you might putt her away in game, some younge rake would snapp
at hir.   90

Kinge.   Oh *Voltimar* our gamsters are to subtill,
Noe man of noate that knowes our court and hir,
Will throw at such falce coyne, and her greate hart
Scornes to bee passd awaie to a base groome.

Voltimar.   The sound of this welsh embassador makes (methincks)
such a singinge in my head, if you could fasten this fish vppon
that hooke.

Kinge.   Ha.

Voltimar.   Make ready you your angell, at the lyne hange lordships, sheires, half your exchequer, to make him byte for hir, to 100
make her nibble, lett mee alone to play the flye.

Kinge.   My *Voltimar* doe this and thou shalt bee
A sharer in my kingdome.

Voltimar.   Half a share shall serve mee.

                                           Exeunt.

                  Finis Actus Secundi.

ACT 3ᵘˢ [SCENE i]

Enter Armante *and Clowne.*

Armante.   What ist thou so art scriblinge, art makinge ballads?

Clowne.   Ballads, noe maddam, my muse drincks neither four
shillinge nor six shillinge beere, the liquor I take in is from the
french Hipocrenian hogshead, I lapp out of *Minervas* milkebowle.

Armante.   ⟨[What] — ⟩ a poet?

Clowne.   ⟨   ⟩ a hobberde hoy of hellicon, and maddam
I feare I must bee ⟨[soon]⟩ carried awaie with a furie from you
for I am ravisht, ⟨[I haue g]⟩ott with child a horse that I keepe at
rack and manger, calld *Pegasus* and vppon him am I gallopinge
to the horshoe foote mountaine of *Pernassus.*   10

Armante.   Th'art mad sure.

      99 *Voltimar.*] MSR; *omit* MS *and speech run on with line* 98.
      99 angell] *i.e.* angle   8 that] & MS

Clowne. I am mad with keepinge you companie, the nine muses are all women, and nine women are able to make nine score men mad.

Armante. Come leaue thie fooleries, I am cold this morninge, letts tosse.

Clowne. And tumble too ladie if you please, but before I say *B* to this baddledore Ile tell your ladiship what I am turnd into.

Armante. If into noe terrible monster Ile looke vppon it.

Clowne. Noe loggerhead Ellephant Ile assure you, for a penny 20 loafe serves mee twoe daies when I eate least.

Armante. Well sir what are you turnd into.

Clowne. Oh maddam my head is a meere bagpuddinge.

Armante. Good meate.

Clowne. My braines the flower that makes it, my sweete concipts the plums, when I sweate in my invention thats the suett, iests the salt, my witt the grosse pepper.

Armante. A wise puddinge, has it noe eggs?

Clowne. Yes; my eagernes in writinge are the eggs I putt into it and my scull is the iron pott in which I seeth this puddinge. 30

Armante. And when comes it to'th table.

Clowne. When you see mee pipinge hott then looke for a lick at mee, my pudding⟨[e]⟩ is wholly at your service.

Armante. To putt you into a heate then, play.

Clowne. My cock is vpp longer then yours for a shillinge.

Armante. Done Sir, you are downe before mee.

Clowne. I thinck so, a man is nothinge in a womans hands.

Armante. I ha lost the Kinge quite for I nere was merry
When my thoughts lighted on him; Ile tosse him from mee
As I doe this, trust mee theis shettlcocks 40
Are pritty fine invention.

Clowne. Oh very fine, the'ile putt cullor into your honorable cheekes, make your leggs supple, your armes soluble, quickens the eye, sharpens the stomach (I could eate oats like a horse now) and is the only sword and buckler fight against the greene sicknes; which I'me sure you feele not.

17 In left margin; *bee redy* | *Prince*
44 oats] eate MS

342

Enter the Prince

Prince.   Mother, my grandsir and a heap of lords
Are rusht into your lodgings.

Enter Colchester, Winchester *and* Kent.

Colchester.   All strangers leaue the roome.
Clowne.   Noe english man stirr a foote.   50
Winchester.   Hence with this triviall fellow.
Kent.   What makes hee heere.
Clowne.   I am this young gentlemans tutor for battledoringe and
shittlecockery.
Winchester.   Awaie foole, bee packinge.
Clowne.   Take heed you never fall vnder the dreery dint of my
goosequill, I will pack and peck if you doe.   *Exit.*
Armante.   Whence shootes this thunder.
Colchester.   The kinge takes *Pendas* widdow to his Queene.
Armante.   When?
Winchester.   Instantly, and theres a murmer flyes
Your sonne the prince (like to a braunch lop'd off)   60
Must bee snatch'd from you, if you refuze to send him,
For fetchd hee wilbee.
Kent.   Whilst you from court retird
Must give ore howskeepinge.
Armante.   Anie more arrowes?
Colchester.   Are not theis three enow; does not the first
(That marriage most vnlawful) cleaue thie hart;
Does not the second wound this child to death,
Else whie should hee bee sent for, hee that hates
The mother seldome smiles vppon the sonne.
Thou hast a north starr yett to steere thie course by,
Theres but one shore of safty, thowsands of ruin.   70
Armante.   And which that one to safety.
Winchester.   For you deere ladie,
To shutt your self vpp mongest some cloysterd *Nunnes*,
Danger dares there not looke in; and for the prince,

57 In left margin: *bee redy* | *Voltimar*

343

To keepe him from the kinge.

Armante.   The kinge?

Prince.   My father?
What brauer wings can ore an eaglett spred
Then the old eagles? I doe not thinck my father
Would hurte mee weare I with him.

Armante.   I will not tread
That path you beate (of safety.) Should a destiny
Bringe mee a leafe of brasse grauen with the deathes
Of mee and my poore boy (as the kings act)   80
Ide spitt ith face of fate, and sweare shee lyes.
Noe kinge makes his owne sonne a sacrifize.

Colchester.   Bee wilfull then and rue it.

Enter Voltimar

Winchester.   Heeres the kings earewigg.

Voltimar.   Health to your lordshipes, if it weare still water before
I came, I am sorry the winde of my mouth must raise a storme;
I come from the kinge, and tho I am noe theefe yett I must see
your howse broaken vpp (sweete lady) and your gates (after the
noble mens waie) to stand shutt, your number of chimneyes are
to cozen the beggers and make 'em fall a cursinge, to see noe smoake
in 'em, maddam I am to dischardge all your followers.   90

Prince.   All, and mee too, I am one Sir.

Voltimar.   Yes and you too, I am the kings lambe taker and this
must with mee.

Prince.   Saue mee good grandsir, saue mee mother, my lords,
This man has a doggs looke.

Colchester.   Touch but his nayle, thou better weart to draw —

Voltimar.   What?

Colchester.   A lyons tooth out.

Voltimar.   Dare you draw vppon mee?

Colchester.   Yes and will draw thie hart out, kill the villaine.   100

Voltimar.   Come, haue I been a butt full of arrowes to feare your
weake bowes, whome I paw I teare, death in a white beard is noe
bug beare to fright mee, your duggions this for e'm, my dublet has

75 spred] sped MS   86 In left margin: *bee redy K:* | *Cornewall &* | *Chester*

344

had oylet holes in't with sharper bodkins; will you fight, I challenge
you at all theis weapons, but if youl talke like Iustices of the peace,
looke you, I am a quiet man, only heare this, 'tis the kings hand
putts him into myne my lords.

Colchester.   And ours takes him out of the kings and thine,
So tell him, saie tis *Colchester* that speakes it.

      Exeunt [Colchester *and* Kent *with Prince.*]

Armante.   My lord of *Winchester* pray stopp theire madnes, 110
The kinge and I made vpp a stock of loue,
A royall stock, and puttinge it to vse,
My child must bee sent home for interest,
Shall hee not haue his owne?   *Exit* Winchester.

Voltimar.   Lett em goe lady, when the whirligiggs of theire
braines haue don spininge the'ile stand still. Doe you hold mee
honest?

Armante.   I find thee full waight yett.

Voltimar.   When anie other musique sounds mee, splitt my pipe.
The Kinge will marry.   120

Armante.   Lett him.

Voltimar.   Noe I will not lett him nor shall you, a welsh embassador is to come to court, the kinge meanes to putt you vppon
him, him vppon you (fine hott-cockles), 'tis my plott, my
grindinge.

Armante.   Vppon mee putt his welsh man?

Voltimar.   Pshew theres a dyall for your howers to goe by, hee
will court you in welsh and broken english, hee speakes both.
The divell vnderstands all languages; Ile (to doe you good) bee
one of his schollers. Whie not? scrubbinge fencers teach fine men 130
to play, and greasie cookes dresse lords dynners; I am your
scullion, how like you that gamoth.

Armante.   Well; very wonderous well.

Voltimar.   Gett that little kings fisher (your sonne) out of the
lords netts, bee but ruld and you shalbee merry.

Armante.   Ile tread this maze, tis walkinge still the round,
Or if I fall lower, 'tis but to the ground.

            Exeunt.

    134 little] litt MS

[ACT III, Scene ii]

Florish. Enter Kinge: Cornewall, *and* Chester.

Kinge.   This is the daie of Audience, fetch him in
With an addition of such regall state
As may inflame the welsh men not to bow
Theire knees for feare but loue, and not repine
To paie vs tribute. Nations euen most rude
Stroakd gently feele noe waight of servitude.
What is hee?
Cornewall.   Troath sir a goodly gentleman;
Take that rough barke awaie his cuntry gives him
(Yett growes hee straight and smooth) your self would sweare
Natu⟨[r]⟩e had spent some curiosity   10
⟨W[hen]⟩ shee made him, for with a cunninge hand
⟨[Valor]⟩ and loue ins face, strive for comaund.
Kinge.   Tis fitter for the mould in which weel cast him,
Cornewall, for that greate worke, which in your care
I builded lately.
Cornewall.   Touchinge *Armante.*
Kinge.   That.
Cornewalle.   The wheles must haue no palsie hands to guide 'em.
Kinge.   An engineers, the sinowy *Voltimars*;
Man kind shewes not his equall.
Cornewall.   Is hee trusty?
Kinge.   As the try'd *Atlas* that vpshoulders heaven.
Bringe in that rarity of Nations   20
(Our welsh embassador.) How now *Voltimar,*   *Exit* Chester.

Enter Voltimar

What speakes the Alminake in *Armantes* eyes.
Voltimar.   Greate winds, blustringe a while, but —
Kinge.   Out with it man aloud, the noble *Cornewall*

3 In left margin: *bee redy Voltimar*   4 knees] kneeues MS
22 In left margin, braced: *bee redy Penda* | *Eldred; winchest'* | *Chest' Colchest* | *Kent*

346

Is in our plott a partener.

Voltimar.   Whie then Sir I ha so 'plyd the lady with warme
perswations, shees supple; yf your bould brittaine dares plant his
ramm of battery, shee'l abide the assault.

Kinge.   My excellent soldier, —
Wee must vse art to arme him, and take tyme.   30

Voltimar.   That greate grumblinge organ pipe likewise of muteny,
the lords of her faction, by a trick that I tund em with, are all
musicall and come to court, to honor your entertainement of the
strangers with theire presences.

Cornewall.   Rather to spie.

Kinge.   Noe matter, weel haue eyes
As peircinge as theire owne, bee quiett, they come.

Hoboyes.   Enter Winchester; Colchester, Chester, Kent; *then* Penda
the welsh Embassador braue; Eldred *as a welsh seruingman:*
Winchester *and his faction kiss the Kings hand; and then place
them selues for Audience.*

Penda.   Awle the showers aboue vs, power downe vppon your
mighty heads —

Voltimar.   Wee shalbee sure to haue rayne enough then.

Penda.   Her benidictions, and remunerations, and exaltations of 40
all monarchall dignities.

Voltimar.   Theres no hurte in this.

Penda.   In *Wales* (oh magnanimous kinge *Athelstanes*) wee haue
noe vniversities to tawge in vplandish greekes and lattins, wee
are not so full of our rethoriques as you are heere, and therefore
your great and masesticall eares was not to looke for fyled
oratories and pig high stiles.

Kinge.   Wee doe not.

Penda.   You are landlord of *Wales*, my master a prince of royall
prittish pludd your tenants; hee and awle the sentillmen of *Wales* 50
send comendations to you awle and sweare with true welse harts,
and longe welse hooke, to fyde vppon your side when they can
stand, till our *Bardhes* play on twincklinge harpes the praverys of
your victories.

32 tund] turnd MS

Kinge.   Wee are beholdinge to them; is not the daie
Of payinge their tribute yearely now at hand?
Omnes.   It is sir.
Penda.   And was come to give significations to Kinge *Athelstans*
that awle our tributes is heere pye and pye vppon ten daies hence
to come.   60
Eldred.   Twilbee awle heere vppon *Lamas* day was senight.
Voltimar.   Latter *Lamas*, ha ha.
Penda.   Whie is your teehies and wehies? is hobby-horse heere
or shacknapes, or logger-head Elephant with flappinge poptayle
snowtes?
Cornewall.   Grow not my lord to coller.
Penda.   Collers? had I the petter of vs awle in powis land to
fleere and seere and sneere in our faces was as good to eate a welse
goate, haires and hornes, and puddings and awle in her pelly
pipinge hott.   70
Kinge.   Who is it that dares ieere.
Eldred.   Pray tell her whoe is it, shall fyde (diggon) from welse
hooke to a prick noe longer as this of a putchers when any tares
sallenge my lord or *Reese* his man vppon duellos, and combatts,
and battalios, and pells mells, welse plud is vpp and can canogg
and rore.
Colchester.   Is that your man my lord.
Penda.   Yes and a sentill man of an old as anie *Wales*.
Kent.   Hees very furious.
Eldred.   Furies, a true welse man scornes redicles and laughins.   80
Penda.   And is mighty sellous of grinings, and is loose her best
pludd in ⟨   ⟩ wounds sooner as loose an inse, inse, nay
a crum⟨b⟩s wa⟨[ight]   ⟩ in the scales of honor.
Kinge.   I faine would know whoe v⟨[sd]⟩ him ⟨[thus]   .⟩
Voltimar.   I laughd, but not at him royall Sir.
Penda.   You logh; wud vs twoe both now weare on the balld pate
of Penmawer.
Voltimar.   Would wee weare.
Eldred.   Should trye whoe was finest tumbler downe, one's neck
must cry twange for't.   90
Penda.   Good *Reese* bee wise.

348

Kent.   Whats your followers name.

Eldred.   Tis *Reese ap meridith, ap shon, ap lewellin, ap morris,*
yet noe dancers. For awle you are english lords, you are made of
noe petter wole then a welse man is, a little finer spunne and petter
carded thats awle; our pludd is as well dyed, and our spirrits as
good a napp vppon her.

Kinge.   Tis so, wee like your sperritts and haue tryde them.

Penda.   Your kinglines had twoe fine sentillmen your brothers, one
prince *Edmonds* and prince *Eldreds*, they did kanaw our prittish 100
sperritts, they fought in *Wales* very finely vppon vs. *Reese* you
saw them all pluddy about Clanvelthin.

Eldred.   Yes, and after they drinck metheglin diggon.

Penda.   And was mighty merry.

Eldred.   And loue to gabble a little welse too.

Penda.   Pray sir what threads of lyfe does they twoe sentill men
spin now.

Kinge.   None, they both dyd ith feild.

Penda.   Mercy vppon vs, in feilds as peggers doe?

Voltimar.   No master comrague, in a battaile.   110

Kinge.   In a french noble feild those princes fell.

Penda.   Was praue men, pogs on knog'd em downe.

Kinge.   Tho they are lost, heere sitts a brother kinge
To bid you welcome; call our english court
Your owne, *England* your *Wales*; wee are so strunge
Wee will in nothinge differ but in tongue.

Penda.   Welse tongue I can tell you is lofty tongue.

Eldred.   And praue sentill men as are in the vrld tawge it.

Kinge.   Shew to this noble lord what rarities
Our court is furnisht with —   120

Penda.   Follow *Reese.*

Eldred.   Not as mouse in sees I warrant her.

     Florish. Exeunt Penda, Eldred, *and* Voltimar.

Kinge.   Whilst I bestow
My second thancks vppon theis worthie lords
By whome our court (a heaven ecclipsed before)
Recouers a new light.

  99 In left margin, braced: *bee redy* | *Edmond &* | *Voltimar*

Colchester.   What light wee give is borrowd from your sunn
      beames.

Kinge.   I am prowd to see your browes so smooth.

Omnes.   Our browes are as our harts.

Enter Voltimar *and* Edmond *like an Irish man.*

Voltimar.   Looke sirra, thats the kinge.   130

Kinge.   Whats hee?

Voltimar.   The embassadors Irish footman full of desire to see
how much you and an Irish kinge differ in state. Which of the
Irish kings know you sirrah?

Edmond.   I once serve and runne alonge by *Morrogh mac Breean*
kinge of *Leinster* and I know all de oder Irish princes.

Kinge.   How does the kinge of *Leinster.*

Edmond.   Yfaatla passinge merry; hee loues dee deerely; *Dæardæry*
his queene too speake well of dee, and *Osha Hanassah* de kings
broder wid *Dermott Lave-yarach* tell mee and I come into *England* 140
to giue dee a towsand comendacons.

Kinge.   Whats thie name.

Edmond.   *Teage mac Breean.*

Kinge.   How farr canst runne in a daie.

Edmond.   Yfaatla I shalbee loate to haue dine owne horse runne so
farr in a day as I can. Euer since I came awaie from de salt water
into *Wales* and out of *Wales* hidder, my toes and my feete never
stawnd still, for bee my gossips hawnd I had a greate desire to see
dee, and dat sweete face a dine.

Kinge.   The kinge of *Leinster* is a noble soldier.   150

Edmond.   Crees sa mee, hee does not care for de divill.

Voltimar.   Wiser man hee.

Kinge.   The Queene is wonderous faire sirrah, is shee not.

Edmond.   Queene *Dæardæry* yfaatla now as white as de inside of
a pome water, and as vppright as anie dart in *Ireland.*

Colchester.   Goes your kinge in such clothes?

Edmond.   ⟨In⟩ trooses a pox a die face, I priddy what should
h⟨[ee g]o[e i]⟩n besides?

      Exeunt Kinge, Cornewall, Chester, Voltimar, Edmond.

   135 In left margin: *bee redy Carintha* | *at a Table*

350

⟨[*Winchester*.]   ⟩ — ⟨*V*⟩*oltim*⟨[*a*]*r*.⟩
Colchester.   So th'ice is thaw'd and tho the water runne   160
  Smooth yett tis deepe, our torrent must rore on.
Omnes.   On.

                                                             Exeunt.

[ACT III, Scene iii]

Enter Carintha *at a Table readinge*.

Carintha.   A contract signd by his owne royall hand,
  The Iudges that weare by (besides her father)
  Twoe dukes, and all theis earles, a full grand Iury
  To passe vppon the life and death of honor;
  Yett hee stands laughinge at the barr. This lady
  Hee wore as a rich Iewell, on his very hart;
  Now tis by him defact and broake in peices
  And swept awaie like rubbish from his court.
  Wicked man, had fate a hand to give mee to him
  (How fast so euer in a golden charme   10
  My finger should bee bound) his wandringe eye
  Meetinge new bewties, wold in scorne view myne,
  And then (as hers) my ioyes should cease to shine.
  Tis better as it is.

Enter a seruant.

Seruant.   Heers a gentlewoman maddam come to see you.
Carintha.   What gentlewoman.
Seruant.   Shee lookes like a lady of the tyme.
Carintha.   Whie how lookes a lady of the tyme.
Seruant.   Shee lookes like a poore lady, for shee has ne're a man,
  but only a shrimping boy and her cheekes are as thin as if shee   20
  had not dynd.
Carintha.   Bringe her in sir.

            2 In left margin: *bee redy* | *seruant*

                              351

Enter Armante *and Prince.*

Seruant.   Theres my lady.
Carintha.   Gett you gon.   *Exit* [*seruant.*]
Ha are you the wrong'd *Armante?*
Armante.   And you the Queene
Of the assendant now? Loue hath resignd
The glories of his raigne (his troath, his honor)
To a fresh brid, whilst wee whoe are the scorne
Of his neglect and foyles of your vprisinge
Are hurld downe lower then the eyes of pitty   30
Can shed a teare for; I am the wrongd *Armante.*
Carintha.   You come Armd in hate;
Tempests of womans mallice and revenge
Muster vppon your forhead; is this your sonne?
Prince.   Yes marry am I maddam.
Carintha.   His very brow
Is bent with frownes vppon mee.
Prince.   I never hard anie say that I euer frownd yett.
Carintha.   There may bee danger
For mee to trust mee in your companies.
Prince.   I am noe fighter, lady, and my mother   40
(My poore wrong'd mother) is to full of sorrow
Now to turne swaggerer. Neither of vs both
Carry a knife about vs.
Armante.   Looke gentle ladie
On this faire braunch sprunge from a royall tree
But now growne crooked; for th'unnaturall roote
Keepes back the vigor that should give it groath.
What thinck you I come for?
Carintha.   I cannot guesse.
Armante.   The generall voyce proclames you the kings mistris.
Carintha.   Kings mistris, so?
Armante.   Queene of the tymes, the starr of *Englands* court,   50
The glorious spheare in which the kinge (once myne)
Moues, and there only. Oh as you are a woman,

29 his] his his MS   32 hate] MSR; fate MS

352

The daughter of a mother, as you can
Pertake the sence of passion (greefes and pitty)
The torments of contempt (disgrace and ruin)
The miseries of honor (scorne and basenes)
Lett mee beseech you ere you tread the path
(The path that must conduct you to the monument
Of a lost name) remember by whose fall
You clyme to a kings bed; think on't what tis   60
To sleep in sheetes forbidden; on a stolne pillow
A royall concubine can bee noe more
Then a greate glorious vncontrolled whore.
Shee whoe for freedome in that state will thrive
Must plead her pattent by prerogative.
Carintha.   I snatch noe pattent from you.
Prince.   Lady methincks your brow is now bent with frownes.
Armante.   If not for my sake,
Yett for my childs sake pitty mee.
Prince.   Pray doe,
For sure there can bee none my fathers wife   70
But shee whoe is my mother.
Carintha.   What first tempted
Your blood to that impression which stampd on you
The seale of theis deepe sorrows?
Armante.   Kingly periuries,
Contracted falshood; theres a true bond drawne
Betwene the kinge and mee in a faire letter
And tis inrolld in yonder court, by tyme
Never to bee rac'd out.
Carintha.   Cursd bee the hand
(Should heere the writinge lye) would crosse one lyne out.
I am so far from vexinge you I'le rather
Spin out a widdow hood in streacht miseries   80
Then play the royall theefe and steale from you
Whats yours, a kings embraces and name of Queene.
'Twas never neare my thought.

Prince.   Whie la you mother, this lady is a good woman.

Carintha.   To cleire your doubts, behold this very letter
I now was writinge, was directed lady
To your owne hands, pray read it.

Armante.   Excellent goodnes.   [*Reads.*]

Carintha.   Sweete prince, oh that thie father on thie cheekes
Would read the story of a hopeful yssue;
Hee cannot bee so cruell in the view   90
Of him self heere, but to the world make knowne
That ruininge thie life hee shakes his owne.

Prince.   I would my father weare so good a man
As you are a woman madam; if hee bee not,
'Twilbee the worse for mee.

Carintha.   Deere soule a guard of angells will waite on thee.

Prince.   Will they trulie, when shall I see them, pray.

Carintha.   When thou shalt neede them.
                                   You haue perusd my letter?

Armante.   I haue and am astonisht; you lock this secret
Within a chest of Adamant?

Carintha.   With it lock this;   100
See the kings hand which him self snatcht away
I putt agen in yours.

Armante.   This brings new life,
And all that life I trust you with.

Carintha.   Then with your leaue
My purpose is to entertaine the kinge
With all the fulnes of his hopes, nay vrge him
To speede the hight of his desires, bee instant
To haue him crowne mee Queene, but lett mee dye
In name, dye in my comforts, in the thoughts
Of all that honor virtue, if my plotts
Ayme farder then your peace, and to awake   110
The kinge out of this dreame.

Prince.   Y'are a braue lady; I may bee a kinge one daie and then —

Armante.   Ought but my prayers I haue not left to thanck you.

Prince.   Yes and myne too.

    99 astonisht;] ~ , MS   100 Adamant?] ~ ₐ MS

Armante.   I can shew to you other wheeles sett goinge
Whose motion the king dreames not of.
Carintha.   Tis happie,
Shall I direct you?
Armante.   Gladlie.
Carintha.   Ere wee then parte,
Weel ioyne our councells by what art wee can
To turne a greate kinge, to a greate good man.

                                                    Exeunt.

               Finis Actus Tertij.

               ⟨[ACT]⟩ 4ᵘˢ [Scene i]

     Florish.   Enter Kinge; Cornwall; Chester, *and* Penda.

Kinge.   How does my noble *Powis* like the lady.
Penda.   Lige her laty out of awle cry.
Cornewall.   Comes shee vpp close, wilt bee a match or noe?
Penda.   Close? shall make her come close enough or pull her
to with a longe welse hooke I haue in corners.
Chester.   Does shee vnderstand your meaninge?
Penda.   I make noe dumbe signes to her, noe wincks nor pinckes.
Chester.   Is shee a hawke fitt for the game, or noe?
Penda.   Kanaw not that, for never can I flye vpp yett.
Chester.   Ha you toucht her home with amorous parliance?   10
Penda.   Toush her home, has toushd her and towsd her, and mowze
her to vppon her soft pedds in fine wanton kanaveries, so as lords
doe ladies, but noe dishonesties; for awle my lord *Powis* is come to
buy as a shapman, was scorne to take her laty ware vppon trust,
vnless her will her self.
Cornewall.   You are a noble chapman and most worthie
To haue the richest ware putt into your hands.
Kinge.   Beside her bewtious buildinge to the eye,
The ornaments within her are much fairer.

───────────────

   4 In left margin: *bee redy* | *Armante &* | *Eldred* [*Eldred* substituted for deleted
Edmond]   6 meaninge] meainge MS

Penda.   Shall trye what is in her ornaments I warrant her.   20
Cornewall.   Shees of high birth too. *Colchesters* only daughter.
Kinge.   And to that golden scale in which her father
Shall lay her portion, our royal hand shall add
Anie twoe sheires in *England* next to *Wales*
To you and yours for euer.
Penda.   Twoe shieres, tis a greate teale of ground to fatten welse
runt vppon.
Kinge.   Whie does shee staie thus longe, knowinge wee are come
To make the musique of her free consent
Fuller and sweeter, knowinge but how shees tund.   30
Penda.   Shee puttinge fine kanaggs vppon her head, and is come
awaie py and py. Harge you is her laty *Armante* a right maid
I tro?
Cornewall.   Thinck you the kinge would so him self dishonor
Or wee blast our owne names to sett before you
A glasse thats falce and crackt, to bid you drinck
In a cupp that has held poyson?
Penda.   I kanaw not, for your greatest men now and then are
greatest whoremasters.

Enter Armante *and* Eldred.

Kinge.   Shees come, how fresh shee lookes, theres in her eyes   40
Sunn beames of power to bringe to life agen
A summer weare it dyinge.
Armante.   Sir all my wishes
Are that myne eyes may serve but as twoe stars
To guide this noble Navigator safely
To that blest haven of marriage, to which hee tells mee
Hees honorably bound, for tho your voyce
Is a sufficient charme to tune my thoughts
To anie limitation yett this gentleman
Has those good parts in him —
Penda.   See not awle her parts neither.   50
Armante.   Gott such a conquest
Ouer my maiden yeildinge, that what fortresse

47 tune] MSR; tyme MS   48 limitation] limitatio MS

356

My chaste hart holds to him I must surrender
On promist composition.
Kinge.   I am glad to heare it.
Penda.   Was not a fine pinckanies laty and tauge out acry well?
Chester.   Oh shees an excellent creature.
Kinge.   Wee shall ha no more thundringe?
Armante.   Not a clapp.
Kinge.   Your hart dwells in your tongue?
Armante.   Are chamber fellowes.
Kinge. So.
Penda.   And when is it the pleasures of ⟨[y]⟩our gre⟨[ate]⟩ 60
masst⟨[ers] ho   pl   ett   st   ⟩
Kinge.   The self same daie in which I take my Queene
You shall my lord bee cald my fellow bridgroome.
Omnes.   Twilbee a princely honor.
Penda.   Tis noe more to doe then, but when her tay comes to
walke to surch and marry and daunce and feast, and then to ride
awaie to *Wales* and shew her fine wife. *Sidannen* was never more
looke vppon so.
Cornewall.   Twilbee a glorious triumph.
Penda.   Pray Sir lett awle her writings bee drawne for portions 70
and towries and agreaments and putt the twoe shiers in.
Kinge.   By anie means.
Penda.   And when the scrivenary pills is awle pend downe our
laty and her self shall putt our markes to it togeither.
Armante.   You promist mee my lord that I should heare
Some of your poetrie, a sonnett you would write
In praise of some thinge in mee, but what I know not
Because nothinge is worth praisinge.
Penda.   Will you awle heare her welse muses pallad or madrigalls?
Omnes.   Rather then anie other.   80
Penda.   Tawsone then.   *Reads.*
Wud you kanaw her mistris face?
See the moone with starrs in shace.
Wud you kanaw her mistris nyes?
Lure downe a goshawke from her skyes.

79 In left margin: *bee redy* | *Voltimar and* | *Clowne*

Kinge. Good.

Penda. Would you kanaw her mistris nose?
Tis fine pridge ore which pewtie goes.

Armante. A flatteringe painter.

Cornewall. Nay on.   90

Penda. Wud you kanaw her mistris seekes?
'Tis sattin white and red as leekes.

Cornewall. How, how red, leekes are greene.

Penda. And greene is younge, and her mistris is younge too, so
leekes in seekes is fine younge tender ones.

Kinge. Nay nay tis well, a welsh metaphor beares it, more.

Penda. Wud you kanaw her mistris lip?
Your fingers in metheglin dip.

Omnes. Excellent.

Penda. Heeres pest, —   100
Oh wud you feele her mistris skin?
Buy kidsleather gloues and so putt in.

Cornewall. Passinge good.

Penda. Wud you heare her mistris tongue?
Lett twincklinge welse harp well bee strunge.

Chester. Braue.

Penda. Her mistris tuggs wud you see pare?
Aske *Cupitt* where his pillowes are.

Chester. By my troath.

Penda. Marge heere now —   110
Sweeter as goates milke wud you tipple?
You then must suck her mistris nipple.

Cornewall. How, suck her nipple?

Armante. Shees beholdinge to you, would you have your mistris
Give suck before shee has a child?

Penda. Shall gett her with child one daie and tis awle one.

Kinge. Is there anie more?

Penda. More, heeres prauest of awle—
Wud you stroake her mistris pelly?
Oh tis smoth as sweete warme Iellie;   120
Beinge come now to her mistris thighes,
Turne againe laine in that parte lyes,

358

And so I dare goe noe farder.

Cornewall.   You haue gon wonderous well.

Kinge.   An excellent poet too.

Come, wee your muse will highten with rich wines,

And drincke to *Hymen* whoe sweete loue combines.

Florish. Exeunt.

[ACT IV, SCENE ii]

Enter Voltimar *and the Clowne.*

Voltimar.   How saist thou, turnd awaie?

Clowne.   Iust as a cutpurse turnd of the ladder of the law, so was
I that very day when you came and tould my ladie shee must give
vpp howskeepinge.   Within an hower after, that old mumble
crust lord her father coyted mee out of doores.

⟨*V*⟩*oltimar.*   But the kinge and shee are in tune againe and thou
maist feed vppon her.

⟨[*Clowne.*]⟩   The divell feed vppon her, they saie the welsh embassador will haue her, and ⟨[wil]l⟩ car⟨r⟩y her into *Wales*; and
what should I doe there?   10

⟨[*Voltimar.*   Eate toasted cheese.]⟩

Clowne.   Whie, I never eate cheese in my life, and if I should but
cry foh when tis a toastinge, ⟨[I]⟩ should haue my throate cutt
before my face and bee nere the wiser.

Voltimar.   A serving mans life thou seest walkes butt vppon
rotten crutches.

Clowne.   Crutches, when I see a horse that has done good to his
cuntrie lye dead in a cart to bee carried to the doghowse, thinck
I to my self theres the reward of service.

Voltimar.   A good observation.   20

Clowne.   Or when I spie a catt hang'd for some petty cryme, that
has been an excellent hunter, saie I heeres the fagg end of a poore
soldier that has rid his cuntry of enimyes.

Voltimar.   You rascall, compare a soldier to a catt?

Clowne.   Oh deere Captaine cry you mercy, I did not mynd you.
Ile bee noe longer a creature, what shift soeuer I putt my self to.

359

Voltimar.	What then.

Clowne.	A meere Animall rather, theres one Image of invention
if you cold carve mee into't I weare made for euer.

Voltimar.	What Image.					30

Clowne.	Gett the kings or some of his lords letters to create mee
cronicler.

Voltimar.	Cronicler, thart not fitt for't, th'ast noe learninge nor
witt to doe it.

Clowne.	Noe witt? I must putt out nothinge but once in ten yeare;
in meane tyme I can creepe into opinion by balductum rymes and
play scrap fooleries. Witt? an arrant asse may carry that burthen
and never kick for it.

Voltimar.	Since th'art so sett vppon it, I'le speake and warrant
thee the tytle of a cronicler.					40

Clowne.	The name, the foolish style is all I desire to climbe ouer.

Voltimar.	When anie of your collections are mellow shew e'm to
the kinge, I muse they come not.

Clowne.	Whoe Captaine?

Voltimar.	The embassadors man, and the Irish footman new come
ouer; wee promist to bee merry heere in my chamber for a spurt
or so, they are a cupple of honest harted mad rascalls.

Enter Edmond *and* Eldred.

Clowne.	See Capten.

Voltimar.	Welcome.

Edmond.	By did hawnd Capten *Voltimar* de kinge bid mee seeke	50
for dee and to come away apace to him.

Voltimar.	Tyme enough; since wee are mett, Ile steale out of
the kinges glasse one quarter of an hower to bee Iouiall.

Eldred.	But where is wine and good seere to be Iawfall and pipes
and fiddles to shake our heele at.

Voltimar.	Your good seere looke you is in bottles; heeres my
Armory, theis are head peices will fitt you.

Clowne.	With a murren.

Voltimar.	And now you talke of fidlinge, a musition dwells at

35 Noe] nott MS

very next wall, I'le step to him, entertaine thou theis gentlemen 60
the whilst, as wee drinck they shall sound.

Edmond.   Crees sa mee if I heare de pipes goe I cannot forbeare
to daunce an Irish hay.

Eldred.   As good hay in *Wales, Rees ap meridith* was daunce too.

Clowne.   Hey then for *England*; if my leggs stand still, hange mee.

Voltimar.   Good sport, I'le goe stringe the musique for you.   *Exit.*

Clowne.   Ith meane tyme because tis scurvie to bee Idle, pray
master *Reese ap shon* what is the reason that wee english men when
the cuckoe is vppon entrance saie the welsh embassador is cominge.

Eldred.   Lett anie rascall sonne of whores come into *Cardigan,* 70
Flint, Merioneth, Clamorgan or *Brecknock* and dare prade so.
Was such a mighty wonder to see an embassador of *Wales?* whie
has her not had kings and Queens and praue princes of *Wales?*

Edmond.   Yfaat hast tow.

Eldred.   But I now can tell you, for manie summers agoe our
valliant comragues and feirce prittons about cuckoe tymes, come
and with welse hooke hack and hoff and mawle your english
porderers, and so fright the ymen that they to still theire wrawlinge
bastards cry out, husht the welsh embassador comes.

Clowne.   I am satisfied. Now master Crammo one question to you. 80
What is the reason all the chimny sweepers in *England* are for the
most parte Irishmen.

Edmond.   I shall tell dee whie. Saint *Patrick* dow knowst keepes
purgator⟨[y. So if Saint]⟩ *Patrick* bee content to make de fyers
tis noe shame fo⟨[r Irishmen]⟩ to sweepe de chimneys.

Eldred.   Tis praue answer.

Clowne.   And I hugg thee sweete Tor⟨y⟩ for it.

Enter Voltimar.

Voltimar.   I give but the Q: and the musique speakes. I cannot
staie; come, on your knees; a health to kinge *Athelstane.*

Eldred.   Was pledge her in noe liquors but her owne cuntries 90
whay or metheglin.

Voltimar.   Theres metheglin for you.

Edmond.   And Ifaatla I shall pledge kinge *Aplestanes* in vsque
bah or notinge.

Voltimar.   Theres vsqua for you.

Clowne.   Ile pledge it in Ale, in Aligant, Cider, Perry, metheglin, vsquebagh, minglum, manglum, purr, in hum, mum, Aquam, quaquam, clarrett or sacum, for an english man is a horse that drincks of all waters.

Voltimar.   To'ot then — when?   *Florish.* 100

Clowne.   Off.

Eldred.   Super naglums.   *Daunce.*

Edmond.   Hey for Saint *Patricks* honor.

Eldred.   Saint *Tavy* for *Wales*.

Clowne.   Saint *George* for *England*.

Voltimar.   Enough, drinck what you will, I must hence.   *Exit.*

Edmond.   Kara magus.

Clowne.   This dauncinge ioggs all my dynner out of my belly, I am as hungry as a huntsman; and now I talke of meate, whie does a welsh man loue tosted cheese so well.   110

Eldred.   Whie does cockny pobell loue toast and putter so well.

Clowne.   And whie onions and leekes you.

Eldred.   And whie a whores plind seekes you awle cuntries loue one tevices or others.

Clowne.   True, you loue freeze and goates, and welsh hookes and whay and flanell and fighting⟨e⟩.

Eldred.   And you loue vdcocks, and praveries, and kanaveries, and fidlings and fistings and praue enches with rotten trenches, and a great teale of prablings but little fightings.

Clowne.   One for one, and what loues my Irish man heere.   120

Edmond.   Yfaatla I loue shamrocks, bonny clabbo, soft boggs, a great many cowes, a garron, an Irish-harpe, cleene trooses and a dart.

Clowne.   But not a fart.

Edmond.   In dy nose, in dy teet, all de farts lett in *Ireland* are putt into bottles for english men to drinck off; a pox vppon dy nyes, by dis hawnd I shall trust my skeene into dy rotten gutts when agen tow anger mee.   *Exit.*

Penda within.   What *Resse*, wa ho *ap shon*.

106 In left margin: *bee redy* | *Colchester* | *Winchester* | *& Kent*

Eldred.   Was heere, was heere.   *Exit.* 130

Clowne.   So; now pumpe I for invention full sea swell
  Of witt that I may write a cronicle.

                                                               Exit.

[ACT IV, Scene iii]

Enter Colchester; Winchester; *and* Kent.

Colchester.   Its a strange creature,
  A daughter and so disobedient.
  Her braines are wilder then a trobled sea,
  Noe clowd is so vnsetled, shees an engine
  Driven by a thowsand wheeles, a german clock
  Never goinge true.
Kent.   That shewes shees a right woman.
Winchester.   Shee and the widdow whome the kinge so doates on
  I heare haue mett and parlied, and sure theire breath
  Blowes downe all that wee build.
Kent.   One glib tongud woman
  Is a shrew witch to annother.
Colchester.   Tis voycd for certaine   10
  That now shees growne so mad to haue the welshman,
  The kinge is quite lost to her.
Kent.   May bee shee longs
  To study all the neighboringe languages.
Winchester.   Tis now noe wonder that a kinge tooke captive
  Her maiden honor when to a new come stranger
  Shee yeilds without assault; I do not thinck
  Shee vnderstands his lofty brittish tongue,
  Hee courts her sure by signes.
Kent.   Hange mee for a signe then, a welsh man make signes
  to a woman?   20
Colchester.   Alls one what signes hee makes, for a dumbe man
  May woe a woman if his face bee good,
  An able promisinge body, a neate legg,

          9 *Kent.*] MSR; *om.* MS   10 voycd] voyd MS

                              363

⟨[Fin]⟩e cloth⟨e⟩s, and lands, and money, and noe coxcombe.
⟨[Whore]⟩s w⟨ou⟩ld scratch out one anothers eyes
To haue such bitts alone. Now this welsh lord
Is all this, rich and well formd, a faire out side,
A mynd nobly furnished, the match weare fitt
But that our heapd vpp wrongs are slaud by it.
It brands both vs and our posteritie   30
To haue a daughter strumpited, a kinswoman
Texted vppon dishonorable fyle,
A grand child branded with a bastards name.
Wee must not therefore swallow it.
Kent.   Wee will not.
Should wee doe nothinge our opposed faction
Might Ieere vs to our faces, comon people
Revile vs, call vs cowards.
Colchester.   Sawcy witts
Will dip theire pens in gall and whett base rymes
To stabb our fames more then to mend our crymes.
Winchester.   Whats to bee done then.
Colchester.   This is to bee done.   40
You know that staringe soldier came for the prince
And wee denyd him.
Kent.   Had wee not cause?
Colchester.   And yett
On more wey'd counsell you my lord hold it fitt
To leaue him in's fathers hands. I thinck hee has not
A knife to cutt his owne hart. Ile presently
Write to the kinge that since tis his high pleasure
To snatch the distaff of my daughters fate
And cutt her golden thred, wee all consent
To this her second fortune. Hee'l thinck vs quiet,
Nor shall hee spell hard letters on our browes.   50
The night before the marriage is a masque;
Wee'l all to court and when the winds lye still
And not a leafe of murmeration stirs
(Suspition sealinge vpp her hunderd eyes)

32 dishonorable] dishorable MS

364

Then breake wee forth, like lighteninge from a clowd
And force him feele our fury.
Winchester.   Feele what fury?
Tho hee has struck a dagger throw my sides,
Bee but a finger held vpp at his life
My brest shalbee a wall to beate back danger
From him on your owne heads.
Colchester.   My lord of *Winchester*,   60
Our arrowes fly not at his life.
Winchester.   Doe fairely what you will doe, I am yours.
Kent.   Not doinge so, leaue vs.
Colchester.   Wee'l only to the kings masque ad our daunce
And vaile our wrongs in smotherd ignorance.   *Exeunt.*

Finis Actus Quarti.

ACTUS 5us [SCENE i]

Florish. Enter Kinge, Cornewall *and* Chester.

Kinge.   *Cornewall.*
Cornewall.   My lord.
Kinge.   Whie shines not brauery
Throughout our court in rich habiliments
Of glory? *Chester.*
Chester.   Sir.
Kinge.   Bee it proclaimd
That whoe soer'e presents most curious sports
Of art or chardge to grace our nuptiall feasts
Shall haue a lardge reward, wee wilbee royall.
Chester.   Ile vndertake the taske.
Kinge.   Doe and bee speedy.

Enter Winchester *like a fryer leadinge the prince vaild.*

Winchester.   Angells of peace waite round about th⟨[y throne]⟩
Greate *Athelstane* the kinge.

2 In left margin: *bee redy* | *Winchester* | *& Prince*

Kinge. Whence art thou fryer?

Winchester. Few words I haue ⟨t[o]⟩ speak⟨[e,] m⟩y lesons c⟨　⟩ 10
⟨T　le　o　s　⟩

Kinge. Yes, wee'l heare it.

Winchester. A sad creature crost in life
For beinge neither maide nor wife,
Hath left the world at last, and reads
Her better hopes vppon her beads.
Shee thincks noe more what shee hath been
Nor dreames what 'tis to bee a Queene,
For goes her bewtie, youth and state
'Timbrace a holier happier fate;
By prayers, sighes, shee weepes, shee dyes, 20
To live a saint in paradice.
Armantes requiem tis I singe,
Once lou'd by *Athelstan* the kinge;
The sad *Armante*, whoe tho strange
Hath made a heavenly sweete exchange;
Insted of marryinge pompe and glory,
Married her to a monestary.
One only token sends shee heere,
More deere then life or whats most deere,
The pawne of her first troath, her sonne, 30
The prince tis hee; loe, I haue done. *Vnvailes him.*
Shee bids thee of this child make store
For shee shall never see thee more;
What ells shee said the boy can tell,
Ile to my beads, now kinge farwell. *Exit.*

Kinge. Staie father, gentle father, holy man.

Cornewall. Hees trugd awaie sir.

Kinge. Gon alreadie? strange:
Exceedinge strange.

Omnes. Vnlookt for.

Kinge. Welcome boy;
Thie mother turnd a nunne, shee whoe so lately
Seemd pliant to the pleasures wee presented 40
Now alterd on a suddaine? tis a riddle

366

I vnder stand not yett.
Prince.   I haue a message 'tee,
And tis her last.
Kinge.   What pritty boy.
Prince.   She prayes yee
Youd vse mee kindly, trulie I can scarce
Refraine from cryinge to remember how
Vnhandsomly wee parted. Oh my child
(My mother, my good mother said and deed la
Shee wept to when shee spoake yt) now my boy
Thou art lost, for euer lost, to mee, the world,
Thie birth, thie freinds, thou hast not one freind left;   50
Goe to thie father, child, thie cruell father;
She bad mee aske you blessinge to, pray give it mee,
Father your blessinge.
Kinge.   For thie mothers sake
Ile keepe a blessinge for thee boy, a greate one;
Rise, tis a good child.
Prince.   But dee loue mee indeed?
Kinge.   Hartylie, hartilie.
Prince.   If cause my blood is yours
You thinck my life may bee some danger 'tee
Or that my mother in law, when next you marry
Cannot abide mee; yett Ile doe the best
I can to please her, but theis stepmothers   60
They saie doe seldome loue theire husbands children.
Or if for beinge your heire some wicked people
Give you bad counsaile that I must not grow
To bee a man, for growinge to fast vpwards,
⟨[Safer]⟩ you cutt mee off betimes;
⟨[Yett as y]⟩ou are a kinge I doe beseech you
⟨[Lett not]⟩ a comon villaine bee my butcher,
⟨[But I]⟩ die like a prince. Sir will you promise mee
⟨   nto   s   for   ⟩
Kinge.   Pestilent ape,
His mother taught him this, fye boy no more,   70

45 In left margin: *bee redy* | *Carintha and* | *Voltimar*

367

I wilbee lovinge, thou shalt find it.
Prince.   Shall I?
Indeed I never went to bed but e're
I slept I praid for the good kinge my father;
I never rose but e're I had my breake fast
I said heaven blesse my father, that is you;
There was no hurte in this?
Cornewall.   Well prated little one.
Kinge.   Enough, I wilbee tender ore thee boy,
As tender as thie mother.
Prince.   Will yee, thanck yee.

Enter Carintha *and* Voltimar

Carintha.   Wheres now this royall louer.
Kinge.   My *Carintha,*
Melt heere all passions from mee, my soules empresse.   80
Carintha.   And when's this daie forsooth, this daie of Queeneship?
I'me made a goodlie foole.
Kinge.   Bee not impatient,
Thie glories and my ioyes shalbee the fuller.
Voltimar.   Now for a shower of raine downe right, theres a
horrible clap of thunder towards; take heed of lighteninge kinge,
you are in danger of being blasted.
Prince.   What angrie womans this, blesse mee hir lookes
Affright mee, father, kinge.
Carintha.   Your bastard heere?
I thought I was your mockery; whie lives hee
To bee my torment?
Kinge.   Prithee sweete.
Prince.   Howes this,   90
Las what must I doe now?
Cornewall.   I like not this.
Chester.   Nor I.
Carintha.   Hast thou nor hart nor hands?
Kinge.   *Carintha* —
Carintha.   How say by that; give mee the bratt, I'le haue him,

93 say] shay MS

368

T'shall saue yee chardges too, oh I am vext,
Not yett dispatcht, a shall with mee.
Kinge.　　　　　　　　　　You must not.
Will you vndoe all what I strive to build
For your advauncement?
Carintha.　　　　　Pish.
Kinge.　　　　　　　　　For my sake doe not,
For your owne sake doe not. — *Voltimar?*
Voltimar.　　　　　　　　My lord.
Kinge.　　Take him aside awhiles.
Voltimar.　　　　　　　I will; come.
Prince.　　　　　　　　　　Heaven,
　Bee thou a father to mee; sure this woman　　　　　　100
　Was never mother to a child, shee's cruell
　Even in her very frowne.
Voltimar.　　　　　　Noe pratinge; come.
　　　　　　　　　　　Exeunt Prince and Voltimar.
Kinge.　　Thou are not well advisd.
Carintha.　　　　　　　You haue broake your promise;
　Make it your practize; would you play the tyrant
　Ouer my wrongs, as ouer hirs whose honor
　Y'aue whor'd and strumpited to your vild lust?
　You'd cast mee off too. Heare mee lords and witnes
　How much my sperrit scornes to fawne on slauery;
　My first borne shall not bee a bastards second.
　Intollerable.
Kinge.　　　Deere *Carintha* —
Carintha　　　　　　　Shall not.　　　　　　110
　Kinge, till I know thie bed and pleasures free,
　Weart thou ten tymes a kinge thou art not for mee.
　Thinck on't, I am not thie bride yet.　　　*Exit.*
Kinge.　　　　　　　Stay — fly after,
　Intreate her back.
Cornewall.　　　　Comaund her.
Chester.　　　　　　　Fetch her, force hir.
Kinge.　　Not so, I haue some privat thoughts require

105 In left margin: *Bee redy* | *Voltimar*

Consideration — leave vs all — none staie.
Omnes.   You are obayd Sir.   *Exeunt.*
Kinge.   Impudent and bloody,
  Twoe attributes fitt only for deformity;
  Trew bewty dwells in meeknes, love with pitty
  Keepes leagues, there is a plurisie within mee   120
  Requires a skillfull surgion that can launce it.

Enter Voltimar.

Voltimar.   Heere, heere, heere my lord, I am heere, what ist you
  call for?
Kinge.   Foe, thou art too officious, I am busie.
Voltimar.   Shall I bee gon sir?
Kinge.   Gon Sir?
Voltimar.   Blesse your maiestie, I dare not bide the noyse.
Kinge.   Stay, send the boy in,
  And waite some twoe roomes of, not within hearinge.
Voltimar.   Tis good; you little one?   130

Enter Prince

Prince.   The kinge.
Kinge.   Awaie, doe as you are comaunded.
Voltimar.   Touch him home, tis my suite heaven I beseech thee.
                                                          Exit.
Kinge.   Come heather, doe not feare mee, yett nearer.
Prince.   Noe sir, beinge with you alone
  I will not feare; doe what you will with mee,
  Ile stand you like a little harmelesse lambe,
  I will not cry out neither.
Kinge.   It has been tould mee,
  That thou art like mee boy.
Prince.   My grand sir swore
  My chin and nose weare yours, and my good mother
  Said I was but your picture.
Kinge.   She was deceaud,   140
  For thou art fairer far.
Prince   Thats cause I am

But yett a child, and if you doe not lay mee
In some vntimely pitt hole ere I grow
To mans estate, I shalbee as you are.
Kinge.   A kinge thou meanest?
Prince.   Noe I meane a man
That shalbee iust like you.
Kinge.   Lett mee looke on thee.
Prince.   Pray doe.
Kinge.   Heeres a white forehead
Of inocence whose allablaster sweetnes
Rebates my cruelties. Tell mee my boy
Didst never heare thie mother curse thie father,   150
Or did shee not teach thee to curse mee?
Prince.   Trulie
My lord I cannot lye, nor doe I vse to sweare
An oath, but by my troath you may beleeue mee
I never hard her curse, but often pray for yee,
And so haue I too, hartilie, euery daie
I learnt it from her mouth.
Kinge.   Gon to a nunnery?
Ile hie mee thether to, by her example
Learne to bee good and reconcile my peace
To hirs, alas poore soule how haue I wrongd hir.
Prince.   Whie did yee?
Kinge.   Gentle boy wilt thou forgive mee?   160
Prince.   I? yes indeed father.
Kinge.   My blessings on thee,
Ile call thee now myne heire — lett mee bethinck mee.
Prince.   If euer a poore childs prayer was accepted
Good heaven I begg thee pitty my poore mother,
And turne my fathers hart now I beseech thee.
How does the kinge my father?
⟨[*Kinge.*]⟩   I ⟨[haue]⟩ for gon,
An angell for a divill, a companion
⟨[Whose soule was]⟩ soft as doues, for a thinge framd
⟨[Of nothinge but]⟩ ambition.

145 meanest] meanst MS   149 In left margin: *bee redy* | *Voltimar*

⟨[*Prince.*]⟩   ⟨   ⟩ke⟨   s⟩
You promist mee to loue mee as my mother doth,   170
And shee would talke to mee, shee would my lord.
Kinge.   It shalbee so; Ile try to what strange hight
Th'ones wickednes will mount, to what humility
The others goodnes creeps. Ioy of my soule,
Desires may stray, our soules are pretious things,
All men are deere to heaven, but cheefely kings.
Attendance.

Enter Voltimar.

Voltimar.   I am heere.
Kinge.   Lock fast the dore,
'Tis death to enter — come you back.   180
Voltimar.   I shall.   *Exit.*
Kinge.   Bee not afraid child.
Prince.   Well I will not then.
Kinge.   Ile teach thee
A pollicy of state euen in thie cradle.
Prince.   Ile learne it if I can.

Enter Voltimar.

Kinge.   Now is all sure?
Voltimar.   As fast as key and boult can ward.
Kinge.   Thine eare, this boy must bee dispatcht.
Voltimar.   How?
Kinge.   Suddenly.
Voltimar.   Good; hee dyes.   190
Kinge.   Shall I depend?
Voltimar.   Remember the words *Tis done.*
Prince.   I doe not like this mans wild lookes; methincks
Vppon his forhead hange a thowsand earthquakes.
Pray stand betwene vs sir.
Kinge.   But dost thou know
What tis to cut off a younge inocent infant?
Voltimar.   Yes, to cutts throate, knock out his braines, writh his
neck off, anie thinge.

174 creeps] creepd MS   175 may] MSR; my MS

Prince.   Blesse mee,
 What does this fellow talke?
Kinge.   A villaines language;   200
 A minister of horror, borne to live
 And dye a monster.
Voltimar.   Fine stuff kinge, admirable dissimulation, it becomes
 yee.
Kinge.   Marke what remaines for thee.
Voltimar.   A braue reward?
Kinge.   I will resigne my royall office vpp
 And plant my crowne heere on this princely head,
 Hee shalbee kinge, for since thou hast my promise
 Of pardon, Ile not bee thie iudge; that daie   210
 Where on my boy makes entrance to his raigne
 Shalbee renowned for an act of Iustice
 On such a man of mischeif as thou art.
Voltimar.   Hey daie how scurvilie it shewes.
Kinge.   The evidence
 Against thee I my self will give; the world
 Shall know how miserable I haue been
 By *Pendas* ruine acted by thie hand.
Prince.   Tis very strange and very pittifull.
Kinge.   My self in person shalbee thie accuser.   220
Voltimar.   Dare yee?
Kinge.   Oh boy if not for my sake for thie mothers
 I chardge thee by the dutie of a sonne,
 Give him a heavie doome, lett him dye groaninge,
 Revenge the manly *Penda*, that braue soldier.
 Take heede, my chardge is greate.
Prince.   Should this bee true,
 When I am kinge a smarts for't.
Kinge.   Guard, a guard.
Voltimar.   Sir what dee meane?
Kinge.   Ile never heare thee againe, Ile call ⟨   ⟩
Prince.   Whie dost not speake? trust mee I'le ou⟨[t]   ⟩   230
 Rath⟨[er] th[en]   e   no   ⟩s ⟨   ⟩
Voltimar.   Will you babble?

Kinge.   Heel infect thee or doe thee mischeif.
Prince.   But a shall not, nay
I'le tell my father, my good father now;
My lord —
Voltimar.   Peace or —
Prince.   Indeed this souldier if a bee not
An honest man, a very honest man,
Is trulie a very knaue. Twas hee that taught mee
What I should saie, hee fetchd mee from my mother,
Shee loues him, chardg'd mee to bee ruld by him,   240
Tould mee hee was not cruell as hee seemd
But of a gentle nature, and indeed
To speake the truth, hee still has vsd mee kindly
As if a had been my man.
Kinge.   Would yett a had
A hart to melt in penitence for *Penda,*
Vnluckily by him misdone.
Voltimar.   The prince
Some what to earely hath prevented mee
In my dissignes. Vppon my knee my lord
I humbly craue your favor.
Kinge.   Kneele to heaven,
I am too low to bee crept to.
Voltimar.   Then know sir   250
That heither to I haue but given you phisick
And now your health is purchast.
Kinge.   Oh whie wilt thou
Flatter myne infinitt guilt.
Voltimar.   I can restore
All your discomforts in a rich discouery
Of honest duty would you bee but pleasd
To take truce with your greefes.
Kinge.   Thou canst not *Voltimar.*
Penda is falne.
Voltimar.   Heaven can work by miracles;

239 In left margin: *bee redy Clowne* | *& Eldred*
246 In left margin: *sett out* | *a Table*

374

I'le cure that wound too.
Kinge.   Ha?
Prince.   I'le passe my word;
I haue comission for it from my mother.
Kinge. Oh boy —
Voltimar.   Sir bee but counsaild.
Prince.   Ile intreate you.   260
Kinge. Doe what you will, I am lost as I am found,
All present ioyes are short, the best come after,
Better to lyve in teares then dye in laughter.
Come child thie hand.
Prince.   Heere father, weel attend yee.

                                        Exeunt.

[ACT V, SCENE ii]

Enter Clowne in his study writinge: one Knockes within.

Clowne. Whoe does molest our contemplations, what are you?
Eldred. Tis *Reece ap meridith, ap shon, ap Vaughan, ap lewellins,
ap morris.*
Clowne. So many of you? come all in.

                Enter Eldred.

Eldred. Plesse you master kernicler from all your good studies
and wise meditations.
Clowne. Oh master *Rice*, I thought more of your cuntry men had
knockt at dore with you; bringe em all in.
Eldred. More, yes and more will come to her and kanog som
bodies night capps, there is a great teale of prapples and high   10
vrds goe vpp and towne to yon rascalls *Brian mac Teages* about
our cuntries, I beseese you now vppon your quarnicle bookes, tell
her which is prauer cuntrie *Wales* or *Ireland* for antickities, and
for ⟨[fin]⟩e sentle men and awle materialls besides.
⟨[*Clowne.* Brau]⟩er cuntry; oh *Wales* by anie meanes.

                *10 prapples] quarrells MS
                12 In left margin: *bee redy* | ⟨E[dmon]d⟩

                        375

⟨[*Eldred.*   I thinck]⟩ so to, *Wales* for *ap shons* money.

⟨   ⟩

Clowne.   Looke how much a Saint *Thomas* onion is a sweeter sallad
then poore ⟨s   ⟩

Eldred.   Right, tis well spoken and in elegancies.   20

Clowne.   Or as a fatt shropsheire cheese outwaies a pound of
hairie Irish b⟨   ⟩, so *Wales* with her mountaines is higher in
stature and therefore older in antiquities then *Ireland.*

Eldred.   Noe cambro-brittaine in the vrld can tauge finer.

Clowne.   Welsh men, whie you are discended from the warlike
Troians and the mad greekes.

Eldred.   Tis awle true as steele.

Clowne.   So that twoe famous nations iumbled togeither to make
vpp a welshman, but alas Irish men make one another.

Eldred.   Now you tawge of greekes and troshans, it was a troshan   30
pare awaie the laty *Hellenes* and praue greekes fought almost
a towzen yeares for her. So a welse man that has true prittish plud
in her, ere hee loose his ense will sweare and fide, and runne vpp to
his nose aboue his chin in embruings and bee awle dyed in sanguins.

Clowne.   Nay you awle carry mettale enough about you, thats
certaine.

Eldred.   *Mac Breean* also saies that *Cupit* was an Irish boy, putt
I say a welse boy because welse men are so lovinge.

Clowne.   What cuntry boy *Cupid* is I know not but I'm sure
Mercury was a welsh man and kept both sheep and goates, and your   40
welsh hooke came from his sheepe hooke.

Eldred.   Tis mighty praue, and I am sure *Arion* was a welse man
and plaid passinge melodiously vppon her harpe.

Clowne.   Hee did so and it was a welsh dolphin hee rod vppon.

Eldred.   I thinck your kernicles some tymes tell lyes, for in *Wales*
are noe dolphins but at Inne dores as signes.

Clowne.   I haue read it so in heathen greeke.

Eldred.   Not in christian welse I assure you, but pray sustifie awle
this of *Wales* vnder your pens and inckhorns, for *mac Teages* and

17 Unless a fresh line was given to another remark by Eldred, it is hard to account
for some evidence of letters at the tattered foot of the leaf. There would not seem to
have been enough room for two lines.

I are to kill one of vs vppon it. I will paie you and bee euer pound 50
in my poddies to you, shall come anon py and py.   *Exit.*

Knock within. Enter Edmond.

Clowne.   Come in; oh master *mac Teage*, this may bee cronicled to
see you heere.
Edmond.   Sawst thou *Reece* datt coggin rascalls?
Clowne.   Not I.
Edmond.   I priddy tell mee, for *Reece* and I quarrell vppon it,
whedder is *Ireland* ore *Wales* more antient or finer cuntry.
Clowne.   Oh *Ireland, Ireland*; anie question of that?
Edmond.   Yfaat I tinck so too, dow and I iump into one hole.
Clowne.   Looke how much difference is betwene myle end and 60
grauesend or betwen⟨e⟩ Dover peere and one of the peeres of
Fraunce, so short comes *Wales* of *Ireland*.
Edmond.   Dow knowst our cuntry too has noe virmine in't.
Clowne.   Oh noe, yett more cattell by far then *Wales*.
Edmond.   And dat der is not a toade or spider in *Ireland*.
Clowne.   Nay thats certen, there are fewer spidercatchers in your
cuntry then in anie else.
Edmond.   *Reece* saies to that a welshman runns faster den an Irish.
Clowne.   Fye fie, *Rice* is an asse, your cuntry men are foote men to
lords and ladies and so runne after honor.   70
Edmond.   Yfaat after a greate teale of honor, and if kinge *Atel-
stanes* himself weare heere, I should tell him I my self was as well
borne in my moders belly as the prowdest comrague in *Wales*.
Clowne.   My head vppon that, *Brian*.
Edmond.   And priddy now tell mee whoe is more terrible in
battailes, de Irish or de welsh.
Clowne.   Oh Irish, Irish, euery Irishman with a dart lookes like
death, only death has not so much haire ons head.
Edmond.   Yett *ap morris* saies in warrs his brittaine is more feirce.
Clowne.   *Ap morris* lyes.   80

55 In left margin: *bee redy* | *Eldred*

Enter Eldred.

Eldred. Which *ap morris*; lugg you, you master hobbadery coscombe, the same *ap morris* can mage your learned crono-logicall nose lye heere n⟨[ow.]⟩

Edmond. Crees sa mee, one Irish man and one welsh man is abl⟨[e to make]⟩ fooles of ten bushells such as dow art.

Eldred. You cutt out thred bare questions vp⟨   ⟩ of your left handed witts, and tis now an ⟨   ⟩

Edmond. Sholl de crow tow horshon teefe b⟨   ⟩ to p⟨[e]⟩ck ⟨   y   m   s   d   ⟩

Eldred. And to nay downe her eares so her hearinge was not 90 vrse for it.

Edmond. And ifaatla ripe awaie di gutts only in meriments.

Clowne. And I (now your bowlts are shott) to see you both like hangtiloes in new suites handsomly trusd vpp, caperinge ith ayre, leapinge at a dazie and to accord togeither in a noose of brother hood not to bee vndone and then that knott would I cronicle.

Edmond. Der is one knott for anoder den.

Eldred. And so awle freinds.

Clowne. Is the masque to night at court?

Eldred. So master Capten *Voltimars* sends his petitionary vrds 100 to your vrship to pring your quarnicles alonge by you and to shage your heeles amonge the masquers.

Edmond. Wutt dow putt in dy ten toes for a share into der company?

Clowne. For a share yes, and theis my ten hobnailes too, I am to speake in the masque, braue sporte. One english dauncer and twoe harpers; whoe mew at all three are malitious carpers. Come I am ready for a caranto already.

Edmond. Tree merry men, and Tree merry men.

Eldred. And tree merry men was wee a.

Clowne. English.   110

Edmond. Irish.

Eldred. And praue welse.

Omnes. And turne aboute knaues all three a.   *Exeunt.*

93 In left margin: ⟨[*bee*]⟩ *redy K: winchest'* | *Cornewall; Colchester* | ⟨[*K*]⟩*ent Carintha* | *Armante &* | *Voltimar*

378

[ACT V, SCENE iii]

Florish. Enter Kinge, Winchester, Cornewall, Carintha; Armante
and Voltimar *followinge.*

Kinge.   My lord of *Winchester* thancks for this phisick,
But ere you came I had an Antidot
T'expell the strongest poyson.
Winchester.   But sir how euer —
Kinge.   Your loue is not the lesse, and I shall pay you
In better coyne then words.

Enter Colchester: *and* Kent.

                    Oh my good lord
For all methincks I am compast in with freinds
I sitt acould without you.
Colchester.   From an old man sir
There can come little heate, yett what I haue
Is ready for your service.
Kinge.   Where are those lords
Your noble kindred?
Colchester.   Oh busie for the masque sir.   10
Kinge.   This night shall heere fix artificiall starrs
To burne out till the morne bringe in the sunne
To putt theire fires out by his golden flames,
Whilst they shall fall dim too when the twoe brides
Shall dazell with theire eyes the kinge of daie,
Whoe fretts that hee so long must keepe awaie
And not behold our pastimes.
Armante.   Is hee without then?
Voltimar.   Yes maddam.
Armante.   An odd conceited fellow (once my servant)   20
Has (as I'me told) writt some strange cronicle
And is to mee a suitor to speake for him,
To haue your maiesty pleasd to cast awaie

9 In left margin: *bee redy* | *Clowne*

379

A few loose mynutes but to heare what wonders
His witt brings forth.

Kinge.   With all my hart sweete lady.

Carintha.   Twilbee a foyle to the nights brighter glories
As a blackamore by a *Venus*, pray sir letts haue him.

Cornewall.   New cronicler? letts not loose him.

Kinge.   Fetch him in, *Voltimar.*

Voltimar.   I shall sir.   30

Enter Clowne with a Booke.

Kinge.   This hee?

Clowne.   I am hee Sir.

Colchester.   Is that your cronicle — hast writt such a vollume
already?

Clowne.   Noe my lord it is not all of myne owne writinge, this
is a ⟨   ⟩ fire fed from tyme to tyme with the faggots and
some⟨   ⟩ins of other mens witt. I haue only pickd vpp
a bundle ⟨   ⟩ drye sticks to maintaine the blaze.
⟨   ͬ   si   ⟩

Winchester.   Your cronicle begins with *Brute* the sonne of *Silvius* 40
the sonne of A⟨s[tyanax]⟩ the sonne of *Æneas* as other cronicles
of *England* doe, dost not?

Clowne.   *Brute?* noe my lord; thincke you I will make bruite
beasts of cun⟨try [men?]⟩ I weare a sweete Brute then. *Brutus*
was noe more heere then I ⟨[was]⟩ heere. Where was *Cassius* when
Brutus was heere?

Kinge.   Thou saist well for that.

Clowne.   To tell you true, my cronicle is not an egg laid as others
haue been, myne is an ephemerides fore tellinge whatt shall happen
in kings raignes to come, for that thats past wee all know.   50

Cornewall.   This is a harder waie; saddle your horse, pray letts see
what pace it keep⟨[es.]⟩

Voltimar.   Gett vpp and ride, you must spurr, cutt and awaie.

Clowne.   I name noe kings and so beinge nameles you know men
are blamelesse.

Winchester.   So so, to your cronicle.

Clowne.   In such a kings raigne, and in the yeare 1217 in the

moneth of december about Christmas, when euery noble man
meanes to keepe open howse and good hospitallity, such terrible
windes will arise that all the fyers shalbee blowne out of theire 60
kitchens, all the good cheere out of theire halls, all the servinge
men out of theire coates, and all theire poore tennants out of theire
witts.

Colchester.   But sirra when theis winds are laid the spitts may bee
turninge againe.

Clowne.   They may so, they shall goe to the fyer and bee ready to
turne when in shall come a caroach and four flanders mares,
a coachman and a page, and they shall runne awaie with more meate,
then would serve three hunderd creatures in blew that stand at
livery.   70

Carintha.   Heeres a strange cronicle.

Armante.   Hast anie more such stuff?

Clowne.   In the yeare 1231 men and women shall so entaile them
selves one vpon an other, that ladies scarlett peticoates shall make
gentlemen little gallipott breeches.

Kinge.   So; good charity when they couer one annother.

Clowne.   In the yeare 1354 bread wilbee so scarce that lords shalbee
gladd to eate pye crust.

Cornewall.   A terrible tyme.

Clowne.   In the yeare 1472 on Saint *Lawrence* daie at noone must 80
a woman bee burnt in Smith feild and before night five carmen
burnt in Turnball streete, and four gentlemen in Bloomsbury.

Colchester.   Hott doinges.

Clowne.   In the yeare 1499 bawdie howses will so increase that to
suppresse the number of them women shalbee faine to keepe
tobacco shopps.

Cornewall.   A good waie.

Clowne.   In the yeare 1561 capp wilbee so intollerable deere that
Powles shall not gett one to fitt him for anie money.

Winchester.   Pittie the Church should stand bare.   90

Clowne.   In the yeare 1600 New gate shall so swarme with theeues
that millers shalbee faine to grind neare Bun hill and yett a number
of taylors shall liue brauely in the Strand.

71 cronicle] cronicles MS   76–83 Deleted in MS   88–93 Deleted in MS

Colchester.   Theres noe hurt in that.

Clowne.   But now in the raigne of this kinge heere in the yeares
1621 : 22 and 23 such a wooden fashion will come vpp that hee whoe
walkes not with a *Battoone* shalbee held noe gallant.

Winchester.   Battoone, whats that.

Clowne.   A kind of cudgell noe longer then that which a water
spaniell carries crosse his chopps. You haue seene shapperoones   100
and maqueroones and baboones, and laroones, and petoones, and
gogs noones, but this lyninge of plimoth cloake (calld the battoone)
is a stuff but new cutt out of the loome.

Kinge.   What are Battoones good for.

Clowne.   Please your maiesty to heare the virtues, my cronicle
shall bumbast them before you.

Kinge.   Come on then, first whie is it calld a battoone?

Clowne.   Tis a french woord le baston, thats as much to ⟨s[aie that
if]⟩ a professor of the needle raile at a ⟨   ⟩ with his
battoone pay him some thinge ⟨   ⟩   110

Kinge.   Ver⟨[ie goo]d⟩.

Clowne.   Yf a gallant promise a rich gowne or petticoate to a
gentlewoman so shee will vnder take a busines for him, hee needes
troble noe taylor to take the altitude, longitude or profundity of
her body, for his owne measure is within reach.

Colchester.   What other properties has it.

Clowne.   This; if a gentleman bee disarm'd by a broker of his
weapon, hee looses noe honor if hee stick to his wooden dagger.

Cornewall.   What more?

Clowne.   In cold weather a crew of roringe boyes beinge in a   120
taverne with little money, may to save fyre make faggotts of theire
battoones and burne em in one place, and cutt battoones out of
faggotts in annother.

Carintha.   Pritty comodities.

Winchester.   But what are now the discomodities.

Clowne.   One only inconvenience my lord leanes vppon it and

---

95 the raigne...heere in the] deleted in MS
96 1621] final digit is blotted and may just possibly be formed over an original O
100 In left margin: *bee redy* | *Edmond*
125–129 Deleted in MS

that is that the battoone beinge a kind of french crutch, many by
walkinge with it may bee suspected to haue cornes on his toes when
they are as sound as I am.

Voltimar.   The masquers sir are readie.   130
Cornewall.   Hence with the cronicler.
Kinge.   Wee'l heare him out at leasure.
Clowne.   At leasure then I shall give my attendance.   *Exit.*

Hoboyes. Enter Edmond.

Edmond.   Leaue di catter wawlinge noyse, cutt of de goose necks
of di fiddles and hange dine owne neck in de strings.
Kinge.   Whie how now *Teage*, whats the matter that your tongue
runnes so.
Edmond.   It runnes out a myne Irish witts, crees sa mee de maskers
(de halters eate em) bee all togeider by de eares, der scurvy wodden
faces bee tore in a towsand peices.   140
Winchester.   How? the maskers quarrell?
Kinge.   See *Cornewall, Colchester*, Capten you to.

Exeunt [they three.]

Edmond.   A little lowsie boy tell twoe hunderd a di self and a
woman dow gotts widd child and so anger my master de embassador hee takes so terrible deale of welsh pepper vpp into his nose
tis y faatla as read as a hott warden pie.

Enter Penda *and* Eldred.

Penda.   Pud trigs vppon a welse man, yes, when can tell? does
her masesty invite to fine seere of cunny pies, and sett your
shraps and offals and pones and toggs meate was awle knawne
before her?   150
Kinge.   The meaninge of this furie?
Penda.   *Reece* tell her furies is mad as horne pull.
Eldred.   Heere is awle her furies — her laties there, whoe was to
marry into her lords consanguinities is a cow has a greate calf
runne by her sides, has porne a pastard.
Kinge.   Whoe dares report this.
Penda.   There are porters enow, see, yett shall fide for her too.

148 In left margin: *bee redy Lords* | *& Prince*

383

Enter Cornewall *with his sword drawne, after him* Colchester *and*
Kent *drawne, the prince like* Cupid, Voltimar *keepes in the midst,*
Penda, Edmond *and* Eldred *draw and guard the Kinge;* Winchester
and Ladies step betwene all.

Cornewall.   Looke to your life sir, traitorous *Colchester*
  And his falce harted faction envyinge the peace
  Of your court pastimes, thus with weapons drawne   160
  Sett your whole court in vprore.
Kinge.   Maske turnd to massacre?
Colchester.   Not royall sir to touch your life.
Omnes.   What then?
Prince.   Ile tell you what tis, I begunne this broyle
  And lett mee end it. I to this welsh lord
  Swore hee should never call mee sonne in law
  Nor call my mother wife.
Penda.   Wife, yes when was hange and trawne in her quarters.
Prince.   I tould him that my father was a kinge
  And that my mother should not dwell in *Wales*
  But bee a Queene in *England.*   170
Eldred.   *Wales* is well rid vppon her.
Prince.   And this brake of the masque, I should ha been you see
  a cupid in't.
⟨[*Penda.*] And I⟩ master *Vulcans* an antidated cuckolds to cry
  ptrooh at.
⟨[*Kent.*] To aid th]⟩is prince come wee thus armd with iustice.
⟨[*Colchester.*]   ⟩ wretched, now a fond silly lady
⟨   r fo   s   er w mo   ⟩
  For heers our resolution to proclayme
  This prince your heire, and this contracted lady   180
  Your wife, ere anie else step to your throwne.
Kinge.   Doe you threaten?
Omnes.   Yes.
Kinge.   Oh you weake sighted lords,
  Kings thoughts fly from the reach of common eyes.
  Tis true our first intentions weare poysond arrowes
  Shott att the hart of *Penda*, I then not card

(T'inioye his wife) so half man kind had fell,
Butt better spirritts mee guided *Voltimar*.
This was my diall, whose goinge true sett all   190
My mad howers right.
Voltimar.   I plaid the honest coniurer; when divills to bee raisd
I putt ang⟨e[lls]⟩ into the same circles.
Carintha.   T'increase your Angells number heere are hands
Wrought in this schole of magique.
Armante.   And was not I a good proficient with you?
Prince.   My lords you are gulld, I ha plaid the little Iuggler too.
Kinge.   I all this while
Sufferd this comedy of welsh disguises
Still to goe on, but now my lord embassador   200
Y'are welcome out of *Wales*.
Penda.   In english I thanck your maiesty.

[Penda *and* Eldred *discover.*]

Kinge.   Nay I must flea your skins of too, deere *Edmond*.
Edmond.   I ha lost my tongue on a suddaine, tis shipt for *Ireland*.
                                              [*Discovers.*]
Kinge.   My princely brothers both, a paire of kingdomes
Shall not buy you twoe from mee.
Edmond.   I had noe reason to lacky like an Irish footman thus —
Eldred.   Nor I as a welse sentillman.
Edmond.   But knowinge
By this most honest, most noble soldier
What falce dice you putt in to cozen *Penda*   210
Of all his wealth (his wife) wee sir turnd cheaters
To haue some sport with you.
Kinge.   If worthie *Penda*
I haue wone from thee ought of this rich treasure,
I'me a franck gamster, take it all agen.
This is myne owne stake, none shall draw thee from mee
My best *Armante* nor this princely boy
For a new world.
Armante.   I am happie in theis tryalls.
Kinge.   Are you pleasd now old grand sire?

Colchester.   And on our knees
Craue pardon for our rashnes.
Kinge.   You did but iustice.
Bee anie to bee blam'd it is theis lords   220
Whoe to sett vpp theire kinswoman a Queene
Card not to ruin vtterly this temple
So basely by mee shaken. *Winchester*
Has plaid at this greate shootinge a faire Archer.
Soldier thou shalt not want what thou deservst,   [*To* Voltimar.]
Gold and our loue.

Enter Clowne like Vulcan.

Clowne.   And what I, haue I been at cost to smutt my face, hire
a hammer, buy a polt foote and study a speech in your maske for
Vulcan and now must I hobble without it?
Kinge.   My weddinge with *Armante* shalbee hastend   230
And till then keepe your speech, then bringe your masque in.
Clowne.   Till then I wilbee speechles.
Prince.   And so youl lay aside your croniclinge
I'le begg thee of the king to bee my iester.
Clowne.   Ide as leife you'd begg mee for your foole, if you did
tweare noe great hurt, for a kings foole meetes better fortune
then manie ⟨[wise men.]⟩
Kinge.   More then a goldinge ringe marries your loues,
A kings spred Armes letts rest after ⟨   ⟩
Wee haue had a royall race, a goal ⟨   ⟩   240
'Tis cr⟨o⟩wnd if wee t⟨   ⟩

[*FINIS.*]

225–226 In left margin, braced and deleted: *Enter Clowne like* | *Vulcan*
226–237 Deleted in MS.
239 after] MSR follows with the reading 'oʳ' which is not present in the manuscript
as presently mutilated.
241 t⟨   ] MSR reads 'that', presumably before the mutilation spread.

386

TEXTUAL NOTES

I.ii

89 Not;]   There is some question whether this word does not end Carintha's speech. Although 'not;' is below the horizontal line drawn above the King's speech-prefix, it is not quite on the line with 'Ile doo't. . .' but somewhat above. The scribe seems to be squeezing in the text as he nears the foot of the page; and it is just possible that to save a line he began the King's speech after and slightly below Carintha's final word and then later confused the issue by misplacing the horizontal. However, if we are to consider this as a possibility, we should also have to take it that the semi-colon was subsequently added after 'not' as an assumed correction. And it is most unusual to begin an independent speech in the manner indicated. The odds are, therefore, that the King completes Carintha's speech, as printed in the text.

II.i

201 Thus I fall]   MSR points out that a rule is drawn at this line in error, or else that a speaker's name *Colchester* has been omitted. It is more probable that the rule is in error, for Winchester and Kent appear to be engaged in a dialogue at this point, and line 201 seems to be a reference back to Winchester's lines 193–197. Colchester's line 208 is very likely the point at which he formally approves the faction.

II.ii

35 throwne]   The manuscript reading *thorne* is clearly wrong, as may be seen from *The Noble Spanish Soldier*, II.ii.39–40: 'the Burre that stickes in your throat is a throane'. The error may perhaps suggest that in the original manuscript the spelling was *throne*, not the characteristic *throwne* found in the present manuscript.

V.ii

10 prapples]   See the Textual Introduction for the analysis of the sophistication that involved deleting *prapples &* and substituting *quarrells* at the moment of writing.

EMENDATIONS OF ACCIDENTALS

I.i

S.D. ACT[us]] *Act*
1 busines?] ~ ∧
2 you?] ~ ∧
2 S.D. *in left margin opposite line* 2
3 *Fraunce*] fraunce
3 theis?] ~ ∧
6 *Eldred,*] ~ ∧
6 *Penda,*] ~ ∧
8 regiment] reginent
9 Nor I.] *followed by deleted* from Edmonds tent I come
10 *Eldreds*] l *altered from start of a* d
12 *Eldred's*] Eldreds
12 Ha,] ~ ∧
12 slaine?] ~ ∧
13 togeither;] ~ ,
14 nothinge;] ~ ,
15 hand,] ~ ∧
16 Twins,] ~ ∧
17 lost?] ~ ∧
18 pale,] ~ ∧
19 brothers? Heere] brothers, heere
19 honors:] ~ ∧
21 S.D. *in left margin opposite lines* 21–22
23 thou?] ~ ∧ (*follows deleted* thost)
23 *Fraunce*] fraunce
25 heere,] ~ ∧
27 *Edmond's*] Edmonds
27 newes?] ~ ∧
32 Slaine?] ~ ∧
33 yeares,] ~ ∧

39 black,] ~ ∧
42 noe] *following is deleted* d
42 them;] ~ ,
44 her.] ~ ∧
49 saxon?] ~ ∧
49 fall?] ~ ∧
50 did,] ~ ∧
54 vprores,] ~ ∧
56 *tis done*] tis done
57 Done;] ~ ∧
58 *Fraunce*] fraunce
59 too?] ~ ∧
60 man,] ~ ∧
63 in't. My] in't, my
63 brothers —] ~ ∧
68 yett;] ~ ∧
69 this;] ~ ∧
71 *Penda*∧] ~ ,
71 sonne),] ~) ∧
75 tell?] ~ ∧
76 *Voltimar*;] ~ ∧
77 both.] ~ ∧
78 S.D. *in left margin opposite line* 78
79 right?] ~ ∧
79 mee,] ~ ∧
81–82 Vnles...againe] *one line in* MS
83 staie;] ~ ∧
84 dare] *preceded by deleted* ar
84 convay —] ~ ∧
85 Dare!] ~ ∧
85 So:] ~ ∧

I.ii

1 body,] ~ ∧
3 had] h *altered from*)
3 force,] ~ ∧

4 triumph] trivmph
6 sweete] *interlined above a caret*
7 breakinge. His] breakinge, his

9 desperate;] ~ ˄
11 Th'accompts] thaccompts
11 vallor,] ~ ˄
11 Virtues,] ~ ˄
13 layings] *preceded by deleted* p
15 death.] ~ ˄
19 it.] ~ ,
22 greefe,] ~ ˄
24 you.] ~ ,
24 husband,] ~ ˄
25 you;] ~ ,
25 euen,] ~ ˄
26 heauen.] ~ ˄
27 for's] fors
27 dy'd,] ~ ˄
30 French,] ~ ˄
32 oakes;] ~ ˄
33 stroakes.] ~ ˄
35 yard?] ~ ˄
35 honor.] ~ ˄
37 greater,] ~ ˄
40 S.D. *in left margin opposite line* 40
41 lords,] ~ ˄
41 you,] ~ ˄
42 story,] ~ ˄
47 S.D. *in left marg. opp. l.* 47
51 water.] ~ ˄
54 shee] *preceded by deleted* see
57 Armes?] ~ ˄
59 to] *interlined with a caret above deleted* for
60 crowne. Both] crowne, both
60 remoud,] ~ ˄
61 alone,] *perhaps* a lone ˄
63–64 *one line in* MS
65 thred,] ~ ˄
66 done?] ~ ˄
66 riddle?] ~ ˄
67 mee] *interlined above a caret*
69 fort —] ~ ˄
72 it.] ~ ˄
73 composition —] ~ ˄
76 me, . . . by,] ~ ˄ . . . ~ ˄
77 armes,] ~ ˄

78 mee;] ~ ,
78 it.] ~ ˄
81 musique,] ~ ˄
81 sings;] ~ ˄
85–86 Besides. . . *Armante*] *one line in* MS
86 *Armante*,] ~ ˄
88 sonne;] ~ ˄
88 knott,] ~ ˄
89 bottome,] ~ ˄
89–92 MS *lines:* Not. . . *Winchester* | in. . . phisitian
90 S.D. *in left marg. opp. l.* 88
91 *Winchester*,] ~ ˄
94 hand,] ~ ˄
95 witnesses —] ~ ˄
103 body. Shee] body shee (shee *interlined above a caret*)
108 vndone.] ~ ˄
111 S.D. *in left marg. opp. l.* 111
112 *Colchester*,] ~ ˄
116 myne?] ~ ,
116 girle, . . . mistris;] ~ ˄ . . . ~ ˄
119 too,] ~ ˄
120 nose, . . . lipp,] ~ ˄ . . . ~ ˄
121 yours,] ~ ˄
122 owne,] ~ ˄
123 trap,] ~ ˄
125 doe?] ~ ˄
126 tymes,] ~ ˄
127 saie,] ~ ˄
130 forward?] ~ ˄
130 sir,] ~ ˄
131 oh!] ~ ˄
131 mother?] ~ ˄
132 sir, . . . whore?] ~ ˄ . . . ~ ˄
133 mercy, . . . concubine,] ~ ˄ . . . ~ ˄
137 sir, . . . dome,] ~ ˄ . . . ~ ˄
139 Awaie] *possibly* a waie
140 falne,] ~ ˄
142 off;] ~ ,
144 rebound?] ~ ˄
148–149 Are. . . ended,] *one line in* MS

149 welcome; ...ended,] ~ ∧   152 man,] ~ ∧
    ... ~ ∧   153 horse,] ~ ∧
150 *Colchester.*] *Clo:*   154 still,] ~ ∧
150 grace?] ~ ∧   155 heede;] ~ ∧
151 anie.] ~ ,

I.iii

1 this?] ~ ∧   58 shall] *mended from* shalt
1 it,] ~ ∧   60 dissolvinge.] ~ ∧
4 him,] ~ ∧   61 hee?] ~ ∧
6 Noe,] ~ ∧   63 marry that] *followed by deleted*
6 S.D. *in left marg. opp. l. 6*   that
8 roome?] ~ ∧ (the roome *inter-*   63 that,] ~ ∧
    lined above a caret)   65 him.] ~ ∧
8 you] *preceded by deleted* it   66 off,] ~ ∧
9 landlord. Avoyd] landlord   68 mettall?] ~ ,
    avoyd   68 mee,] ~ ∧
9 warninge?] ~ ∧   69 you,] ~ ∧
13 *Armante.*] *substituted for*   70 it,] ~ ∧
    smudged-out Win   71 goe,] ~ ∧
13 Game?] ~ ∧   71 Las,] ~ ∧
15 you.] ~ ,   73 sir,] ~ ∧
17 lord,] ~ ∧   75 eyes.] ~ ∧
21 his. My] his, my   76 alone] *preceded by deleted* in it
23 daughter;] ~ ∧   77 behold,] ~ ∧
28 I, ...so,] ~ ∧ ... ~ ∧   79 So,] ~ ∧
29 more,] ~ ∧   81 S.D. *in left marg. opp. l.* 82
31 water —] ~ ∧   82 this?] ~ ∧
32–33 MS *lines:* Thou...stay | 83 bedlam?] ~ ∧
    whats...name   84 Yes,] ~ ∧
33 Stay, ...name?] ~ ∧ ... ~ ∧   85 I,] ~ ∧
35 broaker,] ~ ∧   87 gon, ...slaue?] ~ ∧ ... ~ ∧
38 *London?*] ~ /   94 Awaie,] ~ ∧
40 Citty,] ~ ∧   96 S.D. *in left marg. opp. l.* 97
43 S.D. *in left marg. opp. ll.* 42–43   97 now,] ~ ∧
44 Peace,] ~ ∧   99 her;] ~ ,
48 could,] ~ ∧   101 writinge?] ~ ∧
49 wrongs —] ~ ∧   105 writinge?] ~ ∧
50 them,] ~ ∧   107 daughter.] ~ ,
53 noone,] ~ ∧   111 prithee;] ~ ,
58 hast] *preceded by deleted* h   111 ore,] ~ ∧

II.i

1 faire,] ~ ∧
5 wee] *follows deleted* be
6 princes;] ~ ∧
7 hooke] *follows deleted* hoope
10 offers?] ~ ∧
15 feild,] ~ ∧
18 afishinge,] ~ ∧
19 fate,] ~ ∧
20 kinge] e *altered from* s
22 *Edmond.*] *substituted for* Eld
23–25 MS *lines:* Vppon...earle |
    great...*Gildas*
23 duke,] ~ ;
24 earle, ... by,] ~ ∧ ... ~ ∧
25–26 The...*Vffa.*] *one line in* MS
26 *Conon,*] ~ ∧
27 *Cornewalle* —] ~ ∧
29 th'] *interlined*
29 of] *interlined above a caret*
29 prithee] *follows deleted* I
31 prowdlie,] ~ ∧
32 heere,] ~ ∧
32 *below is the deleted line:* heere
    wheele a troope of horse
33 eares:] ~ ∧
34 there,] ~ ∧
38 courage;] ~ ∧
40 *Dieu;*] ~ ,
41 fell,] ~ ∧
46 mammocks.] ~ ,
46 high,] ~ ∧
47 truth,] ~ ∧
47 earle] *follows deleted* eal
51 kinge,] ~ ∧
54 not,] ~ ∧
54 *Voltimar,*] ~ ∧
54 S.D. *Florish.*] *in left margin*
    opposite line 53, *a cross being made*
    before the speech-prefix for Ed-
    mond
55 all,] ~ ∧
56 *Fraunce,*] ~ ∧

57 *Voltimar?*] ~ ∧
58 sir,] ~ ∧
61 all.] ~ ∧
62 thrifty,] ~ ∧
63 *Capten?*] ~ ∧
65 *Voltimar?*] ~ /
68 dy'd?] ~ ∧
71 fell?] ~ /
73 battaile?] ~ ∧
75 they?] ~ ∧
79 person?] ~ /
87 read;] ~ ∧
88 Whie?] ~ ∧
91 repent?] ~ ∧
92 you? Would] you, would
94 swells,] ~ ∧
100 said,] ~ ∧
105 ha?] ~ ∧
110 ruin, him;] ~ ∧ ~ ,
111 demollisht,] ~ ∧
113 Bawd?] ~ ∧
118 How?] ~ ∧
121 home?] ~ ∧
129 face∧ ...minute,] ~ , ... ~ ∧
129 it:] ~ ,
130 runne] *interlined above deleted*
    words that may be lead you
135 out] *follows deleted* ov
141 peasants,] ~ ∧
142 chastize;] ~ ,
142 pardon,] ~ ∧
146 prison;] ~ ,
147 draw mee,] ~ ~ ∧
149 now?] ~ ∧
152 thee,] ~ ∧
154 shoes,] ~ ∧
155 cutt?] ~ /
157 *Armante.*)] ~ ∧)
160 all?] ~ ,
160 S.D. *in left marg. opp. ll.* 160–161
161 fury,] ~ ∧
164 marry,] ~ ∧

165–166 But...bed?] *one line in* MS
166 bed?] ~ ∧
166–167 A...wife] *one line in* MS
175 kinsmen?] ~ /
175 Sir,] ~ ∧
177 to.] ~ ∧
179 it, noe;] ~ ∧ ~ ∧
180 S.D. *in left marg. opp. l.* 180
182 periury?] ~ ∧
183 frantick?] ~ ∧
184 S.D. *in left marg. opp. ll.* 184–185
186 What,] ~ ∧
186 *Ioue?*] ~ ,
187 him,] ~ ∧
191 niblinge,] ~ ∧

192 it?] ~ ∧
193–195 MS *lines:* I...others |
    when...lady
193 *Cornewall,*] ~ ∧
194 others,] ~ ∧
195 lady,] ~ ∧
196 home,] ~ ∧
196 fill,] ~ ∧
198 *Colchester*] *follows deleted* Ch
198 father,] ~ ∧
200 ours.] ~ ∧
201 blasted,] ~ ∧
202–203 Thus...consult.] *one line in*
    MS

II.ii

5 Noe?] ~ ,
5 not] *interlined above a caret*
8 tormented;] ~ ,
8 birth,] ~ ∧
9 so —] ~ ∧
11 you —] ~ ∧
13 familie —] ~ ∧
15 man∧] ~ —
25 hand,] ~ ∧
25 nourishinge] norinshinge
25 stomach,] ~ ∧
27 oh!] ~ ∧
28 him?] ~ ∧
32 whie?] ~ ∧
32 revenge?] ~ ,
33 frights] *follows deleted* sh
34 you. For] you, for
34 revenge?] ~ ,
35 throwne:] ~ ,
37 another] an *interlined above a*
    caret after the deletion of t *in*
    tother
37 quart;] ~ ,
39 bee.] ~ ,
39 now] *interlined above a caret*
39 market,] ~ ∧
40 done?] ~ ∧

42 villaine,] ~ ∧
45 brazen] *follows deleted* p
46 both?] ~ ∧
49 martingall?] ~ ∧
51 strompitt,] ~ ∧
57 earnest?] ~ ∧
61 goll,] ~ ∧
66 earnest?] ~ ∧
76 S.D. *Florish.*] *added in left marg.*
    opp. l. 76
76 S.D. Chester.] ~ ,
76 S.D. Penda∧] ~ ;
77 before, ...lord,] ~ ∧ ... ~ ∧
78 not,] ~ ∧
80 warrs;] ~ ,
80 beates,] ~ ∧ *(interlined above a*
    caret)
80 call] *altered from* calls
84 meale] *follows deleted* sawce to o
87 mettle] *follows deleted* mettale
88 flyes;] ~ ∧
90 Flyes,] ~ ∧
91 ha,] ~ ∧
91 you?] ~ ∧
92 hee] *follows deleted* a
94 noe,] ~ ∧
97 bootes,] ~ ∧

103 noe?] ~ ∧
106 by∧] ~)
109 many] *follows deleted* may
113 boyes,] ~ ∧
114 bee] *follows deleted* shall
115 *Eldred.*] *substituted for deleted*
     Pen:
121 byas,] ~ ∧
121 I;] ~ ∧
122 could] *follows deleted* I

122 I] *interlined above a caret*
122 sport. You] sport you
122 metheglin:] ~ ∧ (ge *deleted at end*
     of metheglin)
123 *Leinstar,*] ~ ∧
129 Runne,] ~ ∧
129 lord?] ~ ∧
131 dynner. Lord] dynner, lord
136 Arme,] ~ ∧

II.iii

2 bed;] ~ ∧
3 him;] ~ ,
3 husband,] ~ ∧
6 raizd.] ~ ∧
8 see] *follows deleted* he
8 S.D. *in left marg. opp. l.* 7
9 sick,] ~ ∧
11 togeither?] ~ ∧
15 sadnes?] ~ ∧
15 iest?] ~ ∧
22 out] *follows deleted* ut
25 that] *followed by deleted* ty
28 it.] ~ ∧
31 are?] ~ ∧
35 walls,] ~ ∧
37 Yes,] ~ ∧
37 S.D. *in two lines to the right of*
     line 37; *in left margin a hand*
     points across to the direction
37 S.D. *staff.*] ~ ∧
37 Ha,] ~ ∧
40 in] *altered from* int
40 hee] *followed by deleted* th

41 posture?] ~ ∧
42 Noe?] ~ ;
45 *Penda,*] ~ ∧
47 this,] ~ ∧
48 beheld,] ~ ∧
52 sorry,] ~ ∧
53 him —] ~ ∧
54 drakes,] ~ ∧
57 masques —] ~ ∧
57 meanes,] ~ ∧
58 haue] *followed by deleted* eou
59 madd;] ~ ,
64 coronation.] ~ ∧
65 S.D. *in left marg. opp. ll.* 64–65
66–67 *one line in* MS
69 bow?] ~ /
76 heere] *followed by deleted* then
79 S.D. omnes,] ~ ∧
80 welsh] *followed by deleted* a
88 you. Tho] you, tho
91 subtill,] ~ ∧
100 hir,] ~ ∧

III.i

1 ballads?] ~ ∧
3 four shillinge] *followed by deleted*
     or
5 poet?] ~ ∧
8 ravisht,] ~ ∧
9 manger,] ~ ∧
19 looke] *followed by deleted* intoo't

20 you,] ~ ∧
26 plums,] ~ ∧
28 has it noe] *interlined with a caret*
     above deleted without
28 puddinge,   . . . eggs?]   ~ ∧
     . . . ~ ∧
29–30 it and] *interlined above a caret*

34 then,] ~ ₐ
46 S.D. *in left marg. opp. l.* 45
47 Mother,] ~ ₐ
48 S.D. *in left marg. opp. ll.* 47–48
54 foole,] ~ ₐ
59 When? ~ ₐ
61 him,] ~ ₐ
63 arrowes?] ~ ₐ
65 hart;] ~ ₐ
66 death,] ~ ₐ
68 sonne.] ~ ₐ
69 by,] ~ ₐ
71 ladie,] ~ ₐ
72 *Nunnes*,] ~ ₐ
73 in;] ~ ₐ
74 kinge?] ~ ₐ
74 father?] ~ ₐ
76 eagles?] ~ ,
78 safety.) Should] safety) should
81 lyes.] ~ ₐ
83 S.D. *in left marg. opp. l.* 82
87 and your] *followed by deleted* af
94 good] *interlined above a caret*
94 lords,] ~ ₐ
96 nayle,] ~ ₐ
96 draw —] ~ ₐ
97 What?] ~ ₐ

99 mee?] ~ ₐ
103 e'm,] ~ ₐ
104 in't] int
104 bodkins;] ~ ₐ
104 fight,] ~ ₐ
109 him,] ~ ₐ
109 S.D. *Exeunt*] *follows deleted* Eu
110 madnes,] ~ ₐ
111 loue,] ~ ₐ
112 vse,] ~ ₐ
113 interest,] ~ ₐ
114 owne?] ~ —
116 still. Doe] still doe
117 honest?] ~ ₐ
119–120 pipe. The] pipe, the
124 -cockles),] ~) ₐ
124 plott,] ~ ₐ
126 man?] ~ ₐ
128 english,] ~ ₐ
128–129 both. The] both the
129 languages;] ~ ,
130 schollers. Whie not?] schollers,
    whie not,
131 dynners;] ~ ,
136 maze,] ~ ₐ
136 round,] ~ ₐ

III.ii

S.D. *Florish.*] *in left margin opp.*
    III.i.137
1 fetch] *follows deleted* feth
5 tribute. Nations] tribute, nations
6 servitude.] ~ ₐ
7 hee?] ~ ₐ
7 Troath] *follows deleted* what is he
7 gentleman;] ~ ₐ
13 him,] ~ ₐ
14 *Cornewall,*] ~ ₐ
17 *Voltimars*;] ~ ₐ
18 trusty?] ~ ₐ
19 heaven.] ~ ₐ
21 embassador.) How] embassador)
    how

21 S.D. *in left marg. opp. l.* 21
27 supple;] ~ ₐ
28 battery,] ~ ₐ
29–30 *one line in* MS
31 muteny,] ~ ₐ
32 faction,] ~ ₐ
35 *Cornewall.*] *substituted for deleted*
    K:
35 matter,] ~ ₐ
36 quiett,] ~ ₐ
36 S.D. *Hoboyes*] *added in left margin*
36 S.D. *Embassador*] Enbassador
38 heads —] ~ ₐ
53 twincklinge] *followed by deleted*
    we *or* me

56 hand?] ~ ∧
62 Latter] *follows deleted* vpp
62 *Lamas,*] ~ ∧
63 wehies?] ~ ∧
64 logger–head] logger-|head
65 snowtes?] ~ ∧
67 Collers?] ~ ∧
75 battalios,] ~ ∧
90 for't] fort
93 *morris,*] ~ ∧
94 dancers. For] dancers for
98 so,] ~ ∧
99 kinglines] *followed by deleted* at
101 fought] *followed by deleted* very
    finely
101 vs.] ~ ∧
109 vs,] ~ ∧
109 doe?] ~ ∧
110 comrague,] ~ ∧
112 men,] ~ ∧
113 lost,] ~ ∧
114 welcome;] ~ ,
115 *Wales*;] ~ ,
118 vrld] *followed by deleted* tague

120 with —] ~ ∧
122 S.D. *Florish.*] *in left marg. opp. l.*
    122, *which has been indicated by* ♯
    before the speech prefix
129 S.D. *in left marg. starting opp. l.*
    129
130 sirra,] ~ ∧
131 hee?] ~ ∧
133 state. Which] state, which
134 sirrah?] ~ ∧
138 deerely;] ~ ∧
146 can. Euer] can, euer
146 came] *follows deleted* rane
146 de] De
147 hidder,] ~ ∧
148 still,] ~ ∧
151 mee,] ~ ∧
151 not] *followed by deleted* for
153 sirrah,] ~ ∧
156 clothes?] ~ ∧
157 face,] ~ ∧
158 besides?] ~ ∧
160 th'ice] thice

III.iii

1 hand,] ~ ∧
2 (besides...father)] ∧ ~ ... ~ ∧
4 honor;] ~ ∧
5 barr. This] barr, this
6 hart;] ~ ∧
8 court.] ~ ∧
12 myne,] ~ ∧
13 shine.] ~ ∧
14 S.D. *in left marg. opp. l.* 14
22 S.D. *in left marg. opp. l.* 22
24 *Exit*] MS *places after l.* 23
25 *Armante?*] ~ ∧
26 now? Loue] now, loue
27 troath,] ~ ∧
28 the] *altered from* this
29 your] *interlined with a caret above*
    deleted his

30 the] *altered from* th'eyes
32 hate;] ~ ∧
34 forhead;] ~ ,
34 sonne?] ~ ∧
37 I never] *follows deleted* h
38–39 *one line in* MS
40 fighter,] ~ ∧
42 swaggerer. Neither] swaggerer,
    neither
45 th'unnaturall] thunnaturall
46 groath.] ~ ∧
47 for?] ~ ∧
49 mistris, so?] ~ ∧ ~ ∧
50 court,] ~ ∧
52 only. Oh] only, oh
52 woman,] ~ ∧
53 mother,] ~ ∧

54 passion‸] ∼ ,
60 bed;] ∼ ‸
60 on't] ont
61 forbidden;] ∼ ‸
63 whore.] ∼ ‸
67 now] *interlined above a caret*
68–69 If...mee.] *one line in* MS
69–71 Pray...mother.] *prose in* MS
69 doe,] ∼ ‸
73 sorrows?] ∼ ‸
73 periuries,] ∼ ‸
74 falshood;] ∼ ,
78 out.] ∼ ‸
82 Queene.] ∼ ‸
84 mother,] ∼ ‸
86 now] *followed by deleted* as

89 yssue;] ∼ ‸
94 not,] ∼ ‸
97 them,] ∼ ‸
98 letter?] ∼ ‸
100–101 With...away] *one line in* MS
101 which] *followed by deleted* im
102–103 This...with.] *one line in* MS
112 then —] ∼ ‸
113 MS *lines:* Ought...prayers |
  I...you
116–117 Tis...you?] *one line in* MS
117 you?] ∼ ‸
117 parte,] ∼ ‸

IV.i

S.D. *Florish.*] *added in left margin*
3 noe?] ∼ ‸
4 Close?] ∼ ;
6 meaninge?] ∼ ‸
8 noe?] ∼ ‸
10 parliance?] ∼ ‸
12 her to] t *formed over a comma,
  deleting it*
18 eye,] ∼ ‸
21 too.] ∼ ‸
28 longe,] ∼ ‸
30 sweeter,] ∼ ‸
32 py. Harge] py harge
33 tro?] ∼ ‸
37 poyson?] ∼ ‸
39 S.D. *in left marg. opp. ll.* 38–39
  (Eldred *is substituted for deleted*
  Edmond)
49 him —] ∼ ‸
55 tauge] *follows deleted* tag
55 well?] ∼ ‸
57 thundringe?] ∼ ‸
58 Your] *followed by deleted* d
58 tongue?] ∼ ‸
60 the] *altered from* your

67 wife. *Sidannen*] wife, sidannen
69 a] *followed by deleted* grol
79 madrigalls?] ∼ ‸
82 MS *inscribes in Italian hand this
  line only*
82 face?] ∼ ‸
83 shace.] ∼ ‸
84 nyes?] ∼ ‸
87 nose?] ∼ ‸
91 seekes?] ∼ ‸
93 How,] ∼ ‸
97 lip?] ∼ ‸
100–101 *one line in* MS
101 skin?] ∼ ‸
104 tongue?] ∼ ‸
107 pare?] ∼ ‸
108 Aske] *followed by deleted* p
110–111 *one line in* MS
110 Marge] *follows deleted* mag
111 tipple?] ∼ ‸
113 How, ...nipple?] ∼ ‸ ... ∼ ‸
115 child?] ∼ ‸
117 more?] ∼ ‸
118 awle —] ∼ ‸
119 pelly?] ∼ ‸

120 tis] *followed by deleted* soft
120 Iellie;] ~ ∧
121 thighes,] ~ ∧
122 lyes,] ~ ∧

125 too.] ~ ∧
126 Come,] ~ ∧ (*altered from* comes)
127 S.D. *Florish.*] *in left marg. opp. l.*
    126

IV.ii

1 thou, . . .awaie?] ~ ∧ . . . ~ ∧
4 howskeepinge. Within] hows-
    keepinge within
9 *Wales*;] ~ ∧
10 there?] ~ ∧
18 doghowse,] ~ ∧
24 rascall,] ~ ∧
24 catt?] ~ ∧
25 mercy,] ~ ∧
25 mynd you.] ~ ~ ,
26 creature,] ~ ∧
33 for't] fort
35 witt?] ~ ,
35 yeare;] ~ ∧
37 fooleries. Witt?] fooleries witt
43 come] *followed by deleted* co
44 Captaine?] ~ ∧
46 ouer;] ~ ,
46 heere] *followed by deleted* m
47 S.D. *in left marg. opp. l.* 47
51 away apace] *possibly* a way a pace
52 enough;] ~ ,
56 bottles;] ~ ,
57 Armory,] ~ ∧
64 hay] *interlined with a caret above
    deleted* health
65 *England*; . . .still,] ~ ∧ . . . ~ ∧
70 rascall] *altered from* rascally

71 *Merioneth,*] ~ ∧
71–72 so. Was] so, was
72 *Wales?*] ~ ,
73 *Wales?*] ~ ∧
80–81 you. What] you what
83 whie.] ~ ,
87 S.D. *in left marg. opp. l.* 87
88 speakes.] ~ ,
89 staie; come,] ~ , ~ ∧
89 knees;] ~ ∧
90 noe] *followed by deleted* cuntries
96 Ale,] ~ ∧
96 Perry,] ~ ∧
100 when?] ~ ∧
100 *Florish.*] *added in left margin*
102 *Daunce.*] *added in left margin*
106 Enough, . . .will,] ~ ∧ . . . ~ ∧
109 huntsman;] ~ ,
111 does] Does
115 True,] ~ ∧
119 little] *interlined with a caret above
    deleted* noe
121 boggs,] ~ ∧
122 cowes,] ~ ∧
125 nose,] ~ ∧
127 dy] *followed by deleted* sides
129 *within*] *added in left margin*
130 heere,] ~ ∧

IV.iii

1–2 *one line in* MS
1 creature,] ~ ∧
2 disobedient.] ~ ∧
3 sea,] ~ ∧
4 vnsetled,] ~ ∧
9 glib] *altered from* glibd

11 welshman,] ~ ∧
16 not] *followed by deleted* thing
17 tongue,] ~ ∧
20 woman?] ~ ∧
22 good,] ~ ∧
23 legg,] ~ ∧

24 coxcombe.] ~ ∧
26 alone. Now] alone, now
27 side,] ~ ∧
29 it.] ~ ∧
32 fyle,] ~ ∧
33 branded] *followed by deleted* b
33 name.] ~ ∧
34 not.] ~ ∧
37 vs,] ~ ∧
40 done.] ~ ∧
42 cause?] ~ ∧
44 hands.] ~ ,
45 owne] *followed by deleted* throate,
I
45 hart.] ~ ,

48 thred,] ~ ∧
49 fortune. Hee'l] fortune, hee'l
49 quiet,] ~ ∧
50 browes.] ~ ,
51 masque;] ~ ∧
53 murmeration] mvrmeration
56 Feele] *follows deleted* what furie
56 fury?] ~ ∧
57 sides,] ~ ∧
60–61 My...life.] *one line in* MS
60 *Winchester,*] ~ ∧
62 doe,] ~ ∧
63 so,] ~ ∧
65 in] *followed by deleted* sot

V.i

S.D. *Florish.*] *in left marg. opp. l.* 1
3 glory?] ~ ;
5 or] *followed by deleted* spo
9 fryer?] ~ ∧
13 neither] *followed by deleted* w
13 wife,] ~ ∧
15 beads.] ~ ∧
17 Queene,] ~ ∧
18 bewtie,] ~ ∧
19 fate;] ~ ∧
20 prayers, sighes,] ~ ∧ ~ ∧
20 weepes, ...dyes,] ~ ∧ ... ~ ∧
21 paradice.] ~ ∧
22 singe,] ~ ∧
23 kinge;] ~ ∧
25 exchange;] ~ ∧
26 glory,] ~ ∧
27 monestary.] ~ ∧
28 heere,] ~ ∧
29 deere,] ~ ∧
30 troath, ...sonne,] ~ ∧ ... ~ ∧
31 done.] ~ ∧
33 more;] ~ ∧
34 tell,] ~ ∧
37–38 Gon...strange] *one line in*
MS
37 alreadie?] ~ ∧

38 boy;] ~ ∧
41 suddaine?] ~ ∧
42–43 I...last.] *one line in* MS
44 I] *followed by deleted* am sure
44 can] *followed by deleted* scarse
45 Refraine] *follows deleted* to
46 parted. Oh] parted, oh
49 the] *followed by deleted* wol
49 world,] ~ ∧
50 birth,] ~ ∧
50 left;] ~ ∧
51 father, child,] ~ ∧ ~ ∧
51 father;] ~ ∧
52 mee,] ~ ∧
54 one;] ~ ∧
55 Rise,] ~ ∧
55 indeed?] ~ ∧
56 Hartylie,] ~ ∧
59 the] *interlined with a caret above*
deleted my
61 children.] ~ ∧
64 man,] ~ ∧
64 vpwards,] ~ ∧
65 betimes;] ~ ∧
67 butcher,] ~ ∧
68 prince. Sir] prince, sir
69 ape,] ~ ∧

398

70 more,] ∼ ∧
71–72 Shall...e're] *one line in* MS
71 I?] ∼ ;
73 father;] ∼ ∧
75 you;] ∼ ∧
76 this?] ∼ ∧
77 Enough,] ∼ ∧
77 boy,] ∼ ∧
78 S.D. *in left marg. opp. l.* 78
79 *Carintha,*] ∼ ∧
81 forsooth,] ∼ ∧
81 Queeneship?] ∼ ∧
82 impatient,] ∼ ∧
85 towards;] ∼ ∧
87 What] *follows deleted* blesse mee
88 heere?] ∼ ∧
90 torment?] ∼ ∧
90–91 Howes...now] *one line in* MS
91 now?] ∼ ∧
92 hands?] ∼ ∧
92 *Carintha* —] ∼ ∧
93 that;] ∼ ,
93 bratt, ...him,] ∼ ∧ ... ∼ ∧
94 vext,] ∼ ∧
95 not.] ∼ ∧
96 to] *followed by deleted* buid
97 advauncement?] ∼ ∧
97 not,] ∼ ∧
98 not. — *Voltimar?*] ∼ ∧ — ∼ /
102 pratinge;] ∼ ∧
103 promise;] ∼ ∧
106 lust?] ∼ ∧
107 too. Heare] too, heare
108 slauery;] ∼ ∧
109 second.] ∼ ∧
110 *Carintha* —] ∼ ∧
110 not.] ∼ ∧
111 Kinge,] ∼ ∧
111 free,] ∼ ∧
112 mee.] ∼ ∧
113–114 Stay...back] *one line in* MS
113 after,] ∼ ∧
114 her,] ⟨ ∼ ∧⟩

115 so,] ∼ ∧
116 leave] *altered from* leaves
117 bloody,] ∼ ∧
118 deformity;] ∼ ∧
121 S.D. *in left marg. opp. l.* 121
122 Heere, heere,] ∼ ∧ ∼ ∧
122 lord,] ∼ ∧
123 for?] ∼ ∧
124 Foe,] ∼ ∧ (*followed by deleted* I bin)
124 officious,] ∼ ∧
125 sir?] ∼ ∧
126 Sir?] ∼ ∧
130 *in right marg. is deleted* exit
130 S.D. *in left marg. opp. l.* 131
131 The] *followed by deleted* prince
135 feare;] ∼ ,
135 mee,] ∼ ∧
136 lambe,] ∼ ∧
137–138 It...boy.] *one line in* MS
140 deceaud,] ∼ ∧
144 estate,] ∼ ∧
149 cruelties. Tell] cruelties, tell
150 father,] ∼ ∧
151 mee?] ∼ ∧
154 never] *followed by deleted* hard yo
154 yee,] ∼ ∧
156 nunnery?] ∼ ∧
158 my] *followed by deleted* poule
159 soule] *followed by deleted* ha
160 yee?] ∼ ∧
160 mee?] ∼ ∧
161 I?] ∼ ;
164 mother,] ∼ ∧
165 thee.] ∼ ,
166 father?] ∼ ∧
166–167 I...companion] *one line in* MS
168 doues,] ∼ ∧
170 doth,] ∼ ∧
172 so;] ∼ ∧
172 strange] MS *reads* strang *with some final letter deleted, perhaps an* h *as* MSR *gives it*

174 creeps. Ioy] creepd, ioy
174 soule,] ~ ∧
175 stray,] ~ ∧
175 things,] ~ ∧
176 kings.] ~ ∧
177 S.D. *in left marg. opp. l.* 177
179 dore,] ~ ∧
185 S.D. *in left marg. opp. l.* 185
185 sure?] ~ ∧
188 How?] ~ ∧
190 Good;] ~ ∧
191 depend?] ~ ∧
194 forhead] *followed by deleted* hand
194 earthquakes.] ~ ∧
196 infant?] ~ ∧
197–198 MS *lines:* Yes...braines |
     with...thinge
197 Yes, ... braines,] ~ ∧ ... ~ ∧
199–200 Blesse...talke?] *one line in*
     MS
200 this] *followed by deleted* villaine
200 talke?] ~ ∧
200 language;] ~ ∧
203–204 MS *lines:* Fine...dissimula-
     tion | it...yee
203 dissimulation,] ~ ∧
205 Marke] *follows deleted* it
206 reward?] ~ ∧
208 head,] ~ ∧
210 iudge;] ~ ,
215–216 *one line in* MS
216 give;] ~ ∧
221 yee?] ~ ∧
223 sonne,] ~ ∧

224 doome, ...groaninge,] ~ ∧
     ... ~ ∧
225 manly] *followed by deleted* soldier
225 soldier.] ~ ∧
226 heede,] ~ ∧
226 true,] ~ ∧
227 for't] fort
227 Guard,] ~ ∧
228 meane?] ~ ∧
229 againe,] ~ ∧
230 speake?] ~ ∧
232 babble?] ~ ∧
235 father,] *the comma is intended to*
     delete a final s
235 now;] ~ ∧
236 lord —] ~ ∧
237 man, ...man,] ~ ∧ ... ~ ∧
238 knave. Twas] knave, twas
239 mother,] ~ ∧
240 him,] ~ ∧
245 *Penda,*] ~ ∧
246–247 The...mee] *one line in* MS
248 dissignes. Vppon] dissignes
     vppon
249 heaven,] ~ ∧
252–253 Oh...guilt.] *one line in* MS
256 *Voltimar.*] ~ ∧
257 miracles;] ~ ∧
258 Ha?] ~ ∧
258 word;] ~ ∧
260 boy —] ~ ∧
261 found,] ~ ∧
262 short, ...after,] ~ ∧ ... ~ ∧
263 laughter.] ~ ∧

V.ii

1 you?] ~ ∧
2 *lewellins,*] ~ ∧
4 you?]
4 S.D. *in left marg. opp. l.* 4
7 *Rice,*] ~ ∧
8 you;] ~ ∧

10 and high] and *interlined above a*
     caret
12 bookes,] ~ ∧
18 is a] a *interlined above a caret*
20 Right,] ~ ∧
21 shropsheire] shopsheire

25 men,] ~ ∧
29 welshman,] ~ ∧
30 troshans,] ~ ∧
32 her. So] her ⟨　⟩ | so
42 *Arion*] *majuscule altered from minuscule*
45 lyes,] ~ ∧
49 inckhorns,] ~ ∧
50 it.] ~ ,
51 S.D. *in left marg. opp. ll.* 50–51
54 datt] Datt
54 rascalls?] ~ ∧
56 mee,] ~ ∧
56 it,] ~ ∧
58 *Ireland, Ireland*;] ~ ∧ ~ ∧
58 that?] ~ ∧
59 too,] ~ ∧
63 in't] int
65 der] *altered from* ders

66 certen,] ~ ∧
68 welshman] *follows deleted* wes
69 fie,] ~ ∧
74 that,] ~ ∧
75 mee] *followed by deleted* is
76 battailes,] ~ ∧
77 Oh Irish,] ~ ~ ∧
78 death,] ~ ∧
80 S.D. *in left marg. opp. l.* 80
82 coscombe,] ~ ∧
92 di] *some unformed final letter deleted*
94 vpp, . . .ayre,] ~ ∧ . . . ~ ∧
99 court?] ~ ∧
103 company?] ~ ∧
105 sporte. One] sporte, one
106 harpers;] ~ ∧
106 carpers. Come] carpers come

V.iii

S.D. *Florish*.] *added in left marg. opp.* V.ii.112
S.D. *Kinge*,] ~ ∧
S.D. *Carintha*;] ~ ,
 1 phisick,] ~ ∧
 3 T'expell] te'xpell
 4 lesse,] ~ ∧
 5 S.D. *in left margin*
 5 words. Oh] words, oh
10 kindred?] ~ ∧
13 flames,] ~ ∧
14 Whilst. . .] *between l.* 14 *and l.* 15 *is the deleted verse:* whoe fretts that hee so long must keepe awaie
15 daie,] ~ ∧
18 then?] ~ ∧
22 him,] ~ ∧
26 brighter] *followed by deleted* b
28 cronicler?] ~ ∧
29 in,] ~ ∧
30 S.D. *in left marg. opp. l.* 30
31 hee?] ~ ∧
34 already?] ~ ∧

37 witt.] ~ ∧
42 not?] ~ ∧
43 *Brute*?] ~ ∧
43 lord;] ~ ∧
44 then.] ~ ,
45 heere. Where] heere, where
46 heere?] ~ ∧
49 myne] *begins new line after end of line above with a deleted word beginning* my *but the rest mutilated*
49 tellinge] *followed by deleted* s
50 come,] ~ ∧
51 waie; . . .horse,] ~ , . . . ~ ∧
53 spurr,] ~ ∧
56 so,] ~ ∧
57 raigne] raigine
57 1217] *underlined in* MS
62 tennants] *followed by deleted* of
66 so,] ~ ∧
67 mares,] ~ ∧
68 page,] ~ ∧
72 stuff?] ~ ∧
76 So;] ~ ∧

81 Smith] smith
91 1600] *underlined in* MS
91 New] new
92 Bun] bun
93 Strand] strand
94 *Colchester.*] *written before deleted* Cl
98 Battoone,] ~ ∧
100 chopps. You] chopps you
107 battoone?] ~ ∧
108 baston,] ~ ∧
114 altitude,] (*follows deleted* altid)
115 body,] ~ ∧
118 weapon,] ~ ∧
119 more?] ~ ∧
127 crutch,] ~ ∧
133 S.D. *in left marg. opp. l.* 133
134 noyse,] ~ ∧
136 *Teage,*] ~ ∧
138 witts,] ~ ∧
139 eares,] ~ ∧
139 der] *altered from* dere
141 How?   ...quarrell?]   ~ ∧
    ... ~ ∧
145 nose] *followed by deleted* ts
146 S.D. *in left marg. opp. l.* 146
147 man, yes,] ~ ∧ ~ ∧
147 tell?] ~ ∧
150 her?] ~ ∧
151 furie?] ~ ∧
154 cow∧] ~ ,
155 sides,] ~ ∧
157 S.D. Colchester] Colcherster
157 S.D. *drawne,* ...Cupid,] ~ ∧
    ... ~ ∧
157 S.D. Penda,] ~ ∧
160 pastimes,] ~ ∧

161 massacre?] ~ ∧
162 then?] ~ ∧
163 tis,] ~ ∧
164 it.] ~ ,
173 in't] int
182 threaten?] ~ ∧
184 lords,] ~ ∧
185 eyes.] ~ ∧
187 hart] *interlined with a caret above deleted* head
188 (T'inioye...wife)] ∧ ~ ... ~ ∧
188 fell,] ~ ∧
189 *Voltimar.*] ~ /
192 coniurer;] ~ ∧
194 T'increase] 'tincrease
196 you?] ~ ∧
197 gulld,] ~ ∧
204 ha] *followed by deleted* h
204 suddaine,] ~ ∧
205 both,] ~ ∧
207 thus —] ~ ∧
213 treasure,] ~ ∧
214 agen.] ~ ∧
215 stake,] ~ ∧
216 *Armante*] *a second final* e *deleted*
218 sire?] ~ ∧
218–219 And...rashnes.] *one line in* MS
219 iustice.] ~ ∧
223 shaken.] ~ ,
224 Archer.] ~ ∧
225 deservst,] ~ ∧
227 face,] ~ ∧
228 hammer,] ~ ∧
229 it?] ~ ∧
238 loues,] ~ ∧
240 race,] ~ ∧

ERRORS IN THE MALONE
SOCIETY REPRINT

[Differences of transcription in word division are not listed here, since usually these will be a matter of opinion. The first reading is the correct one drawn from the present text; the reading following the bracket is that of MSR. The figure in round brackets is the line number in MSR.]

I.i

1 busines] business (4)
18 beinge] being (30)

45 bee] be (65)

I.ii

3 noe] no (128)
19 er'e] ere (146)
19 thanck] thank (146)

21 methincks] methinks (148)
135 nothinge] nothing (279)

I.iii

3 *line not counted between* 309 *and* 310

25 suspective] suspectiue (334)
44 kinge] king (351)

II.i

35 theire] their (463)
43 beinge] being (472)
67 c)arryinge] C)arrying (502)
84 'twas] twas (519)

127 methincks] methinks (559)
142 thinckst] thinkst (572)
156 self] selfe (585)

II.ii

38 you,] you (679)
44 Arms] Armes (685)
55 ten] then (695)
84 [sawce to o]] [sauce to a] (723)
113 roringe] roring (751)

116 never] neuer (754)
118 lord] Lord (755)
123 the kinge] the king (759)
125 freinds] friends (761)
137 noe] no (773)

II.iii

S.D. *vaild*] *Vaild*
1 drye] Drye (775)
16 like] leke (793)
28 self] selfe (807)
37 S.D. *leadinge*] *Leadinge* (820)

89 rake] rooke (879)
92 knowes] knows (881)
95 methincks] methinks (884)
104 serve] serue (891)

III.i

1 makinge] making (894)
4 minervas] mineruas (897)

76 thinck] think (972)
112 puttinge] putting (1007)

III.ii

36 S.D. *Winchestr*] *Wincheste* (1069)

146 day] daie (1166)
146 De] de (1167)

III.iii

3 (*warning*) seruant] seruan (1186)
85 very] verie (1272)

91 him self] himselfe (1279)

IV.i

6 shee] she (1321)
31 puttinge] putting (1344)

127 drincke] drinke (1439)

IV.ii

33 fort] for't (1468)
37 witt] with (1471)

54 Iawfall] Iawfull (1487)
122 greate] great (1546)

IV.iii

28 mynd] mind (1587)

V.i

3 proclaimd] proclaimed (1639)
34 shee] she (1674)
48 shee] she (1692)

53 thie] the (1698)
118 twoe] two (1787)
137 mee] me (1807)

V.ii

18 is a] *interlining of* a *not recorded* (1979)
88 horshon] horson (2045)

102 amonge] among (2057)
113 aboute] about (2068)

V.iii

60 theire] their (2130)
62 theire coates] their coates (2131)
75 gallipott] gallipot (2142)
77 wilbee] willbee (2144)
85 women] wimen (2152)

112 petticoate] petticoat (2178)
127 beinge] being (2192)
133 give] giue (2198)
192 bee] be (2258)
197 Iuggler] Juggler (2263)

CORRECTIONS
AND REVISIONS OF
VOLUMES I–III

CORRECTIONS AND REVISIONS
OF VOLUMES I–III

Some of these corrections and revisions have been suggested by reviewers in various learned journals; but a number of them have been privately communicated by Messrs J. C. Maxwell and J. George, to whom I am much indebted. The public announcement of the holdings of the Bute Collection in the National Library of Scotland, which brought to light the only known perfect copy of *The Converted Courtesan*, has enabled me to include Dekker's revisions from sigs. K3–4, missing in the two other copies. The textual history of *The Honest Whore, Part One*, is now complete.

VOLUME I

THE SHOEMAKERS' HOLIDAY

Textual introduction, pp. 12–14. The discussion of the two compositors who set this quarto can now be supplemented by the compositorial analysis of other Simmes quartos made by W. Craig Ferguson, 'The Compositors of *Henry IV, Part 2, Much Ado About Nothing, The Shoemakers' Holiday*, and *The First Part of the Contention*', *Studies in Bibliography*, XIII (1960), 19–29. According to Ferguson, the minor workman in the *Holiday* Q1 (his compositor *A*) set sigs. B4, C1–1ᵛ, C4, G1ᵛ, G2, H3ᵛ–4ᵛ, and K4, as remarked, and he confirms the more doubtful attribution to this compositor of sigs. G3ᵛ, I1, I4–4ᵛ, and K3. Ferguson believes that this workman can now be assigned, in addition, sig. G4 (IV.iii.S.D.–IV.iii.28), which completes the inner forme and shows setting by formes from cast-off copy, and sheets H–K complete (IV.iv.5–V.v.191 S.D.).

III.ii.45 *for* wrinkld *read* wicked *and alter footnote to read:* *45 wicked] stent Q1–6.

IV.iv.29 *prefix an asterisk to the footnote number and on p. 92 insert this textual note:* IV.iv.29 lies] Some critics prefer the Warnke-Proescholdt emendation *liues* for Q1 *dies*, instead of Q2 *lies*. Since Q2 has no authority, its reading may be utilized only for convenience as an early editorial guess. If *dies* were exclusively a handwriting error, *lies* would of course be superior to *liues* as an emendation; but memorial failure very likely played as large a part as did misreading. The suggested *liues* makes a sharper contrast with *die* earlier in the line, but in truth the sense would appear to be insufficient evidence to decide the crux.

Textual Notes, p. 91. *Add to note on* IV.i.12: For a recent argument in favour of *vampers*, citing an appearance in 1698 (although still in the sense of stocking), see *R.E.S.*, n.s. v, 418.

OLD FORTUNATUS

I.ii.164 *add footnote:* 164 dost] *i.e.*, does't
I.iii.61 *for* thy *read* this *and add footnote:* 61 this] thy Q
II.i.7 *for* the the *read* the
III.i.296 *for* quiro *read* quiero
III.i.402 *for* tunes *read* times
V.i.90 *for* Agripynes *read* Agripynas *and list the alteration on p.* 205.
V.i.167 *for* Agripyne *read* Agripyna *and list the alteration on p.* 205.
V.ii.77 *add footnote:* 77 beautious] *query* bountious
Textual Notes, p. 199. *for* 38 My pure loue] *read* 38 Blame not mine eyes]
— p. 202. V.ii.98 *for* all editors *read* all editors but Rhys

PATIENT GRISSIL

II.i.40 *for* follower *read* follower.
II.i.63 *for* ar *read* are
II.ii.104 *for* slave *read* slaue
II.ii.123 S.D. *place after line* 122 *and delete footnote to* 123 S.D.
IV.i.124 *for* this *read* theis *and add footnote:* 124 theis] this Q
IV.iii.233 *for* office *read* offices *and add footnote:* 233 offices] office Q
V.ii.50 *for* hee *read* wee *and add footnote:* 50 wee] Collier; hee Q
Emendations of Accidentals, p. 296. *Insert* II.ii.148 hence,] ~ ∧

SATIROMASTIX

Textual Introduction, p. 301, line 24. *for* to this *read* of this
III.i.266 S.D. *for* Exeunt. *read* Exeunt. [Manent Crispinus and Demetrius.]
Delete the heading [ACT III, SCENE II] *and renumber as the continuation of* III.i. *Line* 270 *will be* By this faire Bride remember soone at night

SIR THOMAS WYATT

I.vi.49 *add footnote:* 49 conceal'd] *very likely a corruption of* cancel'd
I.vi.67 *for* persident *read* president *and list the alteration on p.* 462
IV.i.40 *for* baseness *read* basenesse
IV.i.61 *for* blow *read* blowe
V.i.101 *for* me *read* mee
V.ii.182 *for* Highness *read* Highnesse
Emendations of Accidentals, p. 465. *Insert* IV.i.91 fugitiue] fugitue

VOLUME II

THE HONEST WHORE, PART I

THE

Converted Curtezan

With,

The Humours of the Patient Man, and the Longing Wife.

The Same as the Honest Whore.

Tho: Dekker.

LONDON
Printed by V. S. and are to be solde by Iohn
Hodgets at his shoppe in Paules
church-yard 1604.

Textual Introduction, p. 4, line 19. *for* this skeleton also imposes both formes of sheet H. *read* this skeleton, with some running-titles in a different setting, also imposes both formes of sheet H.

— p. 4, line 22. *for* the skeleton of H imposes the outer forme of I. *read* the skeleton of H, with some running-titles in a different setting, imposes the outer forme of I. Running-titles H2^v–H4–I3 and H3–H1^v–I2^v seem to be positively identified, but the swash N running-title E3^v–E4^v–F4–F4^v–H3^v–H4^v is not present in outer I, although, in a most puzzling manner, it reappears in the NLS Q2 revised sheet E.

— p. 5, line 16. *after* the first two sheets. *insert:* The compositor in Q1 and in the Q2 resetting was Simmes's compositor *A*, whose work was identified in Q1 of *The Shoemakers' Holiday*.

— p. 6, line 9. *Add:* The recent identification of a complete copy of Q2 in the Bute Collection of the National Library of Scotland (NLS) may substantiate the opinion that these leaves were lost by accident.

— p. 7, line 17. *insert the following paragraph:* The Bute copy has sheet E in a different state from that in the Bodleian and Folger copies. Instead of the running-titles *The Conuerted Courtizan* the Bute copy has *THE HONEST WHORE*. Moreover, in the E(i) standing type two variants appear. On sig. E2 NLS agrees with Q1 in reading 'A' in III.i.19 as against Bodleian and Folger Q2 'I'; and on E3^v NLS agrees with Q1 in reading 'thrumb' in III.i.98 as against Bodleian and Folger Q2 'thrum'. The Bute copy has been severely trimmed and as a result only the feet of the letters of the running-titles are preserved on sigs. E2, E3, and E3^v. However, so far as can be determined from photographs of the remaining running-titles it would seem that the same set (or substantially the same set) that printed sheets E–F, both formes, of Q1 also printed both formes of the NLS copy of sheet E in Q2, but the NLS sheet has been reimposed. (The swash N appears in NLS on sigs. E4 and E4^v, as in sheet F of Q1, whereas in sheet E of Q1 this swash letter in the running-title occurs on sigs. E3^v and E4^v.) Because of the difficulty, if not perhaps the impossibility, of positively identifying each individual running-title in NLS sheet E, a bibliographical analysis of this anomalous sheet is not at present practicable. (For instance, it is difficult to determine whether the running-titles in the NLS E formes are in exactly the same settings as in E–F of Q1 or else in the somewhat modified setting of sheet H of Q1.) It would be mere guessing to make a choice of the two possibilities that come first to mind: perhaps the NLS sheet was started in error with the Q1 headlines instead of the *Courtesan* titles, either by the printer of Q1 E–K or by the printer of Q2 E–F (if he differed); or perhaps it represents part of a special run to make up a short count in Q1. Speculation at this point is useless without the firm bibliographical evidence on which a hypothesis can be built. The position of the running-title on sig. F1 differs in NLS from that in Bodleian and Folger Q2 although the positioning of F1^v–4^v is identical. Whether this fact has any connexion with the anomaly of sheet E I do not know. Very likely not. Elsewhere NLS contains only one variant reading from Bodleian and Folger. On sig. G4 in IV.iii.16 NLS reads correctly 'let' as against 'le'.

— p. 7, *footnote* 1, line 7. *for* XIII *read* XVIII
— p. 8, lines 9–10. *for* Of the 74 type-pages. . .35 are reset. *read* Of the

78 type-pages of text in Q2, 42 are reimpressed from the standing type of Q1, and 36 are reset.

— p. 8, line 25. *for* sig. K2ᵛ *read* sigs. K2ᵛ, 3 *and in line 26 for* (17 pages) *read* (18 pages). *In the same line, for* sigs. K1ᵛ, 2 of inner K *read* all of inner K *and in line 27 for* sig. K1 *read* sigs. K1, 4ᵛ *and for* (11 pages) *read* (14 pages)

— p. 9, lines 5–13. *for* If the G–K section...in sheet K were also reset. *read* The reset pages in sheet K comprise one vertical half of the quarto's outer forme (K2ᵛ–3). Since it can scarcely be suggested that the printer had started to break up the type before instructions for reprinting arrived, it would seem possible that the imbalance of standing to reset type in this sheet may have been caused by a general equalizing of the proportion in the C–D and G–K sheets taken as one unit. In these six sheets we find 23 reset pages to 25 standing. If G–K be taken as a single unit, it has one complete forme more of reset than of standing type.

— p. 9, lines 15–16. *for* and three pages of K(i, o) *read* K(i) and two pages of K(o).

— p. 12, line 24. *at the end of the paragraph add:* Reset K3 recto in NLS Q2 does not entirely conform to this hypothesis, however, for towards its foot it has extensive authoritative revisions in V.ii.395–397, 401–408. However, sig. K2ᵛ (reset) contains no variants. Thus it would seem that those at the foot of K3 are part of the further extensive revision that continues at the head of standing K3ᵛ and would perhaps not have been made if they had not been of a piece with those ordered for the next page, K3ᵛ.

— p. 15, line 35. *substitute the following:* V.ii.375–410 (calde |) K3 reset. V.ii.410 (| a)–518 K3ᵛ–4ᵛ *standing*

— p. 16, *footnote* 1. *delete footnote* 1 *and substitute:* The Q2 title-page had substituted 'Converted Curtezan' for Q1 'Honest Whore' and had utilized some of the standing type of the Q1 imprint for its variant imprint, 'LONDON | Printed by V. S. and are to be folde by Iohn | Hodgets at his fhoppe in Paules | church-yard 1604.' Q3 took over the standing type of the whole Q2 title with the single substitution of 'Honest Whore' for 'Converted Curtezan'.

— p. 18, line 14. *after* without discovery of any variation. *read* Subsequently the perfect Bute copy in the National Library of Scotland was collated against the Bodleian and Folger copies. The very slight variation has been detailed above on p. 7 (revised).

I.v.100 *alter footnote to read:* 100 mony heare;] ~ ; ~ , Q1–Q2(r) [Q2(r) mony: heere,]

I.v.118 *add footnote:* 118 I] Q1; *I* Q2(s)

I.v.121 *add footnote:* 121 heere] Q1; here Q2(s)

I.v.147 *add footnote:* 147 work] Q1; worke Q2(s)

I.v.152 *add footnote:* 152 I] *I* Q1; I Q2(s)

II.i.8 *alter footnote to read:* *8 I should] Q2(s); *I* should Q1 *and on p.* 112

in the textual note to II.i.8 *delete* However, this is the only place that Q 2 substituted a roman sort.

II.i.29 *add footnote:* 29 What] Q 1; *W*hat Q 2 (s)

II.i.31 *add footnote:* 31 Ile] Q 2 (s); *I*le Q 1

II.i.166 *add footnote:* 166 Is] Q 1; *I*s Q 2 (s)

II.i.247 *for* non *read* none *and add footnote:* 247 none] Q 2 (s); non Q 1

II.i.300–2 *footnote. delete* [yonr]

III.i.19 *alter footnote to read:* 19 I] Q 2 (s) [Bodl., DFo]; A Q 1, Q 2 (s) [NLS]

III.i.98 *alter footnote to read:* 98 thrum] Q 2 (s) [Bodl., DFo]; thrumb Q 1, Q 2 (s) [NLS]

III.ii.75 walk] Q 1; walke Q 2 (s) [sig. F 2ᵛ]

IV.i.101 *add footnote:* 101 has] *i.e.,* h'as

IV.iv.35 *for* for *read* far *and add footnote:* 35 far] Q 2 (r); for Q 1. *Adjust Historical Collation accordingly.*

V.ii.381 *for* meete, *read* meete.

V.ii.384 *for* remedy *read* remedy.

V.ii.388 *for* mad, *read* mad.

V.ii.394 *footnote. for* Q 1 *read* Q 1–2 (r)

V.ii.395–397 *for* Am not I a good...fortune teller. *read:* Am not I a fine fortune teller? gods me you are a braue man: will not you buy me some Suger plums, for telling how the Frier was ith well, will you not? *and add footnote:* 395–397 fine fortune teller...you not?] Q 2 (r) [fortune-teller...frier]; good girle, for finding the Frier in the wel? gods so you are a braue man: will not you buy me some Suger plums because I am so good a fortune teller. Q 1 *Adjust Historical Collation accordingly.*

V.ii.400 *for* Pretty soule, *read* Pretty soule! *and add footnote:* 400 Pretty soule!] Q 2 (r); ~ ~ , Q 1

V.ii.401–408 *delete* I know you: Is not your name *Mathæo. and substitute:*
Math. No.
Bell. Looke fine man, nay? I know you all by your noses, he was mad for me once, and I was mad for him once, and he was mad for her once, and were you neuer mad? yes I warrant. Is not your name *Mathæo.*
Math. Yes Lamb.
Bell. Lamb! baa! am I Lamb? there you lye for I am Mutton. I had a fine iewell once, a very fine iewell and that naughty man stoale it away from me, fine iewell, a very fine iewell.
Add footnote: 401–408 *Math.* No...very fine iewell.] Q 2 (r) [*Math.* You. *Matheo for omitted* (*in phrase* for I am Mutton) Mutton, fine iewellₐ a very fine iewell.]; I know you: Is not your name *Mathæo.* | *Math.* Yes lamb. | *Bell.* Baa lamb! there you lie for I am mutton; looke fine man, he was mad for me once, and I was mad for him once, and he was madde for her once, and were you never mad? yes I warrant. I had a fine iewell once, a very fine iewell and that naughty man stoale it away from me, a very fine iewell. Q 1 *Adjust Historical Collation accordingly.*

V.ii.410–411 *for Bell.* Maide nay...leerer. *read Bell.* Maide nay thats a lie, O twas a golden iewell, harke, twas calde [K3] | [K3ᵛ] a Maidenhead, and that naughty man had it, had you not leerer. *Add footnote: Bell.* Maide nay... leerer.] Q2(r, s) [iewel Q2(r)]; *Bell.* Maide nay thats a lie, O twas a very rich iewell, calde | a Maidenhead, and had not you it leerer. Q1 *Adjust Historical Collation accordingly.*

V.ii.415 *for* then? *read* then, shall he! *and add footnote:* 415 then, shall he!] Q2(s) [then⌄]; then? Q1

V.ii.424 *for* Nay then, father *read* Father *and add footnote:* 424 Father] Q2(s); Nay then, father Q1

V.ii.436–438 *for Mathæo* thou...brest. *read*
Mathæo thou first madst me black, now make me
White as before; I vow to thee Ime now
As chaste as infancy, pure as *Cynthias* brow.
Add footnote: Mathæo thou first...brow.] Q2(s) [before, Ime now, *and* Q2(s) *lines: Mathæo*...black, | Now...Ime now]; *Mathæo* thou didst first turne my soule black, | Now make it white agen, I doe protest, | Ime pure as fire now, chaste as *Cynthias* brest. Q1 *Adjust Historical Collation accordingly.*

V.ii.451 *for* Lord. *read* Lord, *and add footnote:* 451 Lord,] Q2(s); ∼ . Q1 [point uncertain]

V.ii.461 *for* husband mad, *read* husband, that was as patient as *Iob,* to be more mad than euer was *Orlando, and add footnote:* 461 husband, that... *Orlando,*] Q2(s); husband mad, Q1

V.ii.462 *for* placde *read* placed *and add footnote:* 462 placed] Q2(s); placde Q1

V.ii.462 *add footnote:* yonder] Q2(s); youder Q1

V.ii.470 *for* Lord, | Shee had *read*

　　　　　　　　　　　　...Lord.
Duke.　Why Signior came you hether?
Cand.　　　　　　　　　O my good Lord!
　Shee had....

Add footnote: 470–471 *Duke.* Why Signior...good Lord!] Q2(s); *omit* Q1 *Adjust Historical Collation accordingly.*

V.ii.473 *alter footnote to read:* 473 was my] Q2(s); was yet my Q1 *and adjust Historical Collation accordingly*

V.ii.494 *for* Gentleman *read* Gentle-man *and add footnote:* 494 Gentleman] Q2(s); Gentleman Q1

Press-Variants, p. 117. *for* K1 V.ii.343 *read* K2ᵛ V.ii.343

Emendations of Accidentals, p. 121. *Add or substitute the following under* V.ii:
379 friendship:] Q2; ∼ , Q1
379 looke,] ∼ : Q1–5 ±
381 meete.] Q2; ∼ , Q1
387 Frier,] Q2; ∼ . Q1
388 mad.] ∼ , Q1–5 ±

406 warrant.] Q2; ~ ₐ Q1
411 Maidenhead] Q1–3 *text*; mai- Q1–3 *cw*
413–414 Had he...thee.] Q4; *one line in* Q1–3
462 *delete*
474 coate,] Q4; ~ . Q1–3
484 it?] ~ , Q1, 3; ~ . Q2; ~ ! Q4–5
485 tender,] Q4; ~ ₐ Q1–3
488 balme.] Q4; ~ , Q1–3
502 chaine:] ~ . Q1–3; ~ , Q4–5
503 paine.] ~ : Q1–5

THE HONEST WHORE, PART 2

I.i.106 *for* paper *read* Paper
I.i.124 *for* Iacomo *read* Old Iacomo *and for* Florentineₐ *read* Florentine.
Delete footnotes *124 *and* 125 *and textual note* I.i.124 *on p.* 219. *Substitute
footnote* 124 Florentine.] ~ ₐ Q
  I.i.125 *delete* Old
  I.ii.106 *for* al *read* all

THE MAGNIFICENT ENTERTAINMENT

414 *for* attingant *read* attingunt *and add footnote:* 414 attingunt] attingant
Q1–2(s)–3
599 *for* Celebret *read* Celebre *and alter footnote to read:* 599 Celebre]
Celeb: Q1–2(r)–3 *Delete textual note on p.* 304.
599 *for* suos, *read* suos *and add footnote:* 599 suosₐ] ~ , Q1–2(r)–3
646 *for* Aut *read* At *and add footnote:* 646 At] Aut Q1–2(s)–3
1247 *for* de mortui *read* demortui *and for* spe *read* spei and *alter footnotes
to read:* 1247 demortui] Q1(c); de mortui Q1(u) *and* 1247 spei] Q1(c); spe
Q1(u) *Alter Historical Collation accordingly.*
1259 *for* emittuntur *read* emittantur *and add footnote:* 1259 emittantur]
emittuntur Q1(u, c)

WESTWARD HO

Textual Introduction, p. 313, *line* 5. *for* yᵗ *read* yt
— p. 316, *line* 8. *for* Two formes extensively corrected *read* Four formes,
outer A, inner E, inner F, and outer G, were extensively corrected
— p. 316, *line* 10. *before* inner D *insert* outer C,
— p. 316, *footnote* 1, *line* 2. *after* before machining *insert* Something of the
same imbalance may be observed in lightly corrected outer F backing heavily
corrected inner F.
  I.i.33 *for* a tricke *read* the tricke
  I.ii.113 *for* horn-ake *read* horne-ake
  II.i.209 *for* Rhenish *read* Rhenesh

IV.i.63 *for* Counterpane *read* Counterpaine
V.iii.6 *for* Rhenish- *read* Renish-
V.iii.204–205 *for* forth, *Monopoly* Ile cut off your conuoy maist, Sargant *read* forth, Maister *Monopoly* Ile cut off your conuoy, Sargant *and add footnotes:* 204 Maister] *om.* Q *and* 205 conuoy,] conuoy maist, Q

NORTHWARD HO

I.i.87 *for* wiues *read* winnes *and substitute footnote:* 87 winnes] wiues Q. *Delete textual note on p.* 479
II.i.50 *add footnote:* 50 the] Dyce; the the Q
II.i.65 *delete footnote*
II.i.74 *for* heart *read* heare *and add footnote:* 74 heare] heart Q (see II.i.95)
IV.i.162 *for* common *read* comon
V.i.161 *for* bearing *read* bearth *and alter footnote to:* *161 bearth] *stet* Q. *On p.* 485 *delete textual note and substitute:* 485 bearth] Q's reading has caused difficulty and has given rise to the suggestions *breath* and *breadth*, neither of which is satisfactory. On the analogy of *Paradise Lost*, IX, 624, where *bearth* means 'what one bears, produce', it seems likely that the luxuriance of Bellamont's beard and then its fashion, or cut, occasion Kate's comment.
V.i.228 *for* sukket *read* suckket
V.i.328 *for* for the cast *read* for cast

THE WHORE OF BABYLON

I.i.239 *for* doing ill, (would speake ill) *read* (doing ill) would speake ill, *and note accordingly in Emendations of Accidentals.*
II.i.8 *for* Cities. Ther's *read* Cities, Theis, *and add footnote:* 8 Cities, Theis,] Cities‸ Theis‸ Q(u) [Ther's Q(c)]. *In Emendations of Accidentals on p.* 589 *delete* II.i.8
II.i.276 S.D. *for* countries *read* [Low] countries
II.i.277–278 *Above line* 278 *insert direction* [To the King of Portugall.] *and modify accordingly textual note to* II.i S.D. *on p.* 585.
III.ii.62 *for* classe *read* closse *and add footnote:* 63 closse] classe Q1
IV.ii S.D. *for* Elfiron *read* Fideli *and add footnote:* S.D. Fideli] Elfiron Q
IV.iv.95 *for* Montada *read* Moncada *and add footnote:* 95 Moncada] Montada Q
V.iii.23 *for* winges *read* windes *and add footnote:* 23 windes] winges Q

VOLUME III

THE ROARING GIRL

V.i.7 *for* captiuty *read* captiuity *and note alteration from* Q *on p.* 111
V.ii.5 S.D. *for* seruan *read* seruant.

IF THIS BE NOT A GOOD PLAY, THE DEVIL IS IN IT

Textual Introduction, p. 115, lines 15–21. *for* On the other hand, ordinary tests...only one regular compositor. *substitute:* Sequences of colons following speech-prefixes might at first sight suggest that the play was set throughout by only one compositor, but this evidence proves faulty. Dr Gerritsen has pointed out to me that (save for some confusion in sheet B) pages in which the speech-prefixes are *K.* and *Ruff.* should be distinguished from those in which the prefixes are *Ki.*, *Kin.*, or *King.* and *Ruf.* Analysis shows that this is valid evidence for two different compositors.

Compositor I (K., Ruff.) set:

B2(?) I.i.49b–76
B3(?) I.i.101–130a
B3ᵛ–C1 I.i.130b–I.ii.104
C2ᵛ I.ii.169–201
C3ᵛ(?) I.ii.244 S.D.–I.iii.5
D3 I.iii.194–II.i.19
E1ᵛ–2ᵛ II.i.138–II.ii.6
G3ᵛ–H3 III.ii.161–IV.i.18
I1 IV.ii.33–62
K1ᵛ–3 V.i.41b–V.ii.56
K4–4ᵛ V.ii.86c–V.iii.41
L1ᵛ V.iii.70–97a
L2ᵛ–3 V.iii.125b–V.iv.23
M1 V.iv.116–147
M3 V.iv.244–278

Compositor II (Ki., Kin., King., Ruf.) set:

B2ᵛ(?) I.i.77–100
C1ᵛ–2 I.ii.105–I.ii.168
C3 I.ii.202–I.ii.235
C3ᵛ(?) I.ii.236–244
D3ᵛ–E1 II.i.20–II.i.137
F4–4ᵛ III.i S.D.–III.ii.1
I4ᵛ–K1 IV.iv.58–V.i.41a
L1 V.iii.42–V.iii.69
L2 V.iii.97b–V.iii.125a
L4–4ᵛ V.iv.53 S.D.–V.iv.115

A few more pages may be assigned on other evidence. Starting with sig. G1 some shortage of roman capital I's developed and italic *I*'s were substituted. When these were distributed back into the roman box of the case, the italic *I* may appear later sporadically because of foul-case instead of deliberate substitution. The following pages contain one or more italic *I* types where roman was correct: G1, G3ᵛ, H1, H4, I1, I2, K1ᵛ, K2, K2ᵛ, K3, K4ᵛ, L1ᵛ, L3, M2.

Of these fourteen pages, ten have already been assigned to Compositor I on the basis of the speech-prefix evidence (a strong confirmation of its validity), and thus Compositor I may also be given G1 (III.ii.2–35), H4 (IV.i.50–IV.i. 82), I2 (IV.ii.95b–127 [had I |]), and M2 (V.iv.180–210a).

A scattering of italic *k* types in roman words is found in sigs. H1ᵛ–2ᵛ, K1ᵛ, K2ᵛ, and K4, all pages assigned to Compositor I on the evidence of speech-prefixes. Hence when this *k* foul-case is seen on sig. M1 (V.iv.116–V.iv.148), the page may confidently be given to the same compositor.

I.ii.182 *for* 1. Ser. *read* 2. Ser. *and alter footnote to read:* 182 2. Ser.] *Car.* Q

I.iii.143 *for* devise *read* device *and delete* I.iii.143 *note on p.* 219

II.iii.51 *for* wales *read* vales *and add footnote:* 51 vales] wales Q

III.iii.166 *for* Spirit *read* Sport *and add footnote:* 166 Sport] Spirit Q

III.iii.187 *for* Nerenist *read* Neronist *and add note of alteration on p.* 221

IV.ii.51 S.D. *Move stage-direction (except for* Embrace) *to follow line* 50. *Place* Embrace. *as stage-direction to right of line* 51. *Delete footnote and cancel textual note on p.* 213.

IV.ii.99 *before* Exeunt: *add to the stage-direction* Fire. *and delete textual note on p.* 213 *to this line.*

IV.iii.1 *for* Calabriam *read* Calabrian *and note alteration from* Q *on p.* 227

V.i.14 *for* sad-visage *read* sad-visagd *and add footnote:* 14 sad-visagd] sad-visage Q

V.i.25 *for* Lion *read* Lions *and substitute for footnote the following:* 25 Lions] *i.e.,* Lion is

V.iii.90 *for* (father) *read* (father)— *and add note of alteration on p.* 223

V.iii.110 *for* aboue *read* aboue.

Press-variants, p. 217. *In* sheet K (inner forme) *under sig.* K2 *alter to read:* V.i.184 That [*to margin*]] *Stet.* That [*indented as speech-prefix*]

TROIA NOVA TRIUMPHANS

310 *for* Enuy, on: *read* Enuy: On *and add note of alteration on p.* 249

433 *change italic setting to roman, and add note of alteration on p.* 249

MATCH ME IN LONDON

Textual Introduction, p. 253, *line* 2. *for* Buc *read* Herbert

— *p.* 262, *line* 2. *for* K4 *read* F4

I.iv.123 *add footnote* *123 inciferous] *stet* Q *and on p.* 344 *insert the following textual note:* I.iv.123 inciferous] O.E.D. does not recognize this word. If Q is in error, as likely, perhaps some made-up word like *inciterous, incinerous,* or *encinderous* was intended; however, the true reading may be much farther afield.

THE VIRGIN MARTYR

p. 375, line 23 *for* 1897 *read* 1871
I.i.409 S.D. *for* ommes *read* omnes

THE WITCH OF EDMONTON

IV.i.71 *for* Answers? *read* Answers! *and note alteration from* Q *on p.* 567

WONDER OF A KINGDOM

II.iii.129 *for* doe *read* de *and add footnote:* de] doe Q
IV.i.50 *for* Rayot *read* Royet *and add footnote:* 50 Royet] Rayot Q (*but query also* Royat *or* Royot)